Fodor's 7th Edition

Nova Scotia, New Brunswick, Prince Edward Island

The complete guide, thoroughly up-to-date

Packed with details that will make your trip

The must-see sights, off and on the beaten path

What to see, what to skip

Mix-and-match vacation itineraries

City strolls, countryside adventures

Smart lodging and dining options

Essential local do's and taboos

Transportation tips, distances and directions

Key contacts, savvy travel tips

When to go, what to pack

Clear, accurate, easy-to-use maps

Excerpted from *Fodor's Canada*

Fodor's Travel Publications • New York, Toronto, London, Sydney, Auckland
www.fodors.com

Fodor's Nova Scotia, New Brunswick, Prince Edward Island

EDITORS: Shannon Kelly, Christine Swiac

Editorial Contributors: Milan Chvostek, Kim Goodson, Helga Loverseed, Ed Kirby, Susan Randles, Dave Stephens, Isobel Warren, Paul Waters, Ana Watts

Editorial Production: Kristin Milavec

Maps: David Lindroth, *cartographer;* Rebecca Baer and Robert Blake, *map editors*

Design: Fabrizio La Rocca, *creative director;* Guido Caroti, *art director;* Melanie Marin, *photo editor;* Jolie Novak, *senior picture editor*

Cover Design: Pentagram

Production/Manufacturing: Robert Shields

Cover Photograph: Greig Cranna

Copyright

Seventh Edition

ISBN 0–676–90214–6

ISSN 1079–0004

Important Tip

Although all prices, opening times, and other details in this book are based on information supplied to us at press time, changes occur all the time in the travel world, and Fodor's cannot accept responsibility for facts that become outdated or for inadvertent errors or omissions. So **always confirm information when it matters,** especially if you're making a detour to visit a specific place.

Special Sales

Fodor's Travel Publications are available at special discounts for bulk purchases for sales promotions or premiums. Special editions, including personalized covers, excerpts of existing guides, and corporate imprints, can be created in large quantities for special needs. For more information, contact your local bookseller or write to Special Markets, Fodor's Travel Publications, 280 Park Avenue, New York, NY 10017. Inquiries from Canada should be directed to your local Canadian bookseller or sent to Random House of Canada, Ltd., Marketing Department, 2775 Matheson Boulevard East, Mississauga, Ontario L4W 4P7. Inquiries from the United Kingdom should be sent to Fodor's Travel Publications, 20 Vauxhall Bridge Road, London SW1V 2SA, England.

PRINTED IN THE UNITED STATES OF AMERICA

10 9 8 7 6 5 4 3 2 1

CONTENTS

Maps

ON THE ROAD WITH FODOR'S

The more you know before you go, the better your trip will be. One of the most amazing natural sights, most intriguing small museums, or most unique seaside restaurants could be just around the corner from your hotel, but if you don't know it's there, it might as well be on the other side of the globe. That's where this book comes in. It's a great step toward making sure your next trip lives up to your expectations. As you plan, check out the Web as well. Guidebooks have been helping smart travelers find the special places for years; the Web is one more tool. Whatever reference you consult, be savvy about what you read, and always consider the source. Images and language can be massaged to make places appear better than they are. And one traveler's quaint is another's grimy. Here at Fodor's, and at our on-line arm, Fodors.com, our focus is on providing you with information that's not only useful but accurate and on target. Every day Fodor's editors put enormous effort into getting things right, beginning with the search for the right contributors—people who have objective judgment, broad travel experience, and the writing ability to put their insights into words. There's no substitute for advice from a like-minded friend who has just come back from where you're going, but our writers, having seen all corners of Canada's Atlantic provinces, are the next best thing. They're the kind of people you'd poll for tips yourself if you knew them.

Travel writers and broadcasters **Milan Chvostek and Isobel Warren** of Ontario contributed to the Nova Scotia and Prince Edward Island chapters. They headed east for their honeymoon four decades ago and have repeated the journey regularly ever since, maintaining their affection for Nova Scotia and its people, food, and culture.

Food columnist **Kim Goodson,** who updated the Halifax section of the Nova Scotia chapter, indulges her food, wine, and travel passions at every opportunity.

Ed Kirby, editor of the *Newfoundland and Labrador Travel Guide,* lives in St. John's. He combed the area for the latest attractions.

Susan Randles contributed to the Prince Edward Island chapter, and the Cape Breton Island section of the Nova Scotia chapter with her late husband, Dave Stephens. Susan has written extensively on Prince Edward Island for newspapers, books, magazines, and Web sites. She lives in Halifax.

Paul Waters, travel editor of *The Gazette* in Montréal, updated Smart Travel Tips A to Z to make your travels even easier.

Fredericton columnist **Ana Watts** is passionate about her province, New Brunswick; she freshened that chapter for us.

Don't Forget to Write

Keeping a travel guide fresh and up-to-date is a big job. So we love your feedback—positive and negative—and follow up on all suggestions. Contact the Canada editor at editors@fodors.com or c/o Fodor's, 280 Park Avenue, New York, NY 10017. And have a wonderful trip!

Karen Cure

Karen Cure
Editorial Director

Canada

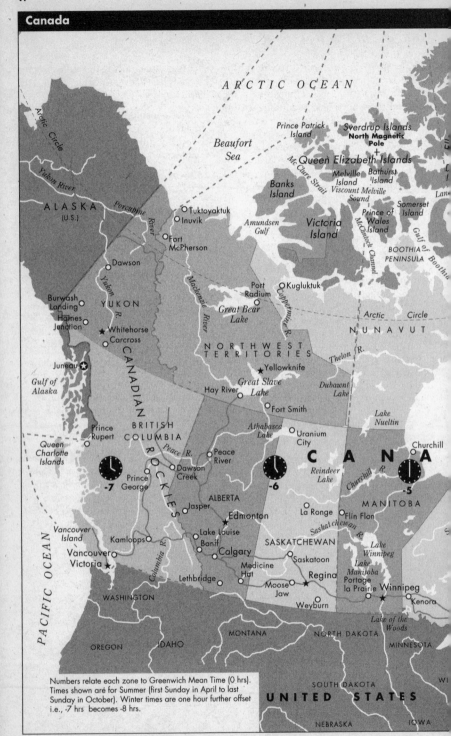

ARCTIC OCEAN

Prince Patrick Island

Sverdrup Islands
North Magnetic Pole
+

Beaufort Sea

McClure Strait

Queen Elizabeth Islands

Banks Island

Melville Island

Bathurst Island

Viscount Melville Sound

Somerset Island

Prince of Wales Island

Lan

BOOTHIA PENINSULA

Gulf of Boothia

Amundsen Gulf

Victoria Island

McClintock Channel

ALASKA (U.S.)

Porcupine

Yukon River

River

Tuktoyaktuk
Inuvik

Fort McPherson

Mackenzie River

Port Radium

Kugluktuk

Coppermine R.

Arctic   Circle

Dawson

Yukon R.

YUKON

Great Bear Lake

N U N A V U T

Burwash Landing

Haines Junction

Whitehorse
Carcross

N O R T H W E S T
T E R R I T O R I E S

Thelon R.

Yellowknife

Dubawnt Lake

Lake Nueltin

Juneau

CANADIAN

Great Slave Lake

Hay River

Gulf of Alaska

ROCKIES

Fort Smith

Prince Rupert

BRITISH COLUMBIA

Athabasca Lake

Uranium City

C A N   A

Churchill

Queen Charlotte Islands

Peace R.

Peace River

Reindeer Lake

A

-7

Dawson Creek

Prince George

-6

Churchill R.

Churchill

-5

PACIFIC OCEAN

ALBERTA

Jasper

Edmonton

La Ronge

Flin Flon

MANITOBA

Vancouver Island

Kamloops

Lake Louise
Banff

Saskatchewan R.

Vancouver
Victoria

Columbia R.

Calgary

SASKATCHEWAN

Saskatoon

Lake Winnipeg

Lethbridge

Medicine Hat

Regina

Lake Manitoba

Portage la Prairie

Winnipeg

WASHINGTON

Moose Jaw

Weyburn

Kenora

Lake of the Woods

OREGON

IDAHO

MONTANA

NORTH DAKOTA

MINNESOTA

Numbers relate each zone to Greenwich Mean Time (0 hrs).
Times shown are for Summer (first Sunday in April to last
Sunday in October). Winter times are one hour further offset
i.e., -7 hrs becomes -8 hrs.

SOUTH DAKOTA

U N I T E D   S T A T E S

NEBRASKA

IOWA

WI

ICELAND

GREENLAND
(Denmark)

Denmark Strait

Ellesmere Island

Devon
Island

Lancaster Sound

*Baffin
Bay*

Davis Strait

Baffin Island

Boothia

Prince
Charles
Island

*Foxe
Basin*

Lake Amadjuak

Iqaluit
Lake Harbour

Hudson Strait

Cape Chidley

'Southampton
Island

Coats
Island

Mansel
Island

Ivujivik

*Ungava
Bay*

Nain

*Labrador
Sea*

Battle
Harbour

*Hudson
Bay*

Belcher
Islands

-4

Scheffervile

Goose Bay

LABRADOR

NEWFOUNDLAND

-2:30

Gander

chill

Fort Severn

Labrador City

St. John's

Severn R.

Fort George

Q U É B E C

Sept-Iles

Anticosti Island

-3

*James
Bay*

*Lake
Mistassini*

GASPÉ
PENINSULA

ST. PIERRE AND
MIQUELON
(France)

Moosonee

O N T A R I O

Rimouski

River

PRINCE
EDWARD
ISLAND

Sydney

*Lake
Nipigon*

Chicoutimi

NEW
BRUNSWICK

Charlottetown

Cochrane

Québec
City★

NOVA
SCOTIA

Thunder
Bay

Timmins

Ste-Agathe-
Des-Monts

Trois-
Rivières

Fredericton

Halifax

Lake Superior

Sudbury

North
Bay

Montréal

Saint John

*Bay of
Fundy*

Sault
Ste. Marie

Ottawa

St. Lawrence

MAINE

A T L A N T I C
OCEAN

WISCONSIN

*Lake
Huron*

Toronto

*Lake
Ontario*

VT.

N.H.

Lake Michigan

Niagara
Falls

MASSACHUSETTS

MICHIGAN

NEW YORK

CONN.

R.I.

ILLINOIS

INDIANA

OHIO

Lake Erie

PENNSYLVANIA

N.J.

0   400 miles

0   600 km

ESSENTIAL INFORMATION

AIR TRAVEL

BOOKING

When you book **look for nonstop flights** and **remember that "direct" flights stop at least once.** Try to avoid connecting flights, which require a change of plane. For more booking tips and to check prices and make on-line flight reservations, log on to www.fodors.com.

CARRIERS

When flying internationally, you must usually choose between a domestic carrier, the national flag carrier of the country you are visiting, and a foreign carrier from a third country. National flag carriers have the greatest number of nonstops. Domestic carriers may have better connections to your hometown and serve a greater number of gateway cities. Third-party carriers may have a price advantage.

Of the major airlines, Air Canada, American Airlines, Continental, Northwest, and United serve Halifax.

Among smaller regional carriers, airNova, Canada 3000, Air Transat, and Air Labrador fly in the Atlantic region; Provincial Airlines serves Newfoundland and Labrador; and WestJet flies to Moncton, NB.

Within Canada, regularly scheduled flights to every major city and to most smaller cities are available on Air Canada and the regional feeder airlines associated with it. Since 1999, when it took over the smaller, financially troubled Canadian Airlines, Air Canada has dominated 90% of Canada's airline industry. The lack of competition has consumers bracing for airfare increases. A few upstart carriers have entered the fray to compete with Air Canada, but at press time one (RootsAir) had already suspended flight operations at least temporarily.

For regulations and for the locations of air bases that allow private flights, check with the regional tourist agencies for charter companies and with the District Controller of Air Services in the territorial (and provincial) capitals. Private pilots should obtain information from the Canada Map Office, which has the "Canada Flight Supplement" (lists of airports with Canada Customs services) as well as aeronautical charts.

➤ MAJOR AIRLINES: **Air Canada** (☎ 800/776–3000, WEB www.air-canada.ca). **Canada 3000 Airlines** (☎ 877/973–3000, WEB www.canada3000.com). **Continental** (☎ 800/525–0280, WEB www.continental.com). **Northwest** (☎ 800/225–2525, WEB www.nwa.com). **United** (☎ 800/241–6522, WEB www.ual.com).

➤ SMALLER AIRLINES: **Air Labrador** (☎ 888/247–2262, WEB www.air-labrador.com). **airNova** (☎ 888/247–2262, WEB www.airnova.ca). **Air Transat** (☎ 877/872–6728, WEB www.airtransat.com). **CanJet** (☎ 800/809–7777). **Provincial Airlines** (☎ 709/576–1666; 800/563–2800 in Atlantic Canada, WEB www.provair.com). **Royal Airlines** (☎ 877/769–2524, WEB www.royal.ca). **WestJet Airlines** (☎ 800/538–5696, WEB www.westjet.com).

➤ CONTACTS FOR PRIVATE PILOTS: **Canada Map Office** (✉ 130 Bentley Ave., Nepean, ON K1A 0E9, ☎ 800/465–6277).

CHECK-IN & BOARDING

Assuming that not everyone with a ticket will show up, airlines routinely overbook planes. When everyone does, airlines ask for volunteers to give up their seats. In return, these volunteers usually get a certificate for a free flight and are rebooked on the next flight out. If there are not enough volunteers, the airline must choose who will be denied boarding. The first to get bumped are passengers who checked in late and those flying on discounted tickets, so **get to the gate and check in as early as possible,** especially during peak periods.

Always **bring a government-issued photo ID to the airport** even when you don't need one; a passport is best. You will be asked to show it before you are allowed to check in. U.S. Customs and Immigration maintains offices at the airports in Montréal, Toronto, and Vancouver; U.S.-bound passengers should arrive early enough to clear customs before their flight.

Security measures at Canadian airports are similar to those in the United States. Be sure you're not carrying anything that could be construed as a weapon: a letter opener, Swiss Army knife, or a toy weapon, for example. Arriving passengers from overseas flights might find a beagle in a green coat sniffing their luggage; he's looking for forbidden agricultural products.

Departing passengers in Montréal and Vancouver must pay a $10 airport-improvement fee before they can board their plane.

CUTTING COSTS

The least expensive airfares to Canada must usually be purchased in advance and are non-refundable. It's smart to **call a number of airlines,** and when you are quoted a good price, **book it on the spot**—the same fare may not be available the next day. Always **check different routings** and look into using different airports. Travel agents, especially low-fare specialists (☞ Discounts & Deals), are helpful.

Consolidators are another good source. They buy tickets for scheduled international flights at reduced rates from the airlines, then sell them at prices that beat the best fare available directly from the airlines, usually without restrictions. Sometimes you can even get your money back if you need to return the ticket. Carefully read the fine print detailing penalties for changes and cancellations, and **confirm your consolidator reservation with the airline.**

➤ CONSOLIDATORS: **Cheap Tickets** (☎ 800/377–1000). **Discount Airline Ticket Service** (☎ 800/576–1600). **Unitravel** (☎ 800/325–2222). **Up & Away Travel** (☎ 212/889–2345). **World Travel Network** (☎ 800/409–6753).

ENJOYING THE FLIGHT

For more legroom, **request an emergency-aisle seat.** Don't sit in the row in front of the emergency aisle or in front of a bulkhead, where seats may not recline. If you have dietary concerns, **ask for special meals when booking.** These can be vegetarian, low-cholesterol, or kosher, for example. On long flights, try to maintain a normal routine, to help fight jet lag. At night, **get some sleep.** By day, **eat light meals, drink water** (not alcohol), and **move around the cabin** to stretch your legs. For additional jet-lag tips consult *Fodor's FYI: Travel Fit & Healthy* (available at bookstores everywhere).

None of the major airlines or charter lines permit smoking.

FLYING TIMES

Flying time to Halifax is 1½ hours from Montréal, 2½ hours from New York, 4½ hours from Chicago (with connection), 8 hours from Los Angeles (with connection), and 6 hours from London.

HOW TO COMPLAIN

If your baggage goes astray or your flight goes awry, complain right away. Most carriers require that you **file a claim immediately.**

➤ AIRLINE COMPLAINTS: U.S. Department of Transportation **Aviation Consumer Protection Division** (✉ C-75, Room 4107, Washington, DC 20590, ☎ 202/366–2220, ⓦⓔⓑ www. dot.gov/airconsumer). **Federal Aviation Administration Consumer Hotline** (☎ 800/322–7873).

AIRPORTS

The major airport is Halifax International Airport (YHZ). For smaller airports, *see* the A to Z sections in each chapter.

➤ AIRPORT INFORMATION: **Dorval International** (☎ 514/394–7377). **Lester B. Pearson International Airport**

(☎ 416/247–7678). **Vancouver International Airport** (☎ 604/276–6101).

BIKE TRAVEL

Despite Canada's harsh climate and demanding landscape, bicycle travel has become very popular since the 1980s, especially on the Atlantic coast. Some terrain is steep and hilly, but it's always varied and interesting.

Many provinces have developed bicycle routes composed of both bike-only trails and specially marked lanes on regular highways. Prince Edward Island, for example, has converted an abandoned rail line into a trail that runs from one end of the province to the other.

Nationally, the Trans-Canada Trail—linking the Atlantic to both the Pacific and Arctic oceans—will allow bicycles along much of its length when the project is finished (parts of it opened in 2000). Though cyclists aren't allowed on most multiple-lane, limited-access highways, much of the Trans-Canada Highway is a two-lane blacktop with broad, paved shoulders that are widely used by cyclists crossing the country. There are also plenty of secondary roads that see little traffic (and almost no truck traffic).

For maps and information on bicycle routes, consult the provincial tourist information offices.

BIKES IN FLIGHT

Most airlines accommodate bikes as luggage, provided they are dismantled and boxed. Bike boxes, often free at bike shops, cost about $5 if you purchase them from airlines; bike bags cost about $100. International travelers can sometimes substitute a bike for a piece of checked luggage at no charge; otherwise, the cost is about $100. Domestic and Canadian airlines charge $25 to $50.

BOAT & FERRY TRAVEL

Car ferries provide essential transportation on the east coast of Canada. Marine Atlantic runs ferries between Nova Scotia and Newfoundland. Northumberland and Bay Ferries Ltd. operates a high-speed catamaran car ferry between Bar Harbor, Maine, and Nova Scotia as well as regular car ferries between New Brunswick and Nova Scotia. Prince of Fundy Cruises sails between Portland, Maine, and Nova Scotia.

For additional information about regional ferry service, *see* individual chapters.

➤ BOAT & FERRY INFORMATION: **Marine Atlantic** (✉ 355 Purves St., North Sydney, NS B2A 3V2, ☎ 800/341–7981, WEB www.marine-atlantic.ca). **Northumberland and Bay Ferries Ltd.** (✉ 121 Eden St., Bar Harbor, ME 04609, ☎ 888/249–7245). **Prince of Fundy Cruises** (☎ 800/341–7540).

BUS TRAVEL

The bus is an essential form of transportation in Canada, especially if you want to visit out-of-the-way towns that do not have airports or rail lines. Greyhound Lines and Voyageur offer interprovincial service. SMT operates bus service throughout Atlantic Canada.

FARES & SCHEDULES

Bus terminals in major cities and even in many smaller ones are usually efficient operations with service all week and plenty of agents on hand to handle ticket sales. In villages and some smaller towns, the bus station is simply a counter in a local convenience store, gas station, or snack bar. Getting information on schedules beyond the local ones is sometimes difficult in these places. In rural Québec, it's advisable to **bring along a French–English dictionary,** although most merchants and clerks can handle a simple ticket sale in English.

➤ BUS INFORMATION: **Greyhound Lines** (✉ 877 Greyhound Way SW, Calgary, AB T3C 3V8, ☎ 800/661–8747 in Canada; 800/231–2222 in the U.S., WEB www.greyhound.ca). **SMT** (☎ 506/859–5105; 800/567–5151 within Nova Scotia, New Brunswick, and Prince Edward Island, WEB www.smtbus.com). **Voyageur** (✉ 505 E. Boulevard Maisonneuve, Montréal, QC H2L 1Y4, ☎ 514/842–2281). In the U.K.: **Greyhound International** (✉ Sussex House, London Rd., E. Grinstead, East Sussex RHI9 1LD, U.K., ☎ 01342/317317).

PAYING

In major bus terminals, most bus lines accept at least some of the major credit cards. Some smaller lines require cash or take only Visa or MasterCard. All accept travelers' checks in U.S. or Canadian currency with suitable identification, but it's advisable to exchange foreign currency (including U.S. currency) at a bank or exchange office. To buy a ticket in really small centers, it's best to use cash.

RESERVATIONS

Most bus lines do not accept reservations. You should plan on picking up your tickets at least 45 minutes before the bus's scheduled departure time.

BUSINESS HOURS

BANKS & OFFICES

Most banks in Canada are open Monday through Thursday 10–3 and Friday 10–5 or 6. Some banks are open longer hours and also on Saturday morning. All banks are closed on national holidays. Most banks (and some gas stations) have automatic teller machines (ATMs) that are accessible around the clock.

GAS STATIONS

Most highway and city gas stations in Canada are open daily (although there's rarely a mechanic on duty Sunday) and some are open around the clock. In small towns, gas stations are often closed on Sunday, although they may take turns staying open.

MUSEUMS & SIGHTS

Hours at museums vary, but most open at 10 or 11 and close in the evening. Some smaller museums close for lunch. Many museums are closed on Monday; some make up for it by staying open late on Wednesday, often waiving admission.

SHOPS

Stores, shops, and supermarkets usually are open Monday through Saturday 9–6, although in major cities supermarkets are often open 7:30 AM–9 PM and some food stores are open around the clock. Blue laws are in effect in much of Canada, but in a growing number of provinces, stores—even liquor stores—have limited Sunday hours, usually noon–5; shops in areas highly frequented by tourists are usually open Sunday. Stores often stay open Thursday and Friday evenings, most shopping malls until 9 PM. Drugstores in major cities are often open until 11 PM, and convenience stores tend to be open 24 hours a day, seven days a week.

CAMERAS & PHOTOGRAPHY

Canada is one of the world's most scenic countries. Particularly intriguing for photographers are the dramatic fogs of the Atlantic shore. Photographers who want to catch the country at its most dramatically beautiful should consider a winter trip. City and country take on a whole new glamour when they're buried deep in snow.

The *Kodak Guide to Shooting Great Travel Pictures* (available at bookstores everywhere) is loaded with tips.

➤ PHOTO HELP: **Kodak Information Center** (☎ 800/242–2424).

EQUIPMENT PRECAUTIONS

Don't pack film and equipment in checked luggage, where it is much more susceptible to damage. X-ray machines used to view checked luggage are becoming much more powerful and therefore are more likely to ruin your film. Always **keep film and tape out of the sun.** Carry an extra supply of batteries, and **be prepared to turn on your camera or camcorder** to prove to security personnel that the device is real. Always **ask for hand inspection of film,** which becomes clouded after repeated exposure to airport X-ray machines, and **keep videotapes away from metal detectors.**

CAR RENTAL

If you prefer a manual-transmission car, check whether the rental agency of your choice offers stick shifts; some companies, such as Avis, don't in Canada.

➤ MAJOR AGENCIES: **Alamo** (☎ 800/522-9696; 020/8759–6200 in the U.K., WEB www.alamo.com). **Avis** (☎ 800/331–1084; 800/879–2847 in Canada; 02/9353–9000 in Australia; 09/525–1982 in New Zealand; 0870/606–0100 in the U.K., WEB www.avis.com). **Budget** (☎ 800/527–0700; 0870/156–5656 in the U.K., WEB www.

budget.com). **Dollar** (☎ 800/800–6000; 0124/622–0111 in the U.K., where it's affiliated with Sixt; 02/9223–1444 in Australia, WEB www.dollar.com). **Hertz** (☎ 800/654–3001; 800/263–0600 in Canada; 02/9669–2444 in Australia; 09/256–8690 in New Zealand; 020/8897–2072 in the U.K., WEB www.hertz.com). **National Car Rental** (☎ 800/227–7368; 020/8680–4800 in the U.K., WEB www.nationalcar.com).

CUTTING COSTS

To get the best deal, **book through a travel agent who shops around.** Also **price local car-rental companies,** although the service and maintenance may not be as good as those of a major player. Remember to ask about required deposits, cancellation penalties, and drop-off charges if you're planning to pick up the car in one city and leave it in another. If you're traveling during a holiday period, also make sure that a confirmed reservation guarantees you a car.

Do **look into wholesalers,** companies that do not own fleets but rent in bulk from those that do and often offer better rates than traditional car-rental operations. Payment must be made before you leave home.

INSURANCE

When driving a rented car you are generally responsible for any damage to or loss of the vehicle as well as for any property damage or personal injury that you may cause. Before you rent, see what coverage your personal auto-insurance policy and credit cards provide.

REQUIREMENTS & RESTRICTIONS

In Canada your own driver's license is acceptable. Some provinces have age restrictions on younger drivers. In Ontario, for example, drivers must be 21; in Québec, drivers under 25 often have to pay a surcharge of $5 a day. Rental-car companies have not set an upper age limit.

SURCHARGES

Before you pick up a car in one city and leave it in another, **ask about drop-off charges or one-way service fees,** which can be substantial. Note,

too, that some rental agencies charge extra if you return the car before the time specified in your contract. To avoid a hefty refueling fee, **fill the tank just before you turn in the car,** but be aware that gas stations near the rental outlet may overcharge.

CAR TRAVEL

Canada's highway system is excellent. It includes the Trans-Canada Highway, which uses several numbers and is the longest highway in the world—running about 8,000 km (5,000 mi) from Victoria, British Columbia, to St. John's, Newfoundland, using ferries to bridge coastal waters at each end. The second-longest Canadian highway, the Yellowhead Highway (Highway 16), follows a route from the Pacific Coast and over the Rockies to the prairies. North of the population centers, roads become fewer and less developed.

FROM THE U.S.

Drivers must carry owner registration and proof of insurance coverage, which is compulsory in Canada. The Canadian Non-Resident Inter-Provincial Motor Vehicle Liability Insurance Card, available from any U.S. insurance company, is accepted as evidence of financial responsibility in Canada. The minimum liability coverage in Atlantic Canada is C$200,000. If you are driving a car that is not registered in your name, carry a letter from the owner that authorizes your use of the vehicle.

The U.S. Interstate Highway System leads directly into Canada along I–95 from Maine to New Brunswick. There are many smaller highway crossings between the two countries as well.

➤ INSURANCE INFORMATION: **Insurance Bureau of Canada** (☎ 416/362–9528; 800/387–2880 in Canada, WEB www.ibc.ca).

GASOLINE

Gas prices in Canada have been on the rise. At press time, the per-liter price was up at 85¢. Gasoline tends to be most expensive in places such as Newfoundland, where transport costs and high provincial taxes boost the price.

Distances are always shown in kilometers, and gasoline is always sold in liters. (A gallon has 3.8 liters.)

RULES OF THE ROAD

By law, you are required to wear seat belts (and to use infant seats). Some provinces have a statutory requirement to drive with vehicle headlights on for extended periods after dawn and before sunset. Radar-detection devices are illegal. Speed limits, given in kilometers, vary from province to province, but they are usually within the 90–110 kph (50–68 mph) range outside the cities.

CHILDREN
IN ATLANTIC CANADA

Travelers crossing the border with children should **carry identification for them** similar to that required by adults (i.e., passport or birth certificate). Children traveling with one parent or other adult should **bring a letter of permission** from the other parent, parents, or legal guardian. Divorced parents with shared custody rights should **carry legal documents establishing their status.**

If you are renting a car, don't forget to **arrange for a car seat** when you reserve.

FLYING

If your children are two or older, **ask about children's airfares.** As a general rule, infants under two not occupying a seat fly at greatly reduced fares or even free. When booking, **confirm carry-on allowances** if you're traveling with infants. In general, for babies charged 10% of the adult fare you are allowed one carry-on bag and a collapsible stroller; if the flight is full, the stroller may have to be checked or you may be limited to less.

Experts agree that it's a good idea to use safety seats aloft for children weighing less than 40 pounds. Airlines set their own policies: U.S. carriers usually require that the child be ticketed, even if he or she is young enough to ride free, since the seats must be strapped into regular seats. Do **check your airline's policy about using safety seats during takeoff and landing.** And since safety seats are not allowed everywhere in the plane, get your seat assignments early.

When reserving, **request children's meals or a freestanding bassinet** if you need them. But note that bulkhead seats, where you must sit to use the bassinet, may lack an overhead bin or storage space on the floor.

LODGING

Most hotels in Canada allow children under a certain age to stay in their parents' room at no extra charge, but others charge for them as extra adults; be sure to **find out the cutoff age for children's discounts.**

SIGHTS & ATTRACTIONS

Places that are especially appealing to children are indicated by a rubber-duckie icon (🦆) in the margin.

CONSUMER PROTECTION

Whenever shopping or buying travel services in Canada, **pay with a major credit card,** if possible, so you can cancel payment or get reimbursed if there's a problem. If you're buying a package or tour, always **consider travel insurance** that includes default coverage (☞ Insurance).

CUSTOMS & DUTIES

When shopping, **keep receipts** for all purchases. Upon reentering the country, **be ready to show customs officials what you've bought.** If you feel a duty is incorrect or object to the way your clearance was handled, note the inspector's badge number and ask to see a supervisor. If the problem isn't resolved, write to the appropriate authorities, beginning with the port director at your point of entry.

U.S. Customs and Immigration has preclearance services at international airports in Calgary, Edmonton, Montréal, Ottawa, Vancouver, and Winnipeg. This allows U.S.-bound air passengers to depart their airplane directly on arrival at their U.S. destination without further inspection and delays.

➤ INFORMATION: **U.S. Customs Service** (✉ 1300 Pennsylvania Ave. NW, Room 6.3D, Washington, DC 20229, WEB www.customs.gov; inquiries ☎ 202/354–1000; complaints c/o ✉ 1300 Pennsylvania Ave. NW, Room 5.4D, Washington, DC 20229; registration of equipment c/o Office of Passenger Programs, ☎ 202/927–0530).

IN AUSTRALIA

Australian residents who are 18 or older may bring home A$400 worth of souvenirs and gifts (including jewelry), 250 cigarettes or 250 grams of tobacco, and 1,125 ml of alcohol (including wine, beer, and spirits). Residents under 18 may bring back A$200 worth of goods. Prohibited items include meat products. Seeds, plants, and fruits need to be declared upon arrival.

➤ INFORMATION: **Australian Customs Service** (Regional Director, ✉ Box 8, Sydney, NSW 2001, Australia, ☎ 02/9213–2000, FAX 02/9213–4000, WEB www.customs.gov.au).

IN CANADA

American and British visitors may bring in the following items duty-free: 200 cigarettes, 50 cigars, and 7 ounces of tobacco; 1 bottle (1.1 liters or 40 imperial ounces) of liquor or wine, or 24 355-ml (12-ounce) bottles or cans of beer for personal consumption. Any alcohol and tobacco products in excess of these amounts is subject to duty, provincial fees, and taxes. You can also bring in gifts up to a total value of C$750.

A deposit is sometimes required for trailers (refunded upon return). Cats and dogs must have a certificate issued by a licensed veterinarian that clearly identifies the animal and certifies that it has been vaccinated against rabies during the preceding 36 months. Seeing-eye dogs are allowed into Canada without restriction. Plant material must be declared and inspected. There may be restrictions on some live plants, bulbs, and seeds. With certain restrictions or prohibitions on some fruits and vegetables, visitors may bring food with them for their own use, providing the quantity is consistent with the duration of the visit.

Canada's firearms laws are significantly stricter than those in the United States. All handguns and semiautomatic and fully automatic weapons are prohibited and cannot be brought into the country. Sporting rifles and shotguns may be imported provided they are to be used for sporting, hunting, or competition while in Canada. All firearms must be declared to Canada Customs at the first point of entry. Failure to declare firearms will result in their seizure, and criminal charges may be made. Regulations require visitors to have a confirmed "Firearms Declaration" to bring any guns into Canada; a fee of $50 applies, good for one year. For more information, contact the Canadian Firearms Centre.

➤ INFORMATION: **Revenue Canada** (✉ 2265 St. Laurent Blvd. S, Ottawa, ON K1G 4K3, ☎ 613/993–0534; 800/461–9999 in Canada). **Canadian Firearms Centre** (☎ 800/731–4000).

IN NEW ZEALAND

Homeward-bound residents 17 or older may bring back NZ$700 worth of souvenirs and gifts. Your duty-free allowance also includes 4.5 liters of wine or beer; one 1,125-ml bottle of spirits; and either 200 cigarettes, 250 grams of tobacco, 50 cigars, or a combination of the three up to 250 grams. Prohibited items include meat products, seeds, plants, and fruits.

➤ INFORMATION: **New Zealand Customs** (Custom House, ✉ 50 Anzac Ave., Box 29, Auckland, New Zealand, ☎ 09/300–5399, FAX 09/359–6730, WEB www.customs.govt.nz).

IN THE U.K.

From countries outside the European Union, including Canada, you may bring home, duty-free, 200 cigarettes or 50 cigars; 1 liter of spirits or 2 liters of fortified or sparkling wine or liqueurs; 2 liters of still table wine; 60 ml of perfume; 250 ml of toilet water; plus £145 worth of other goods, including gifts and souvenirs. If returning from outside the EU, prohibited items include meat products, seeds, plants, and fruits.

➤ INFORMATION: **HM Customs and Excise** (✉ Dorset House, Stamford St., Bromley, Kent BR1 1XX, U.K., ☎ 020/7202–4227, WEB www.hmce.gov.uk).

DINING

The restaurants we list are the cream of the crop in each price category. Properties indicated by an ✕🏠 are lodging establishments whose restaurant warrants a special trip. For information about regional dining, including a price chart, *see* Dining *in* Pleasures and Pastimes at the beginning of each chapter.

RESERVATIONS & DRESS

Reservations are always a good idea: we mention them only when they're essential or not accepted. Book as far ahead as you can, and reconfirm as soon as you arrive. We mention dress only when men are required to wear a jacket or a jacket and tie.

DISABILITIES & ACCESSIBILITY

Travelers with disabilities do not have the same blanket legal protection in Canada that they have in the United States. Indeed, some facilities aren't easy to use in a wheelchair—the subway systems in Montréal and Toronto, for example, and city buses just about everywhere. However, thanks to increased awareness and government-incentive programs, most major attractions—museums, churches, theaters—are equipped with ramps and lifts to handle wheelchairs. National and provincial institutions—parks, public monuments, and government buildings—almost always are accessible.

The Canadian Paraplegic Association National Office has information about touring in Canada. To file a complaint about transportation obstacles at Canadian airports (including flights), railroads, or ferries, contact the Director, Accessible Transportation Directorate, at the Canadian Transportation Agency (www.cta-otc.gc.ca).

➤ COMPLAINTS: In the U.S.: **Aviation Consumer Protection Division** (⊠ C-75, Room 4107, Washington, DC 20590, ☎ 202/366–2220, WEB www. dot.gov/airconsumer) for airline-related problems. **Civil Rights Office** (⊠ U.S. Department of Transportation, Departmental Office of Civil Rights, S-30, 400 7th St. SW, Room 10215, Washington, DC 20590, ☎ 202/366–4648, FAX 202/366–9371, WEB www.dot.gov/ost/docr/index.htm) for problems with surface transportation. **Disability Rights Section** (⊠ U.S. Department of Justice, Civil Rights Division, Box 66738, Washington, DC 20035-6738, ☎ 202/514–0301 or 800/514–0301; 202/514–0383 TTY; 800/514–0383 TTY, FAX 202/307–1198, WEB www.usdoj.gov/crt/ada/adahom1.htm) for general complaints. In Canada: **Accessible Transportation Directorate** (⊠ 15 Eddy St., Hull, QC K1A 0N9, ☎ 819/997–6828 or 800/883–1813). **Council of Canadians with Disabilities** (⊠ 294 Portage Ave., Suite 926, Winnipeg, MN R3C 0B9, ☎ 204/947–0303, FAX 204/942–4625).

➤ LOCAL RESOURCES: **Canadian Paraplegic Association National Office** (⊠ 1101 Prince of Wales Dr., Ottawa, ON K2C 3W7, ☎ 613/723–1033, WEB www.canparaplegic.org).

LODGING

When discussing accessibility with an operator or reservations agent, **ask hard questions.** Are there any stairs, inside *or* out? Are there grab bars next to the toilet *and* in the shower/tub? How wide is the doorway to the room? To the bathroom? For the most extensive facilities meeting the latest legal specifications, **opt for newer accommodations.**

TRAVEL AGENCIES

In the United States, the Americans with Disabilities Act requires that travel firms serve the needs of all travelers. Some agencies specialize in working with people with disabilities.

➤ TRAVELERS WITH MOBILITY PROBLEMS: **Access Adventures** (⊠ 206 Chestnut Ridge Rd., Scottsville, NY 14624, ☎ 716/889–9096, dltravel@prodigy.net), run by a former physical-rehabilitation counselor. **Care-Vacations** (⊠ No. 5, 5110–50 Ave., Leduc, AB T9E 6V4, Canada, ☎ 780/986–6404 or 877/478–7827, FAX 780/986–8332, WEB www.carevacations.com), for group tours and cruise vacations. **Flying Wheels Travel** (⊠ 143 W. Bridge St., Box 382, Owatonna, MN 55060, ☎ 507/451–5005 or 800/535–6790, FAX 507/451–1685, WEB www.flyingwheelstravel.com).

DISCOUNTS & DEALS

Be a smart shopper and **compare all your options** before making decisions. A plane ticket bought with a promotional coupon from travel clubs, coupon books, and direct-mail offers or on the Internet may not be cheaper than the least expensive fare from a discount ticket agency. And always keep in mind that what you get is just as important as what you save.

DISCOUNT RESERVATIONS

To save money, **look into discount reservations services** with toll-free numbers, which use their buying power to get a better price on hotels, airline tickets, even car rentals. When booking a room, always **call the hotel's local toll-free number** (if one is available) rather than the central reservations number—you'll often get a better price. Always ask about special packages or corporate rates.

When shopping for the best deal on hotels and car rentals, **look for guaranteed exchange rates,** which protect you against a falling U.S. dollar. With your rate locked in, you won't pay more, even if the price goes up in the local currency.

➤ AIRLINE TICKETS: ☎ 800/359–2727.

➤ HOTEL ROOMS: **Hotel Reservations Network** (☎ 800/964–6835, WEB www.hoteldiscount.com). **Players Express Vacations** (☎ 800/458–6161, WEB www.playersexpress.com). **RMC Travel** (☎ 800/245–5738, WEB www.rmcwebtravel.com). **Steigenberger Reservation Service** (☎ 800/223–5652, WEB www.srs-worldhotels.com). **Turbotrip.com** (☎ 800/473–7829, WEB www.turbotrip.com).

PACKAGE DEALS

Don't confuse packages and guided tours. When you buy a package, you travel on your own, just as though you had planned the trip yourself. Fly/drive packages, which combine airfare and car rental, are often a good deal.

ECOTOURISM

Canada's rugged wilderness areas often have very delicate ecosystems. Sand dunes in eastern Canada, important nesting grounds for sea birds, often are protected.

EMBASSIES

All embassies are in Ottawa, ON; there are consulates in some major cities. Emergency information is given in the A to Z section at the end of each chapter.

➤ AUSTRALIA: **Australian High Commission** (✉ 50 O'Connor St., Suite 710, Ottawa, ☎ 613/236–0841).

➤ NEW ZEALAND: **New Zealand High Commission** (✉ 99 Bank St., Suite 727, Ottawa, ☎ 613/238–5991).

➤ UNITED KINGDOM: **British High Commission** (✉ 80 Elgin St., Ottawa, ☎ 613/237–1530).

➤ UNITED STATES: **U.S. Embassy** (✉ 490 Sussex Dr., Ottawa, ☎ 613/238–5335).

GAY & LESBIAN TRAVEL

Canada is generally a fairly tolerant country, and same-sex couples should face few problems in the major metropolitan areas. All the big cities actively and avidly compete for gay visitors. Same-sex couples might not get as warm and open a welcome in rural areas as they do in the big cities. Parts of the Atlantic region harbor more conservative views.

➤ GAY- & LESBIAN-FRIENDLY TRAVEL AGENCIES: **Different Roads Travel** (✉ 8383 Wilshire Blvd., Suite 902, Beverly Hills, CA 90211, ☎ 323/651–5557 or 800/429–8747, FAX 323/651–3678, lgernert@tzell.com). **Kennedy Travel** (✉ 314 Jericho Turnpike, Floral Park, NY 11001, ☎ 516/352–4888 or 800/237–7433, FAX 516/354–8849, WEB www.kennedytravel.com). **Now Voyager** (✉ 4406 18th St., San Francisco, CA 94114, ☎ 415/626–1169 or 800/255–6951, FAX 415/626–8626, WEB www.nowvoyager.com). **Skylink Travel and Tour** (✉ 1006 Mendocino Ave., Santa Rosa, CA 95401, ☎ 707/546–9888 or 800/225–5759, FAX 707/546–9891, WEB www.skylinktravel.com), serving lesbian travelers.

HOLIDAYS

Canadian national holidays are as follows: New Year's Day, Good Friday (Friday before Easter), Easter Monday, Victoria Day (Monday before May 25), Canada Day (July 1), Labour Day (first Monday of September), Thanksgiving (second Monday of October), Remembrance Day (November 11), Christmas, and Boxing Day (December 26).

The following are provincial holidays for 2002: New Brunswick Day (August 7); St. Patrick's Day (March 20), St. George's Day (April 24), Discovery Day (June 26), Memorial Day (July 1), and Orangemen's Day (July 10) in Newfoundland; and Civic Holiday (August 7) in Nova Scotia.

INSURANCE

The most useful travel-insurance plan is a comprehensive policy that includes coverage for trip cancellation and interruption, default, trip delay, and medical expenses (with a waiver for pre-existing conditions).

Without insurance you will lose all or most of your money if you cancel your trip, regardless of the reason. Default insurance covers you if your tour operator, airline, or cruise line goes out of business. Trip-delay covers expenses that arise because of bad weather or mechanical delays. Study the fine print when comparing policies.

Always **buy travel policies directly from the insurance company**; if you buy them from a cruise line, airline, or tour operator that goes out of business you probably will not be covered for the agency or operator's default, a major risk. Before making any purchase, **review your existing health and home-owner's policies** to find what they cover away from home.

British and Australian citizens need extra medical coverage when traveling overseas.

➤ TRAVEL INSURERS: In the U.S.: **Access America** (✉ 6600 W. Broad St., Richmond, VA 23230, ☎ 800/284–8300, FAX 804/673–1491, WEB www.etravelprotection.com). **Travel Guard International** (✉ 1145 Clark St., Stevens Point, WI 54481, ☎ 715/345–0505 or 800/826–1300, FAX 800/955–8785, WEB www.noelgroup.com). In Canada: **RBC Travel Insurance** (✉ 6880 Financial Dr., Mississauga, ON L5N 7Y5, ☎ 905/816–2700 or 800/387–4357, WEB www.rbcinsurance.com).

LANGUAGE

Canada's two official languages are English and French. Although English is widely spoken, it is useful to **learn a few French phrases** in the French-Canadian communities in the Maritimes (Nova Scotia, New Brunswick, and Prince Edward Island). Canadian French has many distinctive words and expressions, but it's no more different from the language of France than North American English is from the language of Great Britain.

LANGUAGES FOR TRAVELERS

A phrase book and language-tape set can help get you started. *Fodor's French for Travelers* (available at bookstores everywhere) is excellent.

LODGING

In the cities you have a choice of luxury hotels, moderately priced modern properties, and smaller older hotels with perhaps fewer conveniences but more charm. Options in smaller towns and in the country include large, full-service resorts; small, privately owned hotels; roadside motels; and bed-and-breakfasts. Even here you need to make reservations at least on the day on which you plan to pull into town.

Canada doesn't have a national government rating system for hotels, but many provinces do rate their accommodations.

Expect accommodations to cost more in summer than in the off-season (except for places such as ski resorts, where winter is high season). When making reservations, **ask about special deals and packages.** Big-city hotels that cater to business travelers often offer weekend packages, and many city hotels offer rooms at up to 50% off in winter. If you're planning to visit a major city or resort area in high season, **book well in advance.** Also be aware of any special events or festivals that may coincide with your visit and fill every room for miles around. For resorts and lodges, consider the winter ski-season high as well and plan accordingly.

The lodgings we list are the cream of the crop in each price category. We always list the facilities that are available—but we don't specify whether they cost extra; when pricing accommodations, always ask what's included and what costs extra. Properties indicated by an ✕🏠 are lodging establishments whose restaurant warrants a special trip. For price charts, *see* Lodging *in* Pleasures and Pastimes at the beginning of each chapter.

Assume that hotels operate on the European Plan (EP, with no meals) unless it's otherwise specified that they use the Continental Plan (CP, with a Continental breakfast daily), Breakfast Plan (BP, with a full breakfast), Modified American Plan (MAP, with breakfast and dinner daily), or the American Plan (AP, with all meals).

APARTMENT & VILLA RENTALS

If you want a home base that's roomy enough for a family and comes with cooking facilities, **consider a furnished rental.** These can save you money, especially if you're traveling with a group. Home-exchange directories sometimes list rentals as well as exchanges.

➤ INTERNATIONAL AGENTS: **Hideaways International** (✉ 767 Islington St., Portsmouth, NH 03801, ☎ 603/430–4433 or 800/843–4433, ℻ 603/430–4444, WEB www.hideaways.com; membership $129).

B&BS

Bed-and-breakfasts can be found in both the country and the cities. For assistance in booking these, **contact the appropriate provincial tourist board,** which either has a listing of B&Bs or can refer you to an association that can help you secure reservations. Be sure to **check out the B&B's Web site,** which may have useful information, although you should also find out how up-to-date it is. Room quality varies from house to house as well, so you can **ask to see a room before making a choice.**

CAMPING

Campgrounds in Atlantic Canada range from rustic woodland settings far from the nearest paved road to facility-packed open fields full of sleek motor homes next to major highways. Some of the best sites are in national and provincial parks—well cared for, well equipped, and close to plenty of nature and activity programs for both children and adults. The campgrounds in the coastal regions of the Maritime Provinces are particularly beautiful. Campers tend to be working- or middle-class families with a fair sprinkling of seniors, but their tastes and practices are as varied as the campsites they favor. Some see camping simply as a way to get practical, low-cost lodgings on a road trip, while other, more sedentary campers move into one campground with as much elaborate equipment as they can and set up for a long stay. Wilderness camping for hikers and canoeists is available in national and provincial parks.

HOSTELS

No matter what your age, you can **save on lodging costs by staying at hostels.** In some 4,500 locations in more than 70 countries around the world, Hostelling International (HI), the umbrella group for a number of national youth-hostel associations, offers single-sex, dorm-style beds and, at many hostels, rooms for couples and family accommodations. Membership in any HI national hostel association, open to travelers of all ages, allows you to stay in HI-affiliated hostels at member rates; one-year membership is about $25 for adults (C$26.75 in Canada, £12.50 in the U.K., A$52 in Australia, and NZ$30 in New Zealand); hostels run about $10–$25 per night. Members have priority if the hostel is full; they're also eligible for discounts around the world, even on rail and bus travel in some countries.

➤ ORGANIZATIONS: **Hostelling International—American Youth Hostels** (✉ 733 15th St. NW, Suite 840, Washington, DC 20005, ☎ 202/783–6161, ℻ 202/783–6171, WEB www.hiayh.org). **Hostelling International—Canada** (✉ 400–205 Catherine St., Ottawa, ON K2P 1C3, Canada, ☎ 613/237–7884, ℻ 613/237–7868, WEB www.hostellingintl.ca). **Australian Youth Hostel Association** (✉ 10 Mallett St., Camperdown, NSW 2050, Australia, ☎ 02/9565–1699, ℻ 02/9565–1325, WEB www.yha.com.au). **Youth Hostel Association of England and Wales** (✉ Trevelyan House, 8 St. Stephen's Hill, St. Albans, Hertfordshire AL1 2DY, U.K., ☎ 0870/8708808, ℻ 01727/844126, WEB www.yha.org.uk). **Youth Hostels Association of New Zealand** (✉ Level

3, 193 Cashel St., Box 436, Christchurch, New Zealand, ☎ 03/379–9970, 𝐅𝐀𝐗 03/365–4476, 𝐖𝐄𝐁 www.yha.org.nz).

HOTELS

All hotels listed have private baths unless otherwise noted.

MAIL & SHIPPING

In Canada you can buy stamps at the post office or from vending machines in most hotel lobbies, railway stations, airports, bus terminals, many retail outlets, and some newsstands. If you're sending mail to or within Canada, **be sure to include the postal code** (six digits and letters). Note that the suite number often appears before the street number in an address, followed by a hyphen.

Following are postal abbreviations for provinces and territories: Alberta, AB; British Columbia, BC; Manitoba, MB; New Brunswick, NB; Newfoundland and Labrador, NF; Northwest Territories and Nunavut, NT; Nova Scotia, NS; Ontario, ON; Prince Edward Island, PE; Québec, QC; Saskatchewan, SK; Yukon, YT.

POSTAL RATES

Within Canada, postcards and letters up to 30 grams cost 47¢; between 31 grams and 50 grams, the cost is 75¢; and between 51 grams and 100 grams, the cost is 94¢. Letters and postcards to the United States cost 60¢ for up to 30 grams, 85¢ for between 31 and 50 grams, and $1.30 for up to 100 grams. Prices include GST (Goods and Services Tax).

International mail and postcards run $1.05 for up to 20 grams, $1.60 for 21 to 50 grams, and $2.50 for 51 to 100 grams.

RECEIVING MAIL

Visitors may have mail sent to them c/o General Delivery in the town they are visiting, for pickup in person within 15 days, after which it will be returned to the sender.

MEDIA

NEWSPAPERS & MAGAZINES

Maclean's and *Saturday Night* are Canada's two main general-interest magazines. Both cover arts and culture as well as politics. Canada has two national newspapers, the *National Post* and the *Globe and Mail*—both are published in Toronto and both are available at newsstands in major foreign cities, especially the big weekend editions, which are published on Saturday. The arts-and-entertainment sections of both papers have advance news of major events and exhibitions across the country. Both also have Web sites with limited information on cultural events. For more-detailed information, it is advisable to rely on metropolitan papers. Provincial daily newspapers in Atlantic Canada include the *Halifax Herald* and the *Daily News* in Nova Scotia, the *Telegraph–Journal* in New Brunswick, and the *Guardian* in Prince Edward Island.

RADIO & TELEVISION

U.S. television dominates Canada's airwaves. In border areas—where most Canadians live—Fox, PBS, NBC, CBS, and ABC are readily available. Canada's two major networks, the state-owned Canadian Broadcasting Corporation (CBC) and the private CTV, and the smaller Global Network broadcast a steady diet of U.S. sitcoms and dramas in prime time with only a scattering of Canadian-produced dramas and comedies. The selection of Canadian-produced current-affairs programs, however, is much wider. The CBC also has a parallel French-language network, Radio-Canada. Canadian cable subscribers have the usual vast menu of specialty channels to choose from, including the all-news outlets operated by CTV and CBC.

The CBC operates the country's only truly national radio network. In fact, it operates four of them, two in English and two in French. Its Radio 1 network, usually broadcast on the AM band, has a daily schedule rich in news, current-affairs, and discussion programs. One of the most popular shows, "As It Happens," takes a quirky and highly entertaining look at national, world, and weird events every evening at 6. Radio 2, usually broadcast on FM, emphasizes music and often features live classical concerts by some of Canada's best orchestras, opera companies, and choral groups. The two French-language networks more or less follow the same pattern.

MONEY MATTERS

Throughout this book, unless otherwise stated, all prices, including dining and lodging, are given in Canadian dollars.

Prices throughout this guide are given for adults. Substantially reduced fees are almost always available for children, students, and senior citizens.

ATMS

ATMs are available in most bank, trust-company, and credit-union branches across the country, as well as in many convenience stores, malls, and gas stations.

CREDIT CARDS

Throughout this guide, the following abbreviations are used: **AE**, American Express; **D**, Discover; **DC**, Diners Club; **MC**, MasterCard; and **V**, Visa.

➤ REPORTING LOST CARDS: **American Express** (☎ 800/528–4800). **Diners Club** (☎ 800/234–6377). **Discover** (☎ 800/347–2683). **MasterCard** (☎ 800/307–7309). **Visa** (☎ 800/336–8472).

CURRENCY

U.S. dollars are accepted in much of Canada (especially in communities near the border). However, to get the most favorable exchange rate, **exchange at least some of your money into Canadian funds at a bank or other financial institution.** Traveler's checks (some are available in Canadian dollars) and major U.S. credit cards are accepted in most areas.

The units of currency in Canada are the Canadian dollar (C$) and the cent, in almost the same denominations as U.S. currency ($5, $10, $20, 1¢, 5¢, 10¢, 25¢, etc.). The $1 and $2 bill are no longer used; they have been replaced by $1 and $2 coins (known as a "loonie," because of the loon that appears on the coin, and a "toonie," respectively). At press time the exchange rate was US$1 to C$1.57, £1 to C$2.31, €1 to C$1.43, A$1 to C$.81, and NZ$1 to C$.66.

CURRENCY EXCHANGE

For the most favorable rates, **change money through banks.** Although ATM transaction fees may be higher abroad than at home, ATM rates are excellent because they are based on wholesale rates offered only by major banks. You won't do as well at exchange booths in airports or rail and bus stations, in hotels, in restaurants, or in stores. To avoid lines at airport exchange booths, **get a bit of local currency before you leave home.**

➤ EXCHANGE SERVICES: **International Currency Express** (☎ 888/278–6628 for orders, WEB www.foreignmoney. com). **Thomas Cook Currency Services** (☎ 800/287–7362 for telephone orders and retail locations, WEB www. us.thomascook.com).

NATIONAL PARKS

If you plan to visit several parks in a region, you may be able to **save money on park fees by buying a multipark pass.** Parks Canada passes include the PEI Combo Pass, the Atlantic Regional National Park Pass, and the Eastern Newfoundland National Historic Sites Pass. Parks Canada is decentralized, so it's best to contact the park you plan to visit for information. You can buy passes at the parks covered by the pass.

➤ PARK PASSES: **Parks Canada** (national office: ✉ 25 Eddy St., Hull, QC K1A 0M5, ☎ 800/213–7275, WEB www.parkscanada.pch.gc.ca).

OUTDOORS & SPORTS

BICYCLING

➤ ASSOCIATION: **Canadian Cycling Association** (✉ 702–2197 Riverside Dr., Ottawa, ON K1H 7X3, ☎ 613/248–1353, FAX 613/248–9311, WEB www.canadian-cycling.com).

CANOEING AND KAYAKING

Provincial tourist offices can be of assistance, especially in locating an outfitter to suit your needs. You may also contact the Canadian Recreational Canoeing Association.

➤ ASSOCIATION: **Canadian Recreational Canoeing Association** (✉ Box 398, Merrickville, ON K0G 1N0, ☎ 613/269–2910 or 888/252–6292, FAX 613/269–2908, WEB www.crca.ca).

CLIMBING/MOUNTAINEERING

➤ ASSOCIATION: **Alpine Club of Canada** (✉ Box 8040, Canmore, AB T1W 2T8, ☎ 403/678–3200, FAX 403/678–3224, WEB www.alpineclubofcanada.ca).

GOLF

➤ ASSOCIATION: **Royal Canadian Golf Association** (✉ 1333 Dorval Dr., Oakville, ON L6J 4Z3, ☎ 905/849–9700, FAX 905/845–7040, WEB www.rcga.org).

SCUBA DIVING

➤ ASSOCIATION: **Canadian Amateur Diving Association** (✉ 703–2197 Riverside Dr., Ottawa, ON K1H 7X3, ☎ 613/736–5238, FAX 613/736–0409, WEB www.diving.ca).

TENNIS

➤ ASSOCIATION: **Tennis Canada** (✉ 3111 Steeles Ave. W, Downsview, ON M3J 3H2, ☎ 416/665–9777, FAX 416/665–9017, WEB www.tenniscanada.com).

PACKING

If you plan on camping or hiking in the deep woods in summer, particularly in northern Canada, **always carry insect repellent,** especially in June, which is blackfly season.

In your carry-on luggage, **pack an extra pair of eyeglasses or contact lenses and enough of any medication** you take to last the entire trip. You may also ask your doctor to write a spare prescription using the drug's generic name, since brand names may vary from country to country. In luggage to be checked, **never pack prescription drugs or valuables.** To avoid customs delays, carry medications in their original packaging. And don't forget to carry with you the addresses of offices that handle refunds of lost traveler's checks. Check *Fodor's How to Pack* (available in bookstores everywhere) for more tips.

CHECKING LUGGAGE

You are allowed one carry-on bag and one personal article, such as a purse or a laptop computer. Make sure that everything you carry aboard will fit under the seat or in the overhead bin. Get to the gate early, so you can board as soon as possible.

If you are flying internationally, note that baggage allowances may be determined not by piece but by weight—generally 88 pounds (40 kilograms) in first class, 66 pounds (30 kilograms) in business class, and 44 pounds (20 kilograms) in economy.

Airline liability for baggage is limited to $1,250 per person on flights within the United States. On international flights it amounts to $9.07 per pound or $20 per kilogram for checked baggage (roughly $640 per 70-pound bag) and $400 per passenger for unchecked baggage. You can buy additional coverage at check-in for about $10 per $1,000 of coverage, but it excludes a rather extensive list of items, shown on your airline ticket.

Before departure, **itemize your bags' contents** and their worth, and label the bags with your name, address, and phone number. (If you use your home address, cover it so potential thieves can't see it readily.) Inside each bag, **pack a copy of your itinerary.** At check-in, **make sure that each bag is correctly tagged** with the destination airport's three-letter code. If your bags arrive damaged or fail to arrive at all, file a written report with the airline before leaving the airport.

PASSPORTS & VISAS

When traveling internationally, **carry your passport** even if you don't need one (it's always the best form of I.D.) and **make two photocopies of the data page** (one for someone at home and another for you, carried separately from your passport). If you lose your passport, promptly call the nearest embassy or consulate and the local police.

ENTERING CANADA

Citizens and legal residents of the United States do not need a passport or a visa to enter Canada, but proof of citizenship (a birth certificate or valid passport) and some form of photo identification will be requested. Naturalized U.S. residents should carry their naturalization certificate. Permanent residents who are not citizens should carry their "green card." U.S. residents entering Canada from a third country must have a valid passport, naturalization certificate, or "green card."

Citizens of the United Kingdom need only a valid passport to enter Canada for stays of up to six months.

PASSPORT OFFICES

The best time to apply for a passport or to renew is in fall and winter. Before any trip, check your passport's expiration date, and, if necessary, renew it as soon as possible.

SENIOR-CITIZEN TRAVEL

To qualify for age-related discounts, **mention your senior-citizen status up front** when booking hotel reservations (not when checking out) and before you're seated in restaurants (not when paying the bill). When renting a car, ask about promotional car-rental discounts, which can be cheaper than senior-citizen rates.

➤ EDUCATIONAL PROGRAMS: **Elderhostel** (✉ 11 Ave. de Lafayette, Boston, MA 02111-1746, ☎ 877/426–8056, FAX 877/426–2166, WEB www.elderhostel.org). **Interhostel** (✉ University of New Hampshire, 6 Garrison Ave., Durham, NH 03824, ☎ 603/862–1147 or 800/733–9753, FAX 603/862–1113, WEB www.learn.unh.edu).

SHOPPING

Some smaller regions and towns in Atlantic Canada have become known for particular products. Craftswomen in the tiny Newfoundland outport of St. Anthony's, for example, make parkas, caps, and mittens out of heavy fabric called Grenfell cloth.

SMART SOUVENIRS

The hooked rugs produced by Acadian artisans (usually women) are either kitchy or naively charming, depending on your point of view. The best are available in the Cape Breton village of Chéticamp for prices that range from $15 into the hundreds.

WATCH OUT

Americans should note that it is illegal for them to buy Cuban cigars and to take them home.

STUDENTS IN CANADA

Persons under 18 years of age who are not accompanied by their parents should **bring a letter from a parent or guardian** giving them permission to travel to Canada.

➤ I.D.s & SERVICES: **Council Travel** (CIEE; ✉ 205 E. 42nd St., 15th floor, New York, NY 10017, ☎ 212/822–2700 or 888/268–6245, FAX 212/822–2699, WEB www.councilexchanges.org) for mail orders only, in the United States. **Travel Cuts** (✉ 187 College St., Toronto, Ontario M5T 1P7, Canada, ☎ 416/979–2406; 800/667–2887 in Canada, FAX 416/979–8167, WEB www.travelcuts.com).

TAXES

A goods and services tax (GST) of 7% applies on virtually every transaction in Canada except for the purchase of basic groceries.

In addition to the GST, Newfoundland, Nova Scotia, and New Brunswick have a single harmonized sales tax (HST) of 15%.

GST REFUNDS

You can **get a GST refund** on purchases taken out of the country and on short-term accommodations of less than one month, but not on food, drink, tobacco, car or motor-home rentals, or transportation; rebate forms, which must be submitted within 60 days of leaving Canada, may be obtained from certain retailers, duty-free shops, customs officials, or from the Canada Customs and Revenue Agency. Instant cash rebates up to a maximum of $500 are provided by some duty-free shops when you leave Canada, and most provinces do not tax goods that are shipped directly by the vendor to the purchaser's home. Always **save your original receipts** from stores and hotels (not just credit-card receipts), and **be sure the name and address of the establishment is shown on the receipt.** Original receipts are not returned. To be eligible for a refund, receipts must total at least $200, and each individual receipt must show a minimum purchase of $50.

➤ INFORMATION: **Canada Customs and Revenue Agency** (✉ Visitor

Rebate Program, Summerside Tax Centre, 275 Pope Rd., Suite 104, Summerside, PE C1N 6C6, ☎ 902/432–5608; 800/668–4748 in Canada, WEB www.ccra-adrc.gc.ca).

PROVINCIAL TAX REFUNDS

For provincial tax refunds, **call the provincial toll-free visitor information lines for details** (☞ Visitor Information). Most provinces do not tax goods shipped directly by the vendor to the visitor's home address.

TIPPING

Tips and service charges are not usually added to a bill in Canada. In general, tip 15% of the total bill. This goes for waiters, waitresses, barbers and hairdressers, and taxi drivers. Porters and doormen should get about $2 a bag. For maid service, leave at least $2 per person a day ($3 in luxury hotels).

TOURS & PACKAGES

Because everything is prearranged on a prepackaged tour or independent vacation, you spend less time planning—and often get it all at a good price.

BOOKING WITH AN AGENT

Travel agents are excellent resources. But it's a good idea to collect brochures from several agencies because some agents' suggestions may be influenced by relationships with tour and package firms that reward them for volume sales. If you have a special interest, **find an agent with expertise in that area.** The American Society of Travel Agents (☞ Travel Agencies) has a database of specialists worldwide.

Make sure your travel agent knows the accommodations and other services of the place being recommended. Ask about the hotel's location, room size, beds, and whether it has a pool, room service, or programs for children, if you care about these. Has your agent been there in person or sent others whom you can contact?

Do some homework on your own, too: local tourism boards can provide information about lesser-known and small-niche operators, some of which may sell only direct.

BUYER BEWARE

Each year consumers are stranded or lose their money when tour operators—even large ones with excellent reputations—go out of business. So **check out the operator.** Ask several travel agents about its reputation, and try to **book with a company that has a consumer-protection program.** (Look for information in the company's brochure.) In the United States, members of the National Tour Association and the United States Tour Operators Association are required to set aside funds to cover your payments and travel arrangements in the event that the company defaults. It's also a good idea to choose a company that participates in the American Society of Travel Agents' Tour Operator Program (TOP); ASTA will act as mediator in any disputes between you and your tour operator.

Remember that the more your package or tour includes the better you can predict the ultimate cost of your vacation. Make sure you know exactly what is covered, and **beware of hidden costs.** Are taxes, tips, and transfers included? Entertainment and excursions? These can add up.

➤ TOUR-OPERATOR RECOMMENDATIONS: **American Society of Travel Agents** (☞ Travel Agencies). **National Tour Association** (NTA; ✉ 546 E. Main St., Lexington, KY 40508, ☎ 859/226–4444 or 800/682–8886, WEB www.ntaonline.com). **United States Tour Operators Association** (USTOA; ✉ 342 Madison Ave., Suite 1522, New York, NY 10173, ☎ 212/599–6599 or 800/468–7862, FAX 212/599–6744, WEB www.ustoa.com).

THEME TRIPS

The companies listed below offer multiday tours in Canada. Additional local or regionally based companies that have different-length trips with these themes are listed in each chapter, either with information about the town or in the A to Z section that concludes the chapter.

➤ ADVENTURE: **Gorp Travel** (✉ Box 1486, Boulder, CO 80306, ☎ 303/444–2622 or 800/444–0099, FAX 303/635–0658, WEB www.gorptravel.com).

➤ BICYCLING: **Backroads** (✉ 801 Cedar St., Berkeley, CA 94710-1800, ☎ 510/527–1555 or 800/462–2848, FAX 510/527–1444, WEB www.backroads.com). **Bike Rider Tours** (✉ Box 130254, Boston, MA 02113, ☎ 617/723–2354 or 800/473–7040, FAX 617/723–2355, WEB www.bikeriderstours.com). **Butterfield & Robinson** (✉ 70 Bond St., Toronto, ON M5B 1X3, ☎ 416/864–1354 or 800/678–1147, FAX 416/864–0541, WEB www.butterfield.com). **Easy Rider Tours** (✉ Box 228, Newburyport, MA 01950, ☎ 978/463–6955 or 800/488–8332, FAX 978/463–6988, WEB www.easyridertours.com). **Vermont Bicycle Touring** (✉ Box 711, Bristol, VT 05443-0711, ☎ 800/245–3868 or 802/453–4811, FAX 802/453–4806, WEB www.vbt.com).

➤ FISHING: **Fishing International** (✉ Box 2132, Santa Rosa, CA 95405, ☎ 707/542–4242 or 800/950–4242, FAX 707/526–3474, WEB www.travelsource.com/fishing).

➤ WALKING/HIKING: **Backroads** (✉ 801 Cedar St., Berkeley, CA 94710-1800, ☎ 510/527–1555 or 800/462–2848, FAX 510/527–1444, WEB www.backroads.com). **Butterfield & Robinson** (✉ 70 Bond St., Toronto, ON M5B 1X3, ☎ 416/864–1354 or 800/678–1147, FAX 416/864–0541, WEB www.butterfield.com). **Country Walkers** (✉ Box 180, Waterbury, VT 05676-0180, ☎ 802/244–1387 or 800/464–9255, FAX 802/244–5661, WEB www.countrywalkers.com). **New England Hiking Holidays** (✉ Box 1648, North Conway, NH 03860, ☎ 603/356–9696 or 800/869–0949, WEB www.nehikingholidays.com). **Walking the World** (✉ Box 1186, Fort Collins, CO 80522, ☎ 970/498–0500 or 800/340–9255, FAX 970/498–9100, WEB www.gorp.com/walkingtheworld); specializes in tours for ages 50 and older.

TRAIN TRAVEL

VIA Rail, Canada's Amtrak counterpart, provides transcontinental rail service to Atlantic Canada.

CUTTING COSTS

If you're planning to travel a lot by train, **look into the Canrail pass.** It allows 12 days of coach-class travel within a 30-day period; sleeping cars are available, but they sell out very early and must be reserved at least a month in advance during the high season (June to mid-October), when the pass is $658 (discounts for youths and seniors). Low-season rates (October 16 to May) are $411. The pass is not valid during the Christmas period (December 15 through January 5). For more information and reservations, contact a travel agent in the United States. In the United Kingdom, Long-Haul Leisurail represents VIA Rail.

Train travelers can **check out the 30-day North American RailPass** offered by VIA Rail. It allows unlimited coach–economy travel in the United States and Canada. You must indicate the itinerary when purchasing the pass. The cost is $1,004 from June to October 15, $702 at other times.

➤ TRAIN INFORMATION: **Long-Haul Leisurail** (✉ Box 113, Peterborough, PE3 8HY U.K., ☎ 01733/335599). **VIA Rail Canada** (☎ 800/561–3949).

TRAVEL AGENCIES

A good travel agent puts your needs first. Look for an agency that has been in business at least five years, emphasizes customer service, and has someone on staff who specializes in your destination. In addition, **make sure the agency belongs to a professional trade organization.** The American Society of Travel Agents (ASTA), with more than 26,000 members in some 170 countries, is the largest and most influential in the field. Operating under the motto "Without a travel agent, you're on your own," it maintains and enforces a strict code of ethics and will step in to help mediate any agent-client disputes if necessary. ASTA also maintains a Web site that includes a directory of agents. (If a travel agency is also acting as your tour operator, *see* Buyer Beware *in* Tours & Packages).

➤ LOCAL AGENT REFERRALS: **American Society of Travel Agents** (ASTA; ✉ 1101 King St., Suite 200, Alexandria, VA 22314 ☎ 800/965–2782 24-hr hot line, FAX 703/739–7642, WEB www.astanet.com). **Association of British Travel Agents** (✉ 68–71 Newman St., London W1T 3AH, U.K., ☎ 020/7637–2444, FAX 020/7637–0713, WEB www.abtanet.com).

Association of Canadian Travel Agents (✉ 130 Albert St., Suite 1705, Ottawa, Ontario K1P 5G4, Canada, ☎ 613/237–3657, FAX 613/237–7052, WEB www.acta.net). **Australian Federation of Travel Agents** (✉ Level 3, 309 Pitt St., Sydney NSW 2000, Australia, ☎ 02/9264–3299, FAX 02/9264–1085, WEB www.afta.com.au). **Travel Agents' Association of New Zealand** (✉ Level 5, Paxus House, 79 Boulcott St., Box 1888, Wellington 10033, New Zealand, ☎ 04/499–0104, FAX 04/499–0827, WEB www.taanz.org.nz).

VISITOR INFORMATION

➤ TOURIST INFORMATION: **Canadian Tourism Commission** (☎ 613/946–1000, WEB www.canadatourism.com). **Nova Scotia Tourism** (✉ Box 519, Halifax, B3J 2R7, ☎ 800/565–0000, WEB www.gov.ns.ca/tourism). **Tourism New Brunswick** (✉ Box 12345, Campbellton, E3N 3T6, ☎ 800/561–0123, WEB www. tourismnewbrunswick.ca). **Tourism Newfoundland and Labrador** (✉ Box 8730, St. John's, A1B 4K2, ☎ 800/ 563–6353, WEB www.gov.nf.ca/ tourism). **Tourism PEI** (✉ Box 940, Charlottetown, C1A 7M5, ☎ 888/ 734–7529, WEB www.peiplay.com).

➤ IN THE U.K.: **Visit Canada Center** (✉ 62–65 Trafalgar Sq., London, WC2 5DY, ☎ 0891/715–000, 50p per minute peak rate and 45p per minute cheap rate).

WEB SITES

Do check out the World Wide Web when planning your trip. You'll find everything from weather forecasts to virtual tours of famous cities. Be sure to **visit Fodors.com** (www.fodors.com), a complete travel-planning site. You can research prices and book plane tickets, hotel rooms, rental cars, vacation packages, and more. In addition, you can post your pressing questions in the Travel Talk section. Other planning tools include a currency converter and weather reports, and there are loads of links to travel resources.

For festivals, check out www. festivalseeker.com.

WHEN TO GO

CLIMATE

The following are average daily maximum and minimum temperatures for Halifax.

➤ FORECASTS: **Weather Channel Connection** (☎ 900/932–8437), 95¢ (U.S.) per minute from a Touch-Tone phone.

HALIFAX

Jan.	33F	1C	May	58F	14C	Sept.	67F	19C
	20	– 7		41	5		53	12
Feb.	33F	1C	June	67F	19C	Oct.	58F	14C
	19	– 7		50	10		44	7
Mar.	39F	4C	July	73F	23C	Nov.	48F	9C
	26	– 3		57	14		36	2
Apr.	48F	9C	Aug.	73F	24C	Dec.	37F	3C
	33	1		58	13		25	4

FESTIVALS AND SEASONAL EVENTS

Contact local or provincial tourist boards for more information about these and other festivals.

➤ DEC.: **Newfoundland and Labrador:** In St. John's, **New Year's** revelers gather on the waterfront to ring in the new year.

➤ MAR.: **Newfoundland and Labrador:** From March or April through June, the east coast of Newfoundland from St. Anthony's to St. John's is a great place to see icebergs floating by.

➤ MAY: **New Brunswick:** Celebrations of **Loyalist Day** take place on May 18 in St. John.

Nova Scotia: In the Annapolis Valley, the **Apple Blossom Festival** includes dancing, parades, and entertainment. Truro pays tribute to the tulip with its three-day **Tulip Festival**.

➤ JUNE: **Nova Scotia:** The **International Blues Festival** draws music lovers to Halifax.

Prince Edward Island: Charlottetown Festival Theatre offers concerts and musicals (through September). In Summerside the annual **Summerside Highland Gathering** kicks off a summer of concerts and "Come to the Ceilidh" evenings.

➤ JULY: **New Brunswick:** The **Shediac Lobster Festival** takes place in the town that calls itself the Lobster Capital of the World. There's an **Irish Festival** in Miramichi. The **New Brunswick Highland Games & Scottish Festival** is in Fredericton. In Edmunston the **Foire Brayonne** has music, cultural events, and sports.

Newfoundland and Labrador: The **Exploits Valley Salmon Festival** is in the Grand Falls area; the **Fish, Fun and Folk Festival** in Twillingate; and the **Conception Bay Folk Festival** in Carbonear. **Musicfest** in Stephenville celebrates music, from rock and roll to traditional Newfoundland. **Signal Hill Tattoo** in St. John's (through August) reenacts the final 1762 battle of the Seven Years' War between the British and the French. The **Burin Peninsula Festival of Folk Song and Dance** features traditional entertainment.

Nova Scotia: Antigonish Highland Games, staged annually since 1861, has Scottish music, dance, and such ancient sporting events as the caber toss. Halifax hosts the **Nova Scotia International Tattoo.** The **Atlantic Jazz Festival** is a Halifax highlight. The **Stan Rogers Music Festival** presents three days of gospel, bluegrass, and folk music in an outdoor venue in Canso.

Prince Edward Island: Summerside's Lobster Carnival is a weeklong feast of lobster.

➤ AUG.: **New Brunswick:** At the **Summer Chamber Music Festival** in Fredericton, classical musicians perform and lecture. The **Miramichi Folk Song Festival** has songs steeped in Maritime lore. **Acadian Festival,** at Caraquet, celebrates Acadian heritage with folk singing and food. Saint John's **Festival by the Sea** draws

hundreds of singers, dancers, and musicians. The **Chocolate Festival** in St. Stephen includes suppers, displays, and children's events.

Newfoundland and Labrador: Gander's Festival of Flight celebrates this town as the aviation "Crossroads of the World," with dances, parades, and a folk festival. The **Folk Festival** in St. John's is an outstanding traditional music event.

Nova Scotia: Lunenburg holds the **Nova Scotia Fisheries Exhibition and Fishermen's Reunion.** The **Nova Scotia Gaelic Mod** in St. Ann's celebrates Scottish culture on the grounds of the only Gaelic college in North America. The **Halifax International Buskerfest** has daily outdoor shows by street performers and a food festival.

Prince Edward Island: Old Home Week fills Charlottetown with nostalgia. Kensington stages an annual **Harvest Festival,** the province's biggest country fair.

➤ SEPT.: **New Brunswick:** World-class musicians and up-and-coming Atlantic Canadian talent flood Fredericton with slick jazz, gritty blues, spicy Cajun, and world beat music for five days at the **Harvest Jazz & Blues Festival.** The **Atlantic Balloon Fiesta,** in Sussex, attracts about 30 brightly colored hot-air balloons; it also offers helicopter rides, parachute demonstrations, and other festival fun. Six days of French cinema can be enjoyed at the **Festival du Cinéma Francophone en Acadie** in Moncton; directors and actors from around the world attend.

Prince Edward Island: Festival Acadien de la Région Evangeline is an agricultural fair with Acadian music, a parade, and lobster suppers, at Wellington Station.

➤ OCT.: **Nova Scotia:** The 10-day **Celtic Colors International Festival,** one of the premier Celtic events in the world, celebrates traditional music in two dozen locations across Cape Breton.

➤ NOV.: **Prince Edward Island:** The Prince Edward Island Crafts Council **Annual Christmas Craft Fair** brings craftspeople to Charlottetown.

1

DESTINATION: NOVA SCOTIA, NEW BRUNSWICK, PRINCE EDWARD ISLAND

Of Sea and Land

What's Where

Pleasures and Pastimes

Fodor's Choice

OF SEA AND LAND

CANADA'S MARITIME PROVINCES—Prince Edward Island, New Brunswick, and Nova Scotia—are, along with Newfoundland and Labrador, bound by tradition and geography to the sea. Each province has a distinct personality, but the Atlantic Ocean and the other great bodies of water that flow into it from further inland—the Bay of Fundy with its mighty tides, the warm Baie des Chaleurs, and the Gulf of St. Lawrence, which in pioneer days was part of Canada's nautical highway to the world—have influenced the lifestyle and culture of the more than 2 million people who live here.

The culture manifests itself in the region's language, art, and music. It has been shaped by strong ties to Europe, decades of economic hardship, and a struggle to tame the land. Celtic music, for example, a strong tradition in Cape Breton and other parts of Nova Scotia, has thrived for centuries. The haunting melodies of a lost homeland traveled over the Atlantic in the 18th century when the first Highlanders arrived from Scotland, and mingled with musical influences from the Acadians and Irish. Today Celtic music is being "exported" in a modern form, via young avant-garde performers, to the Scottish homeland from whence it came. In New Brunswick, the toe-tapping fiddle music of the French-speaking Acadians echoes the rhythms of the jigs and reels of Ireland, Scotland, and France. In Newfoundland, too, a lively musical tradition is tempered with folkloric, humorous tales of yesteryear and a vocabulary full of twists and turns that delight the ear.

The Atlantic provinces are strongly rooted in the past, but they are not isolated from the rest of North America—far from it. Those who live in the region have always looked beyond their own borders to wheel and deal with the outside world. The bounty of the ocean (now sadly in decline in certain areas, in part because of mismanagement of resources), marine commerce, and shipbuilding once provided the economic lifeblood of the region, and people sold (and continue to sell) their catches and their expertise around the globe.

Tourism and other service industries have taken over where some of the more traditional occupations have left off. Many national and international technology companies have set up shop here (especially in New Brunswick, which has a large bilingual workforce), attracted by the quality of life and by labor and housing costs that are lower than those in the rest of Canada.

Even Prince Edward Island, Canada's smallest province and a rural enclave of manicured farmland and picturesque villages, is no longer the sleepy backwater of yesteryear. Connected, since 1997, to the mainland by the Confederation Bridge, it is visited by more than 1 million people annually, almost half the entire population of Atlantic Canada.

The Island offers a multitude of outdoor attractions in scenic surroundings, as do all the Atlantic provinces. Gently rolling roads (no hill is higher than 500 ft) make it ideal for cycling. Beaches, many in spectacular settings, abound throughout the region. The Bay of Fundy, which divides Nova Scotia from New Brunswick, is renowned for its whale-watching. On Newfoundland, the birdlife is abundant and moose are so plentiful (125,000 at last count) that locals may warn you not to drive at night.

Atlantic Canada isn't all moose and maritime landscapes, though. Its cities, while small, are attractive, safe, clean, and historic. Charlottetown, on Prince Edward Island, is an intimate, walkable community with old wooden houses and quiet, tree-lined streets. Fredericton, New Brunswick's capital, is a university town on the St. John River. It too, has gracious old buildings, as well as an exceptional regional art museum—the Beaverbrook Art Gallery—named after its benefactor and one of New Brunswick's most famous native sons, Lord Beaverbrook, a renowned Canadian and British press magnate.

St. John's, Newfoundland, has terrific crafts stores (many locals still while away the long winters by knitting sweaters, socks, and woolen hats) and lively pubs, many of them housed in colorfully painted, renovated wooden buildings that march up from the waterfront.

Halifax, Nova Scotia, is the self-proclaimed "capital" of Atlantic Canada. The business center of the region, it is also the area's most populous and sophisticated city. Old and new blend comfortably here. Gracing its harbor skyline are a 19th-century fortress (the Citadel), high-rise hotels, a renovated waterfront collectively known as Historic Properties, and several glass-wall office towers. The present is here but, as in the rest of the region, the past is not forgotten.

— Helga Loverseed

WHAT'S WHERE

New Brunswick
New Brunswick is where the great Canadian forest, sliced by sweeping river valleys and modern highways, meets the Atlantic. To the north and east, the gentle, warm Gulf Stream washes quiet beaches. Besides the seacoast, there are pure inland streams, pretty towns, and historic cities such as Fredericton and Saint John. The province's dual heritage (35% of its population is Acadian French) provides added cultural interest.

Newfoundland and Labrador
The youngest member of the Canadian family, the island of Newfoundland and Labrador on the mainland joined the Confederation in 1949. But the province has a long history. Norsemen settled briefly in L'Anse-aux-Meadows around 1000, and explorer John Cabot landed on the rocky coast in 1497. The land has a raw beauty, with steep cliffs, roaring salmon rivers, and fishing villages that perch precariously on naked rock. Its people are a rich mix of English, Irish, and Scots who have a colorful grasp of language and a talent for acerbic commentary. St. John's, the capital, is a classic harbor city.

Nova Scotia
Almost an island, Nova Scotia is a little province on the Atlantic coast with a long history and a rich culture. Shaped by its rugged coastline and honed by the sea, it has been a haven for blacks arriving as freemen or escaped slaves, Scots, Germans, and Loyalists from the American Revolution, but its earliest colonial history was enriched by the Acadians and scarred by their brutal deportation. This multicultural mix, dating back 400 years, may account for Nova Scotia's rich musical climate, which includes the Gaelic ceilidh—gatherings wild with fiddles and step dancing—and the folk songs of sailors and the sea. Salty little ports dot the coastline, their extravagant Victorian mansions—many of them now hospitable bed-and-breakfasts—bespeaking the wealth of shipwrights and merchants trading with the world a century and more ago. Today, Nova Scotia maintains its unique outlook: worldly, warm, and sturdily independent.

Prince Edward Island
In the Gulf of St. Lawrence north of Nova Scotia and New Brunswick, Prince Edward Island seems too good to be true, with its crisply painted farmhouses, manicured green fields rolling down to sandy beaches, warm ocean water, lobster boats in trim little harbors, and a vest-pocket capital city, Charlottetown, packed with architectural heritage. The opening of the Confederation Bridge in 1997 has made the Island more easily accessible to the mainland.

PLEASURES AND PASTIMES

Dining
Fish and seafood are what Atlantic Canada is known for, although eating out is a relatively new concept in this part of the country. Some dining establishments still serve food the old-fashioned way—deep fried, with lashings of calorie-laden sauce. In the larger cities such as Halifax and St. John's, more choices are available. Along with fish and seafood, you can find a good selection of international and ethnic dishes. If you want to go local, stick to lobster, mussels, scallops, salmon, and cod. In Newfoundland, regional specialties include cod's tongues and seal flipper pie. New Brunswick is known for its fiddleheads—wild ferns picked in early summer before they uncurl (hence their name). In New Brunswick you'll also find dulse,

which is dried, crisp seaweed that can be munched like potato chips or used in powder form to flavor meat and fish.

The Great Outdoors

Atlantic Canada has many provincial and national parks where campers and day-trippers can engage in all kinds of outdoor activities, including water sports such as canoeing, kayaking, and sailing. Fundy National Park, one of New Brunswick's top attractions, has spectacular tides and a unique ecosystem; it is home to an abundance of wildlife such as whales, migrating seabirds, and seals. In Kouchibouguac National Park, on the northeastern shore of the province, sand dunes and grasses protect endangered piping plovers. Sand dunes are also a notable feature of Prince Edward Island National Park, where wide, sandy beaches curve around clean, warm waters that are ideal for swimming, canoeing, or windsurfing. Cape Breton Highlands National Park in Nova Scotia has spectacular drives and great opportunities for wildlife watching as well as hiking and fishing. Newfoundland's Gros Morne National Park, a UNESCO World Heritage Site, offers rugged hiking and camping amid spectacular fjord scenery.

BIKING➤ Eastern Canada offers some of the best bicycling in the country, from the flats of Prince Edward Island to the varied terrain in New Brunswick and Nova Scotia. Write to the provincial tourist boards for their road maps (which are more detailed than the maps available at gas stations) and information on local cycling associations.

BOATING➤ With the Atlantic coastline, major rivers, and smaller lakes, boating in many forms is extremely popular throughout Atlantic Canada. Boat, canoe, and kayak rentals are widely available, and provincial tourism departments can provide lists of sources.

FISHING➤ Anglers can find their catch in Atlantic Canada, although restrictions, seasons, license requirements, and catch limits vary from province to province. In addition, a special fishing permit is required to fish in all national parks; it can be obtained at any national park site, for a nominal fee. Nova Scotia has some of the most stringent freshwater restrictions in Canada, but the availability of Atlantic salmon, speckled trout, and striped bass makes the

effort worthwhile. Salmon, trout, and black bass are abundant in the waters of New Brunswick, and although many salmon pools in the streams and rivers are leased to private freeholders, either individuals or clubs, fly fishing is still readily available for visitors. The waters surrounding Prince Edward Island have some of the best deep-sea tuna fishing. Newfoundland offers cod, mackerel, salmon, and sea trout in the Atlantic and speckled trout and rainbow trout in its fresh waters.

SCUBA DIVING➤ More than 3,000 shipwrecks lie off the coast of Nova Scotia, making it particularly attractive to divers. The provincial Department of Tourism can provide details on the location of wrecks and where to buy or rent equipment.

WHALE-WATCHING➤ The waters around Newfoundland offer excellent whale-watching in season, and giant humpbacks, right whales, finbacks, and minke whales can be seen in the Bay of Fundy. Whale-watching trips are available from Newfoundland, New Brunswick, and Nova Scotia.

Shopping

The residents of Atlantic Canada are consummate craftspeople, and the region abounds with potters, painters, glassblowers, weavers, and photographers. Good buys include handknitted clothing in Newfoundland, hooked rugs and pewter objets d'arts (picture frames, jewelry boxes, candlesticks, and the like) in New Brunswick and Nova Scotia, and pottery on Prince Edward Island. Many of the artisans work from home or from restored barns and farmhouses. If you're driving through the countryside, look for road signs advertising their studios. You should also look for posters listing garage and lawn sales. They're hugely popular in this part of Canada. Some of the stuff on display is just basement junk, but you can find bargains, especially antiques.

FODOR'S CHOICE

No two people will agree on what makes a perfect vacation, but it's fun and helpful to know what others think. We hope you'll have a chance to experience some of Fodor's Choices yourself in Atlantic Canada. For detailed information about each entry, refer to the appropriate chapter.

Historic Sites

Kings Landing Historical Settlement, outside Fredericton, New Brunswick. This reconstructed village—including homes, a school, working farms, and a sawmill—illustrates life in the central Saint John River valley between 1790 and 1900.

Fortress of Louisbourg National Historic Park, Louisbourg, Cape Breton, Nova Scotia. Costumed actors re-create the lives of 18th-century French soldiers, settlers, and tradespeople at this sprawling, reconstructed fortress.

Parks and Gardens

Cape Breton Highlands National Park, Nova Scotia. A wilderness of wooded valleys, plateau barrens, and steep cliffs, it stretches across the northern peninsula of Nova Scotia's Cape Breton Island.

Prince Edward Island National Park, Prince Edward Island. Along the north shore of the Island, sky and sea meet red sandstone cliffs, rolling dunes, and long stretches of sand.

Views to Remember

Signal Hill National Historic Site, St. John's, Newfoundland. Overlooking the snug, punch-bowl harbor of St. John's and the sea, this hilltop was taken and retaken by opposing forces in the 17th and 18th centuries.

Peggy's Cove, Nova Scotia. At the mouth of a bay facing the open Atlantic, the cove, with its houses huddled around the narrow slit in the boulders, has the only Canadian post office in a lighthouse.

Dining

Lion Inn, Lunenburg, Nova Scotia. Scallops with sweet onions, mussels in wine sauce, tender rack of lamb, and sinful desserts are prepared by a chef who cooks for the love of it. The homey yet elegant ambience is accented by candlelight and cool jazz. $$$–$$$$

Lodging

Kingsbrae Arms, St. Andrews by-the-Sea, New Brunswick. The antique furnishings in this restored 1897 estate are eclectic and amusing. Guests are well pampered. $$$$

Gowrie House, Sydney, Nova Scotia. Filled with art and antiques and surrounded by trees and flower beds, this Georgian house is a gem of a country inn; dinners are outstanding. $$

West Point Lighthouse, West Point, Prince Edward Island. A functioning lighthouse in a provincial park, this small inn sits next to the beach. $–$$

2 NOVA SCOTIA

The rugged coastline of this Atlantic
province encloses evergreen forests and
rolling farmland. A wonderful assortment
of cultures exists here but it's no melting
pot, as each pocket of individuality works
fiercely to maintain its identity, traditions,
and language. There are Gaelic street signs
in Mabou, French masses in Chéticamp,
black gospel choirs in Halifax, Mi'Kmaq
handicrafts at Eskasoni, and German
sausage in Lunenburg. Fishing villages
abound, and in Halifax and Dartmouth,
city life coexists with small-town charm.

Updated by
Milan
Chvostek, Kim
Goodson,
Susan Randles,
Dave
Stephens, and
Isobel Warren.

NFINITE RICHES IN A LITTLE ROOM," wrote Elizabethan playwright
Christopher Marlowe. He might have been referring to Nova Scotia, Canada's second-smallest province, which packs an impossible
variety of cultures and landscapes into an area half the size of Ohio.

Water, water everywhere, but that's not all. Within the convoluted coastline of Nova Scotia, you can find highlands to rival Scotland's; rugged
fjords; rolling farmland; and networks of rivers, ponds, and lakes calling out to kayakers and canoers. Fifty-six kilometers (35 miles) is the
farthest you can get from the sea anywhere in the province. Pounding
waves in summer and the grinding ice of winter storms have sculpted
the coastal rocks and reduced sandstone cliffs to stretches of sandy beach.
Inland, the fertile fields of the Annapolis Valley yield peaches, corn,
apples, and plums that are sold at farm stands in summer and fall. A
succession of wildflowers covers the roadside with blankets of color:
purple and blue lupines; yellow coltsfoot; pink fireweed. Each of the
wild habitats—bogs, dry barrens, tidal wetlands, open fields, dense spruce
woods, and climax hardwood forests—has its own distinctive plant life.
Thousands of years ago, scouring glaciers left their scars on the land;
the Halifax Citadel stands atop a drumlin, a round-topped hill left by
the retreating ice. Wildlife abounds: ospreys and bald eagles; moose
and deer; whales in the waters off Cape Breton and Brier Island.

The original people of Nova Scotia, the Mi'Kmaqs, have been here for
10,000 years. In the early days of European exploration, the French
and English navigators found these peoples settled on the shores and
harvesting the sea. In later years, waves of immigrants filled the
province: Germans in Lunenburg County; Highland Scots displaced
by their landlords' preference for sheep; New England Loyalists escaping
the American Revolution; blacks arriving as freemen or escaped slaves;
Jews in Halifax, Sydney, and industrial Cape Breton; Ukranians, Poles,
West Indians, Italians, and Lebanese drawn to the Sydney steel mill.
These people maintain their customs and cultures. There are Gaelic signs
in Mabou and Iona, German sausage and sauerkraut in Lunenburg,
Greek music festivals in Halifax. The Acadians fly their tricolor flag
with pride. Scots step dance to antique fiddle airs. The fragrance of
burning sweet grass mingles with the prayers of the Mi'Kmaqs' Catholic
mass, blending the old ways with the new.

This is a little, buried nation, with a capital city the same size as Marlowe's London. Before Canada was formed in 1867, Nova Scotians
were prosperous shipwrights and merchants, trading with the world.
Who created Cunard Lines? A Haligonian, Samuel Cunard. Those days
brought democracy to the British colonies, left Victorian mansions in
the salty little ports, and created a uniquely Nova Scotian outlook:
worldly, approachable, and sturdily independent.

Pleasures and Pastimes

Dining

Skilled chefs find their abilities enhanced by the availability of succu-
lent blueberries, crisp apples, wild mushrooms, home-raised poultry,
quality beef, fresh-from-the-sea lobster, cultivated mussels, Digby scallops, and fine Atlantic salmon. The quality of ingredients comes from
the closeness of the harvest. Agriculture and fisheries (both wild harvest and aquaculture) are never far away.

Helping travelers discover for themselves the best tastes of the province,
the Nova Scotian culinary industry has formed an organization called
the Taste of Nova Scotia. It pulls together the producers and the pre-

parers, setting quality standards to ensure that patrons at member restaurants receive authentic Nova Scotian food. Look for their symbol: a golden oval porthole framing food and a ship.

CATEGORY	COST*
$$$$	over $32
$$$	$22–$32
$$	$13–$21
$	under $13

per person, in Canadian dollars, for a main course at dinner

Lodging

Nova Scotia's strength lies in a sprinkling of first-class resorts that have retained a traditional feel, top country inns with a dedication to fine dining and high-level accommodation, and a few superior corporate hotels. Bed-and-breakfasts, particularly those in smaller towns, are often exceptional. Most resorts and many B&Bs are seasonal, closing during the winter. Halifax and Dartmouth have some excellent hotels in addition to the reliable chains; reservations are necessary year-round. Expect to pay considerably more in the capital district than elsewhere.

CATEGORY	COST*
$$$$	over $200
$$$	$150–$200
$$	$100–$150
$	under $100

All prices are for a standard double room, excluding 15% harmonized sales tax (HST), in Canadian dollars.

Music

Scottish immigrants brought fiddles and folk airs to eastern Nova Scotia and Cape Breton, where Highland music mingled with that of the Acadians already here and the Irish soon to follow. Today the region enjoys world renown as a center of distinctive Celtic music. Watch for concerts by members of the Rankin Family or the Barra MacNeils; by outstanding fiddlers such as Natalie MacMaster, Ashley MacIsaac, Buddy MacMaster, or Wendy MacIsaac; and the Gaelic-punk sound of singer Mary Jane Lamond. Since these stars grew up here, a visitor stands a good chance of catching them at a square dance in Inverness County or at a milling frolic on Bras d'Or Lake. For 10 days in October, the Celtic Colors International Festival brings musicians from around the world to more than 20 locations throughout Cape Breton.

The Halifax pub scene is a hot spot for other musical styles. Names to watch for include the crooner Johnnie Favorite, country singer Rita MacNeil, the a cappella group Four the Moment, and the lightly punk-flavored Plumptree.

Outdoor Activities and Sports

BEACHES

The province is one big seashore, with the warmest beaches on the Northumberland Strait shore. The west coast of Cape Breton and Bras d'Or Lake also offer fine beaches and warm salt water.

BIRDING

A healthy population of bald eagles nests in Cape Breton, where they reel above Bras d'Or Lake or perch in trees along riverbanks. The Bird Islands boat tour from Big Bras d'Or circles islands where Atlantic puffins, kittiwakes, and guillemots nest in rocky cliffs. In May and August, the Bay of Fundy teems with migrating shorebirds, and the tidal marshes near the end of the Bird Islands, Merrigomish, are home to great blue-heron rookeries. The useful *Where to Find the Birds in*

Nova Scotia, published by the Nova Scotia Bird Society, is available locally in places such as the Nova Scotia Government Bookstore, opposite Province House on Granville Street in Halifax.

FISHING

Nova Scotia has more than 9,000 lakes and 100 brooks; practically all lakes and streams are open to anglers. The catch includes Atlantic salmon (June through September), brook and sea trout, bass, rainbow trout, and shad. You can get a nonresident fishing license from any Department of Natural Resources office in the province and at most sporting-goods stores. Before casting a line in national park waters, it is necessary to obtain a transferrable National Parks Fishing License, available at park offices. In May and June, many rivers and brooks have spectacular spring runs of smelt and *gaspereaux* (river herring or alewives). Limited quantities can be taken without a license; inquire locally for times and sites of good runs. Licenses are not required for saltwater fishing. From Barrington to Digby is the most prosperous fishing region in the province.

FOSSIL HUNTING AND ROCK HOUNDING

Coal seams and shale cliffs along Cape Breton's shores yield fossilized ferns, leaves, and petrified wood. Kempt Head on Boularderie Island, Sutherland's Corner on Sydney Mines's Shore Road, and the beach at Point Aconi are good places to search. The province's richest source of fossils is the Minas Basin, near Joggins and Parrsboro, where dinosaur fossils, agate, and amethyst are found. You can visit the Fundy Geological Museum in Parrsboro and the Joggins Fossil Center. Guided tours of the cliffs are available. Rock hounds are welcome to gather what they find along the beaches, but a permit from the Nova Scotia Museum is required to dig along the cliffs.

Wineries

Nova Scotia's wineries are becoming exceedingly popular. Local wines are featured in many restaurants, and they can be sampled for free and bought by the bottle at local vineyards. Wineries to visit include Jost Vineyards in Malagash and Sainte Famille Winery in Falmouth.

Exploring Nova Scotia

Along the coast of Nova Scotia, the wild Atlantic Ocean crashes against rocky outcrops, eddies into sheltered coves, or flows placidly over expanses of white sand. In the Bay of Fundy, which has the highest tides in the world, the receding sea reveals stretches of red-mud flats; then it rushes back in a ferocious wall that should be treated with respect. Nova Scotia also has dense forests and rolling Annapolis Valley farms. In the province's most dramatic terrain, in Cape Breton, rugged mountains plunge to meet the waves.

When arriving in Nova Scotia from New Brunswick via the Trans-Canada Highway (Highway 104), you have three ways to proceed into the province. Amherst is the first community after the border. From Amherst, Highway 104 takes you toward Halifax, a two-hour drive away. Touring alternatives lie to the north and south. Highway 6, to the north, follows the shore of the Northumberland Strait; farther east is Cape Breton. Highway 2, to the south, is a less-traveled road and a favorite because of nearby fossil-studded shores. Branch roads lead to the Annapolis Valley and other points south. Drivers should be aware that the sharply curving rural roads warrant careful attention.

Great Itineraries

The province is naturally divided into regions that can be explored in three to seven days. Some visitors do a whirlwind drive around, taking in only a few sights, but Nova Scotia's varied cultural landscape deserves careful exploration. If you have more days, try linking two or more regions. Above all, take your time: the back roads and side trips leading down to the shore are often the most rewarding.

Numbers in the text correspond to numbers in the margin and on the Nova Scotia, Halifax, and Cape Breton Island maps.

IF YOU HAVE 3 DAYS

Start in **Halifax** ①–⑭, a port city that combines old maritime charm with new architecture, lively shops, and a musical nightlife centered on a dozen friendly pubs. Explore the South Shore and Annapolis Valley, taking in the Lighthouse Route and Evangeline Trail. The two trails form a loop that begins and ends in Halifax (via Highway 3, 103, or 333, the scenic road around the shore), covering a distance of approximately 850 km (527 mi) with no side trips. Leaving Halifax, head for **Peggy's Cove** ⑯, a picturesque fishing village perched on sea-washed granite and surrounded by coastal barrens. Explore the crafts shops of **Mahone Bay** ⑰ and travel on to ⊡ **Lunenburg** ⑱, where the culture of Atlantic Coast fisheries is explored in the Fisheries Museum. Overnight in Lunenburg before continuing on Highway 3 or 103 to **Shelburne** ⑳ on Day 2. You can visit **Yarmouth** ㉑ and travel on to **Digby** ㉓ for a lunch of scallops. **Annapolis Royal** ㉕, with its gardens, historic sites, and harbor-front boardwalk, is a lovely spot to spend an afternoon, or you may want to drive down Digby Neck to visit **Long Island and Brier Island** ㉔ and catch a whale-watching cruise in season. Travel on to the elm-lined streets of ⊡ **Wolfville** ㉖, home of Acadia University, for an overnight stay. The town is near Grand Pré National Historic Site, a tranquil park and stone church that recount the suffering of Acadians expelled from Nova Scotia in 1755. On Day 3, check tide times and plan a drive to the shore of Minas Basin, where the tides are the highest in the world. A leisurely drive will put you back in Halifax by late afternoon.

IF YOU HAVE 5 DAYS

You can spend a day or two in ⊡ **Halifax** ①–⑭ before exploring the Eastern Shore, the Atlantic Coast east of the city that is perhaps the most scenic and unspoiled stretch of coastline in mainland Nova Scotia. Highway 7 winds along a deeply indented, glaciated coastline of rocky waters interspersed with pocket beaches, long and narrow fjords, and fishing villages. **Musquodoboit Harbour** ㉘ is a haven for fishing enthusiasts. Nearby is Martinique Beach, one of Nova Scotia's best. Continue northeast to **Sherbrooke Village** ㉙, full of refurbished late-19th-century structures. Highway 7 turns inland and follows the St. Mary's River toward **Antigonish** ㉛ on the Sunrise Trail. Historians will appreciate a visit to Hector Heritage Quay in ⊡ **Pictou** ㉝, where the Scots landed in 1773. From Pictou, Highway 6 runs beside an apparently endless string of beaches, with many summer homes in the adjoining fields. Turn right to **Malagash,** where Jost Vineyards invites wine tasting and tours. A half-hour drive will take you to ⊡ **Amherst** ㊱. Continue on to **Joggins** ㊲ and search for souvenirs in its sandstone cliffs. For more fossils, head to **Parrsboro** ㊳, which has the Fundy Geological Museum.

IF YOU HAVE 7 DAYS

With its spectacular scenery, rich musical culture, and meandering seaside highways, Cape Breton Island should not be missed. It's a perfect place for a leisurely seven-day tour. Follow the coastal route, which takes you on a west-to-east loop from the Canso Strait Causeway, taking lots of time to explore side roads. Overnight in ⊡ **Mabou** ㊶, the beating heart of the island's rich musical tradition. From a base in

🔲 **Margaree Harbour** ㊷, take a day or more to explore the Cabot Trail and Cape Breton Highlands National Park and the remote fishing villages north of the park. June and July bring a profusion of wildflowers to highland meadows and bogs. You can photograph the scenery, walk the trails to hidden waterfalls, or whale-watch. There are crafts stores along St. Ann's Bay, but allow time to visit the Alexander Graham Bell National Historic Site in **Baddeck** ㊺, and spend the night in 🔲 **Iona** ㊻. A day or two in 🔲 **Sydney** ㊼ will position you for an afternoon excursion to the Glace Bay Miners' Museum in **Glace Bay** ㊽ and a daylong visit to Fortress of Louisbourg National Historic Park, the largest historic restoration in Canada, and the town of **Louisbourg** ㊾. Take Highway 4 back to Canso Causeway through **Big Pond,** home of singer Rita McNeil, and spend a day wandering the colorful Acadian villages of Isle Madame, such as **Arichat** ㊿.

When to Tour Nova Scotia

The best time of year to visit is mid-June through mid-September; in fact, many resorts, hotels, and attractions are open only during July and August. Nova Scotia, particularly the Cape Breton area, is very popular in fall because of the foliage and the 10-day Celtic Colors International Festival in October. And October—with blazing autumn colors, warm and sunny days, and cool nights—can be spectacular. Love lobster? The popular seafood is plentiful in May and June. Whale-watching and wildlife cruises as well as sea-kayaking outfitters generally operate from July to mid-September. Most golf courses stay open from June until late September, and some into October. Skiing (both downhill and cross-country) is popular at a variety of locations, including Kejimkujik and Cape Breton Highlands, from mid-December to early April.

HALIFAX AND DARTMOUTH

Halifax and Dartmouth, now combined with the surrounding County of Halifax and known as the Halifax Regional Municipality (HRM), gaze upon each other across Halifax Harbour, the second-largest natural harbor in the world. Once the point of entry to Canada for refugees and immigrants, the port remains a busy shipping center, with a flow of container ships and tugboats. Pleasure boats and yachts tie up alongside historic schooners at the Historic Properties Wharf. Pubs, shops, museums, and parks welcome visitors and locals. In summer jazz concerts and buskers, music festivals and sports events enliven the outdoor atmosphere. Art on exhibit, crafts sales, live theater, and fine food bring people here in all seasons. The film *Titanic* brought fresh attention to part of Halifax's history. Some 150 victims of the disaster are buried in three cemeteries here, and the Maritime Museum of the Atlantic has a *Titanic* display. From its harborfront life to its Victorian public gardens, Halifax is big enough to offer the pleasures of an exciting city but intimate enough to retain the ease of a small town.

Halifax

1,137 km (705 mi) northeast of Boston, 275 km (171 mi) southeast of Moncton, New Brunswick.

Salty and urbane, learned and plain-spoken, Halifax is large enough to have the trappings of a capital city, yet small enough that many of its sights can be seen on a pleasant walk downtown.

A Good Walk

Begin on Upper Water Street at **Purdy's Wharf** ① for unobstructed views of Halifax Harbour and the pier and office towers of this wharf. Con-

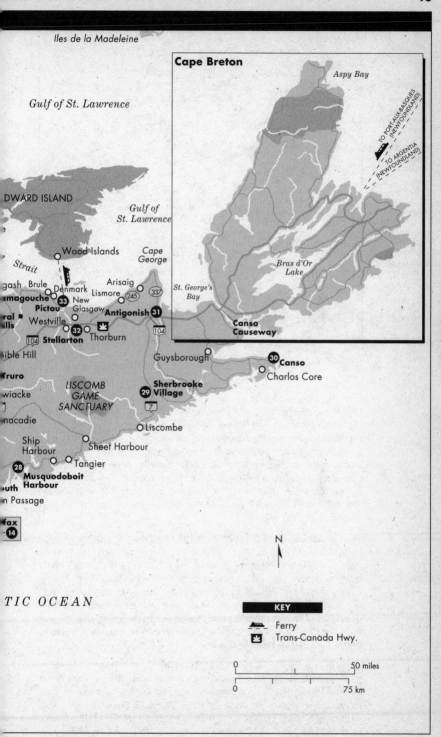

Iles de la Madeleine

Cape Breton

Aspy Bay

Gulf of St. Lawrence

TO PORT-AUX-BASQUES (NEWFOUNDLAND)

TO ARGENTIA (NEWFOUNDLAND)

DWARD ISLAND

Gulf of
St. Lawrence

Bras d'Or
Lake

Strait

Wood Islands

Cape
George

St. George's
Bay

gash Brule

Arisaig

Denmark Lismore

amagouche **33** New **245** **337**

Pictou Glasgow

ral Antigonish **31**

Westville **104**

ills

104 **32**

Thorburn

Stellarton

Canso
Causeway

ible Hill

Guysborough

30 Canso

Truro

Charlos Core

wiacke

LISCOMB
GAME
SANCTUARY

Sherbrooke

29 Village

7

nacadie

Liscombe

Ship
Harbour

Sheet Harbour

28 Tangier

Musquodoboit
Harbour

uth

n Passage

fax

14

N

TIC OCEAN

KEY

Ferry

Trans-Canada Hwy.

0   50 miles

0   75 km

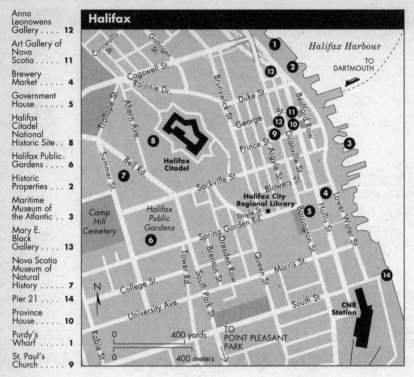

tinue south on Lower Water Street to the restored warehouses of **Historic Properties** ②, a cluster of boutiques and restaurants linked by cobblestone footpaths. Stroll south several blocks along the piers to the **Maritime Museum of the Atlantic** ③: the wharves outside frequently welcome visiting transatlantic yachts and sail-training ships. Walk to the end of the block and cross Lower Water Street to **Brewery Market** ④, a restored waterfront property. Take the elevator at the office end of Brewery Market and emerge on Hollis Street. Turn left, past several elegant Victorian town houses—notably Keith Hall—once the executive offices of the brewery.

Turn right onto Bishop Street and right again onto Barrington Street, Halifax's main downtown thoroughfare. The stone mansion on your right is **Government House** ⑤, the official residence of Nova Scotia's lieutenant governor. Take a detour from Barrington Street onto Spring Garden Road and the attractive shops in the Park Lane and Spring Garden Place shopping centers; then walk west to the **Halifax Public Gardens** ⑥, where you can rest your legs on shaded benches amid flower beds and rare trees. A block to the north, on Summer Street, is the **Nova Scotia Museum of Natural History** ⑦.

On your way back to Barrington Street on Bell Road and Sackville Street, you'll notice the **Halifax Citadel National Historic Site** ⑧, dominated by the fortress that once commanded the city. On a lot defined by Barrington, Argyle, and Prince streets lies **St. Paul's Church** ⑨; one wall within its historic confines contains a fragment of the great Halifax Explosion of 1917. A block farther north and facing City Hall is the Grand Parade, where musicians perform at noon on summer days. From here, the waterfront side of Citadel Hill, look uphill: the tall, stylish brick building is the World Trade and Convention Centre and is attached to the 10,000-seat Halifax Metro Centre—the site of hockey games, rock concerts, and political conventions. Head down the hill on Prince Street, making a left on Hollis Street to **Province House** ⑩, Canada's oldest legislative building. North of Province House, at Cheapside, is the **Art Gallery of Nova Scotia** ⑪, which showcases a large collection of folk art. Walk a block west to Granville Street and two blocks north to the **Anna Leonowens Gallery** ⑫, where you can peruse the work of local artists. Return south two blocks on Barrington to stop by the crafts displays at the **Mary E. Black Gallery** ⑬. A final stop lies to the south: **Pier 21** ⑭, a former immigration center, houses a new museum of immigration.

TIMING

The city of Halifax is fairly compact: depending on your tendency to stop and study, the above tour can take from a half to a full day. Pier 21 could take several hours in itself, so you may want to visit it separately from the walk. You can drive from sight to sight, but parking is a problem, and you will miss out on much of the flavor of the city.

Sights to See

⑫ **Anna Leonowens Gallery.** The gallery is named for the Victorian woman who served the King of Siam as governess and whose memoirs served as inspiration for Rodgers and Hammerstein's *The King and I*. Founding the Nova Scotia College of Art and Design was just another of her life's chapters. Three exhibition spaces serve as a showcase for the college faculty and students. The displays focus on contemporary studio and media art. ⊠ *1891 Granville St.,* ☎ *902/494–8223.* ⊡ *Free.* ⊙ *Tues.–Fri. 11–5, Sat. noon–4.*

⑪ **Art Gallery of Nova Scotia.** Sheltered within this historic building is an extensive permanent collection of more than 4,000 works, including an internationally recognized collection of Maritime and folk art by artists such as wood-carver Sydney Howard and painter Joe Norris. Also here: the actual home of the late folk painter Maude Lewis, whose bright, cheery paintings cover the tiny structure inside and out. The collection of contemporary art has major works by Christopher Pratt, Alex Colville, John Nesbitt, and Dawn McNutt. ⊠ *1741 Hollis St., at Cheapside,* ☎ *902/424–7542,* WEB *www.agns.gov.ns.ca.* ⊡ *$5.* ⊙ *June–Aug., Mon.–Wed. and Fri. 10–6, Thurs. 10–9, weekends noon–5; Sept.–May, Tues.–Fri. 10–5, weekends noon–5.*

④ **Brewery Market.** A popular Saturday market takes place at this sprawling stone complex where Alexander Keith once brewed the beer that still bears his name. You can browse stalls laden with hand-dyed silk scarves, leatherwork, paintings, and stone carvings. Culinary temptations include Chinese and Indian snacks, farm cheese, and home-smoked sausage. Golden mountains of freshly baked bread; colorful displays of fresh local fruits and vegetables; and stalls with lamb, rabbit, and big brown eggs make this a true farmers market. Many of the city's finest chefs are regularly seen shopping here. ⊠ *Between Hollis and Lower Water Sts.,* ☎ *no phone.* ⊙ *Sat. 7 AM–1 PM.*

OFF THE BEATEN PATH

FAIRVIEW CEMETERY – This cemetery is the final resting place of 121 victims of the *Titanic*. The graves can easily be located in a graceful arc of granite tombstones. One grave—marked J. Dawson—attracts particular attention from recent visitors. It's not Jack, the fictional Minnesota artist in the blockbuster film, however, but James Dawson, a coal trimmer from Ireland. Nineteen other victims are buried in Mount Olivet Catholic Cemetery, 10 in the Baron de Hirsch Jewish Cemetery. The Maritime Museum of the Atlantic has an exhibit about the disaster. ⊠ *3720 Windsor St., 3 km (2 mi) north of downtown.*

❺ **Government House.** Built between 1799 and 1805 for Sir John Wentworth, the Loyalist governor of New Hampshire, and his racy wife, Fannie (Thomas Raddall's novel *The Governor's Lady* tells their story), this house has since been the official residence of the province's lieutenant governor (currently Myra Freeman, the first woman to hold the post in almost 400 years). It is North America's oldest consecutively occupied government residence, as the older President's House (the White House) was evacuated and burned during the War of 1812. Its construction, of Nova Scotian stone, was engineered by a Virginian Loyalist, Isaac Hildrith. The house, which has been restored to its original elegance, isn't open to the public. ⊠ *1451 Barrington St.*

★ **❽** **Halifax Citadel National Historic Site.** The Citadel, erected between 1826 and 1856, was the heart of the city's fortifications and was linked to smaller forts and gun emplacements on the harbor islands and on the bluffs above the harbor entrance. Several other forts stood on the site before the present one. Kilted soldiers drill in front of the **Army Museum,** once the barracks, and a cannon is fired every day at noon. Before leaving, take in the view from the Citadel: the spiky downtown crowded between the hilltop and the harbor; the wooded islands at the harbor's mouth; and the naval dockyard under the Angus L. Macdonald Bridge, the nearer of the two bridges connecting Halifax with Dartmouth. The handsome, four-sided **Town Clock** on Citadel Hill was given to Halifax by Prince Edward, Duke of Kent, military commander from 1794 to 1800. ⊠ *Citadel Hill,* ☎ *902/426–5080,* WEB *www.parkscanada. pch.gc.ca.* 🎟 *June–mid-Sept. $6; May 7–May 15 and mid-Sept.–Oct. $3.75; rest of yr free.* ☉ *July–Aug., daily 9–6; Sept.–June 14, daily 9–5.*

❻ **Halifax Public Gardens.** One of the oldest formal Victorian gardens in North America, this city oasis had its start in 1753 as a private garden. Its layout was completed in 1875 by Richard Power, former gardener to the Duke of Devonshire in Ireland. Gravel paths wind among ponds, trees, and flower beds, revealing an astonishing variety of plants from all over the world. The centerpiece is a gazebo erected in 1887 for Queen Victoria's Golden Jubilee. The gardens are closed during the winter but you can take a pleasant walk around the perimeter, along the cast-iron fence. ⊠ *Bounded by Sackville, Summer, and S. Park Sts. and Spring Garden Rd.*

❷ **Historic Properties.** These waterfront warehouses date from the early 19th century, when trade and war made Halifax prosperous. They were built by such raffish characters as Enos Collins, a privateer, smuggler, and shipper whose vessels defied Napoléon's blockade to bring American supplies to the Duke of Wellington. The buildings have since been taken over by quality shops, chic offices, and restaurants, including those in Privateer's Warehouse. ⊠ *Lower Water and Hollis Sts.*

Khyber Center for the Arts. Primarily a gallery for young and emerging artists, the Khyber hosts works in numerous genres, including performance art. Its various galleries are in a historic, turreted building. Also in the building is the Khyber Club bar, where young artists spend time discussing their work and drinking Khybeer. ⊠ *1588 Barrington St.,* ☎ *902/422–9668.* 🎟 *By donation.* ☉ *Wed.–Sat. noon–5.*

❸ **Maritime Museum of the Atlantic.** The exhibits in this restored chandlery and warehouse on the waterfront include small boats once used around the coast, as well as displays describing Nova Scotia's proud sailing heritage, from the days when the province, on its own, was one of the world's foremost shipbuilding and trading nations. Other exhibits explore the Halifax Explosion of 1917, shipwrecks, and lifesaving.

Permanently moored outside, after a long life of charting the coasts of Labrador and the Arctic, is the hydrographic steamer *Acadia.* At the next wharf (summer only) is Canada's naval memorial, HMCS *Sackville,* the sole survivor of a fleet that escorted convoys of ships from Halifax to England during World War II.

Much of the 1997 movie *Titanic* was filmed in Nova Scotia, and the museum has a permanent exhibit about the disaster. With many victims buried in Halifax, the city was, in a sense, the ship's final destination. The display includes 20 artifacts and dozens of photographs. The centerpiece is the only surviving deck chair. Also on display are a section of wall paneling; a balustrade molding and part of a newel from the dual curving staircase; a cribbage board carved from *Titanic* oak by the carpenter of one of the rescue ships; and the log kept by a wireless operator at Cape Race, Newfoundland, on the fateful night. An extensive research library is open to the public by appointment only. ✉ *1675 Lower Water St.,* ☎ *902/424–7490 or 902/424–7491.* ☞ *$6.* ☉ *May–Oct., Mon. and Wed.–Sat. 9:30–5:30, Tues. 9:30–8, Sun. 1–5:30 (10:30–5:30 in Sept.); Nov.–Apr., Wed.–Sat. 9:30–5, Tues. 9:30–8, Sun. 1–5.*

⓭ **Mary E. Black Gallery.** The exhibit space for the Nova Scotia Centre for Craft and Design presents rotating shows of quality crafts. ✉ *1683 Barrington St.,* ☎ *902/424–4062.* ☞ *Free.* ☉ *Weekdays 9–4:30, Sat. 10–4.*

⟳ ❼ **Nova Scotia Museum of Natural History.** You can learn about whales, fossils, dinosaurs, birds, and mushrooms here. The Nature Centre is home to live snakes, frogs, insects, and other creatures; the Butterfly Pavilion is filled with species from around the world. Nature talks, walks, and workshops are designed to appeal to all interests and ages. The museum is most easily recognized by the huge fiberglass model of the tiny northern spring peeper (a frog) that "clings" to the side of the building May through October. ✉ *1747 Summer St.,* ☎ *902/424–7353,* WEB *nature.museum.gov.ns.ca.* ☞ *$4.* ☉ *Mid-May–Oct., Mon.–Tues. and Thurs.–Sun. 1–5:30, Wed. 9:30–8; Nov.–mid-May, Tues. and Thurs.–Sun. 9:30–5, Wed. 9:30–8.*

⓮ **Pier 21.** From 1928 until 1971, refugees, returning troop ships, war brides, and more than a million immigrants arrived on Canadian soil through Pier 21, the front door to Canada. It's now a museum where the immigrant experience is re-created through live performances, multimedia presentations, and displays of photographs, documents, and artifacts. ✉ *1031 Marginal Rd.,* ☎ *902/425–7770.* ☞ *$6.50.* ☉ *June–Sept., daily 9–6; Oct.–May, Tues.–Sat. 10–5, Sun. noon–5.*

Point Pleasant Park. Most of the city's secondary fortifications have been turned into public parks. This one, which encompasses 186 wooded acres with walking trails and seafront paths, is popular with joggers and dog walkers and provides the perfect vantage point from which to watch ships entering and leaving the harbor. The park was leased from the British Crown by the city for 999 years, at a shilling a year. Its major military installation is a massive round martello tower dating from the late 18th century. *About 12 blocks down South Park St. from Spring Garden Rd.*

❿ **Province House.** Charles Dickens proclaimed this structure, now a National Historic Site, "a gem of Georgian architecture." Erected in 1819 to house Britain's first overseas self-government, the sandstone building still serves as the meeting place for the provincial legislature. ✉ *1726 Hollis St.,* ☎ *902/424–4661.* ☞ *Free.* ☉ *July–Aug., weekdays 9–5, weekends 10–4; Sept.–June, weekdays 8:30–4:30.*

❶ **Purdy's Wharf.** Named after a famous shipping family from the 19th century, the wharf is composed of a pier and twin office towers that stand right in the harbor. The buildings actually use ocean water to generate air-conditioning. ✉ *Upper Water St.*

❾ **St. Paul's Church.** Opened in 1750, this is Canada's oldest Protestant church and the burial site of many colonial notables. Inside, on the north end, a piece of metal is embedded in the wall. It is a fragment of the *Mont Blanc,* one of the two ships whose collision caused the Halifax Explosion of December 6, 1917, the largest human-caused explosion prior to that at Hiroshima. ✉ *1749 Argyle St.,* ☎ *902/429–2240.* ☺ *Sept.–May, weekdays 9–4:30; June–Aug., Mon.–Sat. 9–4:30.*

Dining and Lodging

$$$–$$$$ ✕ **Maple.** The fine and artfully presented cuisine served here is simply exquisite. Maple uses ingredients of the highest quality and mixes them up with flair in the open kitchen. The menu changes nightly according to availability. A winter combination of lobster and mango is wrapped in crisp nori and topped with sweet corn shoots. Trust the chef and order his seven-course table d'hôte. It may contain rich and tender duck breast, foie gras, or arctic char. ✉ *1813 Granville St.,* ☎ *902/425–9100. AE, MC, V. Closed Sun.*

$$$ ✕ **da Maurizo's Dining Room.** Dining is a lovely experience at this subdued and elegant Italian restaurant. Chef Maurizo's creativity and attention to detail create meals that are impressive and satisfying. Seared foie gras is napped with a port sauce; pasta shells are stuffed with ricotta, radicchio, and sweet raisins, then sautéed in butter and served with Parmesan on the side. For dessert, the zabaglione is likely to leave you weak. The "specialty wine list" tops out at $400. ✉ *1496 Lower Water St.,* ☎ *902/423–0859. AE, MC, V. Closed Sun.*

$$–$$$ ✕ **Fid.** A fid is a graceful nautical tool used to splice rope. At this minimalist restaurant near the main gates of the Halifax Public Gardens, the chef–owner splices together unusual flavors and textures. Special requests and dietary requirements are accommodated here. The halibut, when available, is the most popular dish on the menu. Chocolate lovers should consider the *moelleau au chocolat,* molten chocolate-custard sauce within a shell of warm cake. ✉ *1569 Dresden Row,* ☎ *902/422–9162. MC, V. No lunch. Closed Mon.*

$$–$$$ ✕ **The Press Gang.** Easily the hippest fine-dining establishment in Halifax, The Press Gang offers only the freshest fish available. Oysters are served with fresh horseradish, black pepper, and lemon, or with one of the house salsas and dressings. A fine muscadet from the well-stocked cellar can complement your seafood. Organic meats, including buffalo, venison, and rabbit, are also a specialty. Built in 1759, this is one of Halifax's oldest buildings; the stone walls may be cold, but the atmosphere is warmed with exquisite decor and lighting. ✉ *5218 Prince St.,* ☎ *902/423–8816. Reservations essential. AE, MC, V.*

$$–$$$ ✕ **Salty's on the Waterfront.** Overlooking Privateer's Wharf and the en-
★ tire harbor, this restaurant gets the prize for the best location in the city. Request a table with a window view and save room for the famous dessert, called Cadix (chocolate mousse over praline crust). The Salty Dog Bar & Grill on the ground level is less expensive and serves lunch outside on the wharf in summer (it can be very windy). ✉ *1869 Upper Water St.,* ☎ *902/423–6818. Reservations essential. AE, DC, MC, V.*

$–$$$ ✕ **MacAskill's Restaurant.** Diners can experience Nova Scotian hospitality in this romantic dining room overlooking beautiful Halifax Harbour. The chefs create a variety of seafood dishes using the finest, freshest fish available. Specialties also include pepper steak, flambéed table-side. ✉ *Dartmouth Ferry Terminal Bldg., 88 Alderney Dr.,* ☎ *902/466–3100. AE, DC, MC, V. No lunch weekends. Nov.–May, closed Sun.*

$–$$$ ✕ **Privateer's Warehouse.** Three restaurants share space in this early 18th-century building with original stone walls and hewn beams. The nautical-theme Upper Deck Waterfront Fishery & Grill has great views of the harbor and offers lobsters from a holding tank. Crawdads has a bistro-style atmosphere and serves innovative pastas along with traditional cuisine; a children's menu is available. Lower Deck Good Time Pub is a boisterous bar with long trestle tables and a patio; fish-and-chips and other pub food are served. ⊠ *Historic Properties, Lower Water St.,* ☏ *902/422–1289, 902/426–1500, or 902/426–1501. AE, DC, MC, V.*

$–$$ ✕ **Cheelin Restaurant.** This small and informal Chinese restaurant with an open kitchen offers some of the most flavorful and freshest dishes available in the region. Each dish is prepared with individual attention and care, and the chef-owner personally checks with diners to make sure they are satisfied. Noodle and dumpling dishes are very popular, but if you're looking for something different, try the amazing fish-stuffed eggplant in black-bean sauce. ⊠ *Brewery Market, 1496 Lower Water St.,* ☏ *902/422–2252. AE, MC, V. Closed Mon.*

$–$$ ✕ **Dharma Sushi.** It's fast-paced here, but the service and food don't suffer as a result; the tidiest sushi, freshest sashimi, and feather-light tempura are artfully presented. The *chawan mushi,* a delicate egg custard with seafood, has the consistency of fine silk. ⊠ *1576 Argyle St.,* ☏ *902/425–7785. AE, MC, V. Closed Sun. No lunch Sat.*

$–$$ ✕ **Il Mercato Ristorante.** Enter this Italian eatery at your own risk: the gleaming display cases of antipasti and desserts—including the *zucotto,* a dome of chocolate and cream—are sure to tempt. On the menu, herbed lamb in wine sauce served with wild mushrooms and barley cakes is a good choice. ⊠ *5475 Spring Garden Rd.,* ☏ *902/422–2866. AE, MC, V.*

$ ✕ **Satisfaction Feast.** This small vegetarian restaurant is informal, friendly, and usually packed at lunchtime. The food is wholesome with lots of ethnic influences (think fresh whole-wheat bread and daily curries). Sweet, sharp ginger beer is brewed on the premises. Enjoy an organic coffee with one of the fine cakes or desserts. ⊠ *1581 Grafton St.,* ☏ *902/422–3540. AE, MC, V.*

$$$$ 🏨 **Cambridge Suites.** This conveniently located all-suites hotel takes pride in its motto, "A suite for the price of a room." There are three suite sizes; all have sitting rooms and kitchenettes. ⊠ *1583 Brunswick St., B3J 3P5,* ☏ *902/420–0555 or 800/565–1263,* ℻ *902/420–9379. 200 suites. Restaurant, bar, kitchenettes, hot tub, sauna, gym. AE, D, MC, V. CP.*

$$$–$$$$ 🏨 **Westin Nova Scotian.** An enormous brick building, this grand hotel sits solidly in downtown Halifax, next door to the VIA Rail station, with the harbor behind it and Cornwallis Park in front. Comfortable, overstuffed chairs and a warm, peachy light fill the lobby, where a nautical theme prevails. Rooms are done in green or peach; some have wicker furniture. The Tradewinds Restaurant ($$–$$$) offers fresh fish and shellfish dishes as well as pastas and meatier fare. ⊠ *1181 Hollis St., B3H 2P6,* ☏ *902/421–1000 or 800/228–3000,* ℻ *902/422–9465,* 🌐 *www.westin.com. 300 rooms, 13 suites. 3 restaurants, in-room data ports, no-smoking rooms, indoor pool, hot tub, sauna, tennis court, gym, baby-sitting, dry cleaning, laundry service. AE, DC, MC, V.*

$$–$$$$ 🏨 **Prince George Hotel.** Contemporary mahogany furnishings in this
★ luxurious and understated business-oriented hotel include writing desks. Georgio's Restaurant ($$) serves eclectic cuisine in a casual setting. The hotel is connected by underground tunnel to the World Trade and Convention Centre; walkways provide access to shops, offices, and entertainment. ⊠ *1725 Market St., B3J 3N9,* ☏ *902/425–1986; 800/ 565–1567 in Canada,* 🌐 *www.princegeorgehotel.com. 207 rooms, 9*

suites. Restaurant, bar, pool, sauna, hot tub, gym, concierge, meeting room. AE, DC, MC, V.

$$–$$$$ ⊡ **Sheraton Halifax.** Built low to match neighboring historic ironstone buildings, this waterfront hotel varies in appearance from others in the chain. Its convenient location in Historic Properties contributes to its elegance. Rooms are fairly spacious, all with desks and sitting areas. A five-minute stroll through a walkway takes you to Halifax's only casino. ⊠ *1919 Upper Water St., B3J 3J5,* ☎ *902/421–1700 or 800/325–3535,* 𝔽𝔸𝕏 *902/422–5805,* 𝕎𝔼𝔹 *www.sheraton.com. 335 rooms, 19 suites. Restaurant, bar, room service, indoor pool, hair salon, health club, dock, concierge, baby-sitting, dry cleaning, laundry service, meeting room, parking (fee). AE, DC, MC, V.*

$$–$$$ ⊡ **Delta Halifax.** This business-class hotel has spacious, attractive rooms, most with a panoramic harbor view. An enclosed walkway provides easy access to the Historic Properties and Scotia Square mall. The Crown Bistro ($$–$$$) includes more-refined dishes as well as lighter fare. ⊠ *1990 Barrington St., B3J 1P2,* ☎ *902/425–6700 or 800/441–1414,* 𝔽𝔸𝕏 *902/425–6214,* 𝕎𝔼𝔹 *www.deltahotels.com. 279 rooms, 21 suites. Restaurant, piano bar, in-room data ports (some), no-smoking rooms, indoor pool, hot tub, sauna, gym, concierge, laundry service, business services, parking (fee). AE, DC, MC, V.*

$$–$$$ ⊡ **Inn on the Lake.** A great value in a quiet location, this small country club–style hotel sits on 5 acres of parkland on the edge of Fall River Lake, 30 minutes from Halifax and 10 minutes from the airport. Rooms are spacious and have balconies. ⊠ *3009 Lake Thomas Dr., Box 29, Waverly B0N 2S0,* ☎ *902/861–3480,* 𝔽𝔸𝕏 *902/861–4883,* 𝕎𝔼𝔹 *www.innonthelake.com. 34 rooms, 12 suites. Restaurant, lounge, beach, airport shuttle, free parking. AE, MC, V.*

$–$$$$ ⊡ **Halliburton House Inn.** A historic property, this hotel is an elegant renovation of three 19th-century town houses. Period antiques, goose-down duvets, and fresh coffee await you in the comfortable rooms, lending a homey ambience. The suites have fireplaces, and there's a lovely garden. The rates here run the gamut, with some topping the $$$$ range. Local game and Atlantic seafood are served in an elegant dining room. ⊠ *5184 Morris St., B3J 1B3,* ☎ *902/420–0658,* 𝔽𝔸𝕏 *902/423–2324,* 𝕎𝔼𝔹 *www.halliburton.ns.ca. 29 rooms, 2 suites. Restaurant, library. AE, DC, MC, V. CP.*

$–$$ ⊡ **Garden View Bed & Breakfast.** This lovely Victorian home sits on a quiet residential street near the Halifax Commons. You can relax in the living room in front of the fire or unwind with a soak in an antique bathtub. The garden is especially charming. Breakfast is served in the dining room or in your room. ⊠ *6052 Williams St., B3K 1E9,* ☎ *902/423–2943 or 888/737–0778,* 𝔽𝔸𝕏 *902/423–4355,* 𝕎𝔼𝔹 *www.interdesign.ca/gardenview. 3 rooms without bath. Dining room. MC, V. BP.*

$ ⊡ **Dalhousie University.** Most Halifax universities offer low prices for no-frills rooms from May through August. Dalhousie University rents single rooms for $38 and two-bedroom apartments for $55. Guests have access to the Dalplex athletic facility and parking. ⊠ *6136 University Ave., B3H 4J2,* ☎ *902/494–8840,* 𝔽𝔸𝕏 *902/494–1219. 420 rooms without bath, 20 apartments. Indoor pool, gym, badminton. MC, V. CP.*

$ ⊡ **Queen Street Tourist Home.** Nova Scotian antiques and paintings fill this charming 19th-century Georgian house. It's just a short walk from busy Spring Garden Road, the heart of the downtown shopping district. ⊠ *1266 Queen St., B3J 2H4,* ☎ *902/422–9828. 6 rooms without bath. No credit cards.*

Nightlife and the Arts

THE ARTS

Halifax has a burgeoning film industry, the product of which is presented at the **Atlantic Film Festival** (☎ 902/422–3456), held the third week in September. The festival also showcases feature films, TV movies, and documentaries made outside Halifax. Admission to films often includes admission to a party or gala event following the screening. During the first week of September, the **Atlantic Fringe Festival** presents 40 shows in eight venues. The **Du Maurier Atlantic Jazz Festival** (☎ 902/492–2225), with an eclectic selection of jazz styles, takes place in mid-July. Some concerts are free. The internationally acclaimed **Scotia Festival of Music** (☎ 902/429–9469) presents classical musicians via concert and master classes each May and June. Pierre Boulez, Philip Glass, Maureen Forrester, and Tafelmusik are just a few of the guest artists who have attended the festival to perform, teach, coach, and lecture.

The **Alderney Theatre** (✉ 2 Ochterloney St., Dartmouth, ☎ 902/461–4698) is home to the Eastern Front Theatre Company, which produces, presents, and hosts professional Canadian theater. **Grafton Street Dinner Theatre** (✉ 1741 Grafton St., ☎ 902/425–1961) holds performances Wednesday through Saturday. **Historic Feast Company** (☎ 902/420–1840) presents shows set in the 19th century at Historic Properties Thursday through Saturday evenings. The **Neptune Theatre** (✉ 1593 Argyle St., ☎ 902/429–7300; 902/429–7070 box office), Canada's oldest professional repertory playhouse, stages year-round performances ranging from classics to contemporary Canadian drama. On mild July and August evenings, **Shakespeare by the Sea** (☎ 902/422–0295) performs the Bard's works in Point Pleasant Park at the southern end of the Halifax peninsula. The natural setting—dark woods, rocky shore, and ruins of fortifications—serves as a dramatic backdrop.

NIGHTLIFE

Haligonians love their pubs and their music. At **Bearly's House of Blues and Ribs** (✉ 1269 Barrington St., ☎ 902/423–2526), a dark, low-ceiling tavern with a couple of pool tables, you can dine on ribs, burgers, and fish-and-chips while listening to outstanding blues artists (except Monday and Wednesday). **Economy Shoe Shop Cafe and Bar, Backstage, and Dimond** (✉ 1663 Argyle St., ☎ 902/423–7463) are actually three establishments with different atmospheres combined in one space with a common menu, making for the trendiest spot in town. The eclectic decor alone is worth a visit. Live jazz can be heard every Monday; author readings are given Tuesday. **The Marquee Club** (✉ 2037 Gottigen St., ☎ 902/429–3020), a cabaret-style venue, presents some of the hottest entertainment in town. The club buzzes until 3:30 AM with live rock, blues, and alternative bands. Downstairs there's jazz, blues, and acoustic evenings. The bar has a good selection of locally brewed beers on tap. **Merrill's Cafe and Lounge** (✉ 5171 George St., ☎ 902/425–5249) is a large, open bar with a DJ. The casual atmosphere is popular with the university crowd. **O'Carroll's Restaurant and Lounge** (✉ 1860 Upper Water St., ☎ 902/423–4405) offers a comfortable, Irish-pub setting and traditional Irish, Scottish, and local music, with the well-known duo Evans and Dougherty as Friday-night regulars. Lots of funky folk art hangs on the walls at the **Soho Kitchen** (✉ 1582 Granville St., ☎ 902/423–3049). Jazz groups perform nightly (except Monday and Wednesday) in the laid-back atmosphere. **Tom's Little Havana Café** (✉ 5428 Doyle St., ☎ 902/423–8667), a cozy pub, offers 30 types of cigars. High ceilings and a state-of-the-art air-purification system ensure that even nonsmokers can enjoy the comfort of a wing chair, bustling bar, or quiet booth.

Outdoor Activities and Sport

PARTICIPANT SPORTS

Ground Zero Climbing Gym (✉ 105 Akerley Blvd., Dartmouth, ☎ 902/468–8788) offers challenging indoor-climbing equipment and supervision.

Within an easy drive of downtown Halifax is **Granite Springs Golf Club** (✉ 1441 Prospect Rd., ☎ 902/852–4653), an 18-hole, par-72, semi-private course open to greens-fee play. Lessons and golf clinics are available. The **Sackville Golf Course** (✉ Hwy. 1, ☎ 902/865–2179) is a 9-hole, par-29 public course; it also offers a driving range and a miniature golf course.

Hatfield Farms Adventures (✉ 1840 Hammonds Plains Rd., ☎ 902/835–5676) offers a wide range of riding experiences for all levels of rider, including overnight camping and pig roasts. **Coastal Adventures Sea Kayaking** (☎ 877/404–2774) has a wide range of tours for the beginner or the experienced kayaker.

SPECTATOR SPORTS

The **Moosehead Premium Dry Speedway** (✉ 200 Prospect Rd., ☎ 902/876–8222) hosts auto races from May through October.

The **Halifax Mooseheads** (☎ 902/496–5993), a Junior A division hockey team, play at the **Halifax Metro Centre** (✉ 1800 Argyle St., ☎ 902/421–8000) September through March.

Shopping

The **Art Gallery of Nova Scotia Shop** (✉ 1741 Hollis St., ☎ 902/424–7542) carries a good selection of arts and crafts; it also has a wonderful café decorated with colorful regional art. You can find fine crafts in the **Barrington Inn Complex** (✉ 1875 Barrington St.). In addition to being a deli and bakery with great takeout, the **Italian Gourmet** (✉ 5431 Doyle St., ☎ 902/423–7880) stocks a wonderful selection of imported gift items, including ceramics, exotic foodstuffs, and cooking gadgets. **Pewter House** (✉ 1875 Granville St., ☎ 902/423–8843) sells locally made and imported pewter goods, from knickknacks and tableware to clocks and jewelry.

Ambience Home Accents (✉ 5431 Doyle St., ☎ 902/423–9200) is packed to the rafters with curios and decorative functional items from all over the province and beyond. **Attica** (✉ 1652 Granville St., ☎ 902/423–2557) presents furniture, objets d'art, and housewares by Canadian and international designers. **Drala Books** (✉ 1567 Grafton St., ☎ 902/422–2504) stocks beautiful ceramics, handmade paper, and guides to meditation and Japanese gardening. At **Nova Scotian Crystal Ltd.** (✉ corner of George and Lower Water Sts., ☎ 902/492–5984), you can watch Waterford master craftspeople blowing glass into graceful decanters and bowls, which can be purchased in the showroom. The **Plaid Place** (✉ 1903 Barrington Pl., ☎ 902/429–6872 or 800/563–1749) has an array of tartans and Highland accessories. The **Wool Sweater Outlet** (✉ 1870 Hollis St., ☎ 902/422–9209) sells wool and cotton sweaters at reasonable prices.

Park Lane (✉ 5657 Spring Garden Rd.) is a stylish, indoor mall with everything from hand-crafted clothing to Canadian books and bath salts. **Spring Garden Road** is the liveliest street in town. Busking musicians serenade shoppers flowing in and out of **Spring Garden Place** (✉ 5640 Spring Garden Rd.), a mall. **Jennifer's of Nova Scotia** (✉ 5635 Spring Garden Rd., ☎ 902/425–3119) sells traditional crafts from around the province, soaps, hooked mats, tartan clothing, ceramics, and pewter.

Dartmouth

⑮ *Just north of Halifax via the A. Murray Mackay and Angus L. Macdonald bridges.*

Suburban in demeanor, Dartmouth was first settled by Quaker whalers from Nantucket. The 23 lakes within Dartmouth's boundaries, which have given Dartmouth the moniker "City of Lakes," provided the Mi'Kmaqs with a canoe route to the province's interior and to the Bay of Fundy. A 19th-century canal system connected the lakes for a brief time, but today there are only ruins, which have been partially restored as historic sites. You can drive or take the ferry from Halifax to Dartmouth. If you walk along the water behind the modern Law Courts in Halifax, near Historic Properties, you'll soon reach the Dartmouth ferry terminal, jammed with commuters during rush hour. The terminal is home to the oldest operational saltwater ferry service in North America, which began in 1732. If you do take the ferry, be sure to enjoy the sculptures by artist Dawn McNutt in the courtyard just outside the Dartmouth terminal. You may also want to head straight up the hill, along Pleasant Street, to explore funky little shops and cafés.

If you'd rather walk to Dartmouth, try the Angus L. Macdonald bridge, which has a walkway and a bicycle path. After you come off the bridge you can follow the wooden boardwalk for a stroll along the water.

The **Black Cultural Centre for Nova Scotia,** in Westphal (a neighborhood of Dartmouth), is in the heart of the oldest black community in the area. The museum, library, and educational complex are dedicated to the preservation of the history and culture of blacks in Nova Scotia, who first arrived here in the 1600s. ⊠ *Hwy. 7 and Cherrybrooke Rd.,* ☎ *902/434–6223.* ⌂ *$5.* ⊙ *Weekdays 9–5, Sat. 10–5.*

Dining and Lodging

$$–$$$ ✕ **La Perla.** This northern Italian restaurant with three separate dining areas, each with a distinctive ambience, overlooks the harbor and has consistently excellent food and a fine wine cellar. The food is rich and the servings are hearty. Calamari tossed with chilies and tomato has never been so tender; snails swim in a heady Gorgonzola cream sauce. ⊠ *73 Alderney Dr.,* ☎ *902/469–3241. Reservations essential. AE, MC, V.*

$–$$$ ⊞ **Sterns Mansion B&B.** This beautifully restored century-old home is on a quiet residential street within walking distance of the Dartmouth ferry terminal. The tastefully decorated house has antique furnishings and hardwood floors. Several rooms have whirlpool tubs and gas fireplaces. Honeymoon packages are a specialty. ⊠ *17 Tulip St., B3A 2S5,* ☎ *902/465–7414 or 800/565–3885,* FAX *902/466–2152. 4 rooms. AE, MC, V. BP.*

$$ ⊞ **Park Place Ramada Renaissance.** In Dartmouth's Burnside Industrial Park, this luxury hotel is aimed at the business traveler as well as families. There is a 108-ft indoor water slide. ⊠ *240 Brownlow Ave., B3B 1X6,* ☎ *902/468–8888; 800/561–3733 in Canada,* FAX *902/468–8765,* WEB *www.ramadans.com. 178 rooms, 30 suites. Restaurant, bar, room service, indoor pool, hot tub, sauna, gym, meeting room, free parking. AE, DC, MC, V.*

THE SOUTH SHORE AND ANNAPOLIS VALLEY

Mainland Nova Scotia is a long, narrow peninsula—no point in the province is more than 56 km (35 mi) from salt water. The South Shore is on the Atlantic side, the Annapolis Valley on the Bay of Fundy side; although they are less than an hour apart by car, the two seem like different worlds. The South Shore is rocky coast, island-dotted bays, fishing villages, and shipyards; the Annapolis Valley is lumberyards, farms, vineyards, and orchards. The South Shore is German, French, and Yankee; the valley, British. The sea is everywhere on the South Shore; in the valley the sea is blocked from view by a ridge of mountains.

Highway 103, Highway 3, and various secondary roads form the province's designated Lighthouse Route, which leads southwest from Halifax down the South Shore. It touches the heads of several big bays and small harbors, revealing a changing panorama of shoreline, inlet, and island. Small towns and fishing villages are spaced out every 50 km (31 mi) or so. The Lighthouse Route ends in Yarmouth and the Evangeline Trail begins, winding along the shore of St. Mary's Bay through a succession of Acadian villages collectively known as the French Shore. Here you notice the Acadian flag, tricolored with a gold star representing *stella maris,* the star of the sea. The star has guided the French-speaking Acadians during troubled times, which have been frequent. In 1755, after residing for a century and a half in Nova Scotia, chiefly in the Annapolis Valley, the Acadians were expelled by the British—an event that inspired Henry Wadsworth Longfellow's famous poem *Evangeline.* Some eluded capture and others slowly crept back; many settled in New Brunswick and along this shore of Nova Scotia. The villages blend into one another for about 32 km (20 mi), each one, it seems, with its own wharf, fish plant, and Catholic church. This tour mostly focuses on the towns along Highway 1, but you should follow the side roads whenever the inclination strikes; the South Shore rewards slow, relaxed exploration.

The Annapolis Valley runs northeast like a huge trench, flat on the bottom, sheltered on both sides by the North and South mountains. Occasional roads over the South Mountain lead to the South Shore; short roads over the North Mountain lead to the Fundy shore. Like the South Shore, the valley is punctuated with pleasant small towns, each with a generous supply of extravagant Victorian homes and churches. The rich soil of the valley bottom supports dairy herds, hay, grain, root vegetables, tobacco, and fruit. Apple-blossom season (late May and early June) and the fall harvest are the loveliest times to visit.

Peggy's Cove

★ ⑯   *48 km (30 mi) southwest of Halifax.*

Peggy's Cove, on Highway 333, marks the entrance to St. Margaret's Bay, which has been guarded for years by its famous octagonal lighthouse. The cove, with its houses huddled around the narrow slit in the boulders, is probably the most photographed village in Canada. A Canadian post office is in the lighthouse perched high on the rocky coast above a restless sea. Don't be tempted to venture too close—many an unwary visitor has been swept away by the mighty surf that sometimes breaks here. You can drive almost to the base of the lighthouse, but you'd do better to park in the spacious public lot below it and enjoy the village's shops and services during your three-minute walk up to the lighthouse.

A simple granite **memorial** (✉ Hwy. 333) for 1998 Swissair Flight 111, which crashed into the waters off Peggy's Cove, commemorates "those who helped and those who died"—the 229 casualties and the courageous Nova Scotia fisherfolk for their recovery work and the unstinting comfort they offered to grieving families. Another memorial stands in the town of Blandford directly across the cove.

Dining and Lodging

$$$$ ✕ **Candleriggs Dining Room.** Authentic Scottish dishes, such as *Forfar bridie* (beef and potato in puff pastry), Scotch mushrooms in cream and whisky, Scotch onion pie, and steak-and-kidney pie, share the menu with Canadian specialties in this pleasant restaurant. ⊠ *8545 Peggy's Cove Rd., Indian Harbour (3 km, or 2 mi, from Peggy's Cove),* ☎ *902/823–2722. AE, D, DC, MC, V. Limited hrs Nov.–mid-Mar.*

$$–$$$ ✕ **Sou'wester Restaurant.** Sou'wester, at the base of the Peggy's Cove lighthouse, serves home-style fare including a wide range of Maritime specialties—try *solomon gundy* (herring and onion with sour cream)—and fish-and-chips. There's also a large souvenir shop. ⊠ *Off Hwy. 333,* ☎ *902/823–2561. AE, DC, MC, V.*

$–$$ ✕ **Gingerbread House.** Flower boxes and dark paneling decorate the outside of this restaurant 15 km (9 mi) from Peggy's Cove; home-style cooking and homemade crafts await inside. Ample portions of chowders, seafood, fettuccine, fish, steaks, and chicken are served in the dining room or out on the patio. ⊠ *10345 Peggy's Cove Rd., Glen Margaret,* ☎ *902/823–1230. MC, V. Closed Nov.–Apr. and Mon.–Tues. in May.*

$–$$$ 🏠 **Havenside B&B.** Multilevel decks overlook a delightful seascape near
★ Peggy's Cove at this luxurious home. Saltwater swimming and canoeing, a serene gathering room with fireplace and library, a games room with a pool table, and a breakfast of fresh homemade muffins, pancakes, French toast, and eggs enhance the package. Four-night packages with two nights aboard a 32-ft yacht and two nights at the B&B are an option. ⊠ *225 Boutillier's Cove Rd., Hackett's Cove B0J 3J0,* ☎ *902/823–9322 or 800/641–8272,* ℻ *902/823–9322. 3 rooms, 1 suite. Dining room, library. MC, V. BP.*

$–$$ 🏠 **Migrate In Bed & Breakfast and Cottage.** Perched on 56 acres overlooking St. Margaret's Bay, this modern home is on the migration route of many birds, including numerous shorebirds, ring-necked pheasants, red-breasted nuthatches, hummingbirds, black-capped chickadees, and robins. Breakfast may offer lobster quiche, homemade granola, or waffles with Nova Scotia blueberries. A restored 1840s cottage has two bedrooms, an eat-in kitchen, and a wood-burning stove. ⊠ *9749 Hwy. 333, Hackett's Cove (7 km, or 4 mi, from Peggy's Cove) B0J 3J0,* ☎ *902/823–1968 or 800/780–7471,* ℻ *902/823–1968,* 🌐 *www.migratein.com. 2 rooms, 1 suite, 1 cottage. Recreation room. MC, V. BP.*

Shopping

Beales' Bailiwick (⊠ 124 Peggy's Point Rd., ☎ 902/823–2099) carries outstanding crafts—Maritime-designed clothing, pewter, jewelry, and more. The adjoining coffee shop affords the best photo opportunity for Peggy's Cove and the lighthouse. **River'B'Quilts** (⊠ 6001 St. Margaret's Bay Rd., Head of St. Margaret's Bay, ☎ 902/826–1991), calling itself "the biggest little quilt shop in Nova Scotia," offers quilts and quilting supplies, including custom-made designs.

Chester

64 km (40 mi) west of Peggy's Cove.

Chester, a charming little town on Mahone Bay, is a popular summer retreat for an established population of well-heeled Americans and Haligonians, whose splendid homes and yachts rim the waterfront. In fact, yachting is the town's principal summer occupation, culminating each August in **Chester Race Week,** Atlantic Canada's largest regatta.

The **Ross Farm Living Museum of Agriculture,** a restored 19th-century farm, illustrates the evolution of agriculture from 1600 to 1925. The animals here are those found on a farm of the 1800s—draft horses, oxen, and older breeds or types of animals. Blacksmithing and other crafts are demonstrated. The Pedlar's Shop sells items made in the community. ✉ *Hwy. 12, New Ross (20-min drive inland from Chester),* ☎ *902/689–2210.* 🎫 *$3.* ☉ *June–mid-Oct., daily 9:30–5:30; Jan.–mid-Mar., by appointment.*

A passenger-only ferry (☎ 902/275–3221) runs from the dock in Chester to the scenic **Big and Little Tancook Islands,** 8 km (5 mi) out in Mahone Bay. Reflecting its part-German heritage, Big Tancook claims to make the best sauerkraut in Nova Scotia. Exploration of the island is made easy by walking trails. The boat runs four times daily Monday through Thursday, six times daily Friday, and twice daily on weekends. The 45-minute ride costs $5 (round-trip ticket).

Dining and Lodging

$$–$$$ ✕ **The Galley.** Decked out in nautical bric-a-brac and providing a spectacular view of the ocean, this restaurant has a pleasant, relaxed atmosphere and an outdoor dining area. The seafood chowder, lobster, and homemade desserts are recommended. Reserve ahead for summer dining. ✉ *Hwy. 3, 115 Marina Rd., Marriot's Cove (Exit 8 off Hwy. 103, 3 km/2 mi west of Chester),* ☎ *902/275–4700. AE, D, MC, V. Closed Nov.–late Mar.*

$–$$ ✕ **Fo'c'sle Tavern.** This rustic midtown pub features nautical touches, including a deliciously ugly ship's figurehead, maps, displays of seamen's knots, and a ship's wheel. The mood is jolly, the food is abundant and affordable, and the potbellied woodstove exudes warmth and goodwill on chilly nights. The hearty pub fare includes hefty servings of fish-and-chips, seafood chowders, and steaks, as well as a Sunday breakfast buffet. ✉ *42 Queen St.,* ☎ *902/275–3912. V.*

$$$$ ✕⌂ **Haddon Hall Inn.** At this luxurious resort near Chester, the large ★ rooms are furnished with antiques—including some canopy beds—working fireplaces, marble baths, and whirlpool tubs. Tennis courts, a pool, mountain bikes, and nature await outdoors. The dining room overlooks Mahone Bay. The three-course prix fixe dinner (reservations required) is $60. The lounge is deep, dark, and rustic, with a fire in the grate on chilly evenings. ✉ *67 Haddon Hill Rd., Box 640, B0J 1J0,* ☎ *902/275–3577,* ℻ *902/275–5159,* ⊞ *www.haddonhallinn.com. 5 rooms, 5 suites. Restaurant, lounge, pool, tennis court, mountain bikes. MC, V. Closed Nov.–Mar. MAP.*

$–$$ ✕⌂ **Dauphinee Inn.** On the shore of Hubbards Cove, about 19 km (12 mi) east of Chester, this charming country inn has first-class accommodations and an excellent restaurant ($–$$). The Hot Rocks is a social dining concept where guests are invited to cook fresh vegetables, seafood, beef, or chicken on a hot slab of South Shore granite. Fresh local seafood is another specialty. Opportunities abound for bicycling, bird-watching, and deep-sea fishing and six golf courses are within a half-hour drive. ✉ *167 Shore Club Rd., Hubbards Cove (Exit 6 off Hwy. 103) B0J 1T0,* ☎ *902/857–1790 or 800/567–1790,* ℻ *902/857–9555,* ⊞ *www.dauphineeinn.com. 4 rooms, 2 suites. Restaurant, lounge, boating, fishing. AE, D, DC, MC, V. Closed Nov.–Apr.*

Mahone Bay

★ ⑰ *24 km (15 mi) west of Chester.*

This quiet town perched on an idyllic bay of the same name comes alive each summer. Many of Nova Scotia's finest artists and artisans are represented in the studios and galleries that line the narrow streets. Three impressive churches stand shoulder to shoulder near the waterfront, their bells vying for attention each Sunday morning. You'll find sailing, kayaking, and walking opportunities. In July the annual **Wooden Boat Festival** celebrates the town's heritage as a shipbuilding center.

Dining and Lodging

$$$–$$$$ ✕ **The Innlet Café.** This pleasant restaurant commands a fine view of the town across the bay. A broad Canadian-style menu has poultry and meats, an understandable emphasis on chowders and seafoods, and a few vegetarian options. ⊠ *249 Edgewater St.,* ☎ *902/624–6363. MC, V.*

$$ ⊞ **Amber Rose Inn.** All the creature comforts plus expert knowledge of this historic area are available at this 125-year-old inn. The three large suites each have a private bath, whirlpool tub, refrigerator, coffeemaker, and handsome antiques. A lavish complimentary breakfast includes French toast or blueberry pancakes. ⊠ *319 W. Main St., Box 397, B0J 2E0,* ☎ *902/624–1060,* FAX *902/624–0997,* WEB *www.amberroseinn.com. 3 suites. Breakfast room. AE, MC, V. BP.*

$–$$ ⊞ **Manse at Mahone Bay Country Inn.** Classical music and fine art, a library of contemporary Canadian literature, and Mahone Bay's three handsome churches just down the hill distinguish this elegant mid-19th-century former Presbyterian manse. Mahone Bay can be viewed from the broad bay window. The inn has an elegant guest parlor plus two spacious rooms in the main house; the carriage house has two huge suites. The menu is exceptional; get set for Stilton cheese, pear omelettes for breakfast, and a range of fresh seafood dishes at dinner (reservations required). ⊠ *88 Orchard St., Box 475, B0J 2E0,* ☎ *902/624–1121,* FAX *902/624–1182,* WEB *www.bbcanada.com/manse. 2 rooms, 2 suites. Dining room. MC, V. BP.*

$ ⊞ **Countryside B&B.** Lessons in llama etiquette are part of the service at this waterfront farm with a private dock. Sheep, poultry, and llamas—who protect the sheep from coyotes—share the meadows and barns. Inside, antiques and original art share space with your host's naval memorabilia. Breakfast might include homemade treats such as jams, wild-blueberry crepes, and baked fat-free French toast. ⊠ *28 Silver Point Rd., R.R. 2, B0J 2E0,* ☎ *902/627–1308,* FAX *902/627–1112,* WEB *www.countrysidebandb.com. 3 rooms. Dining room, dock. V. BP.*

Shopping

Amos Pewter (⊠ 589 Main St., ☎ 902/624–9547 or 800/565–3369) has been using traditional methods to make pewter for 25 years. A studio in an 1888 seaside building offers interpretive displays and demonstrations. Jewelry, sculptures, ornaments, and sand dollars are among the items available along with a new original-design Christmas ornament each year. The **Moorings Gallery & Shop** (⊠ 575 Main St., ☎ 902/624–6208) sells the work of Atlantic Canada's fine artists and artisans in many media. The **Rags to Rugs Shoppe** (⊠ 374 Clearland Woodstock Rd., ☎ 902/624–8075) specializes in the traditional hooked rugs for which Nova Scotia is famous. The owner offers her own designs and those of many other artisans.

Lunenburg

★ ⑱ *9 km (6 mi) south of Mahone Bay.*

A feast of Victorian-era architecture, wooden boats, steel draggers (a fishing boat that operates a trawl), historic inns, and good restaurants, Lunenburg delights all the senses. The center of town, known as Old Town, is a UNESCO World Heritage Site, and the fantastic old school on the hilltop is the region's finest remaining example of Second Empire architecture, an ornate style that began in 19th-century France.

Lunenburg is home port to the **Bluenose II** (☎ 902/634–1963 or 800/763–1963), a tall ship ambassador for Canada sailing out of Lunenburg, Halifax, and other ports. She's a replica of the first *Bluenose,* the great racing schooner depicted on the back of the Canadian dime—a winner of four international races and the pride of Canada. When in port, the *Bluenose II* is open for tours through the Fisheries Museum of the Atlantic. Two-hour harbor sailings in summer cost $20.

The **Fisheries Museum of the Atlantic,** on the Lunenburg waterfront, gives a comprehensive overview of Nova Scotia fisheries with demonstrations such as sail making, dory building, boat launching, and fish splitting. A touch tank with starfish, shellfish, and anemones; participatory demonstrations of rug hooking and quilting; and a day-long schedule of films at the theater make visiting here a busy yet rich experience. Add to that the *Bluenose* exhibit, celebrating the tall ship that won acclaim for Canada, plus a gift shop and seafood restaurant, and your day is full. ⊠ *68 Bluenose Dr.,* ☎ *902/634–4794.* 🖪 *$7.* ☉ *Mid-May–mid-Oct., daily 9:30–5:30; mid-Oct.–mid-May, by appointment.*

Dining and Lodging

$$–$$$ ✕ **Grand Banker Seafood Bar & Grill.** This bustling, big-menu establishment dispenses a wide variety of seafoods at modest prices. You can dine on scallops, shrimp, lobster in season, or all of the above in a seafood platter for those with hearty appetites. ⊠ *82 Montague St.,* ☎ *902/634–3300. AE, D, MC, V.*

$$–$$$ ✕ **The Old Fish Factory Restaurant.** In the Fisheries Museum of the Atlantic, the Old Fish Factory overlooks Lunenburg Harbour. It specializes in seafood, but you can also get steaks and other dishes here. ⊠ *68 Bluenose Dr.,* ☎ *902/634–3333 or 800/533–9336. AE, D, MC, V. Closed Nov.–early May.*

$–$$ ✕🏠 **Arbor View Inn.** The host is a young chef whose fresh menu ideas, based on a variety of ethnic influences, lend culinary sparkle to the gracious dining room ($$–$$$) of this grand, early-20th-century house. Though the menu changes frequently, his white-chocolate crème brûlée is a fixture. Leaded and stained-glass windows, extravagant wood trim, and handsome antiques enhance every room here. The top-floor suite has a queen-size canopy bed, a two-person whirlpool tub, and a deck. The spacious grounds invite strolls. ⊠ *216 Dufferin St., B0J 2C0,* ☎ *800/890–6650,* 🖷 FAX *902/634–3658,* WEB *www.arborviewinn.ns.ca. 4 rooms, 2 suites. Restaurant. MC, V. Closed Jan. BP.*

$ ✕🏠 **Lion Inn B&B.** Original works by Lunenburg artists—for show and
★   for sale—adorn the walls of this three-story 1835 town house, where the host's collection of owls stares out from all sides. Three interesting guest rooms are decorated in rich greens and burgundies and have sloping ceilings, eclectic antiques, and original artwork. The inn is noted for its outstanding dinners ($$$–$$$$); the star of the menu is rack of lamb, but you can also order good seafood and poultry and a wonderfully delicate mocha crème brûlée. ⊠ *33 Cornwallis St., Box 487, B0J 2C0,* ☎ *902/634–8988 or 888/634–8988,* FAX *902/634–3386. 3 rooms. Restaurant. AE, MC, V. BP.*

$–$$$ 🏠 **Pelham House Bed & Breakfast.** Close to downtown, this sea captain's home, circa 1906 and decorated in the style of the era, has a large collection of books about the sea and sailing. The veranda overlooks the harbor. Full breakfast and afternoon tea are included in the room rate. ⊠ *224 Pelham St., Box 358, B0J 2C0,* ☎ *902/634–7113,* FAX *902/634–7114. 3 rooms. Business services. MC, V. BP.*

$–$$ 🏠 **Boscawen Inn and MacLachlan House.** Period antiques adorn and fireplaces warm this elegant 1888 mansion and its 1905 annex in the middle of Lunenburg's historic Old Town. Guests can take afternoon tea in one of the drawing rooms or on the balcony. All rooms and suites have either water or park views. ✉ *150 Cumberland St., Box 1343, B0J 2C0,* ☎ *902/634–3325 or 800/354–5009,* FAX *902/634–9293,* WEB *www3.ns.sympatico.ca/boscawen. 20 rooms. Restaurant. AE, D, DC, MC, V. Closed Jan.–Easter.*

$–$$ 🖭 **Lunenburg Inn.** JFK's father, Joseph Kennedy, patronized this hostelry long before it became the gracious inn it is today. In those days it had 13 tiny rooms and a single shared bathroom. Today it has two suites and seven rooms, each with a private bath, and all are spacious and furnished with fine antiques. An elegant main-floor parlor, awash in books, adjoins the bright dining room. A top-floor 775-square-ft suite includes a tiny kitchenette with a microwave and a refrigerator. ✉ *26 Dufferin St., B0J 2C0,* ☎ *902/634–3963 or 800/565–3963,* FAX *902/ 634–9419,* WEB *www.lunenburginn.com. 7 rooms, 2 suites. Dining room, kitchenettes (some), no smoking rooms. AE, MC, V. BP.*

$ 🖭 **Blue Rocks Road B&B.** Bike enthusiasts and vegetarians can settle in comfortably at this friendly smoke-free, meat-free home that has a bicycle shop and bike rentals. Your host is a quilter, potter, and artist; her unique stencil designs decorate floors, walls, and ceilings in every room. An enthusiastic dog shares hosting duties. Breakfast is home-made, and often made with fresh herbs and vegetables from the garden. ✉ *579 Blue Rocks Rd., RR 1, B0J 2C0,* ☎ *902/634–8033 or 800/ 818–3426,* FAX *902/634–7147. 3 rooms, 1 with bath. Bicycles. V. Closed mid-Oct.–mid-May. BP.*

$ 🖭 **1826 Maple Bird House B&B.** This B&B is just steps away from the Fisheries Museum and Lunenburg's fascinating waterfront. A huge garden overlooking the harbor and a golf course, an outdoor pool, and a piano in the drawing room create a relaxing ambience that characterizes this home. The hosts know a thing or two about breakfast— crepes, omelettes, cereals, and fruits appear in ample amounts. ✉ *36 Pelham St., Box 278, B0J 2C0,* ☎ FAX *902/634–3863 or 888/395–3863,* WEB *www3.ns.sympatico.ca/barry.susie. 4 rooms. Pool. MC, V. BP, CP.*

Outdoor Activities and Sports

June through October **Lunenburg Whale-Watching** (☎ 902/527–7175) offers three-hour trips daily from the Fisheries Museum Wharf for $35. You may spot fin, pilot, humpback, and minke whales; dolphins; seals; and myriad seabirds such as puffins, razorbills, and gannets. You can also arrange for bird-watching excursions and tours of Lunenburg Harbour.

Shopping

Black Duck Gallery and Gifts (✉ 8 Pelham St., ☎ 902/639–3190) sells handmade kites, local art, books, and an imaginative selection of gifts. The **Houston North Gallery** (✉ 110 Montague St., ☎ 902/634–8869) represents both trained and self-taught Nova Scotian artists as well as Inuit soapstone carvers and printmakers. It's closed in January. The **Lunenburg Forge & Metalworks Gallery** (✉ 146 Bluenose Dr., ☎ 902/ 634–7125) is a traditional artist/blacksmith shop in a bright-blue building on the waterfront. One-of-a-kind handcrafted wrought-iron items and custom orders, including both time-honored designs and whimsical creations, are available.

Bridgewater

18 km (11 mi) west of Lunenburg.

This is the main market town of the South Shore. The **DesBrisay Museum** explores the history and people of Lunenburg County and has changing exhibits on art, science, technology, and history. The gift shop carries books by local authors and local arts and crafts. ✉ *130 Jubilee Rd.,* ☎ *902/543–4033.* 🎟 *$2 mid-May–Sept.; free rest of yr.* ☉ *Mid-*

May–Sept., Mon.–Sat. 9–5, Sun. 1–5; Oct.–mid-May, Tues. and Thurs.–Sun. 1–5, Wed. 1–9.

The **Wile Carding Mill,** a water-powered mill with an overshot wheel, operated from 1860 to 1968. Interpreters tell the story of Dean Wile's woolen mill. ⊠ *242 Victoria Rd.,* ☎ *902/543–8233.* ▧ *By donation.* ☉ *June–Sept., Mon.–Sat. 9:30–5:30, Sun. 1–5:30.*

Liverpool

⑲ *46 km (29 mi) south of Bridgewater.*

Nestled on the estuary of the Mersey River, Liverpool was settled around 1760 by New Englanders and is now a fishing and paper-milling town. During the American Revolution and the War of 1812, Liverpool was a privateering center; later, it became an important shipping and trading port.

The **Hank Snow Country Music Centre Museum,** housed in a renovated CN railway station, commemorates the great country singer whose childhood home is nearby. A country-music archive and library and memorabilia of the singer's career are on view. ⊠ *Off Hwy. 103,* ☎ *902/354–4675 or 888/450–5525.* ▧ *$3.* ☉ *June–mid-Oct., Mon.–Sat. 9–6, Sun. noon–6.*

The **Sherman Hines Museum of Photography** contains vintage photos and cameras and the work of the noted photographer. Changing exhibits in the galleries feature top Canadian photographers, and the research center offers a good collection of photographic books and thousands of photographs. ⊠ *219 Main St.,* ☎ *902/354–2667.* ▧ *Free.* ☉ *Apr.–late Dec., Mon.–Sat. 10–5:30.*

Fort Point Lighthouse Park, on the site where explorers Samuel de Champlain and Sieur de Monts landed in 1604, overlooks Liverpool Harbour. Interpretive displays and models in the 1855 lighthouse recall the area's privateering and shipbuilding heritage. Special events include a legal marriage in 1780s style, an encampment of the King's Orange Rangers (a group that reenacts the exploits of a pro-British American Revolution brigade posted to Nova Scotia 1778–83), and opportunities to meet local artisans. ⊠ *End of Main St., off Hwy. 103,* ☎ *902/354–5260.* ▧ *By donation.* ☉ *Mid-May–mid-Oct., daily 9–8.*

The **Simeon Perkins House,** built in 1766, is the historic home of privateer-turned-leading-citizen Simeon Perkins, who kept a detailed diary about colonial life in Liverpool from 1760 until his death in 1812. Built by ships' carpenters, the house gives the illusion of standing in the upside-down hull of a ship. ⊠ *105 Main St.,* ☎ *902/354–4058.* ▧ *By donation.* ☉ *June–mid-Oct., Mon.–Sat. 9:30–5:30, Sun. 1–5:30.*

About 25 km (16 mi) southwest of Liverpool, **Kejimkujik Seaside Adjunct,** one of the last untouched tracts of coastline in Atlantic Canada—with isolated coves, broad white beaches, and imposing headlands—is protected by Kejimkujik National Park. A 6-km (4-mi) hiking trail leads to a pristine coastline that is home to harbor seals, eider ducks, and many other species. To protect nesting areas of the endangered piping plover, parts of the St. Catherine's River beach, the main beach, are closed to the public from late April to early August. ⊠ *Off Hwy. 103, Port Joli,* ☎ *902/682–2772.* ▧ *Free.*

Dining and Lodging

$ ✕▥ **Lane's Privateer Inn and Bed & Breakfast.** Famed buccaneer Captain Joseph Barss once occupied this 200-year-old inn overlooking the Mersey River. Today it has 27 comfortable guest rooms as well as a restaurant serving Canadian fare ($$$–$$$$), a pub, a bookstore café, and a specialty-food shop. Next door there's a B&B, which serves a complimentary full breakfast; the inn serves a complimentary Continental breakfast. Lane's is within walking distance of Liverpool's major attractions and within 15 km (9 mi) of the Kejimkujik Seaside Adjunct. ⊠ *27 Bristol Ave., B0T 1K0,* ☎ *902/354–3456 or 800/794–3332,* FAX *902/354–7220,* WEB *www3.ns.sympatico.ca/ron.lane. Inn 27 rooms, B&B 3 rooms. AE, D, MC, V. B&B closed Nov.–May. BP, CP.*

Outdoor Activities and Sports

The **Mersey River** drains Lake Rossignol, Nova Scotia's largest freshwater lake, and provides trout and salmon fishing.

Kejimkujik National Park

67 km (42 mi) northwest of Liverpool.

The gentle waterways of this 381-square-km (147-square-mi) park have been the canoe routes of the Mi'Kmaq for thousands of years. Today the routes and land trails are well marked and mapped, permitting canoeists, hikers, and campers to explore the landscape; swim in the warm lake; and glimpse white-tailed deer, beaver, owls, loons, and other wildlife. Canoes and camping equipment can be rented here. Park staffers lead interpretive hikes and canoe trips, or you can explore on your own. In late September and early October, the park's deciduous forests blaze with color. ⊠ *Hwy. 8, between Liverpool and Annapolis Royal, Maitland Bridge,* ☎ *902/682–2772.* ☞ *$3.25 per day; camping $14–$19 a day.*

Dining and Lodging

$–$$ ✕ **Bonnie's Diner.** An unpretentious diner serves satisfying food in a homey setting. You can order a home-cooked breakfast at any time of the day, or roasted turkey, baked haddock, and other seafood. Finish off the meal with a slice of homemade cheesecake or pie. ⊠ *Hwy. 8, Caledonia,* ☎ *902/682–3481. No credit cards. Closed Mon. Sept.–mid-June.*

$ ✕ **Personal Touch Bakery.** Homemade breads, cakes, and cookies are served in a casual setting at the Personal Touch Bakery. You can also order chowders, pizza, and lasagna. ⊠ *Hwy. 8, Caledonia,* ☎ *902/682–3175. No credit cards. Closed Sun.*

$ ✕🏠 **Whitman Inn.** Just next door to Kejimkujik Park, this restored 1900 farmstead offers wilderness and learning experiences. The dining room serves interesting full breakfasts and dinners ($$; reserve ahead) that feature seafood, poultry, pasta, and a vegetarian dish. The appealing rooms are furnished with antiques. Nature and canoeing packages are available, and weekend workshops range from quilting, photography, and writing to stress management or wine tasting. ⊠ *12389 Hwy. 8, Kempt B0T 1B0,* ☎ *902/682–2226 or 800/830–3855,* FAX *902/682–3171,* WEB *www.whitman.ns.ca. 8 rooms, 1 2-bedroom apartment. Restaurant, indoor pool, hot tub, sauna, recreation room, video games, library, meeting room. MC, V.*

$$$–$$$$ 🏠 **White Point Beach Resort.** This wilderness seafront resort has something special: bunnies. They're everywhere, and bunny food is doled out at the front desk. But there's more. Just about any physical activity you can think of—including kayaking, nature trails, nature cruises, and birding—is here. In the summer you can catch a theater performance on the premises. Choose from a room in one of the lodges, or a housekeeping cottage with sitting area and fireplace, set among trees or along the beach. ⊠ *Hwy. 103, Exit 20A, White Point, Queens County B0T 1G0,* ☎ *902/354–2711 or 800/565–5068,* FAX *902/354–7278,* WEB *www.whitepoint.com. 77 rooms, 44 cottages. Dining room, indoor pool, spa, 9-hole golf course, 4 tennis courts, hiking, horseback riding,*

beach, surfing, fishing, mountain bikes, shop, recreation room, theater, playground, meeting room. AE, MC, V.

$–$$$ 🏨 **Mersey River Chalets.** Barbecues and sing-alongs around the bon-
★ fire, workshops on building kayaks or dreamcatchers, a hot tub, swim-
ming, and outdoor sports such as canoeing and kayaking fill the agenda
at this 375-acre wilderness resort. A boardwalk offers nearly 2 km (1
mi) of close-up nature, river, and waterfall scenery. Seven two-bedroom
chalets are nestled in dense forest and are excellent for people with mo-
bility problems: exterior ramps, wide doors, and roll-in showers make
these accessible. And for closer encounters with nature, there are te-
pees built on platforms on the shore of Lake Harry. The restaurant serves
Canadian fare ($–$$$); Friday night's special is planked salmon. ✉
Off Hwy. 8, General Delivery, Caledonia B0T 1B0, ☎ *902/682–2443,*
FAX *902/682–2332,* WEB *www.merseyriverchalets.ns.ca. 7 chalets, 5 te-
pees. Restaurant, hot tub. MC, V.*

$–$$ 🏨 **Apple Pie B&B.** Your host may pick up his guitar and serenade you
or pick up woodworking tools and demonstrate how he crafts his handsome pine furniture. For sure, he'll welcome you to join the family in
the sitting room of their century-old home for music and lively talk. The
upstairs two-bedroom suite accommodates up to four visitors. For breakfast you may enjoy muffins, homemade rhubarb and wild-cherry jam,
or bacon and eggs. Nearby is the Kejimkujik Seaside Adjunct and three
fine beaches, including Carter's Beach, which is usually deserted and strewn
with shells. ✉ *Exit 21, Hwy. 103, Box 32, Central Port Mouton B0T
1T0,* ☎ *902/683–2217 or 888/722–7753,* FAX *902/683–2180,* WEB *www.
applepiebedandbreakfast.ns.ca. 1 suite. Closed Nov.–Mar. BP.*

$ 🏨 **Old Homestead Bed & Breakfast.** Your host, "Auntie Pat" to nu-
merous international visitors, offers down-home hospitality and home-
cooked food in her 150-year-old farm home near Caledonia. Her
breakfasts include jams, jellies, breads, and muffins. The sunroom
overlooks hayfields and cattle, and you can take a dip in the lake. A
golf course and the wilderness of Kejimkujik Park are nearby. Pat's handmade quilts and comforters adorn the beds. ✉ *71 Canning Rd., West
Caledonia B0T 1B0,* ☎ *902/682–2654. 3 rooms without bath. Lake,
boating. V.*

Outdoor Activities and Sports

Peter Rogers of **Loon Lake Outfitters** (☎ 902/682–2220) is an 18-year
veteran in canoe outfitting who offers summer canoe instruction, complete and partial canoe outfitting, and recreational guiding in and
around Kejimkujik Park. At Jakes Landing, within Kejimkujik Park,
Wildcat River Outfitters (☎ 902/682–2196 or 902/682–2822), a company owned and operated by local Mi'Kmaqs, rents bicycles and camping supplies, as well as kayaks and canoes.

Shelburne

★ ⑳ *69 km (43 mi) south of Liverpool.*

The high noon of Shelburne occurred right after the American Revolution, when 16,000 Loyalists briefly made it one of the largest communities in North America—bigger than either Halifax or Montréal
at the time. Today it is a fishing and shipbuilding town at the mouth
of the Roseway River.

Many of Shelburne's homes date to the late 1700s, including the **Ross-
Thomson House,** now a provincial museum. Inside, the only surviving
18th-century store in Nova Scotia contains all the necessities of that
period. ✉ *9 Charlotte La.,* ☎ *902/875–3141.* 🎫 *$2.* ☉ *June–mid-Oct.,
daily 9:30–5:30; call for winter hrs.*

Tours of some of Shelburne's historic homes are offered during periodic fund-raising endeavors. The **South Shore Tourism Association** (☎ 902/624–6466) has information.

Dining and Lodging

$–$$ ✕ **Charlotte Lane Café.** This café serves up seafood, meats, pastas, salads, and Swiss specialties. The 150-year-old historic building has a pleasant garden patio and a shop selling local crafts. ⊠ *13 Charlotte La., ☎ 902/875–3314. MC, V. Closed Sun.–Mon. and Jan.–mid-Apr.*

$–$$$ ✕⌂ **Cooper's Inn and Restaurant.** One of the last cooperages in North America, on Shelburne's historic waterfront, is also a unique inn where you may purchase barrels and planters. Inside the elegant 1784 inn seven rooms are furnished with antiques and fine art. Two dining rooms ($$–$$$) offer candlelight dining with an emphasis on seafood; consider ordering scallops with pine-nut butter followed by homemade ice cream. A specialty at breakfast is Belgian waffles with maple syrup, but there are many other choices. ⊠ *36 Dock St., B0T 1W0, ☎ FAX 902/875–4656 or 800/688–2011. 7 rooms. 2 restaurants. AE, DC, MC, V. Closed Nov.–Mar. BP.*

$ ⌂ **Clyde River Inn.** Queen Victoria and her pals peer down from every wall of this inn, once the main stagecoach stop between Tusket and Shelburne. The parlor, with a working organ that belonged to the host's grandmother, is as busy with artifacts and decor as its Victorian forebear might have been. Unusual bric-a-brac and fine china decorate the dining room, where a full breakfast emphasizes blueberry pancakes, homemade jams, and jellies. A golf course is a five-minute walk away, and three beaches are within a 15-minute drive, including shell-strewn Round Bay Beach, which is usually deserted. ⊠ *10525 Hwy. 103, Box 2, Clyde River B0W 1R0, ☎ 902/637–3267 or 877/262–0222, FAX 902/637–1512. 4 rooms. MC, V. BP.*

Barrington

40 km (25 mi) south of Shelburne.

Tiny Barrington has a long history reflected in a clutch of interesting museums. The **Barrington Woolen Mill Museum** represents a thriving late-19th-century industry in which the mill produced durable wool for fishermen's clothing. Today it features demonstrations of hand spinning and details about sheep raising and wool processing. ⊠ *2368 Hwy. 3, ☎ 902/637–2185. ✍ By donation. ☉ June–Sept., Mon.–Sat. 9:30–5:30, Sun. 1–5:30.*

The **Old Meeting House Museum** served as a church, town hall, and election center for New England settlers in the late 1700s. It's the oldest Nonconformist house of worship in Canada, with a historic graveyard next door. ⊠ *2408 Hwy. 3, ☎ 902/637–2185. ✍ By donation. ☉ June–Sept., Mon.–Sat. 9:30–5:30, Sun. 1–5:30.*

The replica **Seal Island Lighthouse** is a lighthouse interpretation center that houses the original light and affords a fine view of the coastline. ⊠ *Hwy. 3, ☎ 902/637–2185. ✍ By donation. ☉ June–Sept., Mon.–Sat. 9:30–5:30, Sun. 1–5:30.*

The **Western Counties Military Museum** displays historic military artifacts such as uniforms, medals, and pictures. ⊠ *Old Courthouse, Hwy. 3, ☎ 902/637–2161. ✍ By donation. ☉ Early June–Aug.; days and hrs vary so call ahead.*

Cape Sable Island

8 km (5 mi) south of Barrington over the causeway.

Nova Scotia's southernmost extremity is the 21-km (13-mi) road that encircles Cape Sable Island, a Yankee community with fine beaches, connected to the mainland by a bridge. On the island the fishing village of Clark's Harbour sits on an appealing harbor sprinkled with colorful fishing boats. Hawk Point, just beyond the town, has excellent bird-watching and a fine view of the 1861 Cape Sable Island Lighthouse.

The **Archelaus Smith Museum,** named for an early New England settler, recaptures late-1700s life with household items such as quilts, toys, and cradles plus fishing gear and information about shipwrecks and sea captains. ⊠ *Hwy. 330,* ☎ *902/745–3361.* ☎ *Free.* ☉ *Mid-June–Sept., Mon.–Sat. 9:30–5:30, Sun. 1:30–5:30.*

Pubnico

48 km (30 mi) northwest of Barrington.

Pubnico marks the beginning of the Acadian milieu; from here to Digby the communities are mostly French-speaking. Favorite local fare includes *rappie* pie, made of meat or poultry with potatoes from which much of the starch has been removed. Most restaurants along the shore between Pubnico and Digby serve some variation on rappie pie.

No fewer than seven towns bear the name Pubnico: Lower West Pubnico, Middle West Pubnico, and West Pubnico, all on the west shore of Pubnico Harbour; three East Pubnicos on the eastern shore; and just plain Pubnico, at the top of none other than Pubnico Harbour. These towns were founded by Phillipe Muis D'Entremont, and they once constituted the only barony in French Acadia. D'Entremont was a prodigious progenitor: to this day, many people in the Pubnicos are D'Entremonts, and most of the rest are D'Eons or Amiraults.

Dining and Lodging

$ ✕⊡ **Red Cap Motel and Restaurant.** This venerable establishment overlooks Pubnico Harbour and includes a six-unit motel and a café that serves an acclaimed version of a favorite Acadian dish, rappie pie. ⊠ *Hwy. 335, Middle West Pubnico B0W 2M0,* ☎ *902/762–2112,* FAX *902/762–2887,* WEB *www.tusket.com/present/rest/redcap. 6 rooms. Café. MC, V.*

Yarmouth

㉑ *41 km (25 mi) north of Pubnico.*

Visitors have been arriving in Yarmouth for nearly three centuries, and they're still pouring in, chiefly by car ferry from Bar Harbor, Maine, and cruise ferry from Portland, Maine. In fact, the town's status as a large port city and its proximity to New England accounted for its early prosperity, and its great shipping heritage is reflected in its fine harbor, two marinas, and its museums. Handsome Victorian architecture, a pleasantly old-fashioned main street lined with friendly shops, and easy access to the Acadian villages to the north or the Lighthouse Trail to the south make Yarmouth much more than just a ferry dock.

★ The **Yarmouth County Museum** presents one of the largest collections of ship paintings in Canada; artifacts associated with the *Titanic*; exhibits of household items displayed in period rooms; musical instruments, including rare mechanical pianos and music boxes; and items that richly evoke centuries past. The museum has a preservation wing and an archival research area, where local history and genealogy are documented. Next door is the **Pelton-Fuller House,** summer home of the original Fuller Brush Man; it's maintained and furnished much as the family left it. ✉ *22 Collins St.,* ☎ *902/742–5539,* WEB *www.ycn. library.ns.ca/museum/yarcomus.htm.* 🖰 *Museum $2.50, museum and Pelton-Fuller House $4, archives $5 per half day.* ☉ *Museum June– mid-Oct., Mon.–Sat. 9–5, Sun. 2–5; mid-Oct.–May, Tues.–Sun. 2–5. Pelton-Fuller House June–mid-Oct., Mon.–Sat. 9–5.*

🖰 The **Firefighters Museum of Nova Scotia** recounts Nova Scotia's fire-fighting history through photographs and artifacts, including vintage pumpers, hose wagons, ladder trucks, and an 1863 Amoskeag Steamer. Children love to don a fire helmet and take the wheel of a 1933 Bickle Pumper. ✉ *451 Main St.,* ☎ *902/742–5525.* 🖰 *$2.* ☉ *June and Sept., Mon.–Sat. 9–5; July–Aug., Mon.–Sat. 9–9, Sun. 10–5; Oct.–May, weekdays 9–4, Sat. 1–4.*

Dining and Lodging

$-$$ ✕ **Harris' Quick 'n Tasty.** This venerable establishment 4 km (2 mi) northeast of Yarmouth is a no-nonsense '50s-style diner with laminated tables, vinyl banquettes, and bright lights. It's also a penny-pincher's delight: a three-course Piggy Bank Special is only $6.95. Dishes include fresh seafood and old standbys such as turkey burgers and club sandwiches. Best of all is the rappie pie, a baked and crisply refried potato and chicken casserole. ✉ *Hwy. 1, Dayton,* ☎ *902/742–3467. MC, V. Closed mid-Dec.–Feb.*

$ ✕ **Ceilidh Desserts Plus.** Homemade soups, breads, and desserts—all free of additives and preservatives—have won a loyal clientele locally and beyond for this cinnamon-scented café on Yarmouth's Main Street. The owner starts at dawn to whip up the day's baked goods and tasty lunches, which are modestly priced and served at simple wooden tables. ✉ *276 Main St.,* ☎ *902/742–0031. AE, V. Closed Sun. mid-Oct.– mid-May.*

$ ✕🖰 **Manor Inn.** A circular rose garden is the highlight of this 9-acre waterfront property near Yarmouth. Fifty-three guest rooms are spread throughout the inn, coach house, and handsome white main lodge. Dinner specialties are fresh Nova Scotia seafood, prime rib, chicken, and pasta ($$–$$$$). The dining rooms also serve breakfast and lunch. ✉ *Hwy. 1, Box 56, Hebron B0W 1X0,* ☎ *902/742–2487 or 888/626–6746,* FAX *902/742–8094,* WEB *www.manorinn.com. 53 rooms. 2 restaurants, 2 bars, café, pool, tennis court, boating, bicycles. AE, DC, MC, V. CP.*

$$$$ 🖰 **Trout Point Lodge.** This luxury resort consists of 200 acres situated among more than 500,000 acres of protected wilderness—the Tobeatic Wilderness Preserve to the south and Kejimkujik National Park to the north. Built of massive spruce logs with chiseled granite walls, Trout Point has eight rooms, two suites, the Great Room, a library, and a dining room. Outdoor activities include swimming, canoeing, kayaking, and wildlife-watching. Food Learning Vacations of three to five days include culinary instruction by La Ferme d'Acadie, a seaside farm at Cheboque Point. About a 40-minute drive out of Yarmouth, the lodge provides transportation from Yarmouth Airport or ferry terminal. You can arrange packages with or without meals. ✉ *East Branch Rd., off Hwy. 203, East Kemptville (R.R. 2, Box 2690, Yarmouth B5A 4A6),* ☎ *902/742–0980 or 877/812–0112,* FAX *902/742– 1057,* WEB *www.troutpoint.com. 8 rooms, 2 suites. Dining room, hiking, boating, fishing, mountain bikes, meeting room. AE, MC, V. Closed Jan.–Mar.*

$$-$$$ 🖰 **Charles C. Richards House B&B.** One of Nova Scotia's most distinc-
★ tive B&Bs, this grand 1893 Queen Anne–style structure in the historic district was the home of a wealthy industrialist, and was built with the

finest imported materials. It later served as the Women's Army Corps barracks, the town library, and an apartment building. The energetic owners rescued the inn and are restoring it themselves. Rooms are spacious, there's a patio and an orchid conservatory that opens onto a wide veranda, and the corporate suite has a data port. Breakfast is an elegant affair. The Yarmouth County Museum is across the street. ☒ *17 Collins St., B5A 3C7,* ☏ FAX *902/742–0042,* WEB *www.charlesrichardshouse.ns.ca. 3 rooms, 1 suite. Dining room. AE, MC, V. BP.*

$ ☷ **Harbour's Edge B&B.** Spectacular views of Yarmouth Harbour can be had from the veranda of this serene 1864 home. Ornate wrought-iron fireplaces dominate the parlor and dining room. At high tide the water laps against the lawn; at low tide birds pay frequent visits. Harbour's Edge was reclaimed after a disastrous fire, and its phoenixlike restoration from burnt shell to elegant completion is revealed in a photo album. At press time, the restoration process had moved to the exterior of the house to the large garden with its century-old rhododendrons, quince, laburnum, and Japanese cherry trees. ☒ *12 Vancouver St., B5A 2N8,* ☏ *902/742–2387,* FAX *902/742–4471. 4 rooms. Dining room. MC, V. BP.*

$ ☷ **Murray Manor B&B.** The distinctive, pointed windows of this handsome 1825 Gothic-style house are reminiscent of a church. Century-old rhododendrons bloom in the garden and at the long dining room table, where guests share a hearty breakfast of fresh fruit, eggs with fresh garden herbs, specially ordered smoked bacon, and homemade apricot compote, and choose from a display of dozens of elegant bone china cups and saucers. ☒ *225 Main St., B5A 1C6,* ☏ *902/742–9625 or 877/742–9629,* FAX *902/742–9625. 4 rooms without bath. V. BP.*

Shopping

Professional potters Michael and Frances Morris, tired of craft shows, opened a craft shop, **At the Sign of the Whale** (☒ 543 Hwy. 1, R.R. 1, Dayton, ☏ 902/742–8895), in their own home on the outskirts of Yarmouth. Antique furniture forms a handsome backdrop for the work of 150 artisans. Wood, textiles, pewter, clothing, lovely Nova Scotian crystal, and the Morris's own excellent stoneware can be found here.

Point de l'Eglise

㉒ *70 km (43 mi) north of Yarmouth.*

Point de l'Eglise (Church Point) is the site of **Université Ste-Anne** (☒ 1695 Hwy. 1, ☏ 888/338–8337), the only French-language institution among Nova Scotia's 17 degree-granting colleges and universities. Founded in 1891, this small university off Highway 1 is a focus of Acadian studies and culture in the province. The university offers five-week immersion French courses in summer.

St. Mary's Church, along the main road that runs through Point de l'Eglise, is the tallest and largest wooden church in North America. Completed in 1905, it is 190 ft long and 185 ft high. The steeple, which requires 40 tons of rock ballast to keep it steady in the ocean winds, can be seen for miles on the approach. Inside the church is a small museum containing an excellent collection of vestments, furnishings, and photographs. Tours are given by appointment. ☒ *Main road,* ☏ *902/769–2832.* ☏ *Free.* ☉ *July–mid-Oct., daily 9:30–5:30.*

Nightlife and the Arts

Evangeline, Longfellow's famous epic poem about the Acadian expulsion, comes to life in a very visual musical drama presented in Acadian French with English translation. Performances are held at 8 PM Tuesday and

Saturday nights at the Université Ste-Anne (☎ 902/769–2114) June through September.

En Route **St. Bernard,** a few miles north of Point de l'Eglise, marks the end of the French Shore. Thanks to magnificent acoustics, internationally acclaimed choirs sometimes perform in the town's impressive granite Gothic church, which seats 1,000. For information on performances call ☎ 902/837–5687.

Digby

㉓ *35 km (22 mi) northeast of Point de l'Eglise.*

Digby is an underappreciated city—people tend to race to or from the ferry service connecting the town with Saint John, New Brunswick. But there's much more to Digby, including a rich history that dates to the arrival in 1783 of Loyalist refugees from New England; a famous scallop fleet that anchors in colorful profusion at the waterfront; and the plump, sweet scallops that are served everywhere. The waterfront begs leisurely strolls to view the Annapolis Basin and the boats; here you can buy ultrafresh halibut, cod, scallops, and lobster—some merchants will even cook them up for you on the spot. You can also sample Digby chicks—salty smoked herring—in pubs or buy them from fish markets. **Digby Scallop Days** is a four-day festival replete with parades, fireworks, and food in early August.

The **Admiral Digby Museum** relates the history of Digby through interesting collections of furnishings, artifacts, paintings, and maps. ⊠ *95 Montague Row,* ☎ *902/245–6322.* ▣ *Free.* ☉ *June–Aug., daily 9–5.*

Dining and Lodging

$ ✕ **Digby's Café and Bookstore.** Bookworms with appetites will appreciate this appealing café, with a fine view of the waterfront, combined with a bookshop offering previously loved books of all persuasions. You can even browse through tomes while drinking coffee. All the food, from hearty seafood chowder to decadent pecan-butter tarts, is homemade, and the daily special, usually a soup-and-sandwich combo, pampers budgets. ⊠ *9 Water St.,* ☎ *902/245–4081. MC, V.*

$$$ ✕▣ **Pines Resort Hotel.** Complete with fireplaces, sitting rooms, walking trails, and a view of the Annapolis Basin, this casually elegant property offers myriad comforts. It contains a Norman château–style hotel, 30 cottages, and lavish gardens. Local seafood with a French touch is served daily in the restaurant ($$–$$$$), and the lounge is perfect for quiet relaxation. ⊠ *103 Shore Rd., Box 70, B0V 1A0,* ☎ *902/245–2511 or 800/667–4637,* FAX *902/245–6133,* WEB *www.signatureresorts.com. 144 rooms. Restaurant, bar, pool, sauna, 18-hole golf course, 2 tennis courts, health club. AE, D, DC, MC. Closed mid-Oct.–May.*

$–$$ ▣ **Thistle Down Country Inn.** A flowery haven overlooks the Annapolis Basin and Digby's fishing fleet at this historic 1904 home where wicker and antiques furnish the rooms. An annex is decorated with colonial furniture. For breakfast, consider ordering the scallop omelette. The 6:30 dinner (reservations required) celebrates fresh local seafood and ends with rich desserts. ⊠ *98 Montague Row, Box 508, B0V 1A0,* ☎ *902/245–4490 or 800/565–8081,* FAX *902/245–6717,* WEB *www.thistledown.ns.ca. 12 rooms. Restaurant. DC, MC, V. Closed Nov.–Apr. BP.*

$ ▣ **Coastal Inn Kingfisher Motel.** Your affable host's encyclopedic knowledge and contagious enthusiasm for his adopted province open the door to little-known sights and adventures. This traditional strip motel handy to all Digby's features has wheelchair-accessible rooms (call for specifics) and a dining room. ⊠ *111 Warwick St., Box 280,*

B0V 1A0, ☎ 902/245–4747 or 800/665–7829, ℻ 902/245–4866, 🆆🅴🅱
www.coastalinns.com. 36 rooms. AE, DC, MC, V.

Bear River

A thriving arts-and-crafts center in summer, and almost a ghost town
in winter, Bear River is called the Switzerland of Nova Scotia for the
delightful vista of its deep valley, dissected by a tidal river. Some buildings have been built on stilts to stay above the tides. Craft and coffee
shops line the main street, and the community center, **Oakdene Centre** (✉ 1913 Clementsvale Rd., ☎ 902/467–3939), contains an artist-
run gallery, craft workshops, and live theater and music.

The **Riverview Ethnographic Museum** houses a collection of folk cos-
tumes and artifacts from around the world. ✉ *18 Chute Rd.,* ☎ *902/
467–3762.* 🄳 *$2.* ⊙ *Nov.–Sept., Tues.–Sat. 10–5.*

Long Island and Brier Island

㉔ *Two brief ferry rides between islands at East Ferry and Freeport.*

Digby Neck is extended seaward by two narrow islands, Long Island
and Brier Island. Because the surrounding waters are rich in plankton,
the islands attract a variety of whales, including finbacks, humpbacks,
minkes, and right whales, as well as harbor porpoises. Wild orchids
and other wildflowers abound here, and the islands are also an excellent spot for bird-watching.

Ferries (☎ 902/839–2302) linking the islands must scuttle sideways
to fight the ferocious Fundy tidal streams coursing through the narrow gaps. They operate hourly, at a cost of $2 each way for car and
passengers. One of the boats is the *Joshua Slocum,* named for Westport's most famous native; the second is the *Spray,* named for the 36-
ft oyster sloop that Slocum rebuilt and in which, from 1894 to 1896,
he became the first man to circumnavigate the world single-handedly.
A cairn at the southern tip of Brier Island commemorates his voyage.

Dining and Lodging

$–$$ ✕🏨 **Brier Island Lodge and Restaurant.** Perched high atop a bluff at
Nova Scotia's most westerly point, this rustic lodge commands a
panoramic view of the Bay of Fundy. The lodge has 40 rooms, most
with ocean and lighthouse views. Whale- and bird-watching are the
most popular activities here, but closer to home there are hens, a flock
of sheep, a pig, and some friendly dogs that children can pet. Seafood
chowder, lobster-stuffed haddock, and solomon gundy (marinated herring with sour cream and onion) are dinner specialties in the attractive restaurant ($$–$$$), which also serves breakfast and can pack a
box lunch for day-trippers. ✉ *Water St., Westport, Brier Island B0V
1H0,* ☎ *902/839–2300 or 800/662–8355,* ℻ *902/839–2006,* 🆆🅴🅱
*www.brierisland.com. 40 rooms. Restaurant, lounge. MC, V. Closed
Nov.–Mar.*

$–$$ ✕🏨 **Olde Village Inn.** Halfway along Digby Neck on Highway 217,
quaint Sandy Cove, population 100, snuggles the shore. The town has
one of Nova Scotia's highest waterfalls and a lookout affording
panoramic views of the water and sometimes whales. The Olde Village includes restored 19th-century buildings—the main inn, an annex,
and various cottages—all comfortably furnished with antiques, wicker,
quilts, and local art. Dinner ($$–$$$; reserve ahead) emphasizes fresh
seafood and steaks. ✉ *387 Sandy Cove Rd., Sandy Cove B0V 1E0,*
☎ *902/834–2202 or 800/834–2206,* ℻ *902/834–2927,* 🆆🅴🅱 *www.
oldevillageinn.com. 16 rooms, 1 cabin, 3 cottages. Restaurant. MC,
V. Closed mid-Oct.–mid-May. BP.*

Outdoor Activities and Sports

Brier Island Whale & Seabird Cruises (☎ 902/839–2995 or 800/656–3660) offers whale-watching and seabird tours. Onboard researchers and naturalists collect data for international research organizations. The fare is $37, and a portion of the fee is used to fund the research. **Mariner Cruises** (☎ 902/839–2346 or 800/239–2189) provides whale and seabird tours with an onboard photographer and a naturalist. The three- to five-hour cruises include a light lunch; the fare is $35.

Annapolis Royal

★ ㉕ *29 km (18 mi) northeast of Digby.*

Annapolis Royal's history spans nearly four centuries, and gracious and fascinating remnants of that history abound. The town's quaint and quiet appearance belies its turbulent past. One of Canada's oldest settlements, it was founded as Port Royal by the French in 1605, destroyed by the British in 1613, rebuilt by the French as the main town of French Acadia, and fought over for a century. Finally, in 1710, New England colonists claimed the town and renamed it in honor of Queen Anne. There are approximately 150 historic sites and heritage buildings here, including the privately owned 1708 DeGannes-Cosby House, the oldest wooden house in Canada, on St. George Street, the oldest town street in Canada. A lively **market** with fresh produce, baked goods, local artists, and street musicians takes place every Saturday mid-May through mid-October on St. George Street, next to Ye Olde Town Pub.

Fort Anne National Historic Site, first fortified in 1629, holds the remains of the fourth fort to be erected here and garrisoned by the British as late as 1854. Earthwork fortifications, an early 18th-century gunpowder magazine, and officers' quarters have been preserved. Four hundred years of history are depicted on the Fort Anne Heritage Tapestry. A guided candlelight tour of the historic Garrison Graveyard is a summer specialty. ✉ *St. George St.,* ☎ *902/532–2397 or 902/532–2321.* 🖼 *Grounds free, museum $3.* ☉ *Mid-May–mid-Oct., daily 9–6; mid-Oct.–mid-May, by appointment.*

The **Annapolis Royal Historic Gardens** are 10 acres of magnificent theme gardens, including a Victorian garden and a knot garden, connected to a wildlife sanctuary. ✉ *441 Upper St. George St.,* ☎ *902/532–7018.* 🖼 *$5.* ☉ *Mid-May–mid-Oct., daily 8–dusk.*

The **Annapolis Royal Tidal Power Project,** ½ km (¼ mi) from Annapolis Royal, was designed to test the feasibility of generating electricity from tidal energy. This pilot project is the only tidal generating station in North America and one of only three operational sites in the world. The interpretive center explains the process with guided tours. ✉ *Annapolis River Causeway,* ☎ *902/532–5454.* 🖼 *Free.* ☉ *Mid-May–mid-June and Sept.–mid-Oct., daily 9–5:30; mid-June–Aug., daily 9–8.*

Dining and Lodging

$$$$ ✕ **Newman's Restaurant.** Fresh flowers, fine art, and the host's handmade pottery give this quality establishment a homey air. The excellent cuisine is made with ultrafresh seafood and produce. At press time, Newman's was being put up for sale; it's likely that the restaurant will continue to maintain its good name and reputation despite a possible change of ownership. ✉ *218 St. George St.,* ☎ *902/532–5502. MC, V. Closed Oct.–mid-Apr.*

$–$$$ ✕ **Secret Garden Restaurant.** Light lunches, snacks, and desserts are served in a sheltered open-air setting that overlooks the Annapolis Royal Historic Gardens. ✉ *441 St. George St.,* ☎ *902/532–2200. MC, V. Closed Oct.–May.*

\$–\$\$ ✕ **Charlie's Place.** Fresh local seafood with a Chinese flavor is served at this pleasant restaurant on the edge of town. Lobster, shrimp, scallops, meat dishes, and vegetarian fare are prepared in Cantonese or Szechuan style. ⊠ *38 Prince Albert Rd. (Hwy. 1),* ☎ *902/532–2111. AE, D, MC, V.*

\$ ✕ **Ye Olde Town Pub.** This merry, low-key pub popular with locals serves down-home lunches and dinners, many prepared with regional blueberries. Diners sometimes spill out onto the patio, which is adjacent to a square where markets and music take place in summer. ⊠ *11 Church St.,* ☎ *902/532–2244. MC, V.*

\$–\$\$ ✕🏠 **Queen Anne Inn.** A lovely old Victorian mansion set within a 5-acre garden, this historic property includes fine dining on its list of amenities. The restaurant (\$\$–\$\$\$; reserve ahead) serves an eclectic dinner menu of Continental cuisine that emphasizes seafood. The 10 large guest rooms are handsomely decorated with period furniture and Victorian accessories. ⊠ *494 Upper St. George St., Box 218, B0S 1A0,* ☎ *902/ 532–7850,* FAX *902/532–2078,* WEB *www.queenanneinn.ns.ca. 10 rooms. Restaurant. MC, V. BP.*

\$ ✕🏠 **Garrison House Inn.** This structure, which faces Fort Anne and its extensive parkland, started life as an inn in 1854, when Annapolis Royal was the capital of Nova Scotia. Now carefully restored with period furniture and decor to create a Victorian ambience, it comes complete with a friendly ghost, called Emily, whose playful presence is known only to women. Three intimate dining rooms (\$\$\$–\$\$\$\$) and a dining deck are the settings for dinners that favor fresh seafood, especially scallops and lobster. Breakfast is included in the room rate during summer months. ⊠ *350 St. George St., B0S 1A0,* ☎ *902/532–5750,* FAX *902/532–5501,* WEB *www.queenanneinn.ns.ca. 7 rooms, 1 suite. 3 restaurants. AE, MC, V. Closed Jan.–Mar.*

\$\$ 🏠 **Bread and Roses Country Inn.** Rivalry between a doctor and a dentist gave Annapolis Royal this interesting hostelry. After the town doctor built a fine house in 1880, the dentist-pharmacist, in the spirit of competition, set out to build a better one. Today this Queen Anne–style inn is replete with exquisite architectural details and wood trim made with mahogany, black walnut, black cherry, and more. A traditional fountain is centered on the front lawn, and the garden invites sitting and strolling. The lavish breakfast may feature macadamia-nut French toast, blueberry pancakes, waffles, or quiche. ⊠ *82 Victoria St., B0S 1A0,* ☎ *902/532–5727 or 888/899–0551,* WEB *www.breadandroses.ns.ca. 9 rooms. Dining room. MC, V. BP.*

\$ 🏠 **Hillsdale House.** Princes, kings, and prime ministers have all visited this historic 1849 property, which is furnished with antiques and paintings and is set within 15 acres of lawns and gardens. The renovated coach house has added three bright and spacious rooms to the original 11 bedrooms. Room rates include a large breakfast with homemade breads and jams. ⊠ *519 George St., Box 148, B0S 1A0,* ☎ *902/532– 2345 or 877/839–2821,* FAX *905/532–2345. 14 rooms. MC, V. Closed Nov.–Apr.*

\$ 🏠 **Moorings Bed & Breakfast.** Built in 1881, this tall, beautiful home overlooking Annapolis Basin has a fireplace, tin ceilings, antiques, and contemporary art. One room has a half-bath. ⊠ *5287 Granville St., Box 118, Granville Ferry B0S 1K0,* ☎ FAX *902/532–2146,* WEB *www.bbcanada.com/1000.html. 3 rooms without bath. Bicycles, library. MC, V. BP.*

Port Royal

8 km (5 mi) downriver (west) from Annapolis Royal on the opposite bank.

One of the oldest settlements in Canada, Port Royal was Nova Scotia's first capital (for both French and English) until 1749, and the province's first military base. The **Port Royal National Historic Site** is a reconstruction of a French fur-trading post originally built by Sieur de Monts and Samuel de Champlain in 1605. Here, amid the hardships of the New World, North America's first social club—the Order of Good Cheer—was founded, and Canada's first theatrical presentation was written and produced by Marc Lescarbot. ⊠ *Hwy. 1 to Granville Ferry, then left 12 km (7 mi) on Port Royal Rd.,* ☎ *902/532–2898 or 902/532–5589.* 🎫 *$3.* ☉ *Mid-May–mid-Oct., daily 9–6.*

Wolfville

★ ㉖ *60 km (37 mi) east of Annapolis Royal.*

Settled in the 1760s by New Englanders, Wolfville is a charming college town with stately trees and ornate Victorian homes. Chimney swifts—aerobatic birds that fly in spectacular formation at dusk—are so abundant that an interpretive display is devoted to them at the **Robie Tufts Nature Centre,** on Front Street. Dykes, built by the Acadians in the early 1700s to reclaim fertile land from the unusually high tides, can still be viewed in Wolfville at the harbor and along many of the area's back roads.

The **Atlantic Theatre Festival** (⊠ 356 Main St., ☎ 902/542–4242 or 800/337–6661) stages classical plays mid-June through September; tickets are $21–$28.

The **National Historic Site at Grand Pré,** about 5 km (3 mi) east of Wolfville on Highway 101, commemorates the expulsion of the Acadians by the British in 1755. A statue of the eponymous heroine of Longfellow's epic poem, *Evangeline,* stands outside a memorial stone church, which contains Acadian genealogical records. ⊠ *Hwy. 1, Grand Pré,* ☎ *902/542–3631.* ☉ *Mid-May–mid-Oct., daily 9–6.*

OFF THE BEATEN PATH

HALLS HARBOUR – One of the best natural harbors on the upper Bay of Fundy can be reached via Highway 359. Go for a walk on a gravel beach bordered by cliffs; try sea kayaking or wilderness camping; or seek out the intaglio printmaking studio and other artists' studios, open during summer months.

CAPE BLOMIDON – At Greenwich, take Highway 358 to Cape Blomidon via Port Williams and Canning for a spectacular view of the valley and the Bay of Fundy from the Lookoff.

Dining and Lodging

$$$–$$$$ ✗ **Acton's Grill & Café.** Refugee restaurateurs from Toronto, where their Fenton's Restaurant was *the* place to dine, have created an equally appealing dining establishment with an interesting and eclectic menu here. Consider rabbit pie, Digby scallops in fresh herbed pasta, or Fundy lobster. ⊠ *268 Main St.,* ☎ *902/542–7525. AE, MC, V. Closed Jan.*

$$$–$$$$ ✗ **Chez la Vigne.** Fresh Nova Scotia seafood, meats and poultry, and vegetarian fare are artfully presented in this pleasant century-old home. On warm summer nights, diners gather on the patio. ⊠ *17 Front St.,* ☎ *902/542–5077. AE, D, MC, V.*

$–$$$ ✗🏨 **Blomidon Inn.** Take time for a half-hour ramble through this inn's 3-acre English country garden, with its fish-stocked ponds, roses, cacti, azaleas, and rhododendrons, plus a terraced vegetable garden that serves as a restaurant. Built by a shipbuilder in 1887, the inn still retains its teak and mahogany, marble fireplaces, and painted ceiling mural. Room rates include Continental breakfast and afternoon tea. Fresh Atlantic salmon is a specialty at the restaurant ($$$–$$$$; reserve ahead). A gift shop, in a separate house beside the inn, sells Maritime crafts, linen, garden items, and the books and prints of folk artist Maude Lewis. ⊠ *127 Main St., Box 839, B0P 1X0,* ☎ *902/542–2291 or 800/565–2291,* FAX *902/542–7461,* WEB *www.blomidon.ns.ca. 26 rooms. Restaurant, tennis court, horseshoes, shuffleboard, meeting room. MC, V. CP.*

$–$$$ 🏠 **Fundy Bay Holiday Homes B&B.** The trek to this seaside resort 40 km (25 mi) outside Wolfville is amply rewarded by the spectacular view of the Bay of Fundy and the north shore beyond. Set on 265 rolling wooded acres, this family-owned property has two two-bedroom houses with comfy living rooms, woodstoves, fully equipped kitchens and laundry facilities, and satellite TV. Stays at the three-room B&B include a hearty German breakfast of deli meats and sausages, European cheeses, German breads, and copious amounts of good German coffee. Groomed walking trails traverse the wooded property. ⊠ *2165 McNally Rd., Victoria Harbour, Aylesford B0P 1C0,* ☎ *902/847–1114,* FAX *902/847–1032,* WEB *www.fundyhomes.com. 3 rooms, 2 houses. Beach. V.*

$–$$ 🏠 **Victoria's Historic Inn and Carriage House B&B.** An 8-ft-high stained-glass window imported from Britain over a century ago sets the tone for this fine Victorian home. Richly carved Nova Scotian furniture adds to the ambience. Rooms are spacious and have TVs, VCRs, and CD players; suites have double whirlpool tubs. The lavish complimentary breakfast celebrates the bounty of the Annapolis Valley. Expect plenty of blueberries to find their way to the table, along with a wide selection of breakfast staples. ⊠ *416 Main St., Box 308, B0P 1X0,* ☎ *902/542–5744 or 800/556–5744,* WEB *www.valleyweb.com/victoriasinn. 9 rooms, 5 suites. AE, D, MC, V. BP.*

$ 🏠 **Farmhouse Inn B&B.** This 1860 B&B in Canning has five cozy suites, each with a whirlpool tub, a parlor, a fireplace, quilts, and whimsical dolls and critters warming the canopy beds. A full breakfast and afternoon tea are complimentary. The knowledgeable hosts may suggest day trips to nearby Blomidon Provincial Park and Cape Split, for hiking, or to the 600-ft Lookoff, which affords panoramic views of five counties. Bird-watchers are likely to enjoy the maneuvers of the chimney swifts summer evenings. ⊠ *Box 38, 9757 Main St., Canning B0P 1H0,* ☎ *800/928–4346,* ☎ FAX *902/582–7900,* WEB *www.farmhouseinn.ns.ca. 5 suites. Dining room. MC, V. BP.*

Shopping

The **Carriage House Gallery** (⊠ 246 Main St., ☎ 902/542–3500) displays artwork from Nova Scotia in several media, including oils, acrylics, watercolors, sculpture, and quilting. **Edgemere Gallery and Crafts** (⊠ 215 Main St., ☎ 902/542–1046) carries the work of Nova Scotia artists, with exhibits changing monthly. Artisans from throughout the Atlantic provinces are also represented by unique quality crafts. **The Weave Shed** (⊠ 232 Main St., ☎ 902/542–5504) is a cooperative craft shop selling quality stained glass, pottery, wood, metal, and textiles by local artisans.

Outdoor Activities and Sports

A popular hiking trail, 25 km (16 mi) north of Wolfville, leads from the end of Highway 358 to the dramatic cliffs of Cape Split, a 13-km (8-mi) round-trip.

Windsor

★ ㉗ *25 km (16 mi) southeast of Wolfville.*

Windsor claims to be the birthplace of modern hockey: the game was first played here around 1800 by students of King's-Edgehill School, the first independent school in the British Commonwealth and Canada's oldest private residential school. But the town's history dates further back—to 1703 when it was settled as an Acadian community. **Fort Edward,** an assembly point for the Acadian expulsion, is the only remaining colonial blockhouse in Nova Scotia. ⊠ *Exit 6 off Hwy. 1, 1st left at King St., left up street facing fire station,* ☏ *902/542–3631.* 🎫 *Free.* ☉ *Mid-June–early Sept., daily 10–6.*

The Evangeline Express train makes a 55-km (34-mi) three-hour round-trip from Windsor to Wolfville Sundays in summer (weather permitting). The train stops at the Grand Pré National Historic Site (in Wolfville) and affords views of the Minas Basin and Annapolis Valley. ⊠ *2 Water St.,* ☏ *902/798–5667.* 🎫 *$18.50.* ☉ *Late June–early Sept.; train departs at 11 AM.*

The Windsor Hockey Heritage Centre takes a fond look at Canada's favorite winter sport with photographs and antique equipment and skates. ⊠ *128 Gerrish St.,* ☏ *902/798–1800.* 🎫 *Free.* ☉ *Daily 9–5.*

Ⓒ The **Mermaid Theatre** uses puppets and performers to retell traditional and contemporary children's classics. Props and puppets are on display. ⊠ *132 Gerrish St.,* ☏ *902/798–5841.* 🎫 *By donation.* ☉ *Jan.–Nov., weekdays 9–4:30.*

The **Haliburton House Museum,** a provincial museum on a manicured 25-acre estate, was the home of Judge Thomas Chandler Haliburton (1796–1865), a lawyer, politician, historian, and humorist. His best-known work, *The Clockmaker,* pillories Nova Scotian follies from the viewpoint of a Yankee clock peddler, Sam Slick, whose witty sayings are still commonly used. ⊠ *414 Clifton Ave.,* ☏ *902/798–2915.* 🎫 *Free.* ☉ *June–mid-Oct., Mon.–Sat. 9:30–5:30, Sun. 1–5:30.*

Tours at the family-owned **Sainte Famille Winery** in Falmouth, 5 km (3 mi) west of Windsor, combine ecological history with the intricacies of growing grapes and aging wine. Tasting is done in the gift shop, where bottles are sold at a steal. ⊠ *Dyke Rd. and Dudley Park La.,* ☏ *902/798–8311 or 800/565–0993.* 🎫 *Free.* ☉ *June–Sept., Mon.–Sat. 9–5, Sun. noon–5; call for off-season hrs and tour schedule.*

OFF THE BEATEN PATH
UNIACKE ESTATE MUSEUM PARK – This country mansion was built around 1815 for Richard John Uniacke, attorney general and advocate general to the Admiralty court during the War of 1812. Now a provincial museum, the house is preserved in its original condition with authentic furnishings. The spacious lakeside grounds are surrounded by walking trails. ⊠ *758 Main Rd., 30 km (19 mi) east of Windsor off Hwy. 1, Mount Uniacke,* ☏ *902/866–2560.* 🎫 *Free.* ☉ *June–mid-Oct., Mon.–Sat. 9:30–5:30, Sun. 11–5:30.*

Dining and Lodging

$–$$$ ✕ **Kingsway Gardens Restaurant.** From the Bavarian decor to the homemade sauerkraut to the Black Forest cheesecake, this establishment declares its owner's German origins. Lunch and dinner specialties include German and Canadian variations on seafood, turkey, and chicken. ⊠ *Wentworth Rd., off Hwy. 101, Exit 5A,* ☏ *902/798–5075. AE, D, MC, V.*

$ ✕ **Rose Arbour Café.** True to its name, the Rose Arbour has a bright, flowery interior. Tasty food, a smiling staff, and reasonable prices make this a pleasant find. Try the fish-and-chips. ⊠ *109 Garrish St.,* ☏ *902/798–2322. V.*

$ 🏨 **Hampshire Court Motel and Cottages.** Once an elegant estate, this multi-unit property retains its splendid 1762 home, with four spacious antiques-furnished guest rooms. Four two-bedroom cottages and a strip motel are also on the property. The ample grounds include picnic tables and a tennis court. ✉ *1081 King St., B0N 2T0,* ☎ *902/798–3133,* FAX *902/798–2499,* WEB *www.hampshirecourt.ca. 4 rooms, 11 motel units, 4 cottages. Tennis court. AE, MC, V. Closed mid-Oct.–mid-May.*

THE EASTERN SHORE AND NORTHERN NOVA SCOTIA

From the rugged coastline of the Atlantic to the formidable tides of the Bay of Fundy to the gentle shores of the Northumberland Strait, the area east and north of Halifax presents remarkable contrasts within a relatively small area. The road toward Cape Breton meanders past picturesque fishing villages, forests, and remote cranberry barrens. The Northumberland Strait is bordered by sandy beaches, hiking trails and the rich heritage of its early Scottish settlers. The Bay of Fundy serves up spectacular scenery—dense forests and steep cliffs that harbor prehistoric fossils and semiprecious stones. The mighty Fundy tides—swift and dangerous—can reach 40 ft. When they recede, you can walk on the bottom of the sea.

There are two excellent driving tours you can follow here. The Sunrise Trail Heritage Tour leads to unusual and historic sights along the Northumberland Strait, from the Tantramar Marsh in Amherst to the Heritage Museum at Antigonish and on to the still-active St. Augustine Monastery. The Fundy Shore Ecotour traces 100 million years of geology, the arrival of Samuel de Champlain, the legends of the Mi'K-maq, the Acadians, and the shipbuilders. (Tour details are available at visitor information centers or from Nova Scotia Tourism.)

This region takes in parts of three of the official Scenic Trails, including Marine Drive (315 km, or 195 mi), the Sunrise Trail (316 km, or 196 mi), and the Glooscap Trail (365 km, or 226 mi). Any one leg of the routes could be done comfortably as an overnight trip from Halifax.

Musquodoboit Harbour

28 *45 km (28 mi) east of Dartmouth.*

Musquodoboit Harbour (locals pronounce it *must*-go-*dob*-bit), with about 930 residents, is a substantial village at the mouth of the Musquodoboit River. The river offers good trout and salmon fishing, and the village touches on two slender and lovely harbors.

A 1916 train station, five rail cars, and a fine collection of railway artifacts, including a legion of lanterns dating from the late 1800s, make the volunteer-run **Musquodoboit Railway Museum** (✉ Main St./Hwy. 7, ☎ 902/889–2689) a must for rail buffs. A library is rich in both railway and local historical documentation and photos. The museum is open daily 9–5 late May to mid-October, by donation.

One of the Eastern Shore's best beaches, **Martinique Beach,** is about 12 km (7 mi) south of Musquodoboit Harbour, at the end of East Petpeswick Road. Clam Bay and Clam Harbour, several miles east of Martinique, are also fine beaches.

OFF THE BEATEN PATH   **MOOSE RIVER GOLD MINES AND MUSEUM –** On-the-spot radio coverage of a mine disaster put Moose River on the map in 1936. Today the town is quiet; a provincial park marks the site of the 12-day effort to rescue three miners trapped far underground (two of the men survived). The museum completes the story with displays, photographs, and artifacts. ⊠ *Moose River Rd., off Hwy. 224 (15 km, or 9 mi, from Middle Musquodoboit),* ☎ *902/384–2006.* ⌗ *By donation.* ☉ *June–Aug., daily 10–5.*

Dining and Lodging

$–$$ ✕⌗ **Salmon River House Country Inn.** Seven guest rooms and three cottages (two on the ocean and both intended for stays of a week or more; $650 to $900 a week) provide glorious water and countryside views. Guests may fish from the floating dock; hike the trails of the 30-acre property; or make use of the canoe, kayak, or rowboat. Lunch, dinner ($–$$), and a breakfast-buffet spread are served on the screened Lobster Shack dining deck. ⊠ *9931 Hwy. 7, Salmon River Bridge, Jeddore (10 km, or 6 mi, east of Musquodoboit Harbour), B0J 1P0,* ☎ *902/889–3353 or 800/ 565–3353,* ℻ *902/889–3653,* 🕸 *www.salmonriverhouse.com. 7 rooms, 3 cottages. Restaurant, boating, fishing. AE, MC, V.*

$ ⌗ **Camelot Inn.** Enthroned in her great-grandmother's rocker, surrounded by memorabilia and an enormous hoya plant, Charlie Holgate shares wit and wisdom with international guests as she has for more than 30 years. Her 5-acre wooded property borders the turbulent Musquodoboit River and is home to mink, otter, and an occasional deer. Inside, it's informal, with five unpretentious rooms, shared baths, and a robust homemade breakfast. ⊠ *8094 Hwy. 7, Box 31, B0J 2L0,* ☎ *902/889–2198. 5 rooms. Lounge, library. MC, V. BP.*

En Route As you travel through **Ship Harbour** on Highway 7, take note of the strings of colorful buoys, marking one of North America's largest cultivated mussel farms. Vistas of restless seas and wooded shorelines make for excellent photo opportunities.

Sherbrooke Village

★ ㉙ *166 km (103 mi) northeast of Musquodoboit Harbour.*

A living-history museum set within a contemporary village, Sherbrooke Village contains 30 restored 19th-century buildings that present life as it was lived during the town's heyday, from 1860 to 1914. Back then, this was a prime shipbuilding and lumbering center; it eventually became a gold-rush center. Artisans demonstrate weaving; wood turning; and pottery, candle, and soap making daily. A working waterpowered sawmill is down the road. ⊠ *Hwy. 7, Sherbrooke,* ☎ *902/ 522–2400 or 888/743–7845,* 🕸 *www.museum.gov.ns.ca/sv.* ⌗ *$7.25.* ☉ *June–mid-Oct., daily 9:30–5:30.*

OFF THE **PORT BICKERTON LIGHTHOUSE BEACH PARK –** Two lighthouses share a
BEATEN PATH lofty bluff about 20 km (12 mi) east of Sherbrooke on Highway 211. One is still a working lighthouse; the other, built in 1910, houses the Nova Scotia Lighthouse Interpretive Centre, which recounts the history, lore, and vital importance of these life-saving lights. Hiking trails and a boardwalk lead to a sandy beach. ⊠ *630 Lighthouse Rd., Port Bickerton,* ☎ *902/364–2000.* ⌗ *$3.* ☉ *July–Aug., daily 9–6; Sept., daily 9–5.*

Dining and Lodging

$ ✕⌗ **Black Duck Seaside Inn.** From a third-floor picture window, equipped with binoculars and a telescope provided by the inn, you can observe birds, sea life, and maybe a star or two over Beaver Harbour. In the airy dining room ($–$$), expect lavish breakfasts of fruit and blueberry pancakes; for dinner, try the fisherman's lasagna (seafood and pasta in a cream sauce) or another seafood dish. The Black Duck is 90 km (56 mi) west of Sherbrooke Village. ⊠ *25245 Hwy. 7, Port*

Dufferin (Box 26, Sheet Harbour B0J 3B0), ☎ FAX *902/654–2237. 2 rooms, 2 suites. Restaurant, dock, bicycles. MC, V.*

$ ×🏠 **Sherbrooke Village Inn & Cabins.** Woodsy chalets, a B&B suite, and a motel are all options in this comfy hostelry overlooking the St. Mary's River (open for trout fishing). The inn offers nature walks and a spectacular view. The pleasant dining room ($–$$) serves up homemade meals—full Canadian breakfasts, lunches, and dinners that lean heavily toward seafood. ✉ *7975 Hwy. 7, Box 40, Sherbrooke B0J 3C0,* ☎ *902/522–2235,* FAX *902/522–2716,* WEB *www.atyp.com/sherbrookevillageinn. 1 B&B suite, 14 motel rooms, 3 chalets. Dining room. AE, D, MC, V. Closed Dec.–mid-Apr.*

$ 🏠 **St. Mary's River Lodge.** Sherbrooke Village is steps away from this lodge with fresh and immaculate rooms. The Swiss owners, in love with their adopted countryside, are helpful in planning day trips and tours. You can also rent houses in nearby Liscombe and Port Hilford for week-long stays. ✉ *21 Main St., B0J 3C0,* ☎ *902/522–2177,* FAX *902/522–2515,* WEB *www3.ns.sympatico.ca/lodge. 5 rooms, 2 suites, 3 houses. MC, V. BP.*

Canso

③⓪ *123 km (76 mi) east of Sherbrooke Village.*

One of Nova Scotia's oldest settlements, founded in 1605, Canso today is a busy fishing town. Each July the town hosts the **Stan Rogers Folk Festival** commemorating the much loved Canadian folk singer and composer.

The **Grassy Island National Historic Site** recounts early struggles to control the lucrative fishing industry. A free boat ride takes you to the island for an interpretive tour of what remains of a once-thriving community, a casualty in 1744 of the war between France and England. Graphics, models, and audiovisuals set the scene. ✉ *Canso Waterfront, off Union St.,* ☎ *902/295–2069,* WEB *www.parkscanada.pch.gc.ca.* 🖾 *$2.50.* ☉ *June–mid-Sept., daily 10–6.*

Lodging

$–$$ 🏠 **SeaWind Landing Country Inn.** Perched on a 20-acre coastal estate just south of Canso, this restored sea captain's home—with bird-watching, interpretive nature walks, and sandy beaches—is a luxurious escape from real life. Short boat tours to offshore islands, where seals bask and bald eagles soar, include white-linen lunches served with fine wines. Home-cooked dinners favor fresh seafood. The inn is furnished with antiques, quilts, and fine art. ✉ *1 Wharf Rd., Charlos Cove B0H 1T0,* ☎ FAX *902/525–2108,* WEB *www.seawindlanding.com. 12 rooms. Dining room, beach, boating, mountain bikes. AE, MC, V. Closed mid-Oct.–mid-May.*

Antigonish

★ ③① *85 km (53 mi) northwest of Canso.*

Antigonish, on the main route to Cape Breton Island, is home to **St. Francis Xavier University,** a center for Gaelic studies and the first co-educational Catholic institution to graduate women. The university **art gallery** (☎ 902/867–2303), open year-round, has changing exhibits. **Festival Antigonish** (☎ 902/867–3333 or 800/563–7529, WEB www.festival.antigonish.com) presents a summer-long drama program—matinées for children, evenings for adults—in the 227-seat university theater.

The **Antigonish Heritage Museum,** in a 1908 rail station, depicts the town's early history. ⊠ *20 E. Main St.,* ☏ *902/863–6160.* ☐ *Free.* ☉ *July–Aug., daily 10–5; Sept.–Nov. and Feb.–June, weekdays 10–noon and 1–5; Dec.–Jan., by appointment.*

The biggest and oldest **Highland Games** (☏ 902/863–4275) outside Scotland are held here each July, complete with caber tossing, highland flinging, and pipe skirling.

Dining and Lodging

$–$$$ ✗ **Gabrieau's Bistro Restaurant.** Gabrieau's has earned a place in Antigonish hearts with its pleasant interior, highlighted by a colorful mural, and its epicurean yet affordable menu of Continental cuisine. Seafood, gourmet pizzas, luscious desserts, and several vegetarian selections are available. ⊠ *350 Main St.,* ☏ *902/863–1925. AE, MC, V. Closed Sun.*

$–$$ ✗ **Lobster Treat Restaurant.** This cozily decorated brick, pine, and stained-glass restaurant was once a two-room schoolhouse. The varied menu includes fresh seafood, chicken, pastas, and bread and pies baked on the premises. Families appreciate its relaxed atmosphere and children's menu. ⊠ *241 Post Rd. (Trans-Canada Hwy.),* ☏ *902/863–5465. AE, DC, MC, V. Closed Jan.–mid-Apr.*

$–$$ ✗⊡ **Maritime Inn.** The Main Street Café ($$–$$$) at this inn serves breakfast, lunch, and a tempting dinner menu that's heavy on seafood. Try the haddock glazed with apricot and ginger or chili pepper shrimp. One of five in a Maritime chain, this 32-room property offers standard rooms, mini-suites, and one two-bedroom family suite. ⊠ *158 Main St., B2G 2B7,* ☏ *902/863–4001 or 888/662–7484,* 𝖥𝖠𝖷 *902/863–2672,* WEB *www.maritimeinns.com. 32 rooms. Restaurant. AE, D, DC, MC, V.*

$–$$ ⊡ **Antigonish Victorian Inn.** A mansion fit for politicians and bishops— and in fact occupied by both at various phases of its life—this luxurious establishment is a gateway to many Antigonish attractions. Rooms are commodious and handsomely appointed. The dining room serves a breakfast of cereal, fruits, French toast, and eggs. ⊠ *149 Main St., B2G 2B6,* ☏ 𝖥𝖠𝖷 *902/863–1103 or 800/706–5558. 10 rooms. Dining room. AE, DC, MC, V.*

Outdoor Activities and Sports

A 3-km (2-mi) **walking trail** along the shoreline borders a large tidal marsh teeming with ospreys, bald eagles, and other birds.

Shopping

Lyncharm Pottery (⊠ 9 Pottery La., ☏ 902/863–6970) produces handsome functional stoneware that's sold in its own shop and exported worldwide. The **Lytesome Gallery** (⊠ 166 Main St., ☏ 902/863–5804) houses a good variety of Nova Scotian art for sale at reasonable prices.

En Route The glorious drive on Highway 337 (the Sunrise Trail) along St. George's Bay passes many good swimming beaches before the road abruptly climbs 1,000 ft to Cape George. High above the sea, the road runs west along Northumberland Strait through farmlands and tiny villages such as **Arisaig,** where you can search for fossils on the shore. Just a few miles west, **Lismore** affirms the Scottish origin of its people with a stone cairn commemorating Bonnie Prince Charlie's Highland rebels, who were slaughtered by the English at Culloden in 1746. The town a great place to buy fresh lobster.

Stellarton

32 *60 km (37 mi) west of Antigonish.*

The **Nova Scotia Museum of Industry** brings industrial heritage to life. Like factory and mine workers of old, you punch in with a time card. Hands-on exhibits show how to hook a rag mat, print a bookmark, work a steam engine, or assemble a World War II artillery shell. Interactive computer exhibits explore multimedia as a new tool of industry. Canada's oldest steam locomotives and a historic model railway layout are also displayed, and there's a restaurant. ⊠ *147 N. Foord St. (Hwy. 104, Exit 24),* ☎ *902/755–5425,* WEB *www.industry.museum. gov.ns.ca.* ▦ *$7.*

Pictou

★ **33** *20 km (12 mi) north of Stellarton.*

First occupied by the Mi'Kmaqs, this well-developed town became a Scottish settlement in 1773 when the first boat of Scottish Highlanders landed, giving the town the distinction of being "the birthplace of New Scotland." Thirty-three families and 25 unmarried men arrived aboard the *Hector,* an aging cargo ship that was reproduced in minute detail and launched in September 2000. **The Hector Heritage Quay,** where the new 110-ft fully rigged *Hector* can be toured, recounts the story of the hardy Scottish pioneers and the flood of Scots who followed them. It includes working blacksmith and carpentry shops and an interpretive center. ⊠ *33 Caladh Ave.,* ☎ *902/485–4371 or 877/574–2868.* ▦ *$4.* ☉ *Mid-May–Oct., daily 9–8.*

A lively weekend craft market at the waterfront, from June to September, showcases crafts and crafts people from the area and across the province.

Melmerby Beach, one of the warmest beaches in the province, is about 23 km (14 mi) east of Pictou. To get here, follow the shore road from Highway 104.

Dining and Lodging

$–$$$ ✕▦ **Braeside Inn.** Collectors will covet the treasures displayed in every nook and cranny of this handsome 60-year-old inn perched on a 5-acre hillside. China, crystal, silver, statuary, inlaid lacquer, and gadgets invite hours of browsing. You can stroll to the historic waterfront or watch your ship come into Pictou Harbour from the dining room ($–$$) picture window. Prime rib and seafood are specialties here, and a Sunday brunch is served. ⊠ *126 Front St., Box 1810, B0K 1H0,* ☎ *902/485–5046 or 800/613–7701,* FAX *902/485–1701,* WEB *www.nsis.com/~braeside. 18 rooms. Restaurant, meeting room. AE, MC, V.*

$–$$ ✕▦ **Consulate Inn.** A private home in 1810 and American Consulate from 1836 to 1896, the inn is a showplace for the innkeepers' creativity—she's a skilled quilter and painter; he's an artist in the kitchen. Colorful quilted hangings and original art decorate each spacious room in the main house, the next-door annex, and a two-bedroom cottage that has a full kitchen and a deck overlooking Pictou Harbour. The dining rooms (open Tuesday to Sunday; $–$$) celebrate fresh seafood, especially salmon, plus meats and pastas. ⊠ *157 Water St., Box 1642, B0K 1H0,* ☎ *902/485–4554 or 800/424–8283,* FAX *902/485–1532,* WEB *www.consulateinn.com. 11 rooms, 1 cottage. 2 restaurants. AE, MC, V. CP.*

$$ ▦ **Customs House Inn.** In 1997 a former customs house on Pictou's waterfront metamorphosed into a nifty inn, complete with eight spacious high-ceiling rooms overlooking the water. All have whirlpool baths.

A basement pub offers Celtic entertainment and Sunday brunch. ✉ *38 Depot St., Box 1542, B0K 1H0,* ☎ *902/485–4546,* FAX *902/485–1296,* WEB *www.pictou.nsis.com/customshouseinn. 8 rooms. Pub, in-room data ports, library, business services, meeting room. AE, DC, MC, V. CP.*

$ 🏨 **Auberge Walker Inn.** A registered Heritage Property, the friendly three-story inn is a short walk from the historic Pictou waterfront. A suite with a private patio and a kitchen is on the ground floor of this compact 1865 town house. ✉ *34 Coleraine St., B0K 1H0,* ☎ *902/485– 1433 or 800/370–5553,* FAX *902/485–1222,* WEB *www.pictou.nsis.com/ walkerinn. 10 rooms, 1 suite. Dining room. AE, MC, V. CP.*

Nightlife and the Arts

The **DeCoste Entertainment Centre** (✉ Water St., ☎ 902/485–8848 or 800/353–5338) is a handsome theater presenting a summer-long program of concerts, pipe bands, highland dancing, and *ceilidhs* (Gaelic music and dance).

Shopping

The artisans' cooperative **Water Street Studio** (✉ 110 Water St., ☎ 902/ 485–8398) sells clothing, weaving, silk painting, blankets, pottery, stained glass, jewelry, woodwork, handspun yarns, and other crafts.

New Glasgow

22 km (14 mi) southwest of Pictou.

The largest community along the Sunrise Trail, New Glasgow boasts a rich Scottish heritage. Since the town's prosperity has been linked to the East River, recent redevelopment of the riverfront—with restaurants, shops, and events—seems appropriate. It's the setting, in early August, of the **Riverfront Music Jubilee,** which attracts local and national performers. In mid-July, New Glasgow hosts the **Festival of the Tartans,** which includes highland dancing, piping, and drumming, plus the Pictou County Pipes and Drums on Parade, a kilted golf tournament, concerts, beer gardens, and much more.

Tatamagouche

❸❹ *50 km (31 mi) west of Pictou.*

Despite the size of its population—all of 600 souls—Tatamagouche is a force to be reckoned with. Canada's second-largest Oktoberfest and a major quilt show are held here each fall. Summer brings strawberry and blueberry festivals, lobster and chowder suppers, and a lively farmers' market each Saturday morning. This charming town on Highway 6 on the north shore is at the juncture of two rivers: Tatamagouche is a Mi'Kmaq name meaning "meeting place of the waters." An old rail bed along the river's edge, part of the Trans-Canada Trail, is ideal for hiking, cycling, walking, and bird-watching.

The **Sunrise Trail Museum** traces the town's Mi'Kmaq, Acadian, French, and Scottish roots and its shipbuilding heritage. ✉ *216 Main St.,* ☎ *902/657-3007.* 🎫 *$1.* ☉ *Late June–early Sept., 9–5 daily.*

The **Fraser Cultural Centre** promotes arts, crafts, and cultural activities. The 1889 Gallery displays the work of local artists; a large crafts room is used for displays and demonstrations. ✉ *Main St.,* ☎ *902/ 657-3285.* 🎫 *Free.* ☉ *June–Aug., daily 10–5; Sept., 1–4.*

OFF THE
BEATEN PATH

BALMORAL GRIST MILL MUSEUM – A water-powered gristmill serves as the centerpiece of this museum near Tatamagouche. Built in 1874, it's the oldest operating mill in Nova Scotia. You can observe milling demonstrations, hike the 1-km (½-mi) walking trail, and buy freshly ground flour in the shop. ⊠ *660 Matheson Brook Rd., Balmoral Mills,* ☎ *902/657–3016,* ⎚ *museum.gov.ns.ca/bgm.* ⌸ *$2.* ☉ *June–mid-Oct., Mon.–Sat. 9:30–5:30, Sun. 1–5:30; demonstrations daily 10–noon and 2–4.*

Dining and Lodging

$–$$ ✕ **The Villager Restaurant.** This homey low-key place on Main Street serves steaks, seafood, and salads. ⊠ *Main St.,* ☎ *902/657–2029. V.*

$–$$$ ⌸ **Train Station Inn.** Railway history lives on in Tatamagouche, where
★   this unique inn offers B&B accommodation in a century-old station and in seven cabooses parked nearby. The station master's quarters include three rooms, a guest parlor, and a kitchen and laundry for guest use. Downstairs, a main-floor café, where tasty breakfasts are served, is decorated with authentic railroad memorabilia. The caboose suites include all the creature comforts (including data ports) plus touches of railroad life—signal switches and elevated conductors' cupolas with their revolving chairs. ⊠ *21 Station Rd., B0K 1V0,* ☎ *902/657–3222 or 888/724–5233,* ⎈ *902/657–9091,* ⎚ *www.trainstation.ns.ca.* *3 rooms, 7 suites. Café, in-room data ports. AE, MC, V.*

$ ⌸ **The Balmoral Motel.** This small motel with 18 rooms overlooks Tatamagouche Bay. German and Canadian dishes are served in the Mill Dining Room. ⊠ *Main St., Box 178, B0K 1V0,* ☎ *902/657–2000 or 888/383–9357,* ⎈ *902/657–3343. 18 rooms. Dining room. AE, MC, V. Closed Nov.–late May.*

Shopping

At the **Sara Bonnyman Pottery Studio** (⊠ Hwy. 246, 1½ km, or 1 mi, uphill from post office, ☎ 902/657–3215), you can watch the well-known potter at work each morning, producing her handsome stoneware pieces, bearing sunflower and blueberry motifs, and one-of-a-kind plates and bowls. She also makes 100%-wool hand-hooked rugs in colorful primitive designs. The studio is open Monday through Saturday June through mid-September, by appointment off-season.

Maritime crafts sold at the **Sunflower Crafts Shop** (⊠ 249 Main St., ☎ 902/657–3276) include the work of noted local potter Sara Bonnyman, Chéticamp hooking, pewter, wood, baskets, wrought iron, quilts, candles, and unusual framed pictures made of caribou tufting.

Malagash

17 km (11 mi) west of Tatamagouche.

Malagash is best known for a winery that flourishes in the warm climate moderated by the Northumberland Strait. **Jost Vineyards** produces a surprisingly wide range of award-winning wines, including a notable ice wine (a sweet wine made after frost has iced the grapes). There's a well-stocked wine shop, a deli-bar, a patio deck, a children's playground, and picnic area here. ⊠ *Hwy. 6, off Hwy. 104,* ☎ *902/257–2636 or 800/565–4567,* ⎚ *www.jostwine.com.* ☉ *Mid-June–mid-Sept., Mon.–Sat. 9–6, Sun. noon–6; mid-Sept.–mid-June, Mon.–Sat. 10–5, Sun. noon–5; tours mid-June–mid-Sept., daily at noon and 3.*

Springhill

③⑤   *40 km (25 mi) west of Malagash.*

The coal-mining town of Springhill, on Highway 2, was the site of the famous mine disaster of the 1950s immortalized in the folk song "The Ballad of Springhill" by Peggy Seeger and Ewen McColl. You can tour a real coal mine at the **Spring Hill Miners Museum.** Retired coal miners act as guides and recount firsthand memories of mining disasters.

⊠ *Black River Rd., off Hwy. 2,* ☎ *902/597–3449.* ⊞ *$5.* ⊙ *May–mid-Oct., daily 10–6.*

Springhill is the hometown of internationally acclaimed singer Anne Murray, whose career is celebrated in the **Anne Murray Centre.** ⊠ *Main St.,* ☎ *902/597–8614.* ⊞ *$5.* ⊙ *Mid-May–mid-Oct., daily 9–5.*

OFF THE
BEATEN PATH

WILD BLUEBERRY & MAPLE CENTRE – This center in Oxford, about 10 km (6 mi) outside of Springhill, details the history of two tasty industries—75% of Nova Scotia's blueberry and maple-syrup production occurs in surrounding Cumberland County. Self-guided tours, interactive displays, and a beehive tell the story. ⊠ *15 Lower Main St., Oxford,* ☎ *902/447–2908,* WEB *www.town.oxford.ns.ca.* ⊞ *$2.* ⊙ *Mid-May–mid-Oct., daily 10–6.*

Amherst

㊱ *28 km (17 mi) northwest of Springhill.*

Amherst, near the New Brunswick border, is a quiet town today, but from the mid-1800s to early 1900s it was a bustling center of industry and influence. Four of Canada's Fathers of Confederation hailed from Amherst, including Sir Charles Tupper, who later became prime minister. The town is tame today, but the **Tantramar Marsh,** originally called Tintamarre because of the racket made by vast flocks of wildfowl, is still alive with incredible birds and wildlife. Said to be the world's largest marsh, it's a migratory route for hundreds of thousands of birds, and a breeding ground for more than 100 species.

From Amherst, the Sunrise Trail heads toward the Northumberland Strait, while the Glooscap Trail runs west through fossil country. The **Fundy Shore Ecotour** has been developed by the local tourism authority to highlight this region's six distinct ecozones. Brochures are available at information centers (☎ 902/667–8429 or 902/667–0696 for locations).

Dining and Lodging

$$–$$$ ✕🏠 **Amherst Shore Country Inn.** This seaside country inn, with a beau-
★ tiful view of Northumberland Strait, has comfortable rooms, suites, and a cottage fronting 600 ft of private beach. Well-prepared four-course dinners incorporating home-grown produce are served at one daily seating (by reservation only, $29.50). ⊠ *Hwy. 366, R.R. 2, Lorneville (32 km, or 20 mi, northeast of Amherst), B4H 3X9,* ☎ FAX *902/661–4800 or 800/661–2724,* WEB *www.ascinn.ns.ca. 4 rooms, 4 suites, 1 cottage. Restaurant. AE, DC, MC, V. Closed weekdays Nov.–Apr.*

$$ 🏠 **Wandlyn Inn.** Just inside the Nova Scotia–New Brunswick border, this dependable inn offers a slew of amenities: an indoor pool, a hot tub, a sauna, a gym, and laundry facilities. ⊠ *Trans Canada Hwy., Victoria St. Exit. Box 275, B4H 3Z2,* ☎ *902/667–3331 or 800/561–0000,* FAX *902/667–0475,* WEB *www.wandlyninns.com. 88 rooms. Restaurant, indoor pool, hot tub, sauna, gym, coin laundry. AE, MC, V.*

Joggins

㊲ *35 km (22 mi) southwest of Amherst.*

Joggins's main draw is the coal-age fossils embedded in its 150-ft sandstone cliffs. At the **Joggins Fossil Centre,** you can view a large collection of 300-million-year-old fossils and learn about the region's geological and archaeological history. Guided tours of the fossil cliffs are available, but departure times depend on the tides. Maps are issued for independent fossil hunters. ⊠ *30 Main St.,* ☎ *902/251–2727.* ☞ *Center $3.50, tour $10.* ◷ *June–Sept., daily 9–5:30.*

Cape Chignecto and Cape d'Or

70 km (43 mi) southwest of Joggins.

Two imposing promontories—Cape Chignecto and Cape d'Or—reach into the Bay of Fundy near Chignecto Bay. Cape Chignecto, home to the newest provincial park, **Cape Chignecto Provincial Park** (⊠ off Hwy. 209, West Advocate, ☎ 902/392–2085 or 902/254–3241), is an untouched wilderness of 10,000 acres of old-growth forest harboring deer, moose, and eagles. It's circumnavigated by a 50-km (31-mi) hiking trail along rugged cliffs that rise to 600 ft above the bay. Wilderness cabins and campsites are available.

Farther south is Cape d'Or (Cape of Gold), named by Samuel de Champlain for its glittering veins of copper. The region was actively mined a century ago, and at nearby Horseshoe Cove you may still find nuggets of almost pure copper on the beach as well as amethysts and other semiprecious stones. Cape d'Or's hiking trails border the cliff edge above the Dory Rips, a turbulent meeting of currents from the Minas Basin and the Bay of Fundy punctuated by a fine lighthouse.

At **Advocate Harbour,** named by Samuel de Champlain for a lawyer friend, a delightful beach walk follows the top of an Acadian dyke, built by settlers in the 1700s to reclaim farmland from the sea. Advocate Beach, noted for its tide-cast driftwood, stretches 5 km (3 mi) from Cape Chignecto to Cape d'Or.

The **Age of Sail Museum Heritage Centre** (⊠ Hwy. 209, Port Greville, ☎ 902/348–2030) traces the history of the area's shipbuilding and lumbering industries. You can also see a restored 1857 Methodist church, a blacksmith shop, and a lighthouse. The center ($2) is open late May through September, daily 10–6.

Dining and Lodging

$ ✕ **Harbour Lite Restaurant.** Every bite you eat in this unpretentious roadside diner is home-cooked by the friendly owner, who is on the job 12 hours a day all summer. Clam chowder, lobster in season, and fresh seafood; sandwiches; and sweets such as feather-light cinnamon buns, muffins, pies, and cakes round out the menu. ⊠ *4160 Main St., Advocate,* ☎ *902/392–2277. No credit cards. Closed Dec.–Feb.*

$$ ▥ **Driftwood Park Retreat.** Five mist-blue cottages face the Fundy shore and its powerful tides. Four of the two-story two-bedroom units have cathedral ceilings, pine floors, gas fireplaces, well-equipped kitchens, and upstairs living rooms with fine views of the bay. The fifth cottage is a ranch unit with a sleeping loft. ⊠ *47 Driftwood La., West Advocate B0M 1A0,* ☎ *902/392–2008 or 866/810–0110,* ☏ *902/392–2041,* ⓦⓔⓑ *www.driftwoodparkretreat.com. 5 cottages. MC, V.*

$ ▥ **Lightkeeper's Kitchen and Guest House.** Before automation, two lightkeepers manned the crucial light on the rocky Cape d'Or shore, and their cottages have been transformed—one to an excellent restaurant and the other to a four-room inn with a comfortable lounge and picture windows overlooking the Minas Basin. This wild and lovely place offers hiking, bird-watching, seal sightings, outdoor lobster boils and clambakes, gourmet cooking, and exceptional hosts. Getting here is a bit challenging: a 5½-km (3-mi) road off Highway 209 from Advocate, then a steep gravel path down to the shore. ⊠ *Cape d'Or, Advocate B0M 1A0,* ☎ *902/670–0534,* ⓦⓔⓑ *www.capedor.ca. 4 rooms, 1 with bath. V. Closed mid-Oct.–mid-May.*

$ ⊞ Reid's Tourist Home. Nestled between Cape d'Or and Cape Chignecto, this cattle farm is a working operation where you can enjoy the bucolic pleasures of country life or take a short walk to the Fundy shore. Four suites, each with a sitting area, bedroom, and refrigerator, occupy a separate building near the picturesque farmhouse. Chignecto Park is just over 1 km (½ mi) away. ⊠ *1391 West Advocate Rd., West Advocate (R.R. 3, Parrsboro B0M 1S0),* ☎ *902/392–2592,* F̲A̲X̲ *902/392–2523. 4 suites. No credit cards. Closed Oct.–May.*

$ ⊞ Spencer's Island B&B. Once home to Captain Bigelow, who built the mysterious *Mary Celeste,* the house today is a modest and friendly B&B with three cozy rooms and an antiques-furnished parlor. Wood-burning fireplaces and a vintage woodstove in the kitchen add to the ambience. Blueberry waffles or cheese soufflé are breakfast favorites. The inn is just uphill from the Spencer's Island lighthouse and the Fundy shore, and it's a 10-minute drive from the wilderness of Cape Chignecto. ⊠ *Off Hwy. 209 (R.R. 3, Parrsboro B0M 1S0),* ☎ *902/392–2721. 3 rooms. No credit cards. Closed Sept.–May. BP.*

En Route At **Spencer's Island Beach** on Highway 209, a cairn commemorates the mystery ship *Mary Celeste,* built here in 1861 and found in 1872 abandoned at sea, all sails set, undamaged, but without a trace of the crew and passengers.

Parrsboro

㊳ *55 km (34 mi) east of Cape d'Or.*

A center for rock hounds and fossil hunters, Parrsboro is the main town on this shore and hosts the **Nova Scotia Gem and Mineral Show** (third weekend of August). Among the exhibits and festivities are concerts and geological displays. The fossil-laden cliffs that rim the Minas Basin are washed by the world's highest tides twice daily. The result is a wealth of plant and animal fossils revealed in the rocks or washed down to the shore. Semiprecious stones such as amethyst, quartz, and stilbite can be found at Partridge Island, 1 km (½ mi) offshore and connected to the mainland by an isthmus.

Parrsboro is an appropriate setting for the **Fundy Geological Museum** because it's not far from the Minas Basin area, where some of the oldest dinosaur fossils in Canada were found. Two-hundred-million-year-old dinosaur fossils are showcased here alongside other mineral, plant, and animal relics. ⊠ *162 Two Island Rd.,* ☎ *902/254–3814,* W̲E̲B̲ *www.fundygeomuseum.com.* ⌨ *$4.* ☼ *June–mid-Oct., daily 9:30–5:30.*

The world's smallest dinosaur footprints, along with rare minerals, rocks, and fossils, are displayed at Eldon George's **Parrsboro Rock and Mineral Shop and Museum** (⊠ 39 Whitehall Rd., ☎ 902/254–2981). Mr. George, a goldsmith, lapidarian, and wood carver, sells his work in his shop and offers tours for fossil and mineral collectors (four person minimum, $10 each). The shop closes November to April.

Although fossils have become Parrsboro's claim to fame, this harbor town was also a major shipping and shipbuilding port, and its history is described at the **Ottawa House Museum-by-the-Sea,** 3 km (2 mi) east of downtown. Ottawa House, which overlooks the Bay of Fundy, is the only surviving building from a 1700s Acadian settlement. It was later the summer home of Sir Charles Tupper (1821–1915), a former premier of Nova Scotia who was briefly prime minister of Canada. ⊠ *Whitehall Rd.,* ☎ *902/254–2376.* ⌨ *$1.* ☼ *June–mid-Sept., daily 10–8.*

Dining and Lodging

$–$$ ✕ **Harbour View Restaurant.** Expect fresh seafood at this pleasant beachfront restaurant—the owners maintain their own boats to fish for scallops and lobster, which, along with clams, flounder, and other seafood, are menu staples. The dining room, with windows overlooking the water and the lighthouse, displays paintings and photos of Parrsboro's past. It's open 7 AM–10 PM. ⊠ *476 Pier Rd.,* ☏ *902/ 254–3507. MC, V. Closed mid-Oct.–Apr.*

$–$$ ✕ **Stowaway Restaurant.** The menu is rich in seafood—thick chowder, fish and chips, and scallops—as well as chicken and meat dishes. Friendly and spacious, its deep window wells are stocked with interesting antiques, also for sale. In one wing, a bakery ruins diets with its fresh apple pies, donuts, and bread. There's a take-out counter, too. All three meals are served. ⊠ *69 Main St.,* ☏ *902/254–3371. AE, MC, V.*

$ ✕ **John's Café.** Here's an unexpected find—a funky café serving healthful salads, sandwiches and soups, plus decadent desserts. There's jazz, blues, and Nova Scotia music, indoors or on a pleasant patio. It's open all day. ⊠ *151 Main St.,* ☏ *902/254–3255. No credit cards. Closed mid-Dec.–early Apr.*

$$$$ ⊞ **The Beach House on Hatfield Road.** Fourteen picture windows provide panoramic views of the Bay of Fundy and a saltwater marsh. The two-story house can sleep 8–10 and boasts access to two beaches and all the attractions of the Glooscap Trail. Fully equipped, from beach towels to fax machine, fondue pots to satellite TV, it includes two bedrooms, two bathrooms, a sunroom, balconies, a dining room, and a sitting room with fireplace. The house is rented in one-week increments for summer and shorter breaks in winter. ⊠ *Fox River (19 km, or 12 mi, west of Parrsboro). Reservations: 96 Sherwood Ave., Toronto, ON, M4P 2A7.* ☏ *416/481–4096,* FAX *416/487–4048,* WEB *www.lizyorke.com.*

$–$$ ⊞ **The Maple Inn, Parrsboro.** Room one in this Italianate-style home built 1860–90 is popular with local residents. That's because many of them were born here when the house served time as a hospital and this was the delivery room. These days the inn offers nine dramatic rooms, including one painted black with lush, flowery touches. Parrsboro's center and the Bay of Fundy are within walking distance. ⊠ *2358 Western Ave., Box 457, B0M 1S0,* ☏ *877/627–5346,* ☏ FAX *902/254– 3735,* WEB *www3.ns.sympatico.ca/mapleinn. 9 rooms. AE, MC, V. BP.*

$–$$ ⊞ **Parrsboro Mansion.** This 1880 home, set far back on a 4-acre lawn, presents an imposing face; inside it's brightly modern, with contemporary European art and furnishings. The owners invite guests to join them in a morning jog and to later learn about regeneration and relaxation through magnetic-field therapy. ⊠ *15 Eastern Ave., Box 579, B0M 1S0,* ☏ FAX *902/254–2585,* WEB *www3.ns.sympatico.ca/parrsboro.m.bb. 3 rooms. Sauna, gym. AE, MC, V. Closed Nov.–June. CP.*

$ ⊞ **Gillespie House B&B.** Wild roses border the driveway leading up to this handsome home. Yoga and spa weekends can be arranged for groups; you can enjoy therapeutic massage and reflexology by reserving a few of days ahead. Four rooms with private baths, a lavish vegetarian breakfast, bikes and helmets, and tons of visitor information are all part of the service. ⊠ *358 Main St., B0M 1S0,* ☏ *902/254–3196 or 877/901–3196,* WEB *www.gillespiehouseinn.com. 4 rooms. Dining room, bicycles. AE, MC, V. Closed Nov.–Apr. BP.*

Nightlife and the Arts

Ship's Company Theatre (⊠ 198 Main St., ☏ 902/254–2003 or 800/ 565–7469, WEB www.shipscompany.com) presents top-notch plays, comedy, and a concert series aboard the M.V. *Kipawo,* a former Minas Basin ferry, early July to early September. **Joy Laking Studio Gallery** (⊠ 6730 Hwy. 2, Portaupique, 5 km, or 3 mi, east of Bass River, ☏

902/647–2816 or 800/565–5899, WEB www3.ns.sympatico.ca/lakings), midway between Truro and Parrsboro, is owned by one of Nova Scotia's best-known painters.

Five Islands

24 km (15 mi) east of Parrsboro.

Among the most scenic areas along Highway 2 is Five Islands, which, according to Mi'Kmaq legend, was created when the god Glooscap threw handfuls of sod at Beaver, who had mocked and betrayed him. **Five Islands Provincial Park** (⊠ Hwy. 2, ☎ 902/254–2980), on the shore of Minas Basin, has a campground, a beach, and hiking trails. Interpretive displays reveal the area's interesting geology: semiprecious stones, Jurassic-age dinosaur bones, and fossils. The Five Islands Lighthouse, at Sand Point Campground, has access to good swimming and clamming; you can "walk on the ocean floor" at low tide, when the water recedes nearly a mile, but beware the awesome return of the tides, which can outrun man or beast.

Cobequid Interpretation Centre highlights the geology, history, and culture of the area, with pictures, videos, and interpretive panels. A World War II observation tower offers a sweeping view of the countryside and the impressive tides. The center is home base for **Kenomee Hiking and Walking Trails** which explore the area's varied landscapes—the coast itself plus cliffs, waterfalls, and forested valleys. ⊠ *3248 Hwy. 2, Central Economy,* ☎ *902/647–2600.* ⊠ *By donation. Closed Oct.–May.*

Lodging

$ 🏠 **Gemstow B&B.** At this B&B 20 km (12 mi) east of Parrsboro, breakfast is served in an airy sunporch that overlooks flowery perennial beds and has a fine vista of Five Islands beyond. Photographers nab their best shots of the windswept islands from the front deck. Inside, three rooms and the lounge are tastefully furnished. Your host leads hikes to a hidden waterfall or clamming on the shore. ⊠ *463 Hwy. 2, Lower Five Islands, B0M 1N0,* ☎ *902/254–2924. 3 rooms, 1 with bath.* V.

$ 🏠 **MacLellans Cottages.** Midway between Parrsboro and Truro are four modest seaside units, equipped with everything from hair dryers to rolling pins to clam-digging gear. The large property has direct access to the Minas Basin beach. ⊠ *3120 Hwy. 2, Economy B0M 1J0,* ☎ *902/647–2209 or 877/647–2209,* FAX *902/647–2592. 4 cottages. Basketball, horseshoes, volleyball, fishing, coin laundry. AE, MC, V. Closed mid-Oct.–May.*

Truro

③⑨ *67 km (42 mi) east of Five Islands.*

Truro's central location places it on many travelers' routes, and its museums, golf course, and harness-racing track satisfy a range of interests. Throughout Truro, watch for the Truro Tree Sculptures—a creative tribute to trees killed by the dreaded Dutch Elm disease. Artists Albert Deveau, Ralph Bigney, and Bruce Wood have been transforming the dead trees into handsome sculptures of historical figures, wildlife, and cultural icons.

Truro's least known asset is also its biggest—the 1,000-acre **Victoria Park,** where, smack in the middle of town, you can find hiking trails, a winding stream flowing through a deep gorge with a 200-step climb to the top, and two picturesque waterfalls. ⊠ *Park Rd.,* ☎ *902/893–6078.* ⊙ *Daily dawn–dusk.*

Dining and Lodging

$$$–$$$$ ✕⌂ **John Stanfield Inn.** Rescued from demolition and moved to this
★   site by the owners of Keddy's, the John Stanfield Inn has been re-
           stored to its original Queen Anne glory, with delicate wood carvings,
           elaborate fireplaces, bow windows, and fine antique furniture. Three
           restaurants ($$–$$$) serve unusual seafood specialties including a
           fisherman's plate with half a dozen seafood varieties; desserts such
           as berries Romanoff; and a lavish Sunday brunch. ⊠ *437 Prince St.,
           B2N 1E6,* ☎ *902/895–1651 or 800/561–7666,* ℻ *902/893–4427,*
           WEB *www.johnstanfieldinn.com. 12 rooms. 3 restaurants, lounge, in-
           room data ports. AE, D, MC, V. CP.*

$–$$ ⌂ **Shady Maple B&B.** On this 200-acre farm 15 km (9 mi) outside of
           Truro, guests can hobnob with herds of Highland cattle, llamas, sheep,
           goats, and horses; sleep on sun-dried bed linens; and breakfast on fresh
           eggs and the farm's own maple syrup, jams, and jellies. The 1890 farm-
           house has two rooms and a deluxe suite with a two-person jet tub. A
           heated pool and a hot tub are outside. ⊠ *11207 Hwy. 2, Masstown B0M
           1G0,* ☎ ℻ *902/662–3565 or 800/493–5844,* WEB *www.ns.sympatico.
           ca/emeisses. 2 rooms without bath, 1 suite. Pool, outdoor hot tub. V.*

$ ⌂ **Keddy's Motor Inn.** Part of a five-inn Maritime chain, this comfortable
           establishment caters to business and family travel. The rooms, in-
           cluding those in a well-appointed executive wing, are modern and
           spacious. A large restaurant serves Canadian cuisine. ⊠ *437 Prince St.,
           B2N 1E6,* ☎ *902/895–1651 or 800/561–7666,* WEB *www.keddys.
           ca/truro. 115 rooms. Restaurant, pub, in-room data ports, pool, coin
           laundry, meeting room. AE, D, DC, MC, V.*

$ ⌂ **Suncatcher B&B.** Stained glass adorns every available window, wall,
           and cranny of this modest B&B 10 minutes from Truro. Two-day
           workshops in crafting stained glass are available (reservations re-
           quired). Breakfast may include homemade breads, jams, muffins, sea-
           sonal fruits, and eggs. The hosts, longtime B&B providers, know their
           province from stem to stern and cheerfully advise on itineraries and
           attractions. ⊠ *25 Wile Crest Ave., R.R. 6, North River B2N 5B4,* ☎
           ℻ *902/893–7169 or 877/203–6032,* WEB *www.bbcanada.com/
           1853.html. 3 rooms with shared bath. V.*

Outdoor Activities and Sports

Riding the rushing tide aboard a 16-ft self-bailing Zodiac with **Shube-
nacadie River Runners** (⊠ 8681 Hwy. 215, Maitland, ☎ 902/261–2770
or 800/856–5061, WEB www.tidalborerafting.com) is an adventure you
won't soon forget. Tide conditions and time of day let you choose a
mildly turbulent ride or an ultrawild one. A 3½-hour excursion costs
$65, including gear and a barbecue.

The **Truro Raceway** (⊠ Main St., ☎ 902/893–8075) holds year-round
harness racing.

CAPE BRETON ISLAND

The highways and byways of the Island of Cape Breton, including those
on the Cabot Trail, make up one of the most spectacular drives in North
America. As you wind through the rugged coastal headlands of Cape
Breton Highlands National Park, you can climb mountains and plunge
back down to the sea in a matter of minutes. The Margaree River is a
cultural dividing line: south of the river the settlements are Scottish,
up the river they are largely Irish, and north of the river they are Acadian French. You can visit villages where ancient dialects can still be
heard and explore a fortress where period players bring the past to life.
This is a place where cultural heritage is alive, where the atmosphere

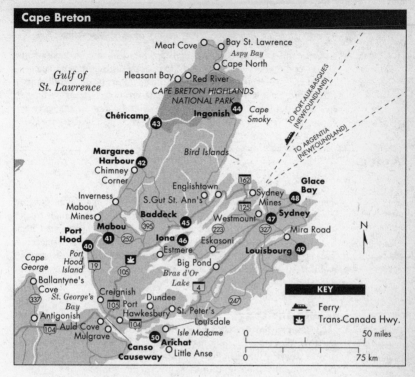

Cape Breton

Meat Cove ○ ○ Bay St. Lawrence
Aspy Bay
○ Cape North

*Gulf of
St. Lawrence*

Pleasant Bay ○ ○ Red River
CAPE BRETON HIGHLANDS
NATIONAL PARK

Chéticamp ○ **43** Ingonish **44** *Cape Smoky*

Margaree Harbour **42**
Chimney Corner ○
Bird Islands

Inverness ○
Mabou Mines ○
Baddeck ○ **45**
Englishtown
S.Gut St. Ann's ○
○ [162]
○ Sydney Mines
Glace Bay **48**

Mabou ○
395
Westmount ○ [125]
Sydney **47**

Port Hood **40** **41** [252]
Iona **46** [223]
Eskasoni ○
○ Mira Road [327]

Cape George
Port Hood Island ○
Estmere ○
Louisbourg **49**

○ Ballantyne's Cove [19]
[105]
Big Pond ○
Bras d'Or Lake

[337] *St. George's Bay*
Creignish ○
Dundee ○
○ Antigonish
[105] Port Hawkesbury ○
St. Peter's ○
Louisdale
[104] Auld Cove [104]
Mulgrave ○
Canso Causeway
50 **Arichat**
Isle Madame
Little Anse

TO PORT-AUX-BASQUES (NEWFOUNDLAND)
TO ARGENTIA (NEWFOUNDLAND)

KEY
⛴ Ferry
Trans-Canada Hwy.

N

0 _____ 50 miles
0 _____ 75 km

is maritime, and where inventors Marconi and Bell share the spotlight with coal miners and singers such as Rita MacNeil. Wherever you go in Cape Breton you are sure to experience warmth and hospitality.

Bras d'Or Lake, a vast, warm, almost-landlocked inlet of the sea, occupies the entire center of Cape Breton. The coastline of the lake is more than 967 km (600 mi) long, and people sail yachts from all over the world to cruise its serene, unspoiled coves and islands. Bald eagles have become so plentiful around the lake that they are now exported to the United States to restock natural habitats. Four of the largest communities along the shore are native Mi'Kmaq communities.

If Halifax is the heart of Nova Scotia, Cape Breton is its soul, complete with soul music—flying fiddles, boisterous rock, velvet ballads. Cape Breton musicians—weaned on Scottish jigs and reels—are among the world's finest, and in summer you can hear them at dozens of local festivals and concerts. In summer, every community in the southern end of Inverness County takes a different night of the week to offer a square dance. Propelled by driving piano and virtuoso fiddling, locals of every age whirl through "square sets," the best of them step dancing and square dancing simultaneously. Local bulletin boards and newspapers have square dance times and locations.

Allow three or four days for this meandering tour of approximately 710 km (440 mi) that begins by entering the island via the Canso Causeway on Highway 104. Turn left at the rotary and take Highway 19, the Ceilidh Trail, which winds for 129 km (80 mi) along the mountainside through glens and farms, with fine views across St. George's Bay to Cape George. This western shoreline of Cape Breton faces the Gulf of St. Lawrence and is famous for its sandy beaches and warm salt water.

Port Hood

40 *45 km (28 mi) northwest of the Canso Causeway on Hwy. 19.*

At this fishing village you can buy lobster and snow crab fresh off the wharf as the boats return in mid-afternoon. With a little persuasion, one of the fisherfolk might give you a lift to **Port Hood Island,** a mile across the harbor. It's a 10-minute walk from the island's wharf to the pastel-color cliffs of wave-mottled alabaster on the seaward shore. Both the village and the island have sandy beaches ideal for swimming.

Mabou

41 *13 km (8 mi) northeast of Port Hood on Hwy. 19.*

The pretty village of Mabou is very Scottish, with its Gaelic signs and traditions of Scottish music and dancing. Most Saturday nights offer a helping of local culture in the form of a dance or kitchen party. Check bulletin boards at local businesses for information about these events. This is the hometown of national recording and performing artists such as John Allan Cameron and the Rankin Family (now defunct). Stop at a local gift shop and buy tapes to play as you drive down the long fjord of Mabou Harbour.

Dining and Lodging

$$$–$$$$ ✕🏠 **Glenora Inn & Distillery Resort.** North America's only single-malt-whiskey distillery adjoins this friendly inn. Here you can sample a "wee dram" of the inn's own whiskey—billed as Canada's first legal moonshine. Even if you don't stay overnight, you can take a tour of the distillery and museum, and enjoy fine cuisine and traditional Cape Breton music. ⊠ *Hwy. 19, Box 181, Glenville B0E 1X0,* ☎ *902/258–2662 or 800/839–0491,* FAX *902/258–3572,* WEB *www.glenoradistillery. com. 9 rooms, 6 chalets. Restaurant, pub, shop, convention center. AE, MC, V. Closed Nov.–mid-June.*

$–$$ ✕🏠 **Duncreigan Country Inn.** These new buildings, on the shore of Mabou Harbour, suggest the early 1900s in design and furnishings. Several decks afford beautiful views and are ideal for relaxing, reading, and leaving your cares behind. The dining room, open to the public, is considered one of the top 100 in Canada. A breakfast buffet is provided in the summer, and a Continental breakfast is available in the off-season. Canoes and bicycles are available for guest use. ⊠ *Rte. 19, Box 59, B0E 1X0,* ☎ *902/945–2207; 800/840–2207 for reservations,* FAX *902/945–2206,* WEB *www.auracom.com/~mulldci. 7 rooms, 1 suite. Restaurant, bicycles. MC, V. CP.*

Mabou Mines

10 km (6 mi) northwest of Mabou.

This quiet area, known locally as the Mines, is a place so hauntingly exquisite that you expect to meet the *sidhe,* the Scottish fairies, capering on the hillsides. Within the hills of Mabou Mines is some of the finest hiking in the province, and above the land fly bald eagles, plentiful in this region. Inquire locally or at the tourist office in Margaree Forks for information about trails.

En Route Take Highway 19 to Highway 219 and follow the coast to **Chimney Corner.** A nearby beach has "sonorous sands": when you step on the sand or drag a foot through it, it squeaks and moans.

Margaree Harbour

42 *33 km (20 mi) north of Mabou.*

The Ceilidh Trail joins the Cabot Trail at Margaree Harbour at the mouth of the Margaree River, a famous salmon-fishing stream and a favorite canoe route. Exhibits at the **Margaree Salmon Museum,** in a former schoolhouse, include fishing tackle, photographs, and other memorabilia related to salmon angling on the Margaree River. ⊠ *60 E. Big Intervale Rd.,* ☎ *902/248–2848.* ⊠ *$1.* ☉ *Mid-June–mid-Oct., daily 9–5.*

Dining and Lodging

$–$$$ ✕▥ **Normaway Inn.** Nestled on 250 acres in the hills of the Margaree Valley at the beginning of the Cabot Trail, this secluded 1920s inn has distinctive rooms and cabins, most with woodstoves and screened porches, and some have hot tubs. There are films or traditional entertainment nightly as well as weekly square dances in the Barn. The restaurant is known for its country cuisine, particularly the vegetable chowders and fresh seafood ragout. ⊠ *Egypt Rd., 3 km (2 mi) off Cabot Trail, Box 101, B0E 2C0,* ☎ *902/248–2987 or 800/565–9463,* 𝖥𝖠𝖷 *902/ 248–2600,* 𝖶𝖤𝖡 *www.normaway.com. 9 rooms, 19 cabins. Restaurant, tennis court, hiking, bicycles. MC, V. Closed mid-Oct.–mid-June.*

Chéticamp

43 *26 km (16 mi) north of Margaree Harbour.*

This Acadian community has the best harbor and the largest settlement on this shore. Even after 200 years of history, Chéticamp's Acadian culture and traditions are still very much a way of life in the region. Nestled on one side by the mountains and on the other by the sea, the community offers the pride, traditions and warmth of Acadian hospitality. Its tall silver steeple towers over the village, which stands exposed on a wide lip of flat land below a range of bald green hills. Behind these hills lies the high plateau of the Cape Breton Highlands. The area is known for its strong southeast winds, called *suêtes,* which are winds of 120–130 km (75–80 mi) per hour. These winds, which may develop into a force up 200 km (125 mi) per hour, have been known to blow the roofs off buildings.

Chéticamp is famous for its hooked rugs, available at many local gift shops. The **Dr. Elizabeth LeFort Gallery and Museum: Les Trois Pignons** (⊠ Cabot Trail B0E 1H0, ☎ 902/224–2642, 𝖶𝖤𝖡 www.lestroispignons. com) displays artifacts and fine hooked embroidery work, rugs, and tapestries. Dr. LeFort created more than 300 tapestries, some of which have been hung in the Vatican, the White House, and Buckingham Palace. The museum is also an Acadian cultural and genealogical information center. Admission is $3.50; the museum is open from mid-October to June, weekdays 8:30–5, and July to mid-October, daily 8–6.

Dining and Lodging

$–$$ ✕ **Le Gabriel.** You can't miss Le Gabriel, with its large lighthouse entranceway. This casual tavern offers simple but good fresh fish dinners and traditional Acadian dishes. Snow crab and lobster specials are available in season. At night things heat up with live music and dancing. ⊠ *Cabot Trail,* ☎ *902/224–3685,* 𝖶𝖤𝖡 *www.legabriel.com. MC, V.*

$$ ▥ **Cabot Trail Sea & Golf Chalets.** Right next to Le Portage Golf Course and overlooking the ocean, these chalets are ideal for families and golfers. One- and two-bedroom chalets have covered decks with gas barbecues. Some units have fireplaces and whirlpool tubs. There is a play area for children, and cribs, cots, and high chairs are available. ⊠ *71 Fraser Doucet La., Box 8, B0E 1H0,* ☎ *902/224–1777 or 877/224–1777,*

FAX 902/224–1999, WEB *www.seagolfchalets.com. 13 chalets. 18-hole golf course, playground. AE, D, MC, V. Closed mid-Oct.–Apr.*

$ ⊞ **Chéticamp Outfitters' Inn B&B.** The clean and cozy rooms at this homey inn operated by a bilingual family overlook the ocean, mountains, and valley. The furniture includes homemade wooden pieces, paintings by the innkeeper, and quilts. Guide and outfitting services are available. ⊠ *Point Cross, Box 448, B0E 1H0,* ☎ FAX *902/224–2776,* WEB *www. sea-trail.com/cheticampoutfitters. 6 rooms, 3 with bath. Fishing. AE, MC, V. Closed mid-Dec.–Mar. BP.*

Outdoor Activities and Sports

Chéticamp is known for its whale-watching cruises, which depart from the government wharf twice daily in May and June, increasing in July and August to three times daily. Expect to see minke, pilot, and fin whales in their natural environment; seabird and bald-eagle sightings are also common. **Whale Cruisers Ltd.** (☎ 902/224–3376 or 800/813–3376, WEB www.whalecruises.com) is a reliable charter company, and the first of its kind in Nova Scotia.

Cape Breton Highlands National Park of Canada

★ *At the northern outskirts of Chéticamp.*

A 950-square-km (367-square-mi) wilderness of wooded valleys, plateau barrens, and steep cliffs, this park stretches across the northern peninsula of Cape Breton from the gulf shore to the Atlantic. The highway through the park (world-renowned Cabot Trail) is magnificent. It rises to the tops of the coastal mountains and descends through scenic switchbacks to the sea. In fact, the road has been compared to a 106-km (66-mi) roller coaster ride, stretching from Chéticamp to Ingonish. Good brakes and attentive driving are advised. Pull-offs provide photo opportunities. For wildlife watchers there's much to see, including moose, eagles, deer, bears, foxes, and bobcats. Your chances of seeing wildlife are better if you venture off the main road at dusk or dawn. Note that it is illegal to feed or approach any animal in the park. Always take care to observe the animals from a safe distance; in particular, you should exercise caution driving in the moose zones, marked by signs on the highway. Moose sometimes claim the road as their own and stand in the middle of it. Hitting one can be damaging to both you and the animal.

High-altitude marshlands are home to delightful wild orchids and other unique flora and fauna. If you plan to hike or camp in the park, or you want to maximize your appreciation for the nature and history of the park, stop at the Chéticamp Information Centre for advice and necessary permits. Inside the Information Centre, you can buy *Walking in the Highlands,* a guide to the park's 28 hiking trails, from the nature bookstore Les Amis du Plein Air. Trails range from easy 20-minute strolls to tough overnight treks. Five hundred fifty campsites in six spectacular locations provide a variety of facilities and services—some are even equipped with showers and cooking shelters. A park permit or pass is required for sightseeing along sections of the Cabot Trail highway when within the National Park and for use of roadside facilities such as exhibits, hiking trails, picnic areas, and washrooms. ⊠ *Entrances on Cabot Trail near Chéticamp and Ingonish,* ☎ *902/285–2535; 902/ 285–2270 in winter; 902/224–3814 bookstore,* WEB *www.parkscanada. gc.ca.* ⊠ *May–Oct. $3.50 per day, multiday and seasonal passes available; additional fees for camping.*

OFF THE   **GAMPO ABBEY -** The only Tibetan Buddhist Monastery in North America,
BEATEN PATH   Gampo Abbey sits at the most northerly tip of the island past the National

Park on a broad flat bench of land high above the sea. To get here, take the spur road (take a left at Pleasant Bay) that creeps along the cliffs to Red River. You can tour the abbey when it's not in retreat; the only way to find out whether tours are available is to drive to the abbey and check the sign at the gate. If the abbey is closed, you can continue down the road for about ½ km (¼ mi) to visit the Stupa, an elaborate shrine.

Outdoor Activities and Sports

On a **Pleasant Bay Whale and Seal Cruise** (☎ 902/224–1316 or 888/754–5112, WEB www.whaleandsealcruise.com) you may see pilot, finback, humpback, or minke whales. If you don't see them, you may at least be able to hear them with the help of an on-board hydrophone. It's also possible to catch sight of dolphins, seals, bald eagles, moose, black bears, and numerous seabirds. Cruises allow for exploration of sea caves, waterfalls, and rock and cliff formations along a remote stretch of unspoiled Cape Breton coastline. There's a money-back guarantee if you don't see a whale. **Pleasant Bay Fiddlin' Whale Tours** (☎ 902/224–2424 or 866/688–2424) and **Wesley's Whale Watching** (☎ 902/224–1919 or 866/273–2593) are among the other outfitters in the area. For those who prefer to stay on dry land to observe sealife, stop by the **Whale Interpretive Centre** (☎ 902/224–1411, WEB www.whaleslife.com) in Pleasant Bay. Using zoom scopes on the whale-spotting deck, visitors may catch a close-up glimpse of many different species of whales that are often frolicking just off shore from the center. Inside the modern structure, exhibits and models explain the unique world of whales. The center ($4.50) is open mid-May through October.

Bay St. Lawrence

76 km (47 mi) north of Chéticamp.

The charming fishing village of Bay St. Lawrence is nestled in a bowl-shape valley around a harbor pond. You can hike along the shore to the east and the Money Point Lighthouse, or find a quiet corner of the shoreline for a wilderness campsite. A "feed of lobster" can be purchased from the fisher who brought it up from the sea an hour before.

OFF THE BEATEN PATH

MEAT COVE – Named for the moose and (now absent) caribou that roamed the highlands and once supplied protein for passing sailing vessels, Meat Cove feels like the end of the earth. It lies at the end of a daunting 12-km (7-mi) mostly unpaved road along a precipitous cliff marked by sudden switchbacks. It's spectacular, but for the adventurous only. To get here, leave the Cabot Trail at Cape North on the Bay St. Lawrence Road. At the foot of the hill leading into St. Margaret's, turn left and follow the sign to Capstick; that road leads to Meat Cove.

The **Meat Cove Campground** (☎ 902/383–2379), high on a cliff overlooking the ocean, attracts an adventurous crowd and is ideal for hiking, mountain biking, ocean swimming, and nature walks.

Lodging

$ 🏠 **Four Mile Beach Inn.** The view of Aspy Bay and the ridge of the highland mountains is spectacular from this large white historic house near Cabot's Landing. Canoeing and kayaking are possible from the small dock on the property. Rooms are clean and have a simple, country look to them. The suites have a kitchen, a private entrance, and a deck. ✉ R.R. 1, Box 3, B0C 1G0, ☎ 902/383–2282 or 888/503–5551, FAX 902/564–5877. 5 rooms, 2 suites. MC, V. Closed mid-Oct.–May. CP.

Outdoor Activities and Sports

Capt. Cox's Whale Watch (☎ 902/383–2981 or 888/346–5556, WEB www.aco.ca/captcox) offers several tours daily—weather permitting—July through August.

Ingonish

🏵 *113 km (70 mi) northeast of Chéticamp.*

Ingonish, one of the leading holiday destinations on the island, is actually several villages—Ingonish Centre, Ingonish Beach, South Ingonish Harbour, and Ingonish Ferry—on two bays, divided by a long narrow peninsula called Middle Head. Each bay has a sandy beach. At Ingonish Harbour, the popular local ski hill also offers ski lift rides in summer and fall. From the 1,000-ft summit, the view of Ingonish and the surrounding highlands is breathtaking.

OFF THE
BEATEN PATH

BIRD ISLANDS – From Big Bras d'Or, 100 km (62 mi) south of Ingonish, notice the small islands on the far side of the mouth of St. Ann's Bay: these are the Bird Islands, breeding grounds for Atlantic puffins, black guillemots, razor-billed auks, and cormorants. Boat tours are offered several times daily mid-May to mid-September from **Bird Island Boat Tour** (☎ 902/674–2384). Landing on the islands is forbidden, however.

Dining and Lodging

$$$$ ✕⊞ **Keltic Lodge.** Spread across cliffs overlooking the ocean, the provincially owned Keltic Lodge sits on the Cabot Trail in Cape Breton Highlands National Park. The setting is glorious, with stunning views of Cape Smokey and the surrounding highlands. Guests can choose among the Main Lodge, Inn at Keltic, and two- or four-bedroom cottages. A wide variety of activities is available, including live professional theater and golfing on the world-class Highlands Links. Seafood stars in the Purple Thistle Dining Room. ⊠ *Middle Head Peninsula, Ingonish Beach B0C 1L0,* ☎ *902/285–2880 or 877/375–6343,* WEB *www.signatureresorts.com. 101 rooms. 2 restaurants, pool, golf, hiking, beaches, theater. AE, D, DC, MC, V. Closed Nov.–mid-May. MAP.*

$–$$ ⊞ **Castle Rock Country Inn.** Surrounded by an idyllic setting of mountains and ocean, and offering the tranquility of a library and lounge, the Castle Rock provides an excellent environment for contemplation and relaxation. This Georgian-style inn is right on the Cabot Trail in Ingonish Ferry. ⊠ *39339 Cabot Trail, B0C 1L0,* ☎ *902/285–2700 or 888/884–7625,* FAX *902/285–2525,* WEB *www.ingonish.com/castlerock. 15 rooms. Dining room, library. AE, MC, V.*

$ ⊞ **Atlantic Beach Resort.** Direct beach access and a large outdoor pool are two of the attractions at this standard motel. Visit the gift shop for a selection of locally made souvenirs and handicrafts. ⊠ *Cabot Trail, Box 187 B0C 1K0,* ☎ *902/285–2519 or 888/821–5551,* FAX *902/285–2538,* WEB *www.atlanticbeachresort.com. 32 rooms. Dining room, pool, beach. MC, V. Closed Nov.–Apr.*

Englishtown

65 km (40 mi) south of Ingonish on Hwy. 312.

A short (five-minute) ferry ride heads from Jersey Cove across St. Ann's Bay to Englishtown, home of the celebrated Cape Breton Giant, Angus MacAskill. Ferries run 24 hours a day; the fare is $3 per car.

The **Giant MacAskill Museum** holds artifacts of the 7'9" man who traveled with P. T. Barnum's troupe in the 1800s. His remains are buried in the local cemetery nearby. ⊠ *Hwy. 312,* ☎ *902/929–2875.* ⊠ *$1.50.* ☉ *Mid-June–mid-Sept., daily 9–6.*

South Gut St. Ann's

12 km (7 mi) south of Jersey Cove.

Settled by the Highland Scots, South Gut St. Ann's is home to North America's only Gaelic College. The **Great Hall of the Clans** (✉ Rte. 205, ☎ 902/295-3411, WEB www.gaeliccollege.edu) at Gaelic College depicts Scottish history and has an account of the Great Migration. The college offers courses in Gaelic language and literature, Scottish music and dancing, weaving, and other Scottish arts. There's also a Scottish gift shop. Admission to the Great Hall is $2.50, daily mid-June to early September.

From the Gaelic College, you can follow the Cabot Trail as it meanders along the hills that rim St. Ann's Bay. The 30-km (19-mi) stretch between St. Ann's and Indian Brook is home to a collection of fine crafts shops.

Baddeck

45 *20 km (12 mi) south of South Gut St. Ann's.*

Baddeck, the most highly developed tourist center on Cape Breton, has more than 1,000 motel beds, a golf course, fine gift shops, and many restaurants. This was also the summer home of Alexander Graham Bell until he died here at the age of 75. In summer the town celebrates the **Centre Bras d'Or Festival of the Arts,** which offers live music and drama every evening. The annual **regatta** of the Bras d'Or Yacht Club is held the first week of August. Sailing tours and charters are available, as are bus tours along the Cabot Trail. On the waterfront, the **Rose Cottage Gallery** overflows with folk art and local crafts.

In summer, a free passenger ferry shuttles between the government wharf and the sandy **Kidston Island beach** by the lighthouse.

The **Celtic Colors International Festival** (☎ 902/295-1414), 10 days spanning the second and third weekends in October, draws the world's best Celtic performers at the height of autumn splendor. International stars such as the Chieftains, the Bumblebees, and Archie Fisher join home-grown performers like Rita MacNeil and Mary Jane Lamond for 30-plus performances in two dozen venues scattered around the island. The cost for each performance is $5 to $15. Workshops and seminars covering all aspects of Gaelic language, lore, history, crafts, and culture fill the festival days.

★ ☾ The **Alexander Graham Bell National Historic Site of Canada** explores Bell's inventions. Experiments, kite making, and other hands-on activities are designed for children. From films, artifacts, and photographs, you learn how ideas led Bell to create man-carrying kites, airplanes, and a marine record-setting hydrofoil boat. The site has reduced services October through May. ✉ *Chebucto St.,* ☎ *902/295-2069,* WEB *www.parkscanada.gc.ca.* ☒ *$4.25.* ☾ *July–Aug. daily 9–8, June and Sept. daily 9–7, Oct.–May daily 9–5.*

At the **Wagmatcook Culture & Heritage Centre,** 16 km (10 mi) west of the town of Baddeck, the ancient history and rich traditions of the native Mi'Kmaq are demonstrated. Mi'Kmaq guides provide interpretations and cultural entertainment. The on-site restaurant highlights traditional foods such as moose and eel dishes, as well as more-contemporary choices. The craft shop has local native products. ✉ *Wagmatcook First Nation, Rte. 105,* ☎ *902/295-2598.* ☒ *$2.* ☾ *Mid-May–Oct.*

Dining and Lodging

$$–$$$$ ✕🏨 **Inverary Resort.** On the shores of the magnificent Bras d'Or Lake, this resort has stunning views and lots of activities. You can choose from cozy pine-paneled cottages, modern hotel units, or the elegant 100-year-old main lodge; some rooms have fireplaces. There's boating and swimming in close proximity to the village, but the resort remains tranquil. Dining choices are the casual Lakeside Café and the elegant main dining room ($$–$$$). ✉ *Hwy. 205 and Shore Rd., Box 190, B0E 1B0,* ☎ *902/295–3500 or 800/565–5660,* 𝔽𝔸𝕏 *902/295–3527,* 🌐 *www.InveraryResort.com. 125 rooms, 14 cottages. Restaurant, café, pub, indoor pool, sauna, 3 tennis courts, boating, playground. AE, D, MC, V.*

$$–$$$ 🏨 **Auberge Gisele's Inn.** An inn and motel share lovely landscaped flower gardens and overlook the Bras d'Or Lake. The atmosphere is one of tasteful hospitality. Some rooms have fireplaces. The chef prepares breakfast, lunch, and dinner by reservation in the dining room. You can also enjoy a cocktail in the smoke-free lounge and art gallery. ✉ *387 Shore Rd., B0E 1B0,* ☎ *902/295–2849,* 𝔽𝔸𝕏 *902/295–2033,* 🌐 *www.giseles.com. 75 rooms, 3 suites. Dining room, in-room data ports, sauna, gym, bicycles, coin laundry. MC, V. Closed Nov.–Apr.*

$$ 🏨 **Duffus House.** Facing the harbor, this quiet inn is furnished with antiques and has cozy sitting rooms and a secluded, well-tended garden. The Continental breakfast is substantial. Smoking isn't permitted. ✉ *108 Water St., Box 427, B0E 1B0,* ☎ *902/295–2172,* 🌐 *www.capebretonet.com/Baddeck/DuffusHouse. 4 rooms, 3 suites. Dock, library. V. Closed mid-Oct.–end of May. CP.*

$ 🏨 **Bain's Heritage House B&B.** In the center of Baddeck sits this tastefully appointed historic home built in the 1850s. On cooler evenings you can relax in front of the fire in the sitting room. ✉ *121 Twining St., B0E 1B0,* ☎ *902/295–1069. 3 rooms, 1 with bath. MC, V. BP.*

Outdoor Activities and Sports

The **Bell Bay Golf Club** (☎ 902/295–1333 or 800/565–3077, 🌐 www.bellbaygolfclub.com) has panoramic views from almost every hole on its par-72, 18-hole course. Bell Bay has the largest practice facilities in Atlantic Canada.

Iona

46 *56 km (35 mi) south of Baddeck.*

Iona, where some residents still speak Gaelic, is the site of a living-history museum. To get here from Baddeck, take Trans-Canada Highway 105 to Exit 6, which leads to Little Narrows, where you can take a ferry to the Washabuck Peninsula. The **Highland Village Museum** (✉ Hwy. 223, ☎ 902/725–2272, 🌐 www.highlandvillage.museum. gov.ns.ca), now part of the Nova Scotia Museum family, is set high on a mountainside, with a spectacular view of Bras d'Or Lake and the narrow Barra Strait. The village's 10 historic buildings were assembled from all over Cape Breton to depict the Highland Scots' way of life from their origins in the Hebrides to the present day. Among the staff at this museum are a smith in the blacksmith shop and a clerk in the store. The complex also houses Roots Cape Breton, a genealogy and family-history center for Cape Breton Island. The village is open from mid-May to mid-October, daily 9–6; admission is $5.

Dining and Lodging

$–$$ ✕🏨 **Highland Heights Inn.** The rural surroundings, the Scottish home-style cooking served near the restaurant's huge stone fireplace, and the view of the lake substitute nicely for the Scottish Highlands. The inn is on a hillside beside the Nova Scotia Highland Village, overlooking

Iona. The salmon (or any fish in season), fresh-baked oatcakes, and homemade desserts are good choices. ✉ *4115 Hwy. 223, Iona B2C 1A3,* ☎ *902/725–2360 or 800/660–8122,* FAX *902/725–2800,* WEB *highlandheightsinn.com. 32 rooms. Restaurant, no-smoking rooms. D, MC, V. Closed mid-Oct.–mid-May.*

En Route The Barra Strait Bridge joins Iona to Grand Narrows. The East Bay route runs through the friendly Mi'Kmaq village of **Eskasoni.** It is the largest native community in the province and has a fascinating cultural heritage.

Sydney

🜨 *60 km (37 mi) northeast of Iona.*

The heart of Nova Scotia's second-largest urban cluster, Sydney is known as industrial Cape Breton. It encompasses villages, unorganized districts, and a half dozen towns—most of which sprang up around the coal mines, which fed the steel plant at Sydney. These are warm-hearted, interesting communities with a diverse ethnic population that includes Ukrainians, Welsh, Poles, Lebanese, West Indians, and Italians. Most residents are descendants of the miners and steelworkers who arrived a century ago when the area was booming.

Sydney has the island's only real airport, its only university, and a lively entertainment scene that specializes in Cape Breton music. It is also a departure point—fast ferries leave from North Sydney for Newfoundland, and scheduled air service to Newfoundland and the French islands of St-Pierre and Miquelon departs from Sydney Airport.

Dining and Lodging

$$ ✕🏨 **Gowrie House.** An unexpected jewel on the Shore Road between
★ North Sydney and Sydney Mines and five minutes from the ferry to Newfoundland, Gowrie House is shaded by towering trees and surrounded by gardens and flowering shrubs. Cherry trees supply the main ingredient for chilled black-cherry soup served in one of Nova Scotia's finest restaurants ($45 prix fixe). Antiques, fine art, and exquisite china add to the elegance. The main house has six rooms; the secluded garden house holds four more; and the caretaker's cottage provides deluxe private accommodation. Whether you stay overnight or are a guest for dinner only, dinner reservations are essential (best to book a week ahead). ✉ *139 Shore Rd., Sydney Mines B1V 1A6,* ☎ *902/544–1050 or 800/372–1115,* WEB *www.gowriehouse.com. 11 rooms. Restaurant. AE, MC, V. BP.*

$$–$$$ 🏨 **Delta Sydney.** This hotel is on the harbor, beside the yacht club and close to the center of town. Guest rooms are attractive and have harbor views. The restaurant specializes in seafood and Continental cuisine. ✉ *300 Esplanade, B1P 1A7,* ☎ *902/562–7500 or 800/565–1001,* FAX *902/562–3023,* WEB *www.deltasydney.com. 152 rooms. Restaurant, lounge, indoor pool, sauna, gym. AE, DC, MC, V.*

$ 🏨 **Rockinghorse Inn.** Alexander Graham Bell was a frequent guest at this historic property, which is beautifully decorated with antiques. A small dining room called the Jack Pitman Library is available for your private use by reservation only. Everything on the menu is made from scratch; the decadent desserts, prepared by the inn's owner, are the main attraction. ✉ *259 Kings Rd., B1S 1A7,* ☎ *902/539–2696 or 888/884–1010,* FAX *902/539–2696,* WEB *www.rockinghorse-inn.com. 7 rooms, 4 with bath. Dining room. MC, V.*

Nightlife and the Arts

Many fiddlers appear at the week-long **Big Pond Concert** (✉ Rte. 4, 1 km, or ½ mi, east of Rita's Tea Room, ☎ 902/828–2373) in mid-July. At the **Casino Nova Scotia** (✉ 525 George St., ☎ 902/563–7777), you can try the slot machines, roulette, or gaming tables or enjoy live entertainment. The **University College of Cape Breton** (⊠ 1250 Grand Lake Rd., ☎ 902/539–5300) has many facilities open to the public, such as the Boardmore Playhouse and the island's only public art gallery.

Glace Bay

48 *21 km (13 mi) east of Sydney.*

★ A coal mining town and fishing port, Glace Bay has a rich history of industrial struggle. The **Glace Bay Miners' Museum** houses exhibits and artifacts illustrating the hard life of early miners in Cape Breton's undersea collieries. Former miners guide you down into the damp recesses of the mine and tell stories of working all day where the sun never shines. ⊠ *42 Birkley St., Quarry Point,* ☎ *902/849–4522,* WEB *www.cbnet.ns.ca.* ☒ *$4.50 museum, $8 museum and mine tour.* ☉ *June–Sept., Wed.– Mon. 10–6, Tues. 10–7; Sept.–June, weekdays 9–4.*

The **Marconi National Historic Site of Canada** commemorates the site at Table Head where in 1901 Guglielmo Marconi built four tall wooden towers and beamed the first wireless messages across the Atlantic Ocean. An interpretive trail leads to the foundations of the original towers and transmitter buildings. The visitor center has large models of the towers as well as artifacts and photographs chronicling the radio pioneer's life and work. ⊠ *Timmerman St., Hwy. 255,* ☎ *902/842–2530,* WEB *www.parkscanada.gc.ca.* ☒ *Free.* ☉ *June–mid-Sept., daily 10–6.*

Nightlife and the Arts

Glace Bay's grand Victorian-style **Savoy Theatre** (⊠ 116 Commercial St., ☎ 902/842–1577), built in 1927, is home to a variety of live drama, comedy, and music performances.

Louisbourg

49 *55 km (34 mi) south of Glace Bay.*

★ Though best known as the home of the largest historical reconstruction in North America, Louisbourg is also an important fishing community with a lovely harborfront. The **Fortress of Louisbourg National Historic Site of Canada** may be the most remarkable site in Cape Breton. After the French were forced out of mainland Nova Scotia in 1713, they established their headquarters here in a walled and fortified town on a low point of land at the mouth of Louisbourg Harbour. The fortress was twice captured, once by New Englanders and once by the British; after the second siege, in 1758, it was razed. Its capture was critical in ending the French empire in America. A quarter of the original town has been rebuilt on its foundations, just as it was in 1744, before the first siege. Costumed actors re-create the activities of the original inhabitants; you can watch a military drill, see nails and lace being made, and eat food prepared from 18th-century recipes in the town's two inns. Plan on spending at least a half day. Louisbourg tends to be chilly, so pack a warm sweater or windbreaker. ⊠ *Hwy. 22,* ☎ *902/ 733–2280 or 800/565–9464,* WEB *www.parkscanada.gc.ca.* ☒ *$11.* ☉ *June and Sept., daily 9:30–5; July–Aug., daily 9–6.*

At the **Sydney and Louisbourg Railway Museum,** a restored 1895 railroad station exhibits the history of the S&L Railway, railroad technology, and marine shipping. The rolling stock includes a baggage car, coach, and caboose. ⊠ *7336 Main St.,* ☎ *902/733–2157.* ☒ *Free.* ☉ *Mid-May–June and Sept.–mid-Oct., daily 9–5; July–Aug., daily 8–8.*

Both live theater performances and traditional Cape Breton music are served up at the **Louisbourg Playhouse,** a 17th-century–style theater, which was originally constructed as part of a Disney movie set. ✉ *11 Aberdeen St.,* ☎ *902/733–2996 or 888/733–2787,* WEB *www.artscapebreton.com.* ⏱ *Mid-June–Oct.*

Dining and Lodging

$–$$$ ✕ **Lobster Kettle Restaurant.** Perched on the wharf, Lobster Kettle offers a pleasant view of the Louisbourg Harbour as well as fine seafood and a variety of other dishes. A huge array of fresh salads awaits you at the all-you-can-eat salad bar. ✉ *Bottom of Strathcona St.,* ☎ *902/733–2723. MC, V.*

$–$$$ 🏨 **Louisbourg Harbour Inn.** In the center of the community, overlooking a fishing wharf, this renovated century-old sea captain's house affords ocean views from most rooms and balconies. All rooms have hardwood floors, high ceilings, queen-size bed, and private bath (some with whirlpool tubs). ✉ *9 Lower Warren St., B1C 1G6,* ☎ *902/733–3222 or 888/888–8466,* WEB *www.louisbourg.com/louisbourgharbourinn. 8 rooms. MC, V. Closed mid-Oct.–May. CP.*

$–$$ 🏨 **Cranberry Cove Inn.** This fully renovated home from the early 1900s is within walking distance of the Fortress of Louisbourg National Historic Park. Inquire about the theme guest rooms, some of which have jet tubs and gas fireplaces. Enjoy a fine meal in an antiques-filled dining room. Smoking is prohibited. ✉ *12 Wolfe St., B1C 2J2,* ☎ *902/733–2171 or 800/929–0222,* FAX *902/733–2449,* WEB *www.louisbourg. com/cranberrycove. 7 rooms. Dining room. AE, MC, V. CP.*

Big Pond

50 km (31 mi) west of Louisbourg.

This little town comprises just a few houses, and one of them is the home of singer-songwriter Rita MacNeil, who operates **Rita's Tea Room.** Originally a one-room schoolhouse, the building has been expanded to accommodate the multitude of visitors who come to sample Rita's Tea Room Blend Tea, which is served along with a fine selection of sandwiches and baked goods. You can visit a display room of Rita's awards and photographs and browse through her gift shop. ✉ *Hwy. 4,* ☎ *902/828–2667.* ⏱ *June–mid-Oct., daily 9–7.*

En Route Highway 4 rolls along Bras d'Or Lake, sometimes by the shore and sometimes in the hills. At **St. Peter's** the Atlantic Ocean is connected with the Bras d'Or Lake by the century-old St. Peter's Canal, still used by pleasure craft and fishing vessels. From St. Peter's to Port Hawkesbury the population is largely Acadian French.

Arichat

🔟 *62 km (38 mi) southwest of Big Pond.*

The principal town of Isle Madame, Arichat is a 27-square-km (10-square-mi) island named for Madame de Maintenon, second wife of Louis XIV. It was an important shipbuilding and trading center during the 19th century, and some fine old houses from that period still remain. Arichat was once the seat of the local Catholic diocese. **Notre Dame de l'Assumption** church, built in 1837, still retains the grandeur of its former cathedral status. Its bishop's palace is now a law office. The two cannons overlooking the harbor were installed after the town was sacked by John Paul Jones during the American Revolution.

To get here from Big Pond, take Highway 247 to Highway 320, which leads through Poulamon and D'Escousse and overlooks Lennox Passage, with its spangle of islands. Highway 206 meanders through the low hills to a maze of land and water at West Arichat. Together, the two routes encircle the island, meeting at Arichat. The island lends itself to biking, as most roads glide gently along the shore. A good half-day hike leads to Gros Nez, the "large nose" that juts into the sea.

LeNoir Forge (⊠ Hwy. 320, off Hwy. 4, ☎ 902/226–9364) is a restored French 18th-century stone blacksmith shop open June through August, daily 9–5.

OFF THE BEATEN PATH	**LITTLE ANSE –** With its red bluffs, cobble shores, tiny harbor, and brightly painted houses, Little Anse may be particularly attractive for artists and photographers. The town is at the southeastern tip of Isle Madame.

NOVA SCOTIA A TO Z

To research prices, get advice from other travelers, and book travel arrangements, visit www.fodors.com.

AIR TRAVEL

Air Atlantic, Air Canada, airNova, Canada 3000, and Northwest Air provide service to Halifax and Sydney from various cities. Air travel within the area is very limited. Air Nova provides regional service to other provinces and to Sydney.

AIRPORTS

The Halifax International Airport (YHZ) is 40 km (25 mi) northeast of downtown Halifax. Sydney Airport (YQY) is 13 km (8 mi) east of Sydney.

➤ AIRPORT INFORMATION: **Halifax International Airport** (⊠ 1 Bell Blvd., Elmsdale, ☎ 902/873–1223). **Sydney Airport** (⊠ 280 Airport Rd., ☎ 902/564–7720).

AIRPORT TRANSFERS

Limousine and taxi services, as well as car rentals, are available at Halifax and Sydney airports. Airport bus service to Halifax and Dartmouth hotels costs $20 round-trip, $12 one-way. Airbus has regular bus service from the airport to most major hotels in Halifax. Regular taxi fare to Halifax is $35 each way, but if you book ahead with Ace–Y, the fare is $22.70—if you share your car with another passenger. The trip takes 30–40 minutes.

➤ CONTACTS: **Ace–Y** (☎ 902/422–4437). **Airbus** (☎ 902/873–2091).

BOAT AND FERRY TRAVEL

Car ferries connect Nova Scotia with Maine and New Brunswick: Prince of Fundy Cruises sails from Portland, Maine, to Yarmouth, Nova Scotia. Bay Ferries Ltd. sails from Bar Harbor, Maine, to Yarmouth, and from Saint John, New Brunswick, to Digby, Nova Scotia. The Bar Harbor–Yarmouth service uses a high-speed catamaran, cutting the trip from 6 to 2¾ hours. The catamaran has become hugely popular recently, so reserve ahead.

From May through December, Northumberland Ferries operates between Caribou, Nova Scotia, and Wood Islands, Prince Edward Island. Marine Atlantic operates year-round between North Sydney and Port aux Basques, on the west coast of Newfoundland, and June through September between North Sydney and Argentia, on Newfoundland's east coast.

Metro Transit runs passenger ferries from the Halifax Ferry Terminal at Lower Water Street to Alderney Gate in downtown Dartmouth and to Woodside Terminal (near Dartmouth Hospital) on the hour and half hour from 6:30 AM to 11:57 PM. Ferries are more frequent during weekday rush hours; they also operate on Sunday in summer (June through September). Free transfers are available from the ferry to the bus system (and vice versa). A single crossing costs $1.50 and is worth it for the up-close view of both waterfronts.

➤ BOAT AND FERRY INFORMATION: **Bay Ferries Ltd.** (☎ 902/566–3838 or 888/249–7245). **Marine Atlantic** (☎ 902/794–5254, 709/772–7701, or 800/341–7981). **Metro Transit** (☎ 902/421–6600). **Northumberland Ferries** (☎ 902/566–3838 or 800/565–0201). **Prince of Fundy Cruises** (☎ 800/341–7540 in Canada; 800/482–0955 in Maine).

BUS TRAVEL

Because of conflicting schedules, getting into Nova Scotia by bus can be problematic. Greyhound Lines, from New York, and Voyageur, from Montréal, connect with Scotia Motor Tours (SMT), through New Brunswick. SMT links (inconveniently) with Acadian Lines and provides interurban service within Nova Scotia. Airbus runs between the Halifax International Airport and major hotels in Halifax and Dartmouth. Shuttle van services with convenient transportation between Halifax and Sydney include Cape Shuttle Service and Scotia Shuttle Service.

There are a number of small, regional bus services; however, connections are not always convenient. Outside of Halifax there are no innercity bus services. For information, call Nova Scotia Tourism.

Metro Transit provides bus service throughout Halifax and Dartmouth, the town of Bedford, and (to a limited extent) the county of Halifax. The base fare is $1.65, exact change only.

➤ BUS INFORMATION: **Acadian Lines** (☎ 902/454–9321). **Airbus** (☎ 902/873–2091). **Cape Shuttle Service** (☎ 800/349–1698). **Greyhound Lines** (☎ 800/231–2222). **Metro Transit** (☎ 902/421–6600). **Nova Scotia Tourism** (☎ 902/424–5000 or 800/565–0000). **Scotia Motor Tours** (☎ 506/458–6000). **Scotia Shuttle Service** (☎ 877/898–5883). **Voyageur Inc.** (☎ 613/238–5900).

CAR RENTAL

Halifax is the most convenient place from which to begin a driving tour. It is recommended that you book a car through your travel agent. Avis, Budget, Hertz, National Tilden, and Thrifty have locations in Halifax.

➤ MAJOR AGENCIES: **Avis** (✉ 5600 Sackville St., Halifax, ☎ 902/492–2847; 902/429–0963 airport). **Budget** (✉ 1558 Hollis St., Halifax, ☎ 902/492–7500 or 800/268–8900). **Hertz** (✉ Halifax Sheraton, 1919 Upper Water St., Halifax, ☎ 902/421–1763; 902/873–3700 airport). **National Tilden** (✉ 2173 Barrington St., Halifax, ☎ 902/422–4439; 902/873–3505 airport). **Thrifty** (✉ 6419 Lady Hammond, Halifax, ☎ 902/422–4455; 902/873–3527 airport).

CAR TRAVEL

Most highways in the province lead to Halifax and Dartmouth. Highways 3/103, 7, 2/102, and 1/101 terminate in the twin cities. Many of the roads in rural Nova Scotia require attentive driving, as they are not well signed, are narrow, and do not always have a paved shoulder. They are generally well surfaced and offer exquisite scenery.

Motorists can enter Nova Scotia through the narrow neck of land that connects the province to New Brunswick and the mainland. The Trans-Canada Highway (Highway 2 in New Brunswick) becomes Highway 104 on crossing the Nova Scotia border at Amherst. It is now possible to drive over the Confederation Bridge from Prince Edward Island into New Brunswick near the Nova Scotia border. Otherwise, car ferries dock at Yarmouth (from Maine), Digby (from New Brunswick), Caribou (from Prince Edward Island), and North Sydney (from Newfoundland).

The province has 10 designated "Scenic Travelways," identified by road-side signs with icons that correspond with trail names. These lovely routes are also shown on tourist literature (maps and the provincial *Travel Guide*). Nova Scotia Tourism provides information.

RULES OF THE ROAD

Highways numbered from 100 to 199 are all-weather, limited-access roads, with 100- to 110-kph (62- to 68-mph) speed limits. The last two digits usually match the number of an older trunk highway along the same route, numbered from 1 to 99. Thus, Highway 102, between Halifax and Truro, matches the older Highway 2, between the same towns. Roads numbered from 200 to 399 are secondary roads that usually link villages. Unless otherwise posted, the speed limit on these and any roads other than the 100-series highways is 80 kph (50 mph).

EMERGENCIES

➤ CONTACTS: **Ambulance, fire, or police** (☎ 911). **Cape Breton Regional Hospital** (✉ 1482 George St., Sydney, ☎ 902/567–8000). **Queen Elizabeth II Health Sciences Centre** (✉ 5909 Jubilee Rd., Halifax, ☎ 902/473–2799 switchboard; 902/473–2043 emergencies).

LODGING

Nova Scotia has a computerized system called Check In that provides information and makes reservations with more than 700 hotels, motels, inns, campgrounds, and car-rental agencies.
➤ TOLL-FREE NUMBERS: **Check In** (☎ 902/425–5781 or 800/565–0000).

OUTDOORS AND SPORTS

BIKING

Bicycle Tours in Nova Scotia ($7) is published by Bicycle Nova Scotia. Atlantic Canada Cycling can provide information on tours and rentals.
➤ CONTACTS: **Atlantic Canada Cycling** (☎ 902/423–2453). **Bicycle Nova Scotia** (✉ 5516 Spring Garden Rd., Box 3010, Halifax B3J 3G6, ☎ 902/425–5450).

BIRD-WATCHING

Nova Scotia is on the Atlantic flyway and is an important staging point for migratory species. A fine illustrated book, *Birds of Nova Scotia,* by Robie Tufts, is a must on every ornithologist's reading list. The Nova Scotia Museum organizes walks and lectures for people interested in viewing local bird life in the Halifax area.
➤ CONTACTS: **Nova Scotia Museum** (✉ 1747 Summer St., ☎ 902/424–6475).

CANOEING

Especially good canoe routes are within Kejimkujik National Park. Canoeing information is available from Canoe NS. The publication *Canoe Routes of Nova Scotia* and route maps are available from the Nova Scotia Government Bookstore.
➤ CONTACTS: **Canoe NS** (☎ 902/425–5450 Ext. 316). **Nova Scotia Government Bookstore** (✉ 1700 Granville St., Halifax, ☎ 902/424–7580).

FISHING

You are required by law to have a valid Nova Scotia fishing license for both freshwater and saltwater fishing. For information about licenses, contact the Department of Natural Resources. Fishing charters are plentiful; contact the Nova Scotia Department of Fisheries and Aquaculture for information.

➤ CONTACTS: **Department of Natural Resources** (☎ 902/424–4467). **Nova Scotia Department of Fisheries and Aquaculture** (☎ 902/485–5056).

GOLF
➤ CONTACTS: **Golf Nova Scotia** (☎ 800/565–0001, WEB www. golfnovascotia.com).

HIKING
The province has a wide variety of trails along the rugged coastline and inland through forest glades, which enable you to experience otherwise inaccessible scenery, wildlife, and vegetation. *Hiking Trails of Nova Scotia* ($12.95) is available through Gooselane Editions.
➤ CONTACTS: **Gooselane Editions** (✉ 469 King St., Fredericton, NB E3R 1E5, ☎ 506/450–4251).

SKIING
➤ CONTACTS: **Nova Scotia Ski Area Association** (☎ 902/798–9501).

SNOWMOBILING
Visiting snowmobilers can get information on trails, activities, clubs, and dealers through the Snowmobile Association of Nova Scotia.
➤ CONTACTS: **Snowmobile Association of Nova Scotia** (☎ 902/425–5450).

TAXIS
In Halifax, rates begin at about $2.50 and increase based on mileage and time. A crosstown trip should cost $6 to $7, depending on traffic. Hailing a taxi can be difficult, but there are taxi stands at major hotels and shopping malls. Most Haligonians simply phone for a taxi service.
➤ TAXI COMPANIES: **Casino Taxi** (☎ 902/429–6666). **Yellow Cab** (☎ 902/420–0000 or 902/422–1551).

TOURS
BOAT TOURS
Boat tours have become very popular in all regions of the province. Murphy's on the Water sails various vessels: *Harbour Queen I*, a paddle wheeler; *Haligonian III*, an enclosed motor launch; *Stormy Weather I*, a 40-ft Cape Islander (fishing boat); and *Mar II*, a 75-ft sailing ketch. All operate from mid-May to late October from berths at 1751 Lower Water Street on Cable Wharf next to the Historic Properties in Halifax. Some tours include lunch, dinner, or entertainment. A cash bar may also be available. Costs vary, but a basic tour of the Halifax Harbour ranges from $15 to $25.

Harbour Hopper Tours offers a unique amphibious tour of historic downtown Halifax and the Halifax Harbour.
➤ CONTACTS: **Harbour Hopper Tours** (☎ 902/490–8687). **Murphy's on the Water** (☎ 902/420–1015).

BUS AND RICKSHAW TOURS
Gray Line Sightseeing and Cabana Tours run coach tours through Halifax, Dartmouth, and Peggy's Cove. Halifax Double Decker Tours offers two-hour tours on double-decker buses that leave daily from Historic Properties in Halifax.

In Halifax, Yellow Cab provides clean, comfortable cars with eloquent, amicable drivers who are well versed in local history and lore. As well as local tours, day trips to locations such as Wolfville or Peggy's Cove are possible with prior arrangement. Prices vary, but you should be sure to set a fee with the tour guide before you begin.

Greater Halifax Rickshaw Service offers intimate narrated tours of downtown Halifax.

➤ CONTACTS: **Cabana Tours** (☎ 902/423–6066). **Gray Line Sightseeing** (☎ 902/454–8279). **Greater Halifax Rickshaw Service** (☎ 902/455–6677). **Halifax Double Decker Tours** (☎ 902/420–1155). **Yellow Cab** (☎ 902/420–0000 or 902/422–1551).

SPECIALIZED TOURS

Explore Halifax's rich tradition of stories of pirates, haunted houses, buried treasure, and ghosts with Halifax Ghost Walk. Tours begin at the Old Town Clock at 8:30 PM on any scheduled night.

➤ CONTACTS: **Halifax Ghost Walk** (☎ 902/469–6716).

TRAIN TOURS

VIA Rail conducts weekly first-class guided rail tours between Halifax and Sydney from May through mid-October.

➤ CONTACTS: **VIA Rail** (☎ 800/561–3949).

VISITOR INFORMATION

Nova Scotia Tourism publishes a wide range of literature, including an invaluable annual travel guide called the *Nova Scotia Doers and Dreamers Guide.* Call to have it mailed to you.

Visiting pilots can obtain aviation-related information for the flying tourist from the Aviation Council of Nova Scotia.

➤ TOURIST INFORMATION: **Aviation Council of Nova Scotia** (✉ Box 100, Debert B0M 1G0, ☎ 902/895–1143). **Nova Scotia Tourism** (✉ Box 130, Halifax B3J 2M7, ☎ 902/424–5000 or 800/565–0000). **Nova Scotia Tourism Information Centre** (✉ Old Red Store at Historic Properties, Halifax, ☎ 902/424–4248). **Tourism Halifax & Nova Scotia Tourism** (✉ International Visitors Centre, 1595 Barrington St., Halifax, ☎ 902/490–5946).

3 NEW BRUNSWICK

With the highest tides in the world carving a rugged coast and feeding more whales than you can imagine, New Brunswick can be a phenomenal adventure. White sandy beaches, lobsters in the pot, and cozy inns steeped in history make it easy to have a relaxing interlude, too. And with fine art galleries, museums, and a dual Acadian and Loyalist heritage, the province is an intriguing cultural destination.

By Ana Watts

NEW BRUNSWICK IS WHERE the great Canadian forest, sliced by sweeping river valleys and modern highways, meets the sea. It's an old place in New World terms, and the remains of a turbulent past are still evident in some of its quiet nooks. Near Moncton, for instance, wild strawberries perfume the air of the grassy slopes of Fort Beauséjour, where, in 1755, one of the last battles for possession of Acadia took place—the English finally overcoming the French. The dual heritage of New Brunswick (35% of its population is Acadian French) provides added spice. Other areas of the province were settled by the British and by Loyalists, American colonists who chose to live under British rule after the American Revolution. If you stay in both Acadian and Loyalist regions, a trip to New Brunswick can seem like two vacations in one.

In fact, a wide range of experience is possible in Canada's only officially bilingual province. For every gesture as grand as the giant rock formations carved by the Bay of Fundy tides, there is one as subtle as the gifted touch of a sculptor in her studio. For every experience as colorful as salmon and fiddleheads served at a church supper, there is another as low-key as the gentle waves of the Baie des Chaleurs. New Brunswick is the luxury of an inn with five stars, or the tranquillity of camping under a million.

At the heart of New Brunswick is the forest, which covers 85% of the province's entire area—nearly all its interior. The forest drives the economy, defines the landscape, and delights hikers, anglers, campers, and bird-watchers.

But New Brunswick's soul is the sea. The largest of Canada's three maritime provinces, New Brunswick is largely surrounded by coastline. The warm waters of the Baie des Chaleurs, Gulf of St. Lawrence, and Northumberland Strait lure swimmers to their sandy beaches. The chilly Bay of Fundy, with its monumental tides, draws breaching whales, whale-watchers, and kayakers.

In this part of the country traditions endure and family ties are strong. It is a strength born of adversity. Rich forests and oceans notwithstanding, the economy here is not robust. Over the years some of the best and the brightest have gone down the road to central and western Canada to make their marks. Now many bright young New Brunswickers are traveling down another road—the Information Highway, with its ever-expanding opportunities for them to stay at home and work "virtually" anywhere.

Pleasures and Pastimes

Beaches

There are two kinds of saltwater beaches in New Brunswick: warm and c-c-c-cold. The warm beaches are along the east coast. At Parlee, it's sand castles, sunscreen, and a little beach volleyball on the side. If sand and solitude are more your style, try Kouchibouguac National Park and its 26 km (16 mi) of beaches and dunes.

The cold beaches are on the Bay of Fundy, on the province's southern coast. The highest tides in the world (a *vertical* difference of as much as 48 ft) have carved some spectacular caves, crevices, and cliffs. There are some sandy beaches, and hardy souls do swim in the "invigorating" salt water. The extreme tides make it possible to explore rich tidal pools and walk on the flats at low tide. Beaches such as Cape Enrage combine salt air and opportunities for thrilling adventures such as rappeling. Others, such as the beach at Marys Point, where you can see thousands of semipalmated plovers take flight, allow you to observe awesome natural sights.

Dining

Cast your line almost anywhere in New Brunswick and you catch some kind of fish-and-chips. Just about any restaurant in any coastal community has its own great chowder, but catching fresh seafood usually means a trip to a better restaurant. New Brunswick's oysters, scallops, clams, crabs, mussels, lobsters, and salmon are worth it. Some seafood is available seasonally, but now that salmon is farmed extensively, this taste of heaven is available anytime, and the price is very reasonable. What New Brunswick serves best and most often is comfort food. Ham and scalloped potatoes, turkey dinners, pork chops, and even liver and onions are staples on many menus. The beer of choice is Moosehead, brewed in Saint John.

A spring delicacy is fiddleheads—emerging ostrich ferns that look like the curl at the end of a violin neck. These emerald gems are picked along riverbanks as the freshet recedes, then boiled and sprinkled with lemon juice or vinegar and butter, salt, and pepper. Summer ends with wild blueberries—delicately flavored dark pearls—sprinkled on cereal, baked in muffins, or stewed with dumplings in a grunt. New Brunswickers also eat dulse, a dried purple seaweed, as salty as potato chips and as compelling as peanuts, whenever the mood hits. You'll find it on Grand Manan Island, in the Old Saint John City Market, and in barrels for tasting at some seafood restaurants.

CATEGORY	COST*
$$$$	over $32
$$$	$22–$32
$$	$13–$21
$	under $13

*per person, in Canadian dollars, for a main course at dinner

Lodging

Among its more interesting options, New Brunswick has a number of officially designated Heritage Inns. These historically significant establishments run the gamut from elegant to homey; many have antique china and furnishings. Cottage clusters are springing up in coastal communities, and Saint John, Moncton, and Fredericton each have a link in first-rate hotel chains. Accommodations are at a premium in summer, so reserve ahead.

CATEGORY	COST*
$$$$	over $200
$$$	$150–$200
$$	$100–$150
$	under $100

*All prices are for a standard double room, excluding 15% harmonized sales tax (HST), in Canadian dollars.

Outdoor Activities and Sports

BIKING

Byroads, lanes, and an emerging network of multiuse trails run through small towns, along the ocean, and into the forest. Bikers can set out on their own or try a guided adventure.

FISHING

Dotted with freshwater lakes, crisscrossed with fish-laden rivers, and bordered by 1,129 km (700 mi) of seacoast, this province is one of Canada's natural treasures. Anglers are drawn by the bass fishing and such world-famous salmon rivers as the Miramichi. Commercial fishers often take visitors line fishing for groundfish.

GOLF

Golf is an increasingly popular sport, and a continuing program to upgrade even the best courses to championship and signature status, and to construct new courses, has enjoyed great success.

WHALE-WATCHING

One unforgettable New Brunswick experience is the sighting of a huge humpback, right whale, finback, or minke. Outfitters along the Bay of Fundy take people to see a variety of whales. Most trips run from May through September.

WINTER SPORTS

New Brunswick can get as much as 16 ft of snow each year, so winter fun often lasts well into spring. Dogsledding is taking off; ice-fishing communities pop up on many rivers; and tobogganing, skating, and snowshoeing are popular. Snowmobiling has boomed: there are more than 9,000 km (5,580 mi) of groomed, marked, and serviced snowmobile trails and dozens of snowmobile clubs hosting special events.

For cross-country skiers, New Brunswick has groomed trails at Mactaquac Provincial Park near Fredericton, Fundy National Park in Alma, and Kouchibouguac National Park between Moncton and Miramichi. Many communities and small hotels offer groomed trails, but skiers can also set off on their own. New Brunswick downhill ski areas usually operate mid-December through April. There are four ski hills—Farlagne, Crabbe, Poley, and Sugarloaf.

Shopping

Fine art galleries display and sell local artists' paintings and sculptures. Crafts galleries, shops, and fairs brim with jewelry, glass, pottery, clothing, furniture, and leather goods. Some of the province's better bookstores have sections devoted to New Brunswick authors. Saint John, Fredericton, and Moncton all have their share of fine art and crafts studios, galleries, and farmers' markets. Saint John has wonderful antiques, Fredericton can claim a bit of haute couture, and the Moncton area has the biggest malls. The shops in the resort town of St. Andrews are artistic, eclectic, and sophisticated.

Exploring New Brunswick

In recent years high-tech companies in New Brunswick have helped lead much of the world onto the Information Highway, but all that has done little to change settlement patterns. The population still clings to the original highways—rivers and ocean. In fact, the St. John River in the west and the Fundy and Acadian coasts in the south and east essentially encompass the province.

The Fundy Coast is phenomenal. Yachts, fishing boats, and tankers bob on the waves at high tide, then sit high and dry on the ocean floor when the tide goes out. The same tides force the mighty St. John River to reverse its flow in the old city of Saint John. The southwestern shores have spawned more than their share of world-class artists, authors, actors, and musicians. Maybe it's the Celtic influence; maybe it's the fog.

Along the Acadian Coast the water is warm, the sand is fine, and the accent is French—except in the middle. Where the Miramichi River meets the sea, there is an island of First Nations, English, Irish, and Scottish tradition that is unto itself, rich in folklore and legend. Many people here find their livelihood in the forests, in the mines, and on the sea.

The St. John River valley scenery is panoramic—gently rolling hills and sweeping forests, with just enough rocky gorges to keep it interesting. The native peoples, French, English, Scots, and Danes who live along the river ensure its culture is equally intriguing.

Numbers in the text correspond to numbers in the margin and on the New Brunswick, Downtown Saint John, and Fredericton maps.

Great Itineraries

IF YOU HAVE 4 DAYS

Plan to concentrate on one region if you have only a few days. Start on the Fundy Coastal Route. Art, history, nature, and seafood abound in the resort community of **St. Andrews by-the-Sea** ⑬. Whale-watching tours leave from the town wharf.

The Fundy Coastal Drive begins in **St. Stephen** ⑫ and winds about 100 km (62 mi) along the shore to the venerable city of **Saint John** ①–⑪, steeped in English and Irish traditions. From the Fundy Coastal Drive, Route 121 moves inland, up the Kennebecasis River past Sussex and meets Route 114; that leads back to the coast and **Fundy National Park** ⑱. Head up to **Cape Enrage** and **Hopewell Cape,** where the Fundy tides have sculpted gigantic flower-pot rocks that turn into islands at high tide. Finish the trip with **Moncton** ⑲, a microcosm of New Brunswick culture.

IF YOU HAVE 7 DAYS

With seven days for exploring you can add an Acadian Coastal experience. The official Acadian Coastal Drive Route is well marked from Aulac to Campbellton, a distance of about 400 km (248 mi). Head north from Moncton and explore the area around **Shediac** ㉑, famous for its lobsters and Parlee Beach. **Bouctouche** ㉒ is just beyond that, with its wonderful dunes and the make-believe land of La Sagouine. Another 50 km (31 mi) north is unspoiled **Kouchibouguac National Park** ㉓, which protects beaches, forests, and peat bogs. The coastal drive from Kouchibouguac Park to **Miramichi City** ㉔, about 75 km (47 mi), passes through several bustling fishing villages. Most of the communities are Acadian, but as you approach Miramichi City, English dominates again. A stopover here positions you perfectly to begin your exploration of the Acadian Peninsula.

It's only about 120 km (74 mi) from Miramichi City to **Caraquet** ㉕, but it might as well be a million. The entire peninsula is so different from the rest of the province it's like a trip to a foreign country: this is a romantic land with a dramatic history and an artistic flair. The Acadian Historical Village is a careful re-creation of the traditional Acadian way of life.

IF YOU HAVE 10 DAYS

With 10 days to explore New Brunswick you can hit most of the highlights. Your explorations of the Acadian Peninsula end in Bathurst, and now you begin the ride over to the western edge of the province. Drive the coast (114 km, or 71 mi) to Campbellton and nearby Sugarloaf Provincial Park. Route 17 from Campbellton to St-Léonard (159 km, or 99 mi) is breathtaking in the autumn, and the detour to Mount Carleton Provincial Park (with the highest peak in the Maritimes) is a must for those who value a wilderness experience.

When you reach St-Léonard, you are on the River Valley Scenic Drive, which begins upriver in St-Jacques and runs all the way down the St. John River valley and back to the city of Saint John. Begin with the New Brunswick Botanical Gardens in **St-Jacques,** just outside **Edmundston** ㉖. The drive from here to **Fredericton** ㉚–㉟ is about 275 km (171 mi) of panoramic pastoral and river scenery, including a dramatic

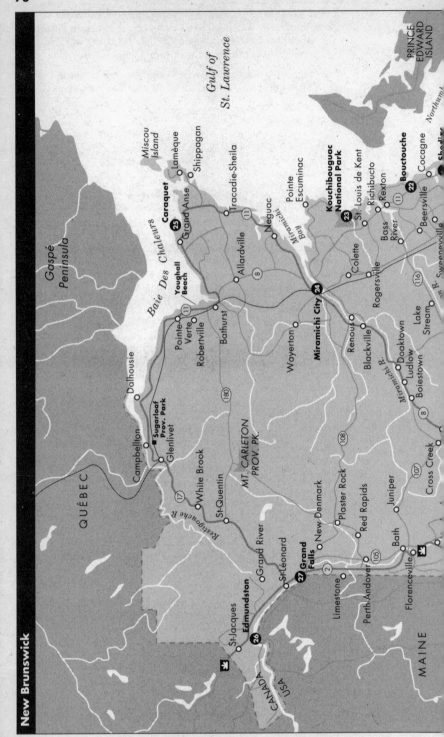

Gulf of
St. Lawrence

PRINCE
EDWARD
ISLAND

*Gaspé
Peninsula*

Miscou
Island

Lamèque

Shippagan

Tracadie-Sheila

Pointe
Escuminac

Kouchibouguac
National Park

Bouctouche

Cocagne

Grand Anse

Caraquet

25

11

Neguac

Miramichi
Bay

St. Louis de Kent

23

Richibucto

Rexton

22

Beersville

Baie Des Chaleurs

**Youghall
Beach**

Allardville

8

Colette

Bass
River

116

Pointe
Verte

Roberville

Bathurst

Miramichi City

24

Rogersville

Dalhousie

11

Wayerton

Renous

Blackville

Doaktown

Lake
Stream

Ludlow

Boiestown

8

**Sugarloaf
Prov. Park**

Glenlivet

180

MT. CARLETON
PROV. PK.

108

Cross Creek

107

Campbellton

QUÉBEC

White Brook

St-Quentin

New Denmark

Plaster Rock

Red Rapids

Juniper

Restigouche R.

17

Grand River

St-Léonard

**Grand
Falls**

27

2

Limestone

Perth-Andover

105

Bath

Florenceville

St-Jacques

Edmundston

26

MAINE

CANADA

USA

Miramichi R.

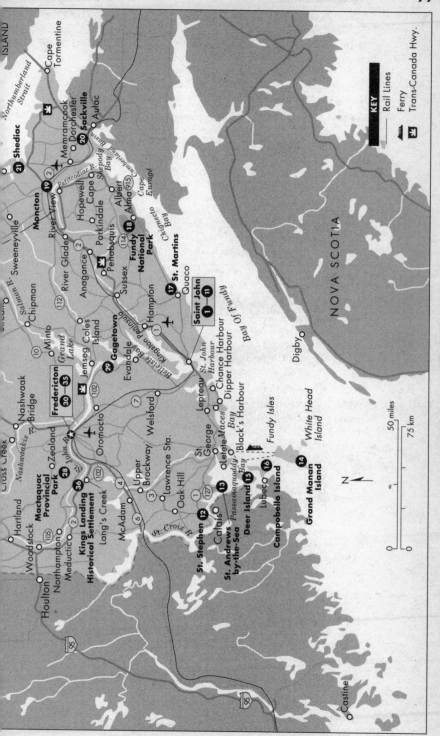

KEY

— Rail Lines

Ferry

Trans-Canada Hwy.

ISLAND

Northumberland Strait

Cape Tormentine

Memramcook

Dorchester

Sackville **20**

Aulac

21 Shediac

19 River View

Moncton

Petitcodiac R.

River Glade

Anagance

(2)

(112)

Salmon R. Sweeneyville

Chipman

Minto

(10)

Grand Lake

Jemseg

Coles Island

29 Gagetown

Evandale

Belleisle Bay

Kingston Peninsula

Hopewell

Cape

Parkindale

Penobsquis

Sussex

Hampton

Albert

18 Alma (915)

Cape Enrage

Fundy National Park

17 St. Martins

Quaco

Shepody Bay

Chignecto Bay

Waterside

Saint John 1 — 11

Lepreau

St. John Harbour

Chance Harbour

Dipper Harbour

Bay Of Fundy

NOVA SCOTIA

Digby

White Head Island

Fundy Isles

Cross Creek

Nashwaak Bridge

Nashwaakis R.

Zealond

28 St. John R.

Oromocto

(102)

(7)

Welsford

Wellsford

Lawrence Sta.

Oak Hill

St. George

Utete Maces Bay

Black's Harbour

Passamaquoddy Bay

16

15 Deer Island

Lubec

Campobello Island

14 Grand Manan Island

Fredericton 30 — 35

(102)

Kings Landing Historical Settlement

Mactaquac Provincial Park 36

Upper Brockway

(3)

(4)

(6)

(1)

(127)

13

12 St. Stephen

Calais

St. Andrews by-the-Sea

Long's Creek

McAdam

St. Croix R.

Woodstock

(105)

Northampton

Meductic

Hartland

Houlton

Cross Creek

(2)

(95)

(95)

Castine

N

50 miles

75 km

gorge and waterfall at **Grand Falls** ㉗. With its Gothic cathedral, Victorian architecture, museums, and riverfront pathways, Fredericton is a beautiful, historic, and cultural stopping place. Nearby **Kings Landing Historical Settlement** ㊱ provides a faithful depiction of life on the river in the last century. The drive from Fredericton to Saint John is just over 100 km (62 mi); about halfway between the two is the village of **Gagetown** ㉙, a must-see for those who love art and history.

When to Tour New Brunswick

Late spring through fall are lovely times to visit, although winter sports lovers have plenty of options. Whales are more plentiful in the Bay of Fundy after the first of August. Festivals celebrating everything from jazz to salmon are held from late spring until early fall. Many communities have festivities for Canada Day (July 1), and on the Acadian Peninsula many festivals, including the unique Blessing of the Fleet, are clustered around the August 15 Acadian national holiday. Fall colors are at their peak from mid-September through mid- or late October. The **Autumn Colours Line** (☎ 800/268–3255) provides daily information on where fall foliage is at its best.

SAINT JOHN

Like any seaport worth its salt, Saint John is a welcoming place, beginning when the natives welcomed Samuel de Champlain and Sieur de Monts, who landed here on St. John the Baptist Day in 1604. Nearly two centuries later, in May 1783, 3,000 British Loyalists fleeing the aftermath of the American Revolutionary War poured off a fleet of ships to make a home amid the rocks and forests. Two years later (1785) the city of Saint John was incorporated, the first in Canada.

Although most of the Loyalists were English, there were some Irish among them. Following the Napoleonic Wars in 1815, thousands more Irish workers found their way to Saint John. It was the potato famine that spawned the largest influx of Irish immigrants though; a 20-ft Celtic Cross on Partridge Island at the entrance to Saint John Harbor stands as a reminder of the hardships and suffering they endured. Their descendants make Saint John Canada's most Irish city, an undisputed fact that is celebrated in grand style each March, with a week-long St. Patrick's festival.

Saint John remains a welcoming place—just ask the thousands of visitors who stream ashore from the dozens of cruise ships that dock at downtown Pugsley Wharf each year. They are greeted with music, flowers and cheerful people ready and willing to help in any way they can.

All the comings and goings over the centuries have exposed Saint Johners to a wide variety of cultures and ideas, and made it a sophisticated city in a friendly Maritime way. Major provincial artists such as Jack Humphrey, Millar Brittain, Fred Ross, and Herzl Kashetsky were born here, as were Hollywood notables such as Louis B. Mayer, Donald Sutherland, and Walter Pidgeon.

Industry and salt air have combined to give parts of this city a weather-beaten quality, but you can also find lovingly restored redbrick homes, as well as modern office buildings, hotels, and shops.

Downtown Saint John

An ambitious urban renewal program undertaken in the early 1980s spruced up the waterfront and converted old warehouses into trendy restaurants and shops. Underground and overhead walkways connect several attractions and shops in the area.

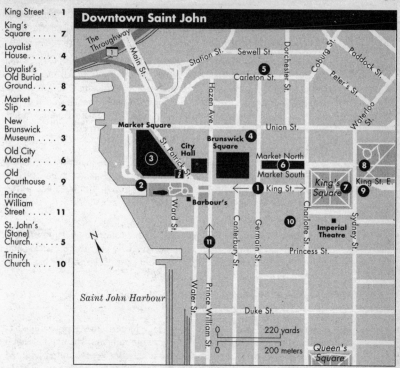

A Good Walk

Saint John is a city on hills, and **King Street** ①, its main street, slopes steeply to the harbor. A system of escalators, elevators, and skywalks inside buildings means you can climb to the top and take in some of the more memorable spots without effort; you can also walk outside if you wish. Start at the foot of King Street, **Market Slip** ②. This is where the Loyalists landed in 1783 and is the site of **Barbour's General Store** and the Little Red Schoolhouse. At Market Square, restored waterfront buildings house historic exhibits, shops, restaurants, and cafés. Also here are the Saint John Regional Library, a year-round visitor information center, and the fine **New Brunswick Museum** ③.

From the second level of Market Square, a skywalk crosses St. Patrick Street, and an escalator takes you up into the City Hall shopping concourse. Here, if you wish, you can branch off to the Canada Games Aquatic Centre and its pools and fitness facilities, or to Harbor Station, with its busy schedule of concerts, sporting events, and trade shows. Once you are through City Hall, another skywalk takes you across Chipman Hill and into the Brunswick Square Complex of shops, offices, and a hotel. To visit historic **Loyalist House** ④, exit onto Germain Street and turn left; it's on the corner at the top of the hill. Continue on for a block to see the venerable **St. John's (Stone) Church** ⑤. In the flavorful **Old City Market** ⑥, across from Brunswick Square, make your way past fish- and cheesemongers, butchers, greengrocers, sandwich makers, and craftspeople. When you leave by the door at the top of the market, you arrive at the head of King Street and right across Charlotte Street from **King's Square** ⑦. Take a walk through the square, past the statues and bandstand, to Sydney Street. Cross Sydney and you're in the **Loyalist's Old Burial Ground** ⑧. Make your way back to Sydney Street and then cross King Street East to the **Old Courthouse** ⑨ with its spiral staircase. Head south on Sydney; turn right on

King's Square South and you're at the handsome Imperial Theatre. Follow King's Square South and cross Charlotte Street to reach the back door of historic **Trinity Church** ⑩.

To end your walk, make your way back to King Street and walk down the hill toward the water. Notice the plaque near the corner of Canterbury Street (at 20 King Street) that identifies a site where Benedict Arnold operated a coffeehouse. **Prince William Street** ⑪ is at the foot of the hill, just steps from where you began at Market Slip. Turn left for antiques shops, galleries, and historic architecture.

TIMING

Allow the better part of a day for this walk, if you include a few hours for the New Brunswick Museum and some time for shopping. You can walk the route in a couple of hours, though. On Sunday some of the indoor walkways are closed, as is the City Market.

Sights to See

Barbour's General Store. This 19th-century shop, now a museum, is filled with the aromas of tobacco; smoked fish; peppermint sticks; and dulse, an edible seaweed. There's an old post office and barber shop, too. ⊠ *Market Slip,* ☎ *506/658–2939.*

❶ **King Street.** The steep main street of the city is lined with solid Victorian redbrick buildings filled with a variety of shops.

❼ **King's Square.** Laid out in a Union Jack pattern, this green refuge has a two-story bandstand and a number of monuments. The mass of metal on the ground in its northeast corner is actually a great lump of melted stock from a neighboring hardware store that burned down in Saint John's Great Fire of 1877, in which hundreds of buildings were destroyed. ⊠ *Between Charlotte and Sydney Sts.*

❹ **Loyalist House.** David Daniel Merritt, a wealthy Loyalist merchant, built this imposing Georgian structure in 1810. It is distinguished by its authentic period furniture and eight fireplaces. July through August the mayor hosts a tea party here each Wednesday afternoon. ⊠ *120 Union St.,* ☎ *506/652–3590.* ⊡ *$3.* ⊙ *June, weekdays 10–5; July–Aug., daily 10–5; Sept.–May, by appointment.*

❽ **Loyalist's Old Burial Ground.** This cemetery, now a landscaped park, is like a history book published in stone. Brick walkways, gardens, and a beaver-pond fountain make it a delightful spot. ⊠ *Off Sydney St., between King and E. Union Sts.*

❷ **Market Slip.** The waterfront area at the foot of King Street is where the Loyalists landed in 1783. Today it's the site of the Saint John Hilton, an amphitheater, restaurants, and Market Square, but it still conveys a sense of the city's maritime heritage. A floating wharf accommodates boating visitors to the city and those waiting for the tides to be right so they can sail up the St. John River.

★ ☚ ❸ **New Brunswick Museum.** Delilah, a suspended full-size right whale skeleton, is on the natural-history level of this fine museum. You can hike along a geologic trail and watch the phenomenal Bay of Fundy tides rise and fall in a glass tube. The province's industrial, social, and artistic history is creatively displayed, and outstanding local, regional, and international art work hangs in fine galleries. The Family Discovery Gallery has lots of fun and educational games. ⊠ *Market Sq.,* ☎ *506/643–2300,* WEB *www.gov.nb.ca/nbmuseum.* ⊡ *$6.* ⊙ *Mid-May–Oct., Mon.–Wed. and Fri. 9–5, Thurs. 9–9, weekends noon–5; Nov.–mid-May, Tues.–Wed., and Fri. 9–5, Thurs. 9–9, weekends noon–5.*

❻ Old City Market. The 1876 inverted ship's-keel ceiling of this handsome market occupies a city block between Germain and Charlotte streets. Its temptations include live and fresh-cooked lobsters; great cheeses; dulse; and tasty, inexpensive snacks, along with plenty of souvenir and crafts items. ⊠ *47 Charlotte St.,* ☎ *506/658–2820.* ◷ *Mon.– Thurs. 7:30–6, Fri. 7:30–7, Sat. 7:30–5.*

❾ Old Courthouse. This 1829 neoclassical building has a three-story spiral staircase, built of tons of unsupported stones. The staircase can be seen year-round during business hours, except when court is in session. ⊠ *King St. E and Sydney St.* ☜ *Free.*

⓫ Prince William Street. South of King Street near Market Slip, this street is full of historic bank and business buildings that now hold shops, galleries, and restaurants. At the foot of the street is the lamp known as the Three Sisters, which was erected in 1848 to guide ships into the harbor.

❺ St. John's (Stone) Church. The first stone building in the city, this church was built for the garrison posted at nearby Fort Howe. The stone was brought from England as ships' ballast. ⊠ *87 Carleton St.,* ☎ *506/ 634–1474.* ◷ *Guided tours weekdays 10–4.*

❿ Trinity Church. The present church dates from 1880, when it was rebuilt after the Great Fire. Inside, over the west door, there's a coat of arms—a symbol of the monarchy—rescued from the council chamber in Boston by a British colonel during the American Revolution. It was deemed a worthy refugee and given a place of honor in the church. ⊠ *115 Charlotte St.,* ☎ *506/693–8558 for hrs.*

Greater Saint John

This may be the largest city in New Brunswick, but you can be on a secluded beach, talking to the harbor seals and listening to the birds, all within the city limits, and only 10 minutes from downtown.

A Good Drive

From Market Square in downtown Saint John, head west in your car (or on any westbound bus) to see the **Reversing Falls.** Go up St. Patrick Street, cross the viaduct, and you are on Main Street. Drive to the top of the hill and turn left on Douglas Avenue, with its grand old homes. A right off Douglas Avenue onto Fallsview Drive takes you to a Reversing Falls lookout and the Reversing Falls Jet Boat Ride. Return to Douglas Avenue, turn right, and keep right to cross the Reversing Falls Bridge. At the end of the bridge, on your left, is the Reversing Falls Tourist Bureau. The west side is home to **Carleton Martello Tower.** Turn left from the Reversing Falls Tourist Bureau, past the Simms Brush Factory, and bear left when the road splits. The rest of the way is well marked. You're also near **Irving Nature Park** (off Route 1 at Catherwood Drive if you're on the highway), 600 acres of volcanic rock and forest that are a haven for wildlife and hikers. There's more exotic wildlife at **Cherry Brook Zoo,** northeast of downtown. The zoo is part of **Rockwood Park,** the largest urban park in Canada.

TIMING

To appreciate the Reversing Falls fully takes time; you need to visit at high, slack, and low tides. Check with any visitor information office for these times to help you plan a visit.

Sights to See

Carleton Martello Tower. The tower, a great place from which to survey the harbor and Partridge Island, was built during the War of 1812 as a precaution against an American attack. Guides tell you about the spartan life of a soldier living in the stone fort, and an audiovisual presentation outlines its role in the defense of Saint John during World War II. ⊠ *Whipple St. at Fundy Dr.,* ☎ *506/636–4011.* 🎫 *$2.50.* ⊙ *June–Labor Day, daily 9–5; Labor Day–mid-Oct. by appointment.*

Cherry Brook Zoo. An entertaining monkey house, wildebeests, and other exotic species are highlights of this small zoo. There's a trail featuring extinct-animal exhibits. ⊠ *901 Foster Thurston Dr.,* ☎ *506/634–1440.* 🎫 *$6.* ⊙ *Daily 10–dusk.*

Irving Nature Park. The ecosystems of the southern New Brunswick coast are preserved in this lovely 600-acre park on a peninsula close to downtown. Roads and seven walking trails (up to several kilometers long) make bird- and nature-watching easy. From downtown take Route 1 west to Exit 107 (Catherwood Road) south; follow Sand Cove Road 4½ km (3 mi) to the park. ⊠ *Sand Cove Rd.,* ☎ *506/634–7135 for seasonal access.* 🎫 *Free.*

Reversing Falls. The strong Fundy tides rise faster than the river can empty twice each day at Reversing Falls Rapids, and the tide water pushes the river water back upstream. When the tide ebbs, the river once again pours over the rock ledges and the rapids appear to reverse themselves. To learn more about the phenomenon, watch the film shown at the Reversing Falls Tourist Bureau. There's a restaurant here, too. A jet boat provides a closer (and wetter) look. A pulp mill on the bank is less scenic, and the smell it occasionally emits is a less charming part of a visit. ⊠ *Rte. 100, Reversing Falls Bridge,* ☎ *506/658–2937.*

Rockwood Park. Encompassing 2,000 acres, this is the largest in-city park in Canada. There are hiking trails through the forest, 13 lakes, several sandy beaches, a campground, a golf course with an aquatic driving range, the Cherry Brook Zoo, and a unique play park for people of all ages. ⊠ *Main entrance off Crown St.,* ☎ *506/658–2883.* ⊙ *Daily 10–dusk.*

Dining and Lodging

$$–$$$ ✕ **Beatty and the Beastro.** This quirky place next to the Imperial Theatre hops at lunchtime as well as before and after the theater. The frequently changing menu, with its distinctive European accent, takes advantage of local and seasonal meat, seafood, and produce. Breads and soups are specialties, with lines on Scotch broth day (the last stop for the local spring lamb). ⊠ *60 Charlotte St., at King's Sq.,* ☎ *506/652–3888. AE, DC, MC, V.*

$$–$$$ ✕ **Billy's Seafood Company.** It's a restaurant, it's an oyster bar, it's a fish market—it's lots of fun, too, with jazzy background music and funny, fishy paintings. The oysters Rockefeller are served with a hint of Pernod. Billy's Seafood Splash is a lobster surrounded by sautéed scallops, steamed clams, and mussels. Live and cooked lobsters can be packed to go. ⊠ *Old City Market, Charlotte St. entrance,* ☎ *506/672–3474 or 888/933–3474. AE, DC, MC, V.*

$$–$$$ ✕ **Suwanna Restaurant.** If you're lucky, Thai duck will be on the menu the night you try this authentic Thai restaurant. The wine cellar is outstanding, and green and yellow curries are always available. The signature dish, Suwanna chicken, is a stir-fry of chicken, sweet peppers, and hot peppers drizzled with dark sauce. The flavor is delicate and unique (and not too spicy, unless you actually eat one of the hot peppers). ⊠ *325 Lancaster Ave.,* ☎ *506/637–9015. MC, V. No lunch.*

$–$$$ ✕ **Grannan's.** Seafood brochette with scallops, shrimp, and lobster tail, sautéed at your table in a white wine and mushroom sauce, is a favorite in this nautically decorated restaurant. The desserts—bananas

Foster flambéed while you watch, for one—are memorable. Dining spills over onto the sidewalk in summer. ⊠ *1 Market Sq.,* ☎ *506/634–1555. AE, DC, MC, V.*

$–$$$ ✕ **Incredible Edibles.** Here you can enjoy down-to-earth food—biscuits, garlic-laden hummus, salads, pastas, and desserts—in cozy rooms or, in summer, on the outdoor terrace. Classic French, vegetarian, and seafood dishes are also available. ⊠ *42 Princess St.,* ☎ *506/633–7554. AE, DC, MC, V. Closed Sun.*

$–$$$ ✕ **Steamer's Lobster Company.** This rustic spot is close to Market Square and across from Pugsley Terminal where the cruise ships dock. Servers dress like fishermen, and the decor is all about fishnets and lobster traps. Lobsters, mussels, and clams are steamed outside on the patio. Children love it. ⊠ *110 Water St.,* ☎ *506/648–2325. AE, DC, MC, V.*

$–$$ ✕ **Taco Pica.** This modest place is a slice of home for the Guatemalan refugees who run it as a worker's co-op. Ornamental parrots and bright colors rule in the dining room, while authentic recipes made with garlic, mint, coriander seeds, and cilantro rule in the kitchen. Frequently, a guitarist entertains on Friday and Saturday evenings. ⊠ *96 Germain St.,* ☎ *506/633–8492. AE, DC, MC, V.*

$–$$ ✕ **Vito's.** The former pizza take-out joint now offers much more. The pizzas in this uptown location are still robust, with lots of fresh toppings, but many pasta choices as well as chicken, seafood, and veal dishes have been added to the menu. The setting is roadhouse meets Mediterranean. Weekends are busy. ⊠ *1 Hazen Ave.,* ☎ *506/634–3900. AE, DC, MC, V.*

$$$ ✕▣ **Delta Brunswick Hotel.** Part of Brunswick Square, this hotel is in the heart of downtown Saint John. MRA's, a venerable department store that presided over the mercantile life of generations of Saint Johners, used to stand here. The hotel honors the old store in the names of some of its function rooms and in its courtly service. Rooms are large, modern, and comfortable. The entire hotel was renovated and refurbished in 2001. Shucker's Restaurant specializes in New Brunswick's best, including dishes made with local seafood, fiddleheads, and blueberries. This property is connected to shopping and entertainment facilities by the walkway that runs through much of Saint John. ⊠ *39 King St., E2L 4W3,* ☎ *506/648–1981,* ᶠᴬˣ *506/658–0914,* ᵂᴱᴮ *www.deltahotels.com. 255 rooms. Restaurant, bar, pool, gym. AE, D, DC, MC, V.*

$$$ ✕▣ **Saint John Hilton.** Rooms overlook the harbor or the town in this Hilton, which is furnished in Loyalist decor. A pedestrian walkway system connects the 10-story property to uptown shops, restaurants, a library, a museum, an aquatic center, and a civic center. The large Turn of the Tide restaurant has terrific views of the harbor. Although the dining, with seafood and meat dishes, is pleasant at all times, the best meal is the Sunday brunch, with a long table full of dishes from the exotic to the tried-and-true. ⊠ *1 Market Sq., E2L 4Z6,* ☎ *506/693–8484; 800/561–8282 in Canada,* ᶠᴬˣ *506/657–6610,* ᵂᴱᴮ *www.hilton.com. 197 rooms. Restaurant, bar, pool, gym. AE, D, DC, MC, V.*

$–$$$ ✕▣ **Shadow Lawn Inn.** This charming inn is in an affluent suburb 10
★ minutes from Saint John that has tree-lined streets, palatial homes, tennis, golf, and a yacht club. With its clapboards and columns, antiques and amenities, this property fits right into the neighborhood. Some of the bedrooms have fireplaces; one suite has a whirlpool bath. The chef honed his skills in some of the finest upper-Canadian kitchens. His creative ideas are reflected in the dining room's Continental and seafood dishes. ⊠ *3180 Rothesay Rd., Rothesay E2E 5V7,* ☎ *506/847–7539 or 800/561–4166,* ᶠᴬˣ *506/849–9238. 9 rooms, 2 suites. Restaurant. AE, DC, MC, V. CP.*

$$ 🛏 **Inn on the Cove and Day Spa.** Near Irving Nature Park, and with
★   its back lawn terraced down to the ocean, this inn has as much char-
acter as its owners, who tape their delightful cooking show in the kitchen.
Bedrooms are furnished with local antiques, and several bathrooms in-
clude whirlpool tubs with ocean views and electric fireplaces. Dinner,
available with advance reservations, is served in the informal Tide's
Table dining room, with its massive fireplace and walls of windows
overlooking the Bay of Fundy. Guests and nonguests can also, with reser-
vations, receive health and beauty treatments at the inn's spa. ⊠ *1371
Sand Cove Rd. (Box 3113, Station B), E2M 4X7,* ☎ *506/672–7799
or 877/257–8080,* FAX *506/635–5455,* WEB *www.innonthecove.com.
3 rooms, 3 suites. Dining room, spa. MC, V. BP.*

$–$$ 🛏 **Homeport Historic Inn c1858.** Graceful arches, fine antiques, Italian marble fireplaces, oriental carpets, and a maritime theme are all at
home in these 19th-century twin mansions built by a prominent Saint
John shipbuilding family. Together the two buildings make a large inn
that commands stunning harbor views and is close to both downtown
and the Reversing Falls. Each oversize room is elegant, unique, and
equipped with modern amenities. One even has a skeleton in the closet.
The hearty Rise & Dine Breakfast, included in the room rate, sets you
up nicely for the day. ⊠ *60–80 Douglas Ave., E2K 1E4,* ☎ *506/672–
7255 or 888/678–7678,* FAX *506/672–7250,* WEB *www.homeport.nb.ca.
6 rooms, 4 suites. Breakfast room, in-room VCRs. AE, MC, V. BP.*

$ 🛏 **Earle of Leinster B&B.** This 1877 three-story brick home in the heart
of one of the city's oldest residential areas is within easy walking distance of theaters, restaurants, and more. Rooms in the main house are
Victorian; rooms in the converted coachhouse in the courtyard include
kitchenettes. Families, and some small pets (call ahead to see if yours
qualifies) can be accommodated. Access to laundry facilities and a games
room is included in the room rate. ⊠ *96 Leinster St., E2L 1J3,* ☎ *506/
652–3275. 7 rooms. Breakfast room, kitchenettes (some), in-room
VCRs, billiards. AE, MC, V. BP.*

Nightlife and the Arts

The Arts

Aitken Bicentennial Exhibition Centre (ABEC; ⊠ 20 Hazen Ave., ☎ 506/
633–4870), in a former Carnegie library, has several galleries display-
ing the work of local artists and artisans as well as a hands-on science
gallery for children. Admission is free. The **Imperial Theatre** (⊠ King's
Sq., ☎ 506/633–9494), a beautifully restored 1913 vaudeville theater,
is home to Saint John's theater, opera, ballet, and symphony productions as well as road shows. Summer tours ($2) are available Monday
through Saturday, 10–6; winter tours are free, but must be arranged
in advance.

Nightlife

Taverns and lounges, usually with music of some kind, provide lively
nightlife. **D'Arcy Farrow's Pub** (⊠ 43 Princess St., ☎ 506/657–8939)
has five rooms and a main stage area that regularly features live Celtic,
jazz, and blues music. Top musical groups and other performers regularly appear at **Harbour Station** (⊠ 99 Station St., ☎ 506/657–1234).
O'Leary's Pub (⊠ 46 Princess St., ☎ 506/634–7135), in the middle of
the Trinity Royal Preservation Area, specializes in old-time Irish fun
complete with Celtic performers; on Wednesday, Brent Mason, a well-
known neofolk artist, starts the evening and then turns the mike over
to the audience. **Tapps Brew Pub and Steak House** (⊠ 78 King St.,
☎ 506/634–1957) pleases the over-30 population with jazz and blues.

Outdoor Activities and Sports

Boat Tours

The **Reversing Falls Jet Boat** (⊠ Fallsview Park, off Fallsview Dr., ☎ 506/634–8987 or 888/634–8987, WEB www.jetboatrides.com) offers you a choice of a 20-minute thrill ride in the heart of the Reversing Falls or a more sedate sightseeing tour along the falls and in through the port. Some age and size restrictions apply on certain rides. The cost is about $25 per person; child and family rates are available.

Kayaking

Kayaking along the Fundy coast is popular. **Eastern Outdoors** (⊠ Brunswick Sq., King and Germain Sts., ☎ 506/634–1530 or 800/565–2925, WEB www.easternoutdoors.com) has single and double kayaks and offers lessons, tours, and white-water rafting. You can make arrangements over the phone or at the Eastern Outdoors retail store in Brunswick Square in downtown Saint John.

GOLF

The **Westfield Golf Club** (⊠ Exit 177 off Rte. 7, ☎ 506/757–2907 or 877/833–4662) is a venerable 18-hole course about 20 minutes outside the city.

Shopping

Brunswick Square (⊠ King and Germain Sts., ☎ 506/658–1000), a vertical mall, has many top-quality boutiques. **Handworks Gallery** (⊠ 12 King St., ☎ 506/652–9787) carries the best of professional crafts and fine art made in New Brunswick. **House of Tara** (⊠ 72 Prince William St., ☎ 506/634–8272) is wonderful for fine Irish linens and woolens. **Peter Buckland Gallery** (⊠ 80 Prince William St., ☎ 506/693–9721), open Wednesday through Saturday or by appointment, is an exceptionally fine gallery that carries paintings, drawings, and sculpture by Canadian artists. **Tim Isaac Antiques** (⊠ 97 Prince William St., ☎ 506/652–3222) has fine furniture, glass, china, Oriental rugs, and a well-informed staff; unique sales are often advertised in local papers. **Trinity Galleries** (⊠ 128 Germain St., ☎ 506/634–1611) represents fine Maritime and Canadian artists.

THE FUNDY COAST

Bordering the chilly and powerful tidal Bay of Fundy is some of New Brunswick's most dramatic coastline. This area extends from the border town of St. Stephen and the lovely resort village of St. Andrews, past tiny fishing villages and rocky coves, through Saint John and on to Fundy National Park, where the world's most extreme tides rise and fall twice daily. The Fundy Isles—Grand Manan Island, Deer Island, and Campobello—are havens of peace that have lured harried mainlanders for generations. Some of the impressive 50-km (31-mi) stretch of coastline between St. Martins and Fundy National Park is now accessible by the new Fundy Parkway, the Fundy Footpath (for hikers), and the Fundy Trail (multiuse, but not for motorized vehicles).

St. Stephen

⓬ *107 km (66 mi) west of Saint John.*

St. Stephen is across the St. Croix River from Calais, Maine. The small town is a mecca for chocoholics, who converge here during the Chocolate Festival held early in August. "Choctails," chocolate puddings and cakes, and even complete chocolate meals should come as no surprise when you learn that the chocolate bar was invented here. There's a

provincial **visitor information center** (⊠ 5 King St., ☎ 506/466–7390)
on King Street.

Ganong's famed, hand-dipped chocolates are available at the factory
store, **Ganong Chocolatier.** ⊠ *73 Milltown Blvd.,* ☎ *506/465–5611.*
☉ *Jan.–Apr., Mon.–Sat. 10–5; May, daily 9–5; June–Aug., weekdays
8–8, weekends 9–5; Sept.–Dec., daily 9–5.*

The Chocolate Museum, behind Ganong Chocolatier, explores the sweet
history of candy making with hand-dipping demonstrations and hands-
on exhibits. ⊠ *73 Milltown Blvd.,* ☎ *506/466–7848.* ☑ *$4.* ☉ *Nov.–
Apr., Tues.–Sat. 9–5; May–Oct., Mon.–Sat. 10–8, Sun. 1–5.*

En Route   **St. Croix Island** can be seen from an interpretive park on Route 127,
between St. Stephen and St. Andrews. An International Historic Site,
St. Croix is where explorers Samuel de Champlain and Sieur de Monts
spent their first harsh winter in North America in 1604.

St. Andrews by-the-Sea

★ ⑬   *29 km (18 mi) southeast of St. Stephen.*

On Passamaquoddy Bay, St. Andrews by-the-Sea, a designated National
Historic District, is one of North America's prettiest resort towns. It
has long been a summer retreat of the affluent (mansions ring the town).
Of the town's 550 buildings, 280 were erected before 1880, and 14 of
those have survived from the 1700s. Some Loyalists even brought
their homes with them piece by piece from Castile, Maine, across the
bay, when the American Revolution didn't go their way.

Knowledgeable costumed guides from **Heritage Discovery Tours** (☎ 506/
529–4011) conduct historical walking tours of St. Andrews. You can
also take ghost tours in summer.

If you'd like to take a self-guided tour, pick up a walking-tour map at
the visitor information center at 46 Reed Avenue (next to the arena) and
follow it through the pleasant streets. A particular gem is the
Court House (⊠ 123 Frederick St., ☎ 506/529–4248), which is still
active. Within these old stone walls is the **Old Gaol,** home of the
county's archives. In summer, tours are given weekdays 9–5. **Greenock
Church,** at the corner of Montague and Edward Streets, owes its exis-
tence to a remark someone made at an 1822 dinner party about the
"poor" Presbyterians not having a church of their own. Captain
Christopher Scott, who took exception to the slur, spared no expense
on the building, which is decorated with a carving of a green oak tree
in honor of Scott's birthplace, Greenock, Scotland. **Water Street,** down
by the harbor, has an assortment of eateries, gift and crafts shops, and
artists' studios.

The **Ross Memorial Museum** is a monument to an American family,
summer residents of St. Andrews, who appreciated beautiful things.
Lovely 19th-century New Brunswick furniture and objets d'art fill the
rooms. ⊠ *188 Montague St.,* ☎ *506/529–5124.* ☑ *Donation.* ☉ *Late
June–Aug., Mon.–Sat. 10–4:30; Sept.–mid-Oct., Tues.–Sat. 10–4:30.*

With more than 40,000 plants on site, **Kingsbrae Gardens** is one of
Canada's top 10 public gardens. It incorporates 27 acres of mature cedar
hedges and rare Acadian old-growth forest from several fine estates
with creative new plantings. Unusual and exotic flowers border the pathways—the rose and daylily collections are amazing—and towering
trees line the woodland trail. There are gardens to attract butterflies,
birds, and children; demonstration gardens that reveal the secrets of
successful horticulture; and a garden maze. An art gallery and gift shop

are housed in a stately mansion along with a café that serves light meals and decadent desserts. ⊠ *220 King St.,* ☎ *506/529–3335.* ⌨ *$7.* ☉ *May–Oct., daily 9–6.*

☺ The **Huntsman Aquarium and Museum** houses marine life and displays, including a teeming touch tank and some very entertaining seals fed at 11 and 4 daily. ⊠ *1 Lower Campus Rd.,* ☎ *506/529–1202.* ⌨ *$5.25.* ☉ *May–June, daily 10–4:30; July–Aug., daily 10–6; Sept.–Oct., Mon.– Tues. noon–4:30, Wed.–Sun. 10–4:30.*

OFF THE
BEATEN PATH
MINISTERS ISLAND – This huge island estate, once completely self-suffi-cient, was the summer home of Sir William Van Horne, chairman of the Canadian Pacific Railway from 1899 to 1915. Touring the island is an adventure: cars line up on Bar Road at low tide (check local schedules) and drive across the sand bar. On the island are the Covenhoven Man-sion, where just a few artifacts are on display, a tidal swimming pool, a livestock barn, a cottage, an old windmill, and the 1790 Minister's House, from which the island takes its name. ⊠ *Bar Rd. (5 km, or 3 mi, north of St. Andrews, off Rte. 127),* ☎ *506/529–5081 for tour informa-tion.* ⌨ *$5.* ☉ *Open June–Oct., sunrise–sunset at low tide.*

Dining and Lodging

$–$$$ ✕ **The Gables.** Salads, fish, and seafood as well as fresh-made desserts are served in this casual harborside eatery. The owner's art decorates the walls, and there's a deck for alfresco dining in summer. ⊠ *143 Water St.,* ☎ *506/529–3440. MC, V.*

$ ✕ **Sweet Harvest Market.** Known for its natural products and made-on-site breads, cookies, cakes, cheesecakes, and preserves, this is a ca-sual bakery-deli that is always experimenting. At press time it was considering dinner items too. ⊠ *182 Water St.,* ☎ *506/529–6249.*

$$$$ ✕⌂ **The Fairmont Algonquin.** This grand old resort hotel, where the
★ bellhops wear kilts and dinner is served on the wraparound veranda in fine weather, presides over town like an elegant dowager. The rooms have a feeling of relaxed refinement; the ones in the newer Prince of Wales wing are especially comfortable. In 2001 most of the rooms got a spruce-up, including new drapes, carpets, and duvets; the traditional bathrooms were also modernized. The Passamaquoddy Dining Room is noted for seafood and for regional dishes such as seared pork loin with local blueberry–balsamic vinegar sauce. Other options are the Right Whale Pub, serving casual lunch and dinner, and the Library Lounge and Bistro restaurant. ⊠ *184 Adolphus St., E0G 2X0,* ☎ *506/529–8823,* FAX *506/529–7162,* WEB *www.cphotels.ca. 238 rooms. 3 restau-rants, 2 bars, pool, hair salon, massage, sauna, 18-hole golf course, 4 tennis courts, health club, racquetball, beach, bicycles, children's pro-grams, meeting rooms. AE, DC, MC, V.*

$$$$ ✕⌂ **Windsor House.** The rooms in this restored 1798 Georgian home are exquisite, with antiques and fabrics true to the period. Note the fine art collection, unusual lighting fixtures, and attention to detail as you wander about the house. The food is amazing—especially the rack of lamb. The menus are built around locally grown produce and freshly baked goods. A good wine cellar, two quiet dining rooms, and a garden courtyard complete the experience. ⊠ *132 Water St., E5B 1A8,* ☎ *506/529–3330 or 888/890–9463,* FAX *506/529–4063,* WEB *www.townsearch.com/windsorhouse. 4 rooms, 2 suites. Dining room, bar, billiards. AE, D, DC, MC, V. BP.*

$$$–$$$$ ✕⌂ **Pansy Patch.** A visit to this B&B, a 1912 Normandy-style farm-
★ house with an art gallery, is a bit like a close encounter with landed gentry who are patrons of the arts and who like their gardens as rich and formal as their meals. Four rooms are in the Corey Cottage next

door. All rooms have period furniture and are individually decorated. Afternoon tea and cookies are served wherever you like—in the dining room, in your room, in the garden, or on the deck overlooking the water. Non-lodgers are welcome for lunch and dinner. Entrées include seafood paella, beef tenderloin, and lobster. The price of a room here entitles you to use the pool and tennis courts of the Fairmont–Algonquin Hotel next door. ⊠ *59 Carleton St., E5B 1M8,* ☎ *506/529–3834 or 888/726–7972,* FAX *506/529–9042,* WEB *www.pansypatch.com. 9 rooms. Restaurant, concierge. MC, V. Closed mid-Oct.–mid-May. BP.*

$$$$ 🔲 **A. Hiram Walker Estate Heritage Inn.** This restored mansion, built for the Hiram Walker Distillery family in 1912, is gracious, elegant, and welcoming. All rooms have fireplaces; most have whirlpool baths. You can ask the owner about everything from the mustard she serves with your breakfast ham to the chandelier over the dining table. A converted carriage house has two additional rooms and an apartment. ⊠ *109 Reed Ave., E5B 2J6,* ☎ *506/529–4210 or 800/470–4088,* FAX *506/529–4311,* WEB *www.walkerestate.com. 9 rooms. Dining room, pool, library. AE, MC, V.*

$$$$ 🔲 **Kingsbrae Arms.** A member of Relais & Châteaux, this restored 1897
★   estate is an experience as much as it is a property. Eclectic and entertaining antique furnishings contribute to the classy decor. Pampering touches are plentiful—roses and Belgian chocolates in the rooms, plush robes, a pantry stocked with biscotti, daily afternoon tea, and farewell gifts from local shops. The owners are gregarious, and you can expect excellent service. Guests celebrating a honeymoon or anniversary get champagne and red roses, as well as tickets to Kingsbrae Garden next door. In high season, breakfast and dinner are included in the room rate. The wine cellar is outstanding. ⊠ *219 King St., E5B 1Y1,* ☎ *506/ 529–1897,* FAX *506/529–1197,* WEB *www.kingsbrae.com. 5 rooms, 3 suites. Dining room, pool. MC, V.*

$–$$$ 🔲 **Treadwell Inn.** Gardens, a huge deck, and balconies all overlook the ocean at this gracious old inn. Built by a ships chandler about 1820, the inn has been faithfully restored and furnished to reflect the era. All the rooms are lovely, though the less expensive ones overlook the street. A healthy, hearty breakfast (included in the rate) is served in the big kitchen, which also has an ocean view. ⊠ *129 Water St., E5B 1A7,* ☎ *506/529–1011 or 888/529–1011,* FAX *506/529–4826,* WEB *www. townsearch.com/treadwell. 6 rooms. Kitchenettes (some), laundry service. AE, MC, V.*

$ 🔲 **Seaside Beach Resort.** If the click of a closing screen door sounds like summer at the beach to you, this waterfront cluster of cottages is your kind of place. At one end of the town's main street, it's close to all the action and a beach. The efficiency units are simple but comfortable and well equipped, right down to big pots for boiling lobsters. This is a terrific, casual spot for children and dogs. ⊠ *339 Water St., E5B 2R2,* ☎ *506/529–3846 or 800/506–8677,* FAX *506/529–4479,* WEB *www.seaside.nb.ca. 24 cottages. Coin laundry. AE, MC, V.*

Outdoor Activities and Sports

St. Andrews Creative Playground (⊠ 168 Frederick St.) is an amazing wooden structure for climbing, swinging, performing, making music, and playing games. The **Sunbury Shores Arts & Nature Centre** (⊠ 139 Water St., ☎ 506/529–3386) offers art workshops in drawing, etching, painting, pottery, and many other media, in conjunction with environmental excursions.

GOLF

The **Algonquin Golf Club** (⊠ off Rte. 127, ☎ 506/529–7124) has an 18-hole, par-72 signature course.

The **Day Adventure Centre** (☎ 506/529–2600), open May through early September, can arrange explorations of Passamaquoddy Bay on various kinds of boats. **Fundy Tide Runners** (☎ 506/529–4481) uses a 24-ft Zodiac to search for whales, seals, and marine birds. The clipper **MV Corey** (☎ 506/529–8116) is an elegant vessel for whale-watching. **Seascape Kayak Tours** (☎ 506/529–4866) provides instruction as well as trips around the area from a half day to a week.

Shopping

Cottage Craft (⌂ Town Sq., ☎ 506/529–3190) employs knitters year-round to make mittens and sweaters from its specially dyed wool. **Garden by the Sea** (⌂ 217 Water St., ☎ 506/529–8905) is an aromatic shop whose owners made a name for themselves with natural, vegetarian soap. You can buy the soap, along with herbal shampoos, rinses, masks, even "Sea Spirit" balls for the bath. Attached to the store is the Garden Party herbal tearoom. **Jon Sawyer's Studio** (⌂ 719 Mowat Dr., ☎ 506/529–3012) has exquisite glass. The **Sea Captain's Loft** (⌂ 211 Water St., ☎ 506/529–3190) specializes in English and New Brunswick woolens, English bone china, and marvelous wool yarn. The **Seacoast Gallery** (⌂ 174 Water St., ☎ 506/529–0005) carries fine arts and crafts by eminent New Brunswick artists. **Serendipin' Art** (⌂ 168 Water St., ☎ 506/529–3327) sells blown glass, hand-painted silks, jewelry, and other crafts by New Brunswick artists. **Steven Smith Designs/The Crocker Hill Store** (⌂ 45 King St., ☎ 506/529–4303), is a special place for those who love gardens, birds, and art. Top-notch Canadian, American, and English antiques—including furniture, rugs, silver, china, paintings, and drawings—can be found at **Windsor House Art & Antiques** (⌂ 136 Water St., ☎ 506/529–3026), which is next door to and affiliated with the Windsor House inn.

Grand Manan Island

⓮ *35 km (22 mi) east of St. Andrews by-the-Sea to Black's Harbour, 2 hrs by car ferry from Black's Harbour.*

Grand Manan, the largest of the three Fundy Islands, is also the farthest from the mainland; it's possible to see spouting whales, sunning seals, or a rare puffin on the way over. Circular herring weirs dot the island's coastal waters, and fish sheds and smoke houses lie beside long wharfs that reach out to bobbing fishing boats. Place names are evocative—Swallowtail, Southern Head, Seven Days Work, and Dark Harbour. It's easy to get around; only about 32 km (20 mi) of road lead from the lighthouse at Southern Head to the one at North Head. Grand Manan attracted John James Audubon, that human encyclopedia of birds, in 1831. More than 240 species of seabirds nest on the island, making it a haven for bird-watchers. The puffin may be the island's symbol, but whales are its visitors' passion. Giant finbacks, right whales, minkes, and humpbacks feed in the rich waters here. A day trip is possible, but your car might not make the infrequent ferry both ways. It's this limited access, however, that keeps the island authentic and relaxing, so you might as well plan to stay a while. Ferry service is provided by **Coastal Transport** (☎ 506/662–3724), which leaves the mainland from Black's Harbour, off Route 1, and docks at North Head on Grand Manan Island.

Dining and Lodging

$ ✕🏠 **Compass Rose.** Two old houses on the water combine to make this small, English-style country inn. The floral-theme guest rooms are bright and comfortable. Morning and afternoon teas, lunch (the lobster rolls are amazing), and dinner are served in a dining room that overlooks the busy fishing wharf. A full English breakfast is included in the rate, and all rooms overlook the water. ✉ *North Head, E0G 2M0,* ☎ FAX *506/662–8570. 7 rooms. Restaurant. MC, V. BP.*

$ ✕▥ **The Inn at Whale Cove Cottages.** This secluded waterfront compound with beach access combines rustic surroundings with elegant furnishings. It includes a lodge with three rooms and three separate cottages, two of which are rented by the week. Full breakfast is included for guests of the lodge and the smaller cottage. The dining room ($$–$$$; reserve ahead) serves everything from local seafood to chicken Oscar (breaded chicken breast stuffed with lobster and Cheddar cheese) from 6 to 8:30 every evening. An on-site food shop offers meals, desserts, bread, tabbouleh, hummus, and sauces to go. ✉ *26 Whale Cove Cottage Rd., E5G 2B5,* ☎ *506/662–3181,* WEB *www.holidayjunction.com/whalecove. 3 rooms, 3 cottages. Dining room, beach, library. MC, V. Closed Nov.–Apr.*

$ ▥ **Marathon Inn.** This gracious mansion built by a sea captain sits on a hill overlooking the harbor. The Marathon has been an inn since 1871, and many of its original furnishings can still be found in the guest rooms. The dining room specializes in seafood; it does not serve lunch but can pack lunches for guests. ✉ *19 Marathon La., North Head, E5G 3A4,* ☎ *506/662–8488,* WEB *www.angelfire.com/biz2/marathon. 28 rooms, 15 with bath. Restaurant, 2 lounges, pool, tennis court. MC, V.*

Outdoor Activities and Sports

For complete information on bird-watching, nature photography, hiking, cycling, horseback riding, sea kayaking, and whale-watching, contact **Tourism New Brunswick** (✉ Box 12345, Fredericton E3B 5C3, ☎ 800/561–0123).

WHALE-WATCHING

A whale-watching cruise from Grand Manan takes you well out into the bay. When the cruise operator tells you to dress warmly, he means it. Some of the boats have winter jackets, hats, and mittens on board for the customers who don't follow the advice. Most of the operators guarantee sightings. **Island Coast Boat Tours** (☎ 506/662–8181), has been around for many years and has a great reputation. **Sea Land Adventure** (☎ 506/662–8997), has the only whale-watching schooner in the Bay of Fundy. Interpreters on **Sea Watch Tours** (☎ 877/662–8552 or 506/662–1081) are very knowledgable about the birds you might encounter on your cruise, as well as the whales.

Deer Island

⑮ *50 km (31 mi) east of St. Andrews by-the-Sea to Letete, 40 min by free ferry from Letete.*

One of the pleasures of Deer Island is walking around the fishing wharves, such as those at Chocolate Cove. Exploring the island takes only a few hours; it's 12 km (7 mi) long, varying in width from almost 5 km (3 mi) to a few hundred feet at some points. At **Deer Point** you can walk through a small nature park while waiting for the ferry to Campobello Island. If you listen carefully, you may be able to hear the sighing and snorting of the **Old Sow**, the second largest whirlpool in the world. If you can't hear it, you'll be able to see it, just a few feet offshore in the Western Passage off Point Park.

Dining and Lodging

$ ▥ **Sunset Beach Cottage & Suites.** A modern property surrounded by natural beauty, this complex is right on a secluded cove. Watch the porpoises and bald eagles during the day, and in the evening enjoy a rare east-coast treat—an ocean sunset. ✉ *21 Cedar Grove Rd., Fairhaven E5V 1N3,*

☏ *506/747–2972 or 888/576–9990,* WEB *www.cottageandsuites. com. 5 suites, 1 cottage. Pool, laundry service. V.*

$ 🏠 **West Isles World B&B.** This white frame house overlooks the cove and has two snug rooms with an informal country feel—the big upstairs suite has a water view. The owners arrange whale-watching cruises and kayaking for guests. ✉ *3 Mountain Side Dr., Lambert's Cove E5V 1G3,* ☏ FAX *506/747–2946. 2 rooms. Hiking, library. No credit cards. BP.*

Outdoor Activities and Sports

Cline Marine Tours (✉ Richardson Wharf, 91 Richardson Rd., Richardson, ☏ 506/529–2287 or 800/567–5880) offers scenic and whale-watching tours. **Sparky Too Scuba Dive Charters** (✉ 108 Richardson Rd., ☏ 506/747–1988) offers whale-watching tours, and scuba excursions for certified divers.

Campobello Island

★ **⑯** *40 min. by ferry (summer only) from Deer Island; 90 km (56 mi) southeast of St. Stephen via bridge from Lubec, Maine.*

Neatly manicured, preening itself in the bay, Campobello Island has always had a special appeal to the wealthy and the famous. It was here that the Roosevelt family spent its summers. The 34-room rustic summer cottage of the family of President Franklin Delano Roosevelt is now part of a nature preserve, **Roosevelt Campobello International Park,** a joint project of the Canadian and U.S. governments. The miles of trails here make for pleasant strolling. President Roosevelt's boyhood home was also the setting for the movie *Sunrise at Campobello.* To drive here from St. Stephen, cross the border to Maine, drive about 80 km (50 mi) down Route 1, and take Route 189 to Lubec, Maine, and a bridge. ✉ *Roosevelt Park Rd.,* ☏ *506/752–2922.* 🎫 *Free.* ☉ *House late May–mid-Oct., daily 10–6; grounds daily year-round.*

The island's **Herring Cove Activity Destination** (✉ Welshpool, ☏ 506/ 752–7010) has camping facilities, a sandy beach, miles of hiking trails, and a 9-hole, par-36 Geoffrey Cornish golf course.

Dining and Lodging

$ ✗🏠 **Lupine Lodge.** Originally a vacation home built by the Adams family (friends of the Roosevelts) in the early 1900s, these three attractive log cabins set on a bluff overlooking the Bay of Fundy are now a modern guest lodge. Nature trails connect Lupine Lodge to Herring Cove Activity Destination. Two of the cabins contain the guest rooms, which are rustic, with modern furniture and homemade quilts. The third cabin houses the dining room ($$–$$$), which specializes in simple but well-prepared local seafood. A deck overlooking the bay connects the three buildings. ✉ *610 Rte. 774, Welshpool E5E 1A5,* ☏ *506/752–2555,* WEB *www.lupinlodge.com. 10 rooms, 1 suite. Restaurant, lounge. MC, V.*

$$$ 🏠 **Water's Edge Villas.** Watch the sun set over the water from the deck of a modern, two-bedroom cottage with all the comforts of home, including a lobster pot and a barbecue. The kitchen appliances are full-size, and the living room couch is a pullout so six can sleep comfortably. The water is just across the road, and the rocky beach is great for explorers. ✉ *37 Hutchins Rd., Welshpool E5E 1H1,* ☏ *506/752–2359 or 800/836–7648. 3 villas. In-room VCRs, laundry service. V.*

St. Martins

⑰ *45 km (28 mi) east of Saint John.*

The fishing village of St. Martins has a rich shipbuilding heritage, whispering caves, miles of lovely beaches, spectacular tides, and a cluster of covered bridges, as well as several Heritage Inns and a couple of restaurants right on the beach. It's also the gateway to the Fundy Parkway. The scenic drive portion of this linear road extends to a new interpretation center at Salmon River. The road closely parallels the cycling–walking Fundy Trail along the shore. There are lots of places to park and many accessible scenic lookouts. The Fundy Parkway, only partially complete at press time, does not extend through Fundy National Park; the Fundy Trail and an expert hiking trail called the Fundy Footpath do, however, continue through to the park.

Some of New Brunswick's finest artists and craftspeople welcome visitors to their galleries and studios. Several of them live and work around St. Martins. Call ahead to arrange a visit. Among the green and rolling hills between St. Martins and Sussex is **Powning Design** (⊠ 610 Markhamville Rd., ☎ 506/433–1188), a studio–gallery operated by Peter and Beth Powning. He has won many awards for his work in clay, cast bronze, and other media. She is a writer and photographer whose work is found in galleries and books throughout North America.

Dining and Lodging

$$　✕⊡ **Weslan Inn.** Fireplaces, antiques, and lots of floral prints give the rooms in this Heritage Inn an English country feel. Breakfast, served in the rooms, is included in the overnight rate. The dining room (reservations required) specializes in seafood; lobster pie is a hot item. ⊠ *45 Main St., E5R 1B4,* ☎ *506/833–2351,* WEB *www.weslaninn.com. 3 rooms. Restaurant. MC, V.*

$–$$　✕⊡ **St. Martins Country Inn.** High on a hill overlooking the Bay of Fundy, this restored sea captain's home is furnished with Victorian antiques. Breakfast is served in the Country Dining Room; formal dinners in the Candlelight Dining Room are excellent. Children are welcome to stay in the carriage house, though not the main inn. ⊠ *303 Main St., E5R 1C1,* ☎ *506/833–4534 or 800/565–5257,* FAX *506/833–4725,* WEB *www.stmartinscountryinn.com. 16 rooms (4 in carriage house). Restaurant. MC, V.*

Alma

135 km (84 mi) northeast of Saint John.

The small seaside town of Alma services Fundy National Park and has some motels, as well as restaurants that serve good lobster and sticky buns. Around this area, much of it in Albert County, there's plenty to do outdoors—from bird-watching to spelunking. The **Albert County Tourism Association** (⊠ Hopewell Cape E0A 1Y0, ☎ 888/228–0444 or 506/882–2004) can provide information by phone or mail.

★ ⑱ **Fundy National Park.** This awesome 206-square-km (80-square-mi) park is a microcosm of New Brunswick's inland and coastal climates. The influence of the Bay of Fundy has also created some climatic conditions not found anywhere else in the region. This has led to a fascinating biological evolution that can clearly be seen in its protected forests. The park has 110 km (68 mi) of varied hiking and mountain-biking trails, some gravel-surface auto trails, year-round camping, golf, tennis, a heated Bay of Fundy saltwater pool, and a restaurant. Park naturalists offer regular programs throughout the summer. Its more than 600 campsites range from full-service to wilderness. ⊠ *Hwy. 114, Box 1001, E4H 1B4,* ☎ *506/887–6000,* WEB *www.parkscanada.pch.gc.ca.* ⊠ *$3.50 per person late May–mid-Oct.; free rest of year.* ☉ *Daily 24 hrs.*

Salem & Hillsborough Railroad Inc. (⊠ 197 Main St., Hillsborough, ☎ 506/734–3195 in summer) offers one-hour train excursions on Sunday and some Wednesdays mid-June through Labor Day. The train skirts the Petitcodiac River and travels near scenic marshlands and wooded areas. The cost is $8.

OFF THE
BEATEN PATH

CRAFTS STUDIOS AND GALLERIES – Along routes 915 and 114 from Alma to Hillsborough are dozens of talented artists and craftspeople, many of whom open their studios and galleries to visitors. For more information and a map, pick up a Fundy Studio Tour pamphlet at visitor information centers. **Cornucopia Great Gifts and Fine Art** (⊠ 2816 Main St., Hillsborough, ☎ 506/734–1118), stocks New Brunswick's finest crafts, including pottery, glass, wood, metal, and jewelry. Lynne Saintonge, an owner of **Joie de Vivre Contemporary Arts & Craft Gallery** (⊠ Rte. 114, Riverside-Albert, ☎ 506/882–2276), is a painter–visual artist who uses computer and sound to enhance her images. Her fascinating work is created in a studio upstairs from the gallery. **Kindred Spirits Stained Glass Studio** (⊠ 2831 Main St., Hillsborough, ☎ 506/734–2342) is where Diana Boudreau creates unique patterns with glass carefully chosen for its color and texture. Brian Blakney's **Lonesome Rose Pottery** (⊠ Waterside Rd., ☎ 506/882–2770) is east of Fundy National Park. At **Oval Door Manor Arts** (⊠ 2666 Main St., Hillsborough, ☎ 506/734–3382), Paul and Elsie Nowlan create wonderful, highly detailed oil and ink works that are cherished in collections throughout North America and Europe. **Samphire Casuals** (⊠ Albert Mines Rd. off Rte. 2114 near Hopewell, ☎ 506/734–2851) is a converted one-room schoolhouse where Judy Tait silk-screens her unique designs on T-shirts, sweatshirts, and even mugs. Lars Larsen's **Studio on the Marsh** (⊠ Mary's Point Rd. off Rte. 915, ☎ 506/882–2917) is the perfect setting for his wildlife art. Many of **Tim Isaac and Karin Bach's** (⊠ Rte. 915 between Alma and Riverside-Albert, ☎ 506/882–2166) wildlife clay sculptures and fountains are on display in a garden outside their studio. **Wendy Johnston's Pottery** (⊠ behind the post office on Main St., Hillsborough, ☎ 506/734–2046) sells contemporary, functional, and brightly-colored pieces with abstract designs.

Dining

$$ ✗ **Adair's Wilderness Lodge.** All of the food at this cedar lodge in the woods is made from scratch in the kitchen; you'll be served hearty portions of just about anything you like, including arctic char, rainbow trout, and sirloin steak. If you want fresh lobster, call ahead. ⊠ *Creek Rd., 12 km (7 mi) past Poley Mountain,* ☎ *506/432–6687. AE, DC, MC, V.*

Outdoor Activities and Sports

BIRD-WATCHING

The bit of shoreline at **Marys Point** (⊠ watch for signs off Rte. 915) draws tens of thousands of migrating birds, including semipalmated sandpipers and other shore birds, each summer. The area, now a bird sanctuary and interpretive center, is near Riverside-Albert.

CAVING

Baymount Outdoor Adventures (⊠ 17 Elwin Jay Dr., Hillsborough, ☎ 506/734–2660, WEB www.baymountadventures.com) has trained interpreters who lead expeditions into the White Caves near the Bay of Fundy. The caving experience is great fun, but not for the faint of heart, as it requires crawling on cave floors and slithering through narrow openings at some points. You can also arrange interpretive walks around Hopewell Rocks and Marys Point.

GOLF

The **Fundy National Park Golf Club** (⊠ Fundy National Park, near the Alma entrance, ☎ 506/887–2970) is near cliffs overlooking the restless Bay of Fundy; it's one of the province's most beautiful and challenging 9-hole courses.

HORSEBACK RIDING

Broadleaf Guest Ranch (⊠ 5526 Rte. 114, Hopewell Hill, ☎ 506/882–2349 or 800/226–5405) can provide an overnight adventure or a short trail ride. The short excursions are through the lowland marsh; longer rides take the high road into the forest.

SEA KAYAKING

Baymount Outdoor Adventures (⊠ 17 Elvin Jay Dr., Hillsborough, ☎ 506/734–2660) offers sea kayaking around the Hopewell Rocks. **Fresh Air Adventure** (⊠ 16 Fundy View Dr., Alma, ☎ 506/887–2249 or 800/545–0020, WEB www.freshairadventure.com) conducts Bay of Fundy sea-kayaking excursions that last from two hours to three days. Guides, instruction, and equipment are provided.

SKIING AND SNOWMOBILING

Poley Mountain Resort (⊠ Waterford Rd., Box 4466, Sussex E4E 5L6, ☎ 506/433–7653), 10 km (6 mi) from Sussex on Waterford Road, has a vertical drop of 660 ft, 23 trails, a snowboard park, and a tubing park with four trails and its own lift that converts to a water-based thrill ride in summer. Poley is also on the groomed Fundy Snowmobile Trail between Saint John and Moncton.

Cape Enrage

15 km (9 mi) east of Alma.

Route 915 takes you to the wild driftwood-cluttered beach at Cape Enrage, which juts out into the bay. A lighthouse, restaurant, gift shop, and some spectacular views can be found here. You can arrange for rappeling and other adventures.

Outdoor Activities and Sports

Cape Enrage Adventures (⊠ off Rte. 114, ☎ 506/887–2273 mid-May–mid-Sept.; 506/856–6081 off-season) offers rappeling and rock-climbing ($49.50 per person for two hours), kayaking ($54.50 per person for four hours), and hiking, including a particularly challenging five-day coastal hike.

Hopewell Cape

40 km (25 mi) north of Alma.

The coastal road (Route 114) from Alma to Moncton winds through covered bridges and along rocky coasts. **Hopewell Rocks** is home to the famous Giant Flowerpots—rock formations carved by the Bay of Fundy tides. They're topped with vegetation and are uncovered only at low tide, when you can climb down for a closer study. There are also trails, an interactive visitor center, and a children's play area. ⊠ *131 Discovery Rd.,* ☎ *877/734–3429.* ⌑ *$5.* ☉ *Late May–June and Sept.–Oct., daily 8–5; July–Aug., daily 8–8; closing hrs vary slightly, so call ahead.*

Dining and Lodging

$–$$ ✕⌹ **Aubergine & Spa.** The young couple that bought and converted this 1854 home (he's a chef, she's a massage therapist) added a section for the spa, which includes a cedar sauna. The rooms are all named for local flowers, and the key fobs are miniature hand-painted replicas of the floral paintings that identify each room. The furniture is antique, and many of the paintings are by young Acadian artists— the combination works amazingly well. A Continental breakfast is included in the rate. The intimate dining room, which features Thai and Indian food in addition to Indonesian specialties, is open to the public. ⊠ *5 Maple St., Riverside-Albert (24 km, or 15 mi, outside Hopewell Cape) E4H 3X1,* ☎ *506/882–1800 or 877/873–1800,* FAX *506/882–1801,* WEB *www.aubergine-spa.com. 4 rooms. Restaurant, in-room data ports, spa, sauna, laundry service. AE, MC, V. CP.*

$–$$ ⊞ **Florentine Manor Heritage Inn.** With silver candlesticks on the dining-room table and handmade quilts on the beds, this restored old shipbuilder's house is a haven for honeymooners and romantics. All the rooms have at least two windows, the better to hear the birds in the trees outside. Two rooms have fireplaces and two have whirlpool baths. Dinner is served by request. ⊠ *356 Rte. 915, Harvey on the Bay E4H 2M2,* ☎ *506/882–2271 or 800/665–2271,* FAX *506/882–2936. 9 rooms. Dining room, bicycles. MC, V. BP.*

Moncton

⑲ *80 km (50 mi) north of Alma.*

A friendly city, often called the Gateway to Acadia because of its mix of English and French and its proximity to the Acadian shore, Moncton has a renovated downtown, where wisely placed malls do a booming business. A walking-tour brochure, available at the tourist information centers at both Magnetic Hill on Route 126, and at City Hall on Main Street, indicates the city's historic highlights.

This city has long touted two natural attractions: the Tidal Bore and the Magnetic Hill. You may be disappointed if you've read too much tourist hype, though. In days gone by, before the harbor mouth filled with silt, the **Tidal Bore** was an incredible sight, a high wall of water that surged in through the narrow opening of the river to fill red mud banks to the brim. It still moves up the river, and is worth seeing, but it's no longer a raging torrent. Bore Park on Main Street is the best vantage point; viewing times are posted there.

♺ **Magnetic Hill** creates a bizarre optical illusion. If you park your car in neutral at the designated spot, you'll seem to be coasting uphill without power. Shops, an amusement park, a zoo, a golf course, and a small railroad are part of the larger complex here; there are extra charges for the attractions. ⊠ *North of Moncton off Trans-Canada Hwy. (watch for signs).* ☞ *$2.* ☉ *May–early Sept., daily 8–8.*

♺ An excellent family water-theme park, **Magic Mountain** is adjacent to Magnetic Hill. ⊠ *North of Moncton off Trans-Canada Hwy.,* ☎ *506/857–9283; 800/331–9283 in Canada.* ☞ *$19.50.* ☉ *Mid–late June and mid-Aug.–early Sept., daily 10–6; July–mid-Aug., daily 10–8.*

♺ The award-winning **Magnetic Hill Zoo,** the largest zoo in Atlantic Canada, has no shortage of exotic species: lemurs, lions, macaques, muntjacs, and more. At Old MacDonald's Barnyard, children can pet domestic animals or ride a pony in summer. ⊠ *North of Moncton off Trans-Canada Hwy.,* ☎ *506/384–0303.* ☞ *$6.* ☉ *Apr.–mid-June, daily 10–6; mid-June–early Sept., daily 9–8; early Sept.–Oct., weekdays 10–6, weekends 9–7; Jan.–Mar., Sun. 11–4.*

A restored 1920s vaudeville theater, the opulent **Capitol Theatre** is a beautiful attraction in itself as well as a venue for plays, musicals, ballets, and concerts. Free tours are available. ⊠ *811 Main St.,* ☎ *506/856–4379; 800/567–1922 in Canada.*

The **Thomas Williams Heritage House,** a neo-Gothic structure built in 1883 by the treasurer of the Intercolonial Railway, is elegantly furnished and contains several original family pieces. The Veranda Tea Room is open in July and August. ⊠ *103 Park St.,* ☎ *506/857–0590.* 🗩 *By donation.* ⊙ *May and Sept., Mon., Wed., and Fri. 10–3; June, Tues.– Sat. 9–5, Sun. 1–5; July–Aug., Mon.–Sat. 9–5, Sun. 1–5.*

The 1821 **Free Meeting House,** a simple and austere National Historic Site operated by the Moncton Museum, is Moncton's oldest standing building. It was built as a gathering place for all religious denominations without their own places of worship. ⊠ *100 Steadman St.,* ☎ *506/856–4383.* 🗩 *By donation.* ⊙ *Mon.–Sat. 9–4:30.*

Comprehensive exhibits trace the city's history from the days of the Mi'Kmaq people to the present at the **Moncton Museum.** ⊠ *20 Mountain Rd.,* ☎ *506/856–4383.* 🗩 *By donation.* ⊙ *Mon.–Sat. 9–4:30.*

The halls of the **Aberdeen Cultural Centre,** a converted schoolhouse, ring with music and chatter. This is home to theater and dance companies, a framing shop, and several galleries. **Galerie 12** represents leading contemporary Acadian artists. **Galerie Sans Nom** is an artist-run co-op supporting avant-garde artists from throughout Canada. The English, artist-run **IMAGO Inc.** is the only print production shop in the province. Guided tours are available by appointment. ⊠ *140 Botsford St.,* ☎ *506/857–9597.* ⊙ *Weekdays 10–4.*

At **Lutz Mountain Heritage Museum** you can find genealogical records of the area's non-Acadian pioneer settlers from as far back as 1766. It's also a hands-on museum. ⊠ *3143 Mountain Rd.,* ☎ *506/384–7719.* 🗩 *Free.* ⊙ *Mon.–Sat. 10–6.*

The **Acadian Museum,** at the University of Moncton, has a remarkable collection of artifacts reflecting 300 years of Acadian life in the Maritimes. There's also a fine gallery showcasing contemporary art by local and Canadian artists. ⊠ *Clement Cormier Bldg., Université de Moncton, 165 Massey Ave.,* ☎ *506/858–4088.* 🗩 *$2.* ⊙ *June–Sept., weekdays 10–5, weekends 1–5; Oct.–May, Tues.–Fri. 1–4:30, weekends 1–4.*

Dining and Lodging

$$–$$$$ ✕ **Fisherman's Paradise.** The enormous dining area at this restaurant seats more than 350 people. Memorable à la carte seafood dishes are served in an atmosphere of candlelight and wood furnishings. ⊠ *375 Dieppe Blvd.,* ☎ *506/859–4388. AE, DC, MC, V.*

$$–$$$ ✕ **Le Château à Pape.** This riverside restaurant in an old Victorian home has it all—crisp white linen, romantic atmosphere, and a well-stocked wine cellar (you go down and select your own). The chef is third generation in a French-Acadian tradition. He prepares everything from steak to seafood with an Acadian flare. Traditional dishes include *fricot* (stew) and *poutine à trou* (apple pastry). ⊠ *2 Steadman St.,* ☎ *506/ 855–7273. AE, DC, MC, V. No lunch.*

$ ✕ **Pump House Brewery.** Metal fermentation tanks and bags of hops are proudly displayed in the laid-back atmosphere of the Pump House. Seasonal ales, such as pumpkin ale for Halloween, are served in addition to the regular house brews. Try the blueberry ale, complete with floating blueberries. A limited menu includes snack foods, burgers, and single-serving pizzas. The veggie pizza is loaded with fresh vegetables. ⊠ *5 Orange La.,* ☎ *506/855–2337. AE, MC, V.*

$ ✕ **Vito's.** This restaurant is the original in what is now a small but successful family chain. The pizza toppings are fresh and generous. Pasta, chicken dishes, seafood, and veal round out the selection. The Mediterranean decor completes the mood. Vito's can be busy on weekends, so reserve ahead. ✉ *726 Mountain Rd.,* ☎ *506/858–5000. AE, DC, MC, V.*

$$–$$$ ✕⊞ **Delta Beauséjour.** Moncton's finest hotel is conveniently located
★ downtown and has friendly service. The decor of the guest rooms echoes the city's Loyalist and Acadian roots. L'Auberge, the main hotel restaurant ($–$$$), has a distinct Acadian flavor. The more formal Windjammer dining room ($$$) is modeled after the opulent luxury liners of the early 1900s. ✉ *750 Main St.,* ☎ *506/854–4344,* FAX *506/858–0957,* WEB *www.deltahotels.com. 299 rooms, 11 suites. 2 restaurants, bar, café, indoor pool, gym. AE, D, DC, MC, V.*

$$–$$$ ⊞ **Best Western Crystal Palace.** Part of an amusement complex, this hotel keeps the fun coming with theme rooms devoted to rock and roll, the Victorian era, and more. The hotel also has movie theaters, a giant bookstore, an indoor pool, and an indoor amusement park. Pets are welcome. Champlain Mall is just across the parking lot. ✉ *499 Paul St., Dieppe E1A 6S5,* ☎ *506/858–8584 or 800/561–7108,* FAX *506/858–5486,* WEB *www.m2000.nb.ca/bestwestern. 92 rooms, 23 suites. Restaurant, indoor pool, gym. AE, D, DC, MC, V.*

$$ ⊞ **Château Moncton Hotel & Suites.** This modern château-like hotel stretches along the Petitcodiac River. The decor is European, with custom-made cherry-wood furniture. Some rooms overlooking the water have decks with great views of the Tidal Bore. Continental breakfast is included in the room rate, but no other meals are served here. ✉ *100 Main St., E1C 1B9,* ☎ *506/870–4444 or 800/576–4040,* FAX *506/870–4445,* WEB *www.chateau-moncton.nb.ca. 106 rooms, 12 suites. In-room data ports, minibars, gym. AE, DC, MC, V. CP.*

$ ⊞ **Victoria B & B.** This historic home in the heart of downtown has antiques-furnished rooms with amenities such as terry robes and aromatic bath gels. The full complimentary breakfast, served in the dining room, often includes chocolate pecan and orange-brandy French toast. ✉ *71 Park St., E1C 2B2,* ☎ *506/389–8296,* FAX *506/389–8296,* WEB *www.sn2000.nb.ca/comp/victoria-b&b. 3 rooms. Dining room, in-room VCRs. MC, V. BP.*

Nightlife and the Arts

THE ARTS

Top musicians and other performers appear at the **Colosseum** (✉ 377 Killam Dr., ☎ 506/857–4100).

NIGHTLIFE

Moncton rocks at night. **Club Cosmopolitan** (✉ 700 Main St., ☎ 506/857–9117) is open Wednesday through Saturday for dancing, rock, jazz, or the blues. It's billed as one cool club with four different atmospheres. **Club Mystique** (✉ 939 Mountain Rd., ☎ 506/858–5861) features major Canadian rock and alternative artists a couple of times a month. **Rockin Rodeo** (✉ 415 Elmwood Dr., ☎ 506/384–4324) is the biggest country-and-western bar in the province. **Voodoo** (✉ 938 Mountain Rd., ☎ 506/858–8844) has lots of room for dancing and caters to the 25-plus crowd.

Shopping

Five spacious malls, retail stores, and numerous pockets of shops make Moncton and nearby suburban Dieppe two of the best places to shop in New Brunswick. This city is also the province's fashion trendsetter, a reputation upheld by several downtown boutiques. Moncton has its share of fine crafts as well. **La Difference Fine Craft and Art** (✉ 181 Main St., ☎ 506/861–1800) specializes in Atlantic Canadian woodwork, jewelry, and pottery, and also features paintings and photographs. **The Moncton Market** (✉ 120 Westmorland St., ☎ 506/383–1749) brims with fresh produce, baked goods, ethnic cuisine, and crafts every Saturday morning 7–1.

Outdoor Activities and Sports

The **All World Super Play Park** (⊠ Cleveland Ave., Riverview), across the river from Moncton, is a giant wooden structure with plenty of room for children to exercise their bodies and imaginations.

GOLF

Royal Oaks Golf Club (⊠ 1746 Elmwood Dr., ☎ 506/384–3330) is an 18-hole, par-72 PGA Championship course, the first Canadian course designed by Rees Jones.

TANTRAMAR REGION

History and nature meet on the Tantramar salt marshes east of Moncton. Bounded by the upper reaches of the Bay of Fundy, the province of Nova Scotia, and the Northumberland Strait, the region is rich in history and culture and is teeming with birds. The marshes provide a highly productive wetland habitat, and this region is along one of North America's major migratory bird routes.

Dorchester and Memramcook

40 km (25 mi) from Moncton.

Acadian roots run deep in Memramcook; on the other side of a marsh, Dorchester was a center of British culture and industry long before the Loyalists landed. Dorchester is home to some of the province's oldest buildings, including **The Bell Inn** on the village square. Now a restaurant, The Bell Inn was built in 1811 as a stagecoach stop; it is reputed to be the oldest stone structure in New Brunswick.

Keillor House & Coach House Museum and Saint James Church is a cluster of historic properties turned into museums. The restored 1813 Keillor House has 16 rooms and nine fireplaces. Saint James Church is home to the Beachkirk textile collection and is a working textile museum. ⊠ 4974 Main St., Dorchester, ☎ 506/379–6633 (seasonal). ⊡ $2 (each property). ⊙ June–mid-Sept., Mon.–Sat. 10–5, Sun. 1–5.

The **Monument Lefebvre National Historic Site** in Memramcook explores the turbulent history of the Acadian people in passionate detail. ⊠ 480 Central St., ☎ 506/758–9808. ⊡ $2. ⊙ June–mid-Oct., daily 9–5; rest of year by appointment.

Outdoor Activities and Sports

Along the beaches at **Johnson's Mills** (⊠ Rte. 935, about 8 km, or 5 mi, south of Dorchester) is part of the internationally recognized staging area for migratory shorebirds such as semipalmated sandpipers. The numbers are most impressive in July and August.

Sackville

20 *22 km (14 mi) from Dorchester and Memramcook.*

Sackville is an idyllic university town complete with a swan-filled pond. Its stately homes and ivy-clad university buildings are all shaded by venerable trees, and there's a waterfowl park right in the town. It makes for a rich blend of history, culture, and nature. The **Sackville Waterfowl Park** in the heart of the town has more than 3 km (2 mi) of boardwalk and trails. The area is dotted with rest benches, viewing areas, and interpretive signs throughout the marsh that reveal the rare waterfowl species that nest here. There's an interpretation center, and guided tours are available in French and English June through August. ⊠ *Main St.,* ☎ *506/364–4968.* ⊆ *Park free, tour $4.* ☼ *Daily 24 hrs.*

The sophisticated **Owens Art Gallery** is on the Mt. Allison University campus. One of the oldest and largest university art galleries in the country, it houses 19th- and 20th-century European, American, and Canadian artwork. ⊠ *61 York St.,* ☎ *506/364–2574.* ⊆ *Free.* ☼ *Weekdays 10–5, weekends 1–5.*

Near the Nova Scotia border in Aulac and 12 km (7 mi) outside Sackville, the **Fort Beauséjour National Historic Site** holds the ruins of a star-shape fort that played a part in the 18th-century struggle between the French and English. The fort has indoor and outdoor exhibits as well as fine views of the marshes at the head of the Bay of Fundy. ⊠ *Rte. 106,* ☎ *506/364–5080 in summer; 506/876–2443 off-season.* ⊆ *$2.50.* ☼ *June–mid-Oct., daily 9–5.*

Dining and Lodging

$–$$ ✕ **Schnitzel Haus.** This unpretentious roadside restaurant is refreshingly authentic. The German owners make everything from schnitzel and bratwurst to spaetzle. ⊠ *153 Aulac Rd., Aulac (12 km, or 7 mi, outside Sackville),* ☎ *506/364–0888. MC, V.*

$$–$$$ ✕▥ **Marshlands Inn.** In this white clapboard inn, a welcoming dou-
★ ble parlor with fireplace sets the comfortable country atmosphere. Bedrooms are furnished with sleigh beds or four-posters. The chefs offer traditional and modern dishes; seafood, pork, and lamb are specialties ($$–$$$). In summer most of the vegetables come from the organic garden in the backyard. ⊠ *55 Bridge St., E4L 3N8,* ☎ *506/536–0170 or 800/561–1266,* ℻ *506/536–0721,* ⱳⱸⰼ *www.marshlands.nb.ca. 20 rooms. Restaurant. AE, DC, MC, V.*

Outdoor Activities and Sports

Without a doubt, bird-watching is the pastime of choice in this region. Several locations around Sackville allow you to observe a variety of species. For information on bird-watching in the area, contact the **Canadian Wildlife Service** (⊠ 17 Waterfowl La., ☎ 506/364–5044). **Cape Jourimain Nature Centre** (⊠ Exit 51 off Rte. 16, at the foot of Confederation Bridge, Bayfield, ☎ 506/538–2220), at the Cape Jourimain National Wildlife Area, covers 1,800 acres of salt and brackish marshes. Large numbers of waterfowl, shorebirds, and other species can be seen here. It includes a fine nature interpretation center, nature store, restaurant, viewing tower, and a 13 km (8 mi) trail network. **Goodwin's Pond** (⊠ off Rte. 970), near the Red-Wing Blackbird Trail in Baie Verte, allows for easy viewing of wetland birds and boasts more birds per acre than anywhere else in the province. The **Port Elgin Rotary Pond and Fort Gaspereaux Trail** (⊠ 30 km, or 19 mi, from Sackville via Rte. 16) offer a diverse coastal landscape that attracts migrating waterfowl, bald eagles, and osprey. At the **Tantramar Marshes** (⊠ High Marsh Rd., between Sackville and Point de Bute) you may be able to spot marsh hawks. The **Tintamarre National Wildlife Area** (⊠ Goose Lake Rd., off High Marsh Rd., ☎ 506/364–5044) consists of 5,000 acres of protected land ideal for sighting several species of ducks, rails, pied-billed grebes, and American bittern.

Shopping

Fog Forest Gallery (⊠ 14 Bridge St., ☎ 506/536–9000) is a small, friendly, and reputable commercial gallery representing Atlantic Canadian artists. The **Sackville Harness Shop** (⊠ 39 Main St., ☎ 506/536–0642) still actually makes harnesses for horses. You can also pick up fine leather belts, wallets, bags, and jewelry. **Tidewater Books** (⊠ 4 Bridge St., ☎ 506/536–0404) offers old-fashioned service and all the latest titles.

THE ACADIAN COAST AND PENINSULA

The white sands and gentle tides of the Northumberland Strait and Baie des Chaleurs are as different from the rocky cliffs and powerful tides of the Bay of Fundy as the Acadians are from the Loyalists. In the Acadian Peninsula, fishing boats and churches define this land where a French-language culture survives. You're not likely to run into any language barriers in stores, restaurants, and attractions along the beaten path, but down the side roads it's a different story altogether.

Shediac

㉑ *25 km (16 mi) east of Moncton.*

Shediac is the self-proclaimed Lobster Capital of the World. It even has a giant lobster sculpture to prove it. But this is not what draws people to this fishing village–resort town. The magnet is **Parlee Beach,** a 3-km (2-mi) stretch of glistening sand. Surveys have named it the best beach in Canada, making it a popular vacation spot for families. It also plays host to beach-volleyball and touch-football tournaments; an annual sand-sculpture contest and a triathlon are held here as well. Services include canteens and a licensed restaurant. ⊠ *Off Rte. 133,* ☎ *506/533–3363.* ⌦ *$5 per vehicle.* ⊙ *Mid-May–mid-Sept., 7 AM–9 PM.*

Parc de L'Aboiteau, on the western end of Cap-Pelé, has a fine, sandy beach as well as a boardwalk that runs through salt marshes where waterfowl nest. The beach complex includes a restaurant and lounge with live music in the evening. Cottages are available for rent. ⊠ *Rte. 15, Exit 53,* ☎ *506/577–2005.* ⌦ *$4 per vehicle.* ⊙ *Beach complex June–Sept., daily dawn–dusk; cottages year-round.*

Dining and Lodging

$–$$$ ✕ **Lobster Deck.** Don't bother trying to wipe the sand off your table at this casual restaurant; it's here to stay. But don't worry—it won't get into your chowder. Lobster is the specialty here, but a platter that includes a half lobster with scallops, haddock, shrimp, and mussels is wonderful. On nice evenings you can eat on the front deck and watch people passing by, or you can dine on the back deck and watch gulls soaring over the water. Reservations are recommended in July and August. ⊠ *312 Main St.,* ☎ *506/532–8737. AE, MC, V. Closed Dec.–Apr.*

$–$$$ ✕ **Paturel Shorehouse Restaurant.** This big "cottage" on the beach is quite cozy, and because it's right next door to a fish-processing plant, you can get nearly anything you want—even a 5-pound lobster. The chef has a way with salmon and sole. Reservations are recommended for July and August. ⊠ *Corner of Cap Bimet and Legere,* ☎ *506/532–4774. AE, DC, MC, V. Closed mid-Sept.–mid-May. No lunch.*

$–$$$ ✕▥ **Little Shemogue Country Inn.** The unusual name (pronounced shim-o-*gwee*; it means "goodfeed for geese") is not nearly as surprising as the inn itself, a jewel in the rough along a rural coastal road. The main inn is a restored country home, exquisitely furnished and decorated with antiques. (One of the common rooms has an African motif: in another life the owner was an engineer who often worked on that continent.) A three-story wall of windows in the common area of the modern Log Point annex overlooks the ocean; the rooms here are large and have ocean views and whirlpool tubs. The 200-acre property has its own white-sand beach, canoes, and trails along a salt marsh. Breakfast (not included in the rate) and a set five-course dinner, for guests and the public, are served in three dining rooms ($$$) by reservation. ⊠ *2361 Rte. 955, Little Shemogue (40 km, or 25 mi,*

When you pack your MCI Calling Card, it's like packing your loved ones along too.

Your MCI Calling Card is the easy way to stay in touch when you travel. Use it to call to and from over 125 countries. Plus, every time you call, you can earn frequent flier miles. So wherever your travels take you, call home with your MCI Calling Card. It's even easy to get one. Just visit **www.mci.com/worldphone**.

EASY TO CALL WORLDWIDE

1. Just enter the WorldPhone® access number of the country you're calling from.

2. Enter or give the operator your MCI Calling Card number.

3. Enter or give the number you're calling.

Aruba ✢	800-888-8
Bahamas ✢	1-800-888-8000

Barbados ✢	1-800-888-8000
Bermuda ✢	1-800-888-8000
British Virgin Islands ✢	1-800-888-8000
Canada	1-800-888-8000
Mexico	01-800-021-8000
Puerto Rico	1-800-888-8000
United States	1-800-888-8000
U.S. Virgin Islands	1-800-888-8000

✢ Limited availability.

EARN FREQUENT FLIER MILES

MCI

SEE THE WORLD
IN FULL COLOR

Fodor's Exploring Guides bring all the great sights vividly to life with hundreds of photographs, fascinating historical background, and colorful anecdotes. Detailed maps and practical information keep you headed in the right direction.

Pair a **Fodor's** Exploring Guide with your trusted Gold Guide for a complete planning package.

Fodor's EXPLORING GUIDES

At bookstores everywhere.

outside Shediac) E4M 3K4, ☎ *506/538–2320,* FAX *506/538–7494,* WEB *www.little-inn.nb.ca. 9 rooms. Dining room, outdoor hot tub, beach, boating, bicycles. AE, MC, V.*

$–$$ ✕⊞ **Le Gourmand Country Inn.** The dining room ($$$), with its table d'hôte menu, is the most outstanding feature of this fine renovated home near the beach. The chef understands and appreciates Maritime flavors, so you're assured an extra fine dining experience. Rooms in the inn are modern and comfortable. The property also includes 10 two-bedroom cottages with cedar walls, cathedral ceilings, gas fireplaces, and fully equipped kitchens. ⊠ *562 Main St., E4P 2H1,* ☎ *506/532–4351 or 888/532–2585,* FAX *506/532–1025. 6 rooms, 10 cottages. Restaurant. AE, DC, MC, V.*

$$ ⊞ **Auberge Belcourt Inn.** This elegant Heritage Inn was built around 1912 and has been carefully restored and furnished with lovely period furniture. In summer the front veranda is an ideal spot for a drink before dinner at the Lobster Deck restaurant next door. The inn doesn't serve dinner in the summer, but in September through May offers authentic Chinese dinners to guests and the public ($45). ⊠ *310 Main St., E4P 2E3,* ☎ *506/532–6098,* FAX *506/533–9398,* WEB *www.sn2000. nb.ca/comp/auberge-belcourt. 7 rooms. Dining room, air-conditioning, laundry service. AE, DC, MC, V. Closed Jan. BP.*

Bouctouche

㉒ *35 km (22 km) north of Shediac.*

Bouctouche is a coastal town with a number of attractions. **Le Pays de la Sagouine** is a theme park with a make-believe island community that comes to life in French in day-long musical and theatrical performances and dinner theater–musical evenings July through September. La Sagouine is an old charwoman–philosopher created by award-winning author Antonine Maillet. ⊠ *Hwy. 11, Exit 32,* ☎ *506/743–1400 or 800/561–9188.* ▧ *$12.* ☉ *Mid-June–Labor Day, daily 10–6; Sept., daily 10:30–4.*

★ **Irving Eco-Centre, La Dune de Bouctouche** is a superb example of a coastal ecosystem that protects the exceptionally fertile oyster beds in Bouctouche Bay. Hiking trails and boardwalks to the beach make it possible to explore sensitive areas without disrupting the environment of one of the few remaining great dunes on the northwest coast of North America. An outstanding interpretive center puts the ecosystem in perspective. Swimming and clam digging are allowed. ⊠ *Rte. 475,* ☎ *506/ 743–2600.* ▧ *Free.* ☉ *Visitor center May–June, daily noon–8; July–Sept., daily 10–8; Sept.–Oct., weekdays noon–5, weekends 10–6.*

Dining and Lodging

$ ✕⊞ **Auberge le Vieux Presbytère de Bouctouche.** This inn, formerly a rectory and then a retreat house complete with chapel (now a conference room), has a courtly staff and is brimming with wonderful New Brunswick art and fascinating collections of antiques and books. The dining room ($$–$$$) is open to the public, serves seafood and Acadian fare, and is supported by a substantial wine cellar. ⊠ *157 chemin du Couvent, E4S 3B8,* ☎ *506/743–5568,* FAX *506/743–5566,* WEB *www.sn2000.nb.ca/comp/presbytere. 19 rooms, 3 suites. Restaurant. AE, MC, V. Closed Oct.–June.*

Kouchibouguac National Park

★ ㉓ *40 km (25 mi) north of Bouctouche, 100 km (62 mi) north of Moncton.*

The park's white, dune-edged beaches, some of the finest on the continent, are preserved here. Kellys Beach is supervised and has facilities.

The park also protects forests and peat bogs, which can be explored along its 10 nature trails. There are lots of nature interpretation programs and you can bicycle, canoe, kayak, and picnic too. Reservations are strongly recommended for the 311 campsites. ✉ *186 Rte. 117, Kouchibouguac,* ☎ *506/876–2443,* WEB *www.parkscanada.pch.gc.ca.* ✆ *Late May–mid-Sept, $3.50 per person; free rest of year.* ⊙ *Year-round.*

Outdoor Activities and Sports

Kouchibouguac National Park conducts **Voyager Canoe Day Adventures** (☎ 506/876–2443), which take you to offshore sandbars to meet gray seals and common terns and to discuss the Mi'Kmaq and Acadian culture in the area. The cost is $28, and outings take place four times a week, twice in English and twice in French. **Kayakouch, Inc.** (☎ 506/876–1199) offers guided, interpretive tours, ranging anywhere from four hours to five days, through the waters of Kouchibouguac National Park.

Miramichi City

㉔ *40 km (25 mi) north of Kouchibouguac, 150 km (93 mi) north of Moncton.*

The fabled Miramichi region is one of lumberjacks and fisherfolk. Celebrated for salmon rivers that reach into some of the province's richest forests, and the ebullient nature of its residents (Scottish, English, Irish, and a smattering of First Nations and French), this is a land of ghost stories, folklore, and lumber kings.

Sturdy wood homes dot the banks of Miramichi Bay at Miramichi City, which in 1995 incorporated the former towns of Chatham and Newcastle and several small villages. This is also where the politician and British media mogul Lord Beaverbrook grew up and is buried.

Dare the Dark for the Headless Nun! (☎ 800/459–3131) is a tragic tale best told in the dark while exploring one of the city's most infamous haunts. Costumed guides meet participants at French Fort Cove (watch for signs along the King George Highway through the city) at 9 PM Monday, Wednesday, and Friday from mid-June through August; the cost is $5.

The **Atlantic Salmon Museum and Aquarium** provides a look at the endangered Atlantic salmon and at life in noted fishing camps along the rivers. ✉ *263 Main St., Doaktown (80 km, or 50 mi, southwest of Miramichi City),* ☎ *506/365–7787.* ✆ *$4.* ⊙ *June–early Oct., daily 9–5.*

The **Central New Brunswick Woodmen's Museum,** with artifacts that date from the 1700s to the present, is in what looks like two giant logs set on more than 60 acres of land. The museum portrays a lumberjack's life through displays, but its tranquil grounds are excuse enough to visit. The Whooper, a 10-passenger amusement train ($2) is a 1½-km (1-mi) woodland adventure. There are picnic facilities and camping sites. ✉ *6342 Rte. 8, Boiestown (110 km, or 68 mi, southwest of Miramichi City),* ☎ *506/369–7214.* ✆ *$5.* ⊙ *May–Sept., daily 9–5.*

Dining and Lodging

$$ ✕🏨 **Rodd Miramichi River.** This grand riverside hotel, with warm natural wood and earth-tone interior, manages to feel like a fishing lodge. The rooms are comfortable, with lots of fishing prints on the walls. One room is specially equipped for guests with disabilities, and has a wheelchair-accessible shower stall. The Angler's Reel Restaurant ($$) is dedicated to fresh salmon. ✉ *1809 Water St., E1N 1B2,* ☎ *506/*

773–3111, FAX 506/773–3110, WEB *www.rodd-hotels.ca. 76 rooms, 4 suites. Restaurant, bar, indoor pool, hot tub, gym. AE, DC, MC, V.*

$ 🏨 **Pond's Chalet Resort.** You'll get a traditional fishing-camp experience in this lodge and chalets, 100 km (62 mi) outside of Miramichi, set among trees overlooking a salmon river. The accommodations in Ludlow, 15 km (9 mi) northwest of Boiestown, are comfortable but not luxurious. You can canoe and bicycle here, too. The dining room turns out reliable but undistinguished food. ⊠ *91 Porter Cove Rd., Ludlow E9C 2J3 (watch for signs on Rte. 8),* ☎ *506/369–2612,* FAX *506/369–2293,* WEB *www.pondsresort.com. 10 rooms, 5-bedroom lodge, 14 cabins. Bar, dining room, tennis court, volleyball, snowmobiling. AE, D, DC, MC, V.*

Shippagan

37 km (23 mi) from Tracadie-Sheila.

Shippagan is an important commercial fishing and marine education center as well as a bustling, modern town with lots of amenities. It's also the gateway to the idyllic islands of Lamèque and Miscou. The wonderful **Aquarium and Marine Centre** has a serious and a fun side. The labs here are the backbone of marine research in the province, and the marine museum houses more than 3,000 specimens. A family of seals in the aquarium puts on a great show in the pool at feeding time. There's a touch tank for making the acquaintance of various sea creatures, and during the fisheries and aquaculture festival in July, there are fish races in a special tank with numbered racing lanes. Place a bet on your favorite fish, and you could win a prize. ⊠ *100 rue de l'Aquarium,* ☎ *506/336–3013.* 🎫 *$6.* ☉ *May–Sept., daily 10–6.*

Across a causeway from Shippagan is Île Lamèque and the **Sainte-Cécile church** (⊠ Rte. 113 at Petite-Rivière-de-l'Île). Although the church is plain on the outside, every inch of it is decorated on the inside. Each July, the **International Festival of Baroque Music** (☎ 506/344–5846) takes place here.

Île Miscou, accessible by bridge from Île Lamèque, has white sandy beaches.

Caraquet

㉕ *40 km (25 mi) from Shippagan.*

Perched along the Baie des Chaleurs, with Québec's Gaspé Peninsula beckoning across the inlet, Caraquet is rich in French flavor and is the acknowledged Acadian capital. Beaches are another draw. The two-week **Acadian Festival** (☎ 506/727–6515) held here in August includes the Tintamarre, in which costumed participants noisily parade through the streets; the Blessing of the Fleet, a colorful and moving ceremony that eloquently expresses the importance of fishing to the Acadian economy and way of life.

★ ☾ A highlight of the Acadian Peninsula is **Acadian Historical Village,** 10 km (6 mi) west of Caraquet. The more than 40 restored buildings recreate Acadian communities between 1770 and 1939. There are modest homes, a church, a school, and a village shop, as well as an industrial area that includes a working hotel with barbershop, a bar and restaurant, a lobster hatchery, a cooper, and tinsmith shops. ⊠ Rte. 11, ☎ 506/726–2600, WEB *www.gov.nb.ca/vha.* 🎫 *$12.* ☉ *June–mid-Sept., daily 10–6. Guided tours through mid-Oct.*

With 86 figures in 23 scenes, the **Acadian Wax Museum** traces the history of the Acadians between 1604 and 1761. ⊠ *Rte. 11, outside the*

ACADIAN CULTURE, PAST AND PRESENT

CULTURE IS OFTEN DEFINED by geographical boundaries. Acadian culture, however, defines Acadia, because it isn't so much a place as it is an enduring French society. In New Brunswick it abides (although not exclusively) above an imaginary line drawn from Edmundston to Moncton. In the heartland you can hear remnants of Norman-French. Around Moncton you're just as apt to hear a melodious Acadian dialect called Chiac, a tweedy kind of French with flecks of English.

French settlers arrived in the early 1600s and brought with them an efficient system of dykes called *aboiteaux* that allowed them to farm the salt marshes. In the 1700s they were joined by Jesuit missionaries who brought the music of Bach, Vivaldi, and Scarlatti along with their zeal. In 1713 England took possession of the region, and authorities demanded Acadians swear an oath to the English crown. Some did, others didn't. But by 1755 it didn't seem to matter. Only those who fled into the forests escaped Le Grand Dérangement—The Expulsion of the Acadians, which dispersed them to Québec, the eastern seaboard, Louisiana (where they became known as Cajuns), France, and even as far as the Falkland Islands. It was a devastating event that probably should have eradicated French language and culture in the Maritimes. It didn't. It did, however, profoundly affect Acadian expression—mobility remains a pervasive theme in the art, literature, and music of Acadian people.

Whether they were hiding deep in Maritime forests or living in exile, Acadians clung tenaciously to their language and traditions. Within 10 years of their deportation, Acadians began to return. They built new communities along coasts and waterways remote from English settlement. In the 1850s Acadians began

to think "nationally." By 1884 there was an Acadian national anthem and a flag.

The Acadian National Holiday on August 15 provides an official reason to celebrate Acadian culture. Le Festival Acadien de Caraquet stretches the celebration out for two weeks. Caraquet is also home to Théâtre Populaire d'Acadie, which mounts original productions for French communities throughout the Maritimes and encourages contemporary Acadian playwrights. Books by Acadian authors, including internationally renowned Antonine Maillet, circulate in Québec, France, and Belgium. Conceptual artist Herménégilde Chiasson pushes the envelope with his poetry and painting, and Paulette Foulem Lanteigne's palate contains the bright colors that have traditionally defined the Acadian spirit.

The earliest Acadian settlers made pine furniture that was elegant in its simplicity. Modern Acadian artisans continue to make functional things, such as pottery and baskets, beautiful. Handmade wooden spoons are doubly beautiful—in pairs they keep time to the music at kitchen parties, where Acadian families have traditionally sung their history around the kitchen fire. But it isn't necessary to have a party to enjoy "music de cuisine." Today, folk singer Edith Butler of Paquetville takes some of that history back to her French cousins in Paris. A lively pop band called Mechants Maquereaux (roughly translated that's "Naughty Mackeral") carries the same messages with a modern spin.

Clearly, the love of music endures here: it rings clear in churches, the cotillion and quadrille are danced at Saturday-night soirées, Acadian sopranos and jazz artists enjoy international renown, and a world-class Baroque Music Festival in Lamèque still celebrates Bach, Vivaldi, and Scarlatti.

— Ana Watts

Acadian Historical Village, ☎ *506/727–6424.* 🎫 *$6.* ☾ *June and Sept., daily 9–6; July–Aug., daily 9–7.*

The **Pope's Museum,** 7 km (4 mi) outside of Caraquet, is the only museum in North America dedicated to papal history. It includes replicas of Saint Peter's Basilica, the cathedral in Florence, and even an Egyptian pyramid. ✉ *184 Acadie St., Grand-Anse,* ☎ *506/732–3003,* 🕸 *www.museedespapes.com.* 🎫 *$5.* ☾ *Mid-June–Aug., daily 10–6.*

Dining and Lodging

$$–$$$$
★ ✕ **La Fine Grobe-Sur-Mer.** North of Bathurst in Nigadoo, about 80 km (50 mi) outside of Caraquet, is one of New Brunswick's finest restaurants. The French cuisine, seafood, and wine are outstanding because the chef–owner never compromises. Sample dishes include seafood crepes, bouillabaisse, and roast leg of lamb. The dining room is small, but has a cozy fireplace and three walls of windows overlooking the ocean. Lunch is available only by special arrangement. ✉ *289 rue Principal,* ☎ *506/783–3138,* 🕸 *www.finegrobe.com. Reservations essential. AE, DC, MC, V. No lunch.*

$ ✕🏨 **Hotel Paulin.** Each pretty room of this quaint property has its own unique look, with old pine dressers and brass beds. An excellent small dining room, open to the public, specializes in fresh fish cooked to perfection, Acadian style. ✉ *143 blvd. St-Pierre W, E1W 1B6,* ☎ *506/ 727–9981,* 📠 *506/727–4808. 4 rooms, 4 suites. Restaurant, in-room data ports. MC, V.*

The Arts

Caraquet is home to **Théâtre Populaire d'Acadie** (✉ 276 blvd. St-Pierre W, ☎ 506/727–0920), a professional theater that mounts original productions by Acadian playwrights.

Outdoor Activities and Sports

Sugarloaf Provincial Park (✉ 596 Val d'Amour Rd., Atholville E3N 4C9, ☎ 506/789–2366) is in Atholville, 180 km (112 mi) north of Caraquet. The eight trails on this 507-ft vertical drop accommodate skiers of all levels. There are also 25 km (16 mi) of cross-country ski trails. Instruction and equipment rentals are available. In summer an Alpine Slide offers fun on the ski hill, and there's lots of space for camping and hiking. The park has a lounge and cafeteria.

ST. JOHN RIVER VALLEY

The St. John River forms 120 km (74 mi) of the border with Maine, then swings inland. Eventually it cuts through the heart of Fredericton and rolls down to Saint John. Gentle hills of rich farmland and the blue sweep of the water make this a lovely area to drive through. The Trans-Canada Highway (Route 2) follows the banks of the river for most of its winding, 403-km (250-mi) course. New highway construction has left Route 102 (the old Route 2) above Fredericton as a quiet scenic drive. In the early 1800s the narrow wedge of land at the northern end of the valley was coveted by Québec and New Brunswick; the United States claimed it as well. To settle the issue, New Brunswick governor Sir Thomas Carleton rolled dice with the governor of British North America at Québec. Sir Thomas won—by one point. Settling the border with the Americans was more difficult; even the lumberjacks engaged in combat. Finally, in 1842, the British flag was hoisted over Madawaska county. One old-timer, tired of being asked to which country he belonged, replied, "I am a citizen of the Republic of Madawaska." So began the mythical republic, which exists today with its own flag (an eagle on a field of white) and a coat of arms.

St-Jacques

280 km (174 mi) north of Fredericton.

This town near the Québec border contains Les Jardins de la République Provincial Park, the Antique Auto Museum, and a botanical garden.

At the **New Brunswick Botanical Garden,** roses, rhododendrons, alpine flowers, and dozens of other annuals and perennials bloom in eight gardens. The music of Mozart, Handel, Bach, or Vivaldi often plays in the background. Two arboretums have coniferous and deciduous trees and shrubs. ⊠ *Main St.,* ☏ *506/737–5383.* 🎫 *$4.75.* ☉ *June and Sept., daily 9–6; July and Aug., daily 9–8.*

Outdoor Activities and Sports

Mont Farlagne (⊠ 360 Mont Farlagne Rd., E7B 2X1, ☏ 506/735–8401) has 20 trails for downhill skiing on a vertical drop of 600 ft. Its four lifts can handle 4,000 skiers per hour, and there's night skiing on eight trails. Snowboarding and tube sliding add to the fun. Equipment rentals are available, and there is a cafeteria and a bar.

Edmundston

㉖ *5 km (3 mi) south of St-Jacques, 275 km (171 mi) northwest of Fredericton.*

Edmundston, the unofficial capital of Madawaska, has always depended on the wealth of the deep forest around it. Even today, the town looks to the Fraser Papers pulp mills as the major source of employment. In these woods the legend of Paul Bunyan was born; tales spread to Maine and beyond. The annual **Foire Brayonne** (☏ 506/739–6608), held over the New Brunswick Day (first Monday in August) long weekend, is the biggest Francophone festival outside Québec. It's also one of the liveliest and most vibrant cultural events in New Brunswick, with concerts by acclaimed artists as well as local musicians and entertainers.

Lodging

$$ 🏨 **Howard Johnson Hotel & Convention Centre.** Its downtown location within a shopping complex near the town's riverside walking trail, and a small restaurant with talented chefs make this chain property worth visiting. ⊠ *100 Rice St., E3V 1T4,* ☏ *506/739–7321 or 800/576–4656,* 𝖥𝖠𝖷 *506/735–9101. 99 rooms, 4 suites. Restaurant, indoor pool, hot tub, sauna, meeting rooms. AE, D, DC, MC, V.*

Grand Falls

㉗ *50 km (31 mi) south of Edmundston.*

At Grand Falls, the St. John River rushes over a high cliff, squeezes through a narrow rocky gorge, and emerges as a wider river. The result is a magnificent cascade, whose force has worn strange round wells in the rocky bed, some as large as 16 ft in circumference and 30 ft deep. A **pontoon boat** operates June through early September at the lower end of the gorge and offers an entirely new perspective of the cliffs and wells. Tickets are available at the LaRochelle Tourist Information Centre. ⊠ *2 Chapel St.,* ☏ *506/475–7760.* 🎫 *$10.* ☉ *Hourly boat trips daily 10–7.*

The **Gorge Walk,** which starts at the Malabeam Tourist Information Center (⊠ 24 Madawaska Rd., ☏ 506/475–7788) and covers the full length of the gorge, is dotted with interpretation panels and monuments. There's no charge for the walk, unless you descend to the wells ($3). Guided walking tours are also available ($6). According to native legend, a young maiden named Malabeam led her Iroquois captors to their deaths over the foaming cataract rather than guide them to her village.

The **Grand Falls Historical Museum** depicts local history. ⊠ *142 Court 209, Suite 103,* ☎ *506/473–5265.* ☜ *Free.* ⊙ *July–Aug., weekdays 9–5.*

En Route   About 75 km (47 mi) south of Grand Falls, stop in Florenceville for a look at the small but reputable **Andrew and Laura McCain Gallery** (⊠ McCain St., Florenceville, ☎ 506/392–6769), which has launched the career of many New Brunswick artists. The Trans-Canada Highway is intriguingly scenic, but if you're looking for less-crowded highways and typical small communities, cross the river to Route 105 at Hartland (about 20 km, or 12 mi, south of Florenceville), via the **longest covered bridge** in the world: 1,282 ft in length.

Mactaquac Provincial Park

🐾 ㉘ *197 km (122 mi) south of Grand Falls.*

Surrounding the giant pond created by the Mactaquac Hydroelectric Dam on the St. John River is Mactaquac Provincial Park. Its facilities include an 18-hole championship golf course, two beaches with lifeguards, two marinas (one for power boats and the other for sailboats), supervised crafts activities, myriad nature and hiking trails, and a restaurant. Reservations are advised for the 300 campsites in summer. Winter is fun, too: there are lots of trails for cross-country skiing, and snowshoeing and sleigh rides are available by appointment. The toboggan hills and skating–ice hockey ponds are even lit in the evening. ⊠ *Rte. 105 at Mactaquac Dam,* ☎ *506/363–4747.* ☜ *$5 per vehicle in summer, free Sept.–June.* ⊙ *Daily; overnight camping mid-May–mid-Oct.*

En Route   Oromocto, along Route 102 from Mactaquac Provincial Park, is the site of the Canadian Armed Forces Base, **Camp Gagetown,** the largest military base in Canada (not to be confused with the pretty village of Gagetown farther downriver). Prince Charles completed his helicopter training here. The base has an interesting military museum. ⊠ *Museum, Bldg. A5, off Tilley St.,* ☎ *506/422–1304.* ☜ *Museum free.* ⊙ *June–Aug., weekdays 8–4, weekends noon–4; Sept.–May, weekdays 8–4.*

Gagetown

㉙ *265 km (164 mi) southeast of Grand Falls, 50 km (31 mi) southeast of Fredericton.*

Historic Gagetown bustles with artisans and the summer sailors who tie up at the marina. The **Queens County Museum** is growing by leaps and bounds. Its original building, **Tilley House,** was the birthplace of Sir Leonard Tilley, one of the Fathers of Confederation. It displays loyalist and First Nations artifacts, early 20th-century medical equipment, Victorian glassware, and more. The museum now also includes the nearby old **Queens County Court House,** which holds county archival material and court house furniture. It also hosts changing exhibits throughout the season. ⊠ *Museum: Front St.; Court House: Court House Rd.,* ☎ *506/488–2966.* ☜ *$2 per building, $3 for both.* ⊙ *June–mid-Sept., daily 10–5.*

Lodging

$ 🏠 **Steamers Stop Inn.** This grand old waterside inn has a screened veranda, antiques, and an art gallery on the premises. Continental breakfast is included in the rate. Dinner is served by reservation from 6 to 9 each evening. ⊠ *74 Front St., E5M 1A1,* ☎ *506/488–2903,* ℻ *506/*

488–1116, WEB *www.heritageinns.com/steamers. 6 rooms. Dining room, outdoor hot tub, boating. AE, MC, V. Closed Oct.–Apr. CP.*

Shopping

Beamsley's Coffee House (☒ 44 Front St., ☎ 506/488–3164) sells lunches, big cookies, sticky buns, and coffee in pottery cups. **Grimcross Crafts** (☒ 17 Mill Rd., ☎ 506/488–2832) represents 30 area craftspeople. **Flo Grieg's** (☒ 36 Front St., ☎ 506/488–2074) carries superior pottery made on the premises. **Juggler's Cove** (☒ 32 Tilley Rd., ☎ 506/488–2574) is a studio-gallery featuring pottery, paintings, and woodwork. **Loomcrofters** (☒ Loomcroft La., off Main St., ☎ 506/488–2400) is a good choice for handwoven items.

FREDERICTON

The small inland city of Fredericton spreads itself on a broad point of land jutting into the St. John River. Its predecessor, the early French settlement of St. Anne's Point, was established in 1642 during the reign of the French governor Villebon, who made his headquarters at the junction of the Nashwaak and the St. John rivers. Settled by Loyalists and named for Frederick, second son of George III, the city serves as the seat of government for New Brunswick's 753,000 residents. Wealthy and scholarly Loyalists set out to create a gracious and beautiful place, and thus even before the establishment of the University of New Brunswick, in 1785, the town served as a center for liberal arts and sciences. It remains a gracious and beautiful place as well as a center of education, arts, and culture. The river, once the only highway to Fredericton, is now a focus of recreation.

Exploring Fredericton

Downtown Queen Street runs parallel with the river, and its blocks enclose historic sights and attractions. Most major sights are within walking distance of one another. An excursion to Kings Landing Historical Settlement, a reconstructed village, can bring alive the province's history.

Dressed in 18th-century costume, actors from the **Calithumpians** theater company (☎ 506/457–1975) conduct free historical walks several times a day in summer and an after-dark Haunted Hike ($12) several evenings a week.

A Good Walk

Start at City Hall, formerly a farmers' market and opera house, on Phoenix Square, at the corner of York and Queen streets. Its modern council chambers are decorated with tapestries that illustrate Fredericton's history. Walk down (as the river flows) Queen Street to Carleton Street to the **Military Compound** ㉚, which includes the New Brunswick Sports Hall of Fame and the **York-Sunbury Museum** ㉛, the latter occupying what used to be the Officers' Quarters in Officers' Square. Here the Calithumpians offer outdoor comedy theater at lunchtime. On a rainy day the show goes on in the nearby Carleton Street Armory. The next stop down the river side of Queen Street is the **Beaverbrook Art Gallery** ㉜, with its sculpture garden outside. Turn right on Church Street and walk to **Christ Church Cathedral** ㉝. Once you have had your fill of its exquisite architecture and stained glass, turn right and start walking back up Queen. The **Provincial Legislature** ㉞ is on your left. Restaurants and cafés along Queen Street provide opportunities for refreshment. Turn left on St. John Street and then take the second right onto Brunswick Street, where the wonders of **Science East** ㉟ await you. If you make your way back to York Street (across

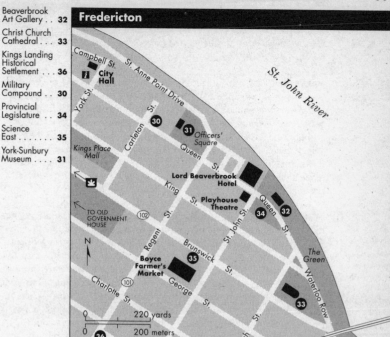

from where you started at City Hall), turn left to visit a chic block of shops. One variation to this walk: if you're touring on Saturday, start in the morning with the **Boyce Farmers' Market,** off George and Brunswick streets, to get a real taste of the city.

TIMING

The distances are not great, so the time you spend depends on how much you like history, science, art, and churches. You could do it all in an afternoon, but start in the morning at the Boyce Farmers' Market on Saturday.

Sights to See

32 Beaverbrook Art Gallery. A lasting gift of the late Lord Beaverbrook, this gallery could hold its head high in the company of some smaller European galleries. Salvador Dali's gigantic *Santiago el Grande* has always been the star, but a rotation of avant-garde Canadian paintings now shares pride of place. The McCain "gallery-within-a-gallery" is devoted to the finest Atlantic Canadian artists. ⊠ *703 Queen St.,* ☎ *506/458–8545.* ⊡ *$5.* ☉ *June–Sept., weekdays 9–6, weekends 10–5; Oct.–May, Tues.–Fri. 9–5, Sat. 10–5, Sun. noon–5.*

Boyce Farmers' Market. It's hard to miss this Saturday-morning market because of the crowds. There are lots of local meat and produce, baked goods, crafts, and seasonal items like wreaths and maple syrup. The market sells good ready-to-eat food, from German sausages to tasty sandwiches. ⊠ *Bounded by Regent, Brunswick, and George Sts.*

33 Christ Church Cathedral. One of Fredericton's prides, this gray stone building, completed in 1853, is an excellent example of decorated neo-Gothic architecture. The cathedral's design was based on an actual medieval prototype in England, and it became a model for many American churches. Inside you'll see a clock known as "Big Ben's little brother," the test run for London's famous timepiece, designed by Lord Grimthorpe. ⊠ *Church St.,* ☎ *506/450–8500.* ☉ *Self-guided tours available year-round. Free guided tours mid-June–Aug., weekdays 9–6, Sat. 10–5, Sun. 1–5.*

<table>
<tr><td>OFF THE
BEATEN PATH</td><td>MARYSVILLE – A National Historic Region, Marysville is one of Canada's best-preserved examples of a 19th-century mill town. Its architecture and social history are amazing and can be appreciated with the help of a self-guided walking-tour booklet available at the York-Sunbury Museum and at Westminster Books on King Street. Marysville itself is on the north side of the St. John River, about 10 km (6 mi) from downtown via Route 8. Knobb Hill Gallery (⊠ 285 Canada St., ☎ 506/450–1986), home of the Catherine Karns Munn Collection, is a sentimental stop, with paintings and crafts depicting the local area and Victorian scenes.</td></tr>
</table>

㉚ Military Compound. The restored buildings of this British and Canadian post, which extends two blocks along Queen Street, include soldiers' barracks, a guardhouse, and a cell block. Local artisans operate studios in the casemates below the soldiers' barracks. In July and August free guided tours run throughout the day and there are outdoor concerts in Officers' Square Tuesday and Thursday evenings. Red Coat soldiers have long stood guard in Officers' Square, and a formal changing-of-the-guard ceremony takes place in summer at 11 and 7. It's even possible for children of all ages to live a soldier's life for a while: each summer afternoon at 2, would-be red coats get their own uniforms and practice drilling ($12 per person, $40 per family). ⊠ *Queen St. at Carleton St.,* ☎ *506/460–2129.* ☉ *Free.*

Old Government House. This imposing 1828 Palladian mansion has been restored as the official seat of office for the province's lieutenant governor. A hands-on interpretation center with multimedia presentations spans 12,000 years of history. Guided tours take in elegantly restored state rooms and art galleries. The 11-acre grounds include a 17th-century Acadian settlement and border an early Maliseet burial ground. ⊠ *Woodstock Rd.,* ☎ *506/453–2505.* ☉ *Free.* ☉ *June–Oct., daily 10–5 (last hourly tour begins at 4); Nov.–May, weekdays by appointment.*

㉞ Provincial Legislature. The interior chamber of the legislature, where the premier and elected members govern the province, reflects the taste of the late Victorians. The chandeliers are brass, and the prisms are Waterford. Replicas of portraits by Sir Joshua Reynolds of King George III and Queen Charlotte hang here. There's a freestanding circular staircase, and a volume of Audubon's *Birds of America* is on display. ⊠ *Queen St.,* ☎ *506/453–2527.* ☉ *Free.* ☉ *Legislature tours June–Aug., daily 9–6; Sept.–May, weekdays 9–4; library weekdays 8:15–5.*

㉟ Science East. This hands-on science center, in what was once the York County Jail, has family fun locked up. The more than 70 exhibits include a giant kaleidoscope you can walk inside, a pattern-making laser beam, and a place where you can create a minitornado. ⊠ *668 Brunswick St.,* ☎ *506/457–2340.* ☉ *$2.* ☉ *June–Sept., Mon.–Sat. 10–5, Sun. 1–4; Oct.–May, Tues.–Fri. noon–5, Sat. 10–5.*

York Street. Here is the city's high-fashion block, with designer shops, a hairdresser-cum-art dealer, an incense-burning boutique, and a general store with an eclectic assortment of gifts and housewares. At the middle of the upriver side of the block is Mazucca's Alley, with more shops and the gateway to several more stores and restaurants in Piper's Lane. King and Queen streets, at either end of the block, have some fun shops, too.

③ **York-Sunbury Museum.** The Officers' Quarters houses a museum that offers a living picture of the community from the time when only First Nations peoples inhabited the area, through the Acadian and Loyalist days, to the immediate past. Its World War I trench puts you in the thick of battle, and the shellacked remains of the giant Coleman Frog, a Fredericton legend, still inspire controversy. ⊠ *Officers' Sq., Queen St.,* ☎ *506/455–6041.* ☒ *$2.* ☉ *May–early Sept., Mon.–Sat. 10–6; July–Aug., Mon. and Fri. 'til 9, Sun. noon–6; early Sept.–mid-Oct., weekdays 9–5, Sat. noon–4; mid-Oct.–Apr., Mon., Wed., and Fri. 11–3, or by appointment.*

Dining and Lodging

$$–$$$$ ✕ **Lobster Hut.** A 200-gallon tank stocked with 1- to 2-pound lobsters adds the finishing touch to the nautical decor of this popular spot. The high end of the price range depends on the market price of lobster. ⊠ *City Motel, 1216 Regent St.,* ☎ *506/455–4413. AE, DC, MC, V.*

$–$$$ ✕ **Brewbaker's.** Downtown's most popular spot for casual dining, Brewbaker's has an old-world Italian atmosphere, California and eclectic cuisine, and a rooftop garden patio. Fabulous salads, authentic pastas, and thin-crust pizzas baked in a wood-fired brick oven assist in drawing the crowds. ⊠ *546 King St.,* ☎ *506/459–0067. Reservations essential. AE, DC, MC, V.*

$–$$ ✕ **Dimitri Souvlaki.** Chicken souvlaki reigns supreme in this downtown authentic Greek eatery, but lots of people make a meal of the appetizers, especially the *pikilia* (hors d'oeuvres) platters and *saganaki* (sautéed goat's milk cheese with lemon juice). ⊠ *349 King St., at Piper's La.,* ☎ *506/452–8882. AE, DC, MC, V.*

$–$$ ✕ **El Burrito Loco.** With family recipes in his head and love in his heart, Perez Huerta moved to his wife's home in Fredericton from his home in Jalisco, Mexico. His authentic Mexican dishes have caught on like wildfire up north—even the huevos rancheros for breakfast. Everything is made on the spot, from the burritos and tacos to the guacamole and salsa. There's a patio for summer, and occasionally local Spanish guitarists or mariachi players from Montréal entertain. ⊠ *304 King St.,* ☎ *506/459–5626. Reservations essential. AE, MC, V.*

$$$$ ▦ **Sheraton Fredericton Hotel.** This stately riverside property is within walking distance of downtown. The elegant country decor is almost as delightful as the sunset views over the river from the patio restaurant and many of the modern rooms. The gift shop carries top-notch crafts. Bruno's Cafe serves legendary buffets, seafood on Friday evening, and brunch on Sunday. ⊠ *225 Woodstock Rd., E3B 2H8,* ☎ *506/457–7000,* ℻ *506/457–4000,* WEB *www.sheraton.com. 208 rooms, 15 suites. Restaurant, bar, indoor-outdoor pool, hot tub, sauna, gym. AE, DC, MC, V.*

$$$ ▦ **Holiday Inn Hotel and Resort Fredericton.** Outside the city and overlooking the Mactaquac Headpond, this modern hotel offers luxurious appointments in a relaxed, country atmosphere. There's a fireplace in the lobby, and the suites have electric fireplaces. Some of the rooms with water views have cathedral ceilings. The cottages are ideal for boating and skiing families. ⊠ *35 Mactaquac Rd., off Rte. 102, French Village, E3E 1L2,* ☎ *506/363–5111 or 800/561–5111,* ℻ *506/363–3000,* WEB *www.holidayinnfredericton.com. 72 rooms, 4 suites, 6 cottages. Dining room, lounge, in-room data ports, indoor pool, hot tub, tennis court, gym, dock. AE, D, DC, MC, V.*

$$ ▦ **Lord Beaverbrook Hotel.** This hotel was acquired by new owners in 2000. At press time it had yet to be re-named, and was still awaiting renovations. No matter what improvements the new owners make, however, the downtown location of this hotel is its most attractive fea-

ture. ⊠ *659 Queen St., E3B 5A6,* ☏ *506/455–3371,* FAX *506/455–1441. 155 rooms, 13 suites. 2 restaurants, bar, no-smoking rooms, indoor pool, hot tub, sauna. AE, DC, MC, V.*

$$ ⊞ **On the Pond Lodge.** This woodland, European-style lodge near the river offers several opportunities for relaxation and rejuvenation, including full spa packages, canoeing, kayaking, and hiking. Everything about the place is elegant yet hearty, from the big stone fireplace and exposed beams in the great room to the well-appointed bedrooms. Dinner in the dining room can be as decadent or as nutritious as you like. ⊠ *20 Rte. 615, Mactaquac E6L 1M2,* ☏ *506/363–3420,* FAX *506/363– 3479,* WEB *www.onthepond.com. 8 rooms. Dining room, sauna, bicycles. MC, V.*

$ ⊞ **Carriage House Inn.** The lovely bedrooms in this venerable mansion are furnished with Victorian antiques. A complimentary breakfast, complete with homemade maple syrup for the fluffy pancakes, is served in the solarium. ⊠ *230 University Ave., E3B 4H7,* ☏ *506/452– 9924 or 800/267–6068,* FAX *506/458–0799,* WEB *www.bbcanada.com/ 4658.html. 11 rooms. Solarium. AE, DC, MC, V.*

$ ⊞ **The Very Best—A Victorian B&B.** This elegant home, with its fine antiques and original artwork, is in the downtown Heritage Preservation Area. The smoked-salmon omelette is an outstanding breakfast choice. ⊠ *806 George St., E3B 1K7,* ☏ *506/451–1499,* FAX *506/454–1454,* WEB *www.bbcanada.com/2330.html. 3 rooms. Dining room, pool, sauna. AE, MC, V. BP.*

Nightlife and the Arts

The Arts

The **Calithumpians** (☏ 506/457–1975) offer free summer outdoor theater daily (12:15 weekdays, 2 PM weekends) in Officers' Square and an evening Haunted Hike ($12) through a historic haunted neighborhood and ghostly graveyards. The **Playhouse** (⊠ 686 Queen St., ☏ 506/458–8344) is the venue for theater and most other cultural performances, including Symphony New Brunswick, Theatre New Brunswick, and traveling ballet and dance companies.

Nightlife

Fredericton has a lively nightlife, with lots of live music in downtown pubs, especially on the weekends. King Street and Piper's Lane, off the 300 block of King Street, have a number of spots. **Bugaboo Creek** (⊠ 422 Queen St., ☏ 506/453–0582) features R&B and blues. **The Capital** (⊠ 362 Queen St., ☏ 506/459–3558) offers an eclectic collection of good acts—jazz, blues, oldies, and folk. **Dolan's Pub** (⊠ 349 King St., ☏ 506/454–7474) features Maritime acts every weekend. The **Lunar Rogue** (⊠ 625 King St., ☏ 506/450–2065) has an old-world pub atmosphere and occasionally showcases acoustic folk, rock, and Celtic music. **Moe's Garage** (⊠ 375 King St., ☏ 506/458–1254) is a venue for rock, blues, folk, and pretty much anything other than country. **Rye's Deli & Pub** (⊠ 73 Carleton St., ☏ 506/472–7937) goes for cozy and romantic with leather booths and soft lights. There's live jazz and blues every weekend.

Outdoor Activities and Sports

Boat Tours

The 80-passenger *Carleton II* (⊠ departs from Regent Street Wharf, ☏ 506/454–2628) is used for sightseeing river cruises. *The Wood Duck* (☏ 506/444–9180 or 506/447–7494), a little water taxi, complete with a canopy, offers nature and exploration tours. It departs from the Sheraton Hotel and Regent Street Wharf.

Canoeing and Kayaking

Shells, canoes, and kayaks can be rented by the hour, day, or week at the **Small Craft Aquatic Center** (⊠ behind Victoria Health Centre, where Brunswick St. becomes Woodstock Rd., ☎ 506/460–2260), which also arranges guided tours and instruction.

Golf

The Lynx At Kingswood Park (⊠ 31 Kingswood Park, ☎ 506/443–3333 or 877/666–0001), opened in 2001, is the first major course to open in many years. It's an 18-hole, par-72 championship course designed by Cooke–Huxham International.

Skiing

Ski Crabbe Mountain (⊠ 50 Crabbe Mountain Rd., Central Hainesville E6E 1E3, ☎ 506/463–8311) is about 55 km (34 mi) west of Fredericton. There are 17 trails, a vertical drop of 853 ft, snowboard and ski rentals, instruction, a skating pond, baby-sitting, and a lounge and restaurant.

Many of Fredericton's 70 km (44 mi) of walking trails, especially those along the river and in Odell and Wilmot parks, are groomed for cross-country skiing. Other trails are broken and useful for skate-skiing.

Walking

Fredericton has a fine network of walking trails, one of which follows the river from the Green, past the Victorian mansions on Waterloo Row, behind the Beaverbrook Art Gallery, and along the riverbank to the Sheraton. The **visitor information center** in City Hall (⊠ Queen St., at York St., ☎ 506/460–2129) has a trail map.

Shopping

Indoor mammoth crafts markets are held in the fall; a Labor Day–weekend outdoor craft fair is held in Officers' Square. You can find pottery, blown glass, pressed flowers, turned wood, leather, and other items, all made by members of the New Brunswick Craft Council.

Aitkens Pewter (⊠ 65 Regent St., ☎ 506/453–9474) makes its own pewter goblets, belt buckles, candlesticks, and jewelry. **Botinicals Gift Shop** (⊠ 65 Shore St., ☎ 506/454–7361) sells crafts by juried Maritime artisans only. **Carrington&Co.** (⊠ 225 Woodstock Rd., ☎ 506/450–8415) in the Sheraton is a gem for crafts and Tilley Endurables clothing. **Eloise** (⊠ 83 York St., ☎ 506/453–7715) carries kinder, gentler women's fashions. **Gallery 78** (⊠ 96 Queen St., ☎ 506/454–5192) has original works by local artists. **Marba Gallery** (⊠ 1565 Woodstock Rd., ☎ 506/454–4862) offers fine art and crafts, antiques, and even Oriental carpets. **The New Brunswick Fine Craft Gallery** (⊠ 87 Regent St., ☎ 506/450–8989) exhibits and sells juried crafts. **Table for Two** (⊠ Kings Place Mall, 440 King St., ☎ 506/455–1401) specializes in New Brunswick crafts and offers fine imported glass and tableware. **The Urban Almanac General Store** (⊠ 59 York St., ☎ 506/450–4334) has an eclectic collection of unique housewares and other items of exemplary design.

Side Trip from Fredericton

30 km (19 mi) west of Fredericton.

★ ☺ ㊱ **Kings Landing Historical Settlement.** This excellent outdoor living-history museum on the St. John River evokes the sights, sounds, and society of rural New Brunswick between 1790 and 1900. The winding country lanes and meticulously restored homes pull you back a century or more, and programs are available to let you cane a chair at the carpenter shop or bake bread on an open hearth. There are daily dramas in the theater, barn dances, and strolling minstrels. You can see how the wealthy owner of the sawmill lived and just how different things were for the immigrant farmer. Hearty meals are served at the Kings Head Inn.

The Kings Landing Historical Settlement was built by moving period buildings to a new shore. The drive from Fredericton takes less than a half hour; to appreciate the museum, plan to spend at least a half day. Route 102 passes through some spectacular river and hill scenery on the way, including the Mactaquac Dam—turn off here if you want to visit Mactaquac Provincial Park. ⊠ *Exit 253, Trans-Canada Hwy. (near Prince William),* ☎ *506/363–4999,* WEB *www.kingslanding.nb.ca.* ⊠ *$12.* ☉ *June–mid-Oct., daily 10–5.*

NEW BRUNSWICK A TO Z

To research prices, get advice from other travelers, and book travel arrangements, visit www.fodors.com.

AIR TRAVEL
Air Canada serves the three major airports in the area. Moncton Airport is also served by Canada 3000 and WestJet.
➤ AIRLINES AND CONTACTS: **Air Canada** (☎ 800/776–3000). **airNova** (☎ 888/247–2262). **Canada 3000 Airlines** (☎ 877/973–3000). **West-Jet Airlines** (☎ 800/538–5696).

AIRPORTS
New Brunswick has three major airports. Saint John Airport (YSJ) is in the east end of the city; Moncton Airport (YQM) is on Champlain Road; and Fredericton Airport (YFC) is minutes from downtown on Lincoln Road.
➤ AIRPORT INFORMATION: **Fredericton Airport** (⊠ Lincoln Rd., ☎ 506/444–6100). **Moncton Airport** (⊠ Champlain Rd., ☎ 506/856–5444). **Saint John Airport** (⊠ Loch Lomond Rd., ☎ 506/638–5555).

BUS TRAVEL
SMT Eastern Ltd. runs buses within the province and connects with most major bus lines.
➤ BUS INFORMATION: **SMT Eastern Ltd.** (☎ 506/859–5100 or 800/567–5151).

CAR RENTAL
➤ LOCAL AGENCIES: **Byways Car & Truck Rental** (☎ 800/668–4233 or 902/469–2620). **Trius Car & Truck Rental** (☎ 506/457–9000).
➤ MAJOR AGENCIES: **Avis** (☎ 800/331–1084; 800/879–2847 in Canada, WEB www.avis.com). **Budget** (☎ 800/527–0700, WEB www.budget.com). **Hertz** (☎ 800/654–3001; 800/263–0600 in Canada, WEB www.hertz. com). **National Car Rental** (☎ 800/227–7368, WEB www.nationalcar. com).

CAR TRAVEL
From Québec, the Trans-Canada Highway (Route 2) enters New Brunswick at St-Jacques and follows the St. John River through Fredericton and on to Moncton and the Nova Scotia border. From Maine, I-95 crosses at Houlton to Woodstock, New Brunswick, where it connects with the Trans-Canada Highway. Those traveling up the coast of Maine on Route 1, cross at Calais to St. Stephen, New Brunswick. New Brunswick's Route 1 extends to Saint John and up to Sussex, where it meets the Trans-Canada Highway.

New Brunswick has an excellent highway system with numerous facilities. The Trans-Canada Highway, marked by a maple leaf, is the same as Route 2. Route 7 joins Saint John and Fredericton. Fredericton is connected to Miramichi City by Route 8. Route 15 links Moncton to the eastern coast and to Route 11, which follows the coast to Miramichi City, around the Acadian Peninsula, and up to Campbellton. You can get a good map at a visitor information center. Tourism New Brunswick has mapped five scenic routes: the Fundy Coastal Drive, the River Valley Scenic Drive, the Acadian Coastal Drive, the Miramichi River Route, and the Appalachian Range.

EMERGENCIES
➤ EMERGENCY SERVICES: **Ambulance, fire, police** (☎ 911).
➤ HOSPITALS: **Campbellton Regional Hospital** (✉ 189 Lilly Lake Rd., Campbellton, ☎ 506/789–5000). **Chaleur Regional Hospital** (✉ 1750 Sunset Dr., Bathurst, ☎ 506/548–8961). **Dr. Everett Chalmers Hospital** (✉ Priestman St., Fredericton, ☎ 506/452–5400). **Dr. Georges Dumont Hospital** (✉ 330 Archibald St., Moncton, ☎ 506/862–4000). **Edmundston Regional Hospital** (✉ 275 Hébert Blvd., Edmundston, ☎ 506/739–2200). **Miramichi Regional Hospital** (✉ 500 Water St., Miramichi City, ☎ 506/623–3000). **Moncton City Hospital** (✉ 135 MacBeath Ave., Moncton, ☎ 506/857–5111). **Saint John Regional Hospital** (✉ Tucker Park Rd., Saint John, ☎ 506/648–6000).

OUTDOORS AND SPORTS
Whale-watching, sea kayaking, trail riding, bird-watching, garden touring, river cruising, and fishing are just a few of the province's Day Adventure programs. Packages cover a variety of skill levels and include equipment. All adventures last at least a half day; some are multiday. Information is available at New Brunswick Day Adventure centers (in some information offices, hotels, and attractions), or contact Tourism New Brunswick (☎ 800/561–0123).

BIKING
B&Bs frequently have bicycles for rent. Tourism New Brunswick (☎ 800/561–0123) has listings and free cycling maps. Baymount Outdoor Adventures operates along the Fundy shore near Hopewell Cape.
➤ CONTACTS: **Baymount Outdoor Adventures** (✉ 17 Elwin Jay Dr., Hillsborough, ☎ 506/734–2660).

FISHING
New Brunswick Fish and Wildlife has information on sporting licenses and can tell you where the fish are.
➤ CONTACTS: **New Brunswick Fish and Wildlife** (☎ 506/453–2440).

GOLF
The most up-to-date information about new courses and upgrades to existing courses is available at the New Brunswick Golf Association.
➤ CONTACTS: **New Brunswick Golf Association** (☎ 506/451–1324, WEB www.golfnb.nb.ca).

HIKING
The New Brunswick Trails Council has complete information on the province's burgeoning trail system.
➤ CONTACTS: **New Brunswick Trails Council** (☎ 506/459–1931 or 800/526–7070).

SNOWMOBILING
For information on snowmobiling, contact the New Brunswick Federation of Snowmobile Clubs, a group that maintains the province's 9,000-km trail system and issues permits.

➤ CONTACTS: **New Brunswick Federation of Snowmobile Clubs** (☎ 506/ 325–2625).

TOURS
Saint John visitor information centers have brochures for three good self-guided walking tours. Guided walking tours sponsored by the City of Saint John are also available (☎ 506/658–2855 for information).

TRAIN TRAVEL
VIA Rail offers passenger service every day but Tuesday from Campbellton, Newcastle, and Moncton to Montréal and Halifax.
➤ TRAIN INFORMATION: **VIA Rail** (☎ 800/561–8630 in Canada; 800/ 561–3949 in the U.S.).

TRANSPORTATION AROUND NEW BRUNSWICK
A car is essential outside Saint John, Moncton, and Fredericton. The inter-city bus line (SMT) has specific routes, and there are a couple of places where there are local shuttle services to small towns from the bus, but these are few and far between.

VISITOR INFORMATION
Tourism New Brunswick can provide information on day adventures, scenic driving routes, accommodations, and the seven provincial tourist bureaus. Also helpful are the city information services in Bathurst, Edmundston–St-Jacques, Fredericton, Moncton, Saint John, and St. Stephen.
➤ TOURIST INFORMATION: **Tourism New Brunswick** (✉ Box 12345, Fredericton E3B 5C3, ☎ 800/561–0123, WEB www.tourismnbcanada.com). **Bathurst** (☎ 506/548–0418). **Edmundston–St-Jacques** (☎ 506/735– 2747). **Fredericton** (☎ 506/460–2041). **Moncton** (☎ 506/853–3590). **Saint John** (☎ 506/658–2990). **St. Stephen** (☎ 506/466–7390).

4 PRINCE EDWARD ISLAND

This island province, in the Gulf of St. Lawrence north of Nova Scotia and New Brunswick, seems too good to be true, with its crisply painted farmhouses, manicured green fields rolling down to sandy beaches, the warmest ocean water north of the Carolinas, and lobster boats in trim little harbors. The vest-pocket capital city, Charlottetown, is packed with architectural heritage.

WHEN YOU EXPERIENCE Prince Edward Island, known locally as "the Island," you'll understand instantly why Lucy Maud Montgomery's novel of youth and innocence, *Anne of Green Gables,* was framed against this land. What may have been unexpected, however, was how the story burst on the world in 1908 and is still selling untold thousands of copies every year. After potatoes and lobsters, Anne is the Island's most important product.

In 1864, Charlottetown, the Island's capital city, hosted one of the most important meetings in Canadian history, which eventually led to the creation of the Dominion of Canada in 1867. Initially, Prince Edward Island was reluctant to join, having spent years fighting for the right to an autonomous government. Originally settled by the French in 1603, the Island was handed over to the British under the Treaty of Paris in 1763. Tensions grew as absentee British governors and proprietors failed to take an active interest in the development of the land, and the resulting parliamentary government proved ineffective for similar reasons. Yet the development of fisheries and agriculture at the beginning of the 19th century strengthened the economy. Soon settlement increased, and those who were willing to take a chance on the Island prospered.

Around the middle of the 19th century, a modern cabinet government was created, and relations between tenants and proprietors worsened. At the same time, talk of creating a union with other North American colonies began. After much deliberation, and although political upheaval had begun to subside, delegates decided that it was in the Island's best economic interest to join the Canadian Confederation.

The 1997 opening of the Confederation Bridge, linking Prince Edward Island's Borden-Carleton with New Brunswick's Cape Jourimain, physically sealed the Island's connection with the mainland. The bridge was not built without controversy. Nobody doubts that it is an engineering marvel: massive concrete pillars—65 ft across and 180 ft high—were sunk into waters more than 110 ft deep in order to cope with traffic that now brings more than 1 million visitors annually. Most locals have gotten used to the bridge, but some fear the loss of the Island's tranquillity. As you explore the crossroads villages and fishing ports, it's not hard to understand why. Outside the tourist mecca of Cavendish, otherwise known as Anne's Land, the Island seems like an oasis of peace in an increasingly busy world.

Pleasures and Pastimes

The Arts
The arts, particularly theater, are an integral part of the Island. Summer productions and theater festivals are highlights. The grandest is the Charlottetown Festival, which takes place June through mid-September at the Confederation Centre of the Arts. Theater in Summerside, Georgetown, and Victoria is also good. Traditional Celtic music, with fiddling and step dancing, can be heard almost daily.

Beaches
Prince Edward Island is ringed by beaches, most of them lightly used. Ask a dozen Islanders to recommend their favorites and you'll hear many different answers. Basin Head Beach, near Souris, is one choice—miles of singing sands, utterly deserted. West Point has lifeguards, restaurants nearby, and showers at the provincial park. At Greenwich, near St. Peter's Bay, a half-hour walk along the floating boardwalk brings you to an endless empty beach. In summer, thanks to a branch of the

Gulf Stream, the ocean beaches have the warmest water north of the Carolinas, which makes for fine swimming.

Dining

On Prince Edward Island, wholesome, home-cooked fare is a matter of course. Talented chefs ensure fine cuisine in each region. The service is friendly—though a little laid back at times—and the setting is generally informal. Seafood is usually good anywhere on the Island, with top honors given to lobster. Lobster suppers are offered commercially and by church and civic groups. These meals feature lobster, rolls, salad, and mountains of sweet home-baked goods. Local papers, bulletin boards at grocery stores, and visitor information centers have information about these events.

CATEGORY	COST*
$$$$	over $32
$$$	$22–$32
$$	$13–$21
$	under $13

per person, in Canadian dollars, for a main course at dinner

Lodging

Prince Edward Island has a variety of accommodations in a range of prices, from full-service resorts and luxury hotels to moderately priced motels, cottages, and lodges. Some farms take guests, too. For July and August, lodgings should be booked early, especially for long stays.

CATEGORY	COST*
$$$$	over $200
$$$	$150–$200
$$	$100–$150
$	under $100

All prices are in Canadian dollars for a standard double room, excluding 10% provincial sales tax and 7% GST.

Outdoor Activities and Sports

BIKING

The Island is popular with bike-touring companies for its moderately hilly roads and stunning scenery; trips take place throughout the province, and the Island's tourism department can recommend tour operators. There are plenty of level areas, especially east of Charlottetown to Montague and along the north shore. However, shoulderless, narrow secondary roads in some areas and summer's car traffic can be challenging. A 9-km (5½-mi) path near Cavendish Campground loops around marsh, woods, and farmland. The Confederation Trail, which extends almost the complete length of the Island, has more than 350 km (217 mi) of flat surface covered with rolled stonedust, making it an excellent family cycling path. Plum-color entry gateways are near roadways at many points. A two-sided map–information sheet is available from Tourism PEI.

FISHING

Deep-sea fishing boats are available along the eastern end of the Island as well as in the north shore region. Although some boats can be chartered for fishing bluefin tuna, most operators offer excursions to fish for mackerel and cod. These trips stay within 6 km (4 mi) of the shore and usually last for three or four hours. The vessels have washroom facilities, approved safety equipment, and all the required gear and bait. Some operators clean and bag the catch if passengers request it.

Freshwater sport fishing for rainbow trout or salmon is also an option. A nonresident one-day fishing license may be purchased for $7 at more than 100 businesses (hardware, tackle, convenience stores) throughout PEI. A few operations rent fishing tackle and offer "no license required" fishing on private ponds.

GOLF

Prince Edward Island is a golfer's paradise with more than two dozen 9- and 18-hole courses open to the public. Several of the more beautiful ones have scenic ocean vistas, and almost all have hassle-free golfing—easily booked tee times, inexpensive rates, and uncrowded courses, particularly in fall. Brudenell River, incorporating the Brudenell Resort Golf Academy, is Atlantic Canada's only 36-hole complex.

HIKING

Hiking within the lush scenic areas of Prince Edward Island National Park and provincial parks is encouraged with marked trails, many of which are being upgraded to provide quality surfaces good for walking, hiking, or cycling. One of the trails is part of Confederation Trail, a provincial trail system created along the flat roadbed of the former railway network, which allows outdoor explorers to travel 350 km (217 mi) within the province. Contact Tourism PEI for a map.

Exploring Prince Edward Island

Prince Edward Island is irregular in shape, with deep inlets and tidal streams that nearly divide the province into three equal parts, known locally by their county names of Kings, Queens, and Prince (east to west). Roughly resembling a crescent, it is 224 km (139 mi) from one end to the other, with a width ranging from 4 km (2½ mi) to 60 km (37 mi). The Island is a rich agricultural region surrounded by sandy beaches, delicate dunes, and stunning red sandstone cliffs. The eastern and central sections consist of gentle hills. Nevertheless, the land never rises to a height of more than 500 ft above sea level, and you are never more than 15 minutes by car from a beach or waterway. To the west, from Summerside to North Cape, the terrain is flatter.

Numbers in the text correspond to numbers in the margin and on the Prince Edward Island and Charlottetown maps.

Great Itineraries

Visitors often tour only the central portion of the Island, taking Confederation Bridge from New Brunswick to Borden-Carleton and exploring Anne country and Prince Edward Island National Park. To experience the Island's character more deeply, you might visit the wooded hills of the east, including compact, bustling Montague. Another choice is to go west to superb, almost private beaches, the Acadian parish of Tignish, and the country around Summerside. Even if you're in a rush, it won't take long to get off and back on the beaten path: in most places you can cross the Island, north to south, in half an hour or so. The four areas identified in this chapter include many Island highlights: a mostly walking tour of Charlottetown, and three tours following the major scenic highways—Blue Heron Drive, Kings Byway, and Lady Slipper Drive. There are plenty of chances to get out of the car, hit the beach, or photograph wildflowers.

IF YOU HAVE 1 DAY

Leaving 🕭 **Charlottetown** ①–⑨ on Route 2 west, take Route 15 north to **Brackley Beach** ⑪. This puts you onto a 137-km-long (85-mi-long) scenic drive, marked with signs depicting a blue heron. Route 6 west takes you to **Cavendish** ⑫, an entryway to **Prince Edward Island National Park** ⑩. Cavendish is home to the fictional character Anne of Lucy Maud Montgomery's *Anne of Green Gables*. This area has enough attractions for a full day, but if you prefer to keep exploring,

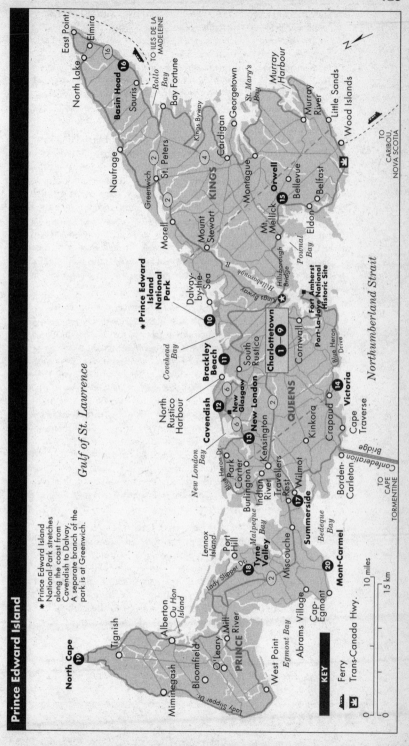

Prince Edward Island

* Prince Edward Island National Park stretches along the coast from Cavendish to Dalvay. A separate branch of the park is at Greenwich.

Gulf of St. Lawrence

TO ÎLES DE LA MADELEINE

East Point
Elmira
North Lake
16
Basin Head
Souris
Rollo Bay
Bay Fortune
Naufrage
Greenwich
St. Peters
Kings Byway
Georgetown
St. Mary's Bay
Cardigan
Murray Harbour
Murray River
Little Sands
Wood Islands
KINGS
Morell
Mount Stewart
Montague
Bellevue
Belfast
Eldon
Mt. Mellick
Orwell
15
Pownal Bay
Prince Edward Island National Park
Dalvay-by-the-Sea
10
Covehead Bay
Brackley Beach
11
Kings Byway
Hillsborough Bridge
Fort Amherst Port-La-Joye National Historic Site
Charlottetown
1-9
Cornwall
South Rustico
North Rustico Harbour
6
12
New Glasgow
Cavendish
6
New London
13
Kensington
2
QUEENS
Victoria
14
Cape Traverse
Blue Heron Drive
New London Bay
Blue Heron Dr.
Park Corner
Burlington
Indian River
Travellers Rest
Wilmot
17
Summerside
Bedeque Bay
Kinkora
Crapaud
Borden-Carleton
Confederation Bridge
TO CAPE TORMENTINE
Northumberland Strait
TO CARIBOU, NOVA SCOTIA
Lennox Island
Port Hill
Tyne Valley
18
Malpeque Bay
Miscouche
Mont-Carmel
20
Cap-Egmont
Egmont Bay
Abrams Village
West Point
Lady Slipper Dr.
PRINCE
O'Leary
Mill River
Bloomfield
Alberton
Ou Hon Island
Tignish
Miminegash
North Cape
19

10 miles
15 km

KEY
Ferry
Trans-Canada Hwy.

continue west on Route 6, where museums vie with fishing wharfs and scenic vistas for your attention. Blue Heron Drive, now Route 20, takes you to the Anne of Green Gables Museum at Silver Bush in Park Corner. Continue west, then south on Route 20 and join Route 2 south (at Kensington) until turning onto Route 1A east (at Travellers Rest). Just north of the Confederation Bridge, follow the Trans-Canada Highway east (Route 1) back to Charlottetown. **Victoria** ⑭ is a scenic fishing town along the way.

IF YOU HAVE 2 DAYS

Leaving 🖭 **Charlottetown** ①–⑨ early in the day, follow Highway 1 east to Kings Byway, a scenic drive marked by signs showing a king's crown, and on to **Orwell** ⑮, where a period farm re-creates life in the 1800s. Continue on to **Montague** for a seal-watching tour. Stay overnight in the area of 🖭 **Bay Fortune.** The next day, pack a picnic lunch and head out for a morning on the soft white-sand beach beside the Basin Head Fisheries Museum in **Basin Head** ⑯. After lunch, continue east on Kings Byway to East Point for a stop at the lighthouse, which marks the easternmost point on the Island. Proceed west along the north shore to the eastern entrance of **Prince Edward Island National Park** ⑩ and end your tour with a swim or hike.

IF YOU HAVE 3 DAYS

From **Charlottetown** ①–⑨, explore the peaceful suburbs of 🖭 **Summerside** ⑰ before heading for its bustling waterfront. The relatively undiscovered area west of Summerside is perfect for those who like a slow pace. Follow Lady Slipper Drive through Acadian country to the Acadian Museum of Prince Edward Island in **Miscouche.** Leave midafternoon and take Route 12 to the scenic and peaceful 🖭 **Tyne Valley** ⑱. This small, friendly village makes a perfect base from which to visit the Mi'Kmaq community at Lennox Island, where some fine traditional crafts are sold. Stop by the historic Green Park in nearby **Port Hill,** where you may stroll through a former shipyard or visit the fine museum to learn about the importance of wooden ships in the history of the Island. On Day 3, make your way up to **North Cape** ⑲ and explore its reef. Plan to arrive early in the afternoon at 🖭 **West Point,** where you can enjoy the beach and walking trails. Finish your time in Prince County with a south-shore tour to **Mont-Carmel** ⑳, home to one of the province's best French dinner theaters.

When to Tour Prince Edward Island

Although Prince Edward Island is considered a summer destination because of its many seasonal attractions, the "shoulder seasons" should not be overlooked. May, June, September, and October usually have spectacular weather and few visitors; some sights and restaurants are closed, however. Fall is an excellent time for exploring, hiking, and golfing. Migratory birds arrive in vast numbers toward the end of summer, many staying until the snow falls. Winters are unpredictable but offer some of the Island's most overlooked activities: cross-country skiing, snowmobiling, and ice-skating on ponds. Nightlife is limited in cold weather although many communities, including Summerside and Charlottetown, offer residents and visitors an array of festivals and cultural events.

CHARLOTTETOWN

Prince Edward Island's oldest city, on an arm of the Northumberland Strait, is named for the stylish consort of King George III. This small city, peppered with gingerbread-clad Victorian houses and tree-shaded squares, is the largest community on the Island (population 33,000).

It's often called the Cradle of Confederation, a reference to the 1864 conference that led to the union of Nova Scotia, New Brunswick, Ontario, and Québec in 1867 and, eventually, Canada itself.

Charlottetown's main activities center on government, tourism, and private commerce. While new suburbs were springing up around it, the core of Charlottetown remained unchanged, and the waterfront has been restored to recapture the flavor of earlier eras. Today the waterfront includes the Delta Prince Edward Hotel; an area known as Peake's Wharf and Confederation Landing Park, with informal restaurants and handicraft and retail shops; and a walking path painted as a blue line on the sidewalk leading visitors through some of the most interesting historical areas of the Old City. Irene Rogers's *Charlottetown: The Life in Its Buildings,* available locally, gives much detail about the architecture and history of downtown Charlottetown.

Exploring Charlottetown

Historic homes, churches, parks, and the waterfront are among the pleasures of a tour of downtown Charlottetown, and you can see many of the sights on foot. The city center is compact, so walking is the best way to explore the area.

A Good Tour

Before setting out to explore Charlottetown, brush up on local history at the **Confederation Centre of the Arts** ① on Richmond Street, in the heart of downtown. Next door, the **Province House National Historic Site** ② is the site of the first meeting to discuss federal union. If you have an interest in churches, turn left off Richmond Street onto Prince Street to see **St. Paul's Anglican Church** ③. Backtrack on Richmond two blocks and turn left onto Great George Street, home to **St. Dunstan's Basilica** ④, with its towering twin Gothic spires. Great George Street ends at the waterfront, where the boardwalks of **Confederation Landing Park** ⑤ lead past small eateries, shops and **Founder's Hall.**

On the city's west end, the work of Robert Harris, Canada's foremost portrait artist, adorns the walls of **St. Peter's Cathedral** ⑥ in Rochford Square, bordered by Rochford and Pownal streets. It's a bit of a walk (¾ km, or ½ mi) to get there, but **Victoria Park** ⑦ provides a grassy respite edging the harborfront. Next, visit one of the finest residential buildings in the city, **Beaconsfield Historic House** ⑧, for panoramic views of its quiet garden and Charlottetown Harbour. Leave time to observe a favorite Prince Edward Island pastime—harness racing at **Charlottetown Driving Park** ⑨.

TIMING

The downtown area can be explored on foot in a couple of hours, but the wealth of historic sites and harbor views warrants a full day.

Sights to See

⑧ Beaconsfield Historic House. Designed by the architect W. C. Harris and built in 1877 for a wealthy shipbuilder, James Peake, Jr., this gracious Victorian home near the entrance to Victoria Park is one of the Island's finest historic homes, with 11 furnished rooms. You can tour the first and second floors and enjoy views of the garden and Charlottetown Harbour. An on-site bookstore features museum publications as well as community histories. Special events such as musical performances and history-based lectures are held regularly. A carriage house on the grounds has activities for children in summer, including a weekday morning Children's Festival during July and August (call for exact times and price). ⌧ *2 Kent St.,* ☎ *902/368–6603.* ⌨ *$3.50.* ☉ *June–early Sept., daily 10–5; late Sept.–June, daily, call for hrs.*

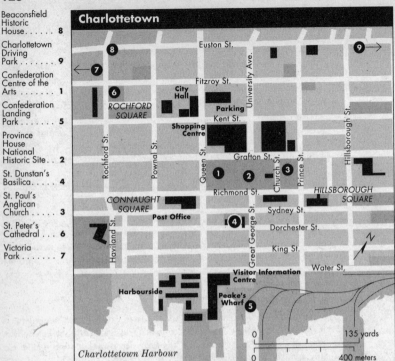

Charlottetown Harbour

❾ Charlottetown Driving Park. Since 1890 this track at the eastern end of the city has been the home of a sport dear to Islanders—harness racing. Standardbred horses are raised around the Island, and harness racing on the ice and on country tracks has been popular for generations. In fact there are more horses per capita on the Island than in any other Canadian province. August brings **Old Home Week,** when eastern Canada's best converge for 15 races in eight days. ⊠ *Kensington Rd.,* ☎ *902/892–6823.* 🎟 *Free.* ☉ *Races June, July, and most of Aug., 3 nights per wk; Old Home Week mid-Aug., Mon.–Sat. twice daily.*

❶ Confederation Centre of the Arts. Set in Charlottetown's historic red-brick core, this modern, concrete structure houses a 1,100-seat main-stage theater and two 190-seat second-stage theaters. The center also has an outdoor amphitheater, a memorial hall, a gift shop with Canadian crafts, a seasonal theater shop, an art gallery and museum, a public library with a special Prince Edward Island collection, including first editions of Lucy Maud Montgomery's famous novel, and a restaurant. The center's art gallery is the largest east of Montréal and provides a varied year-round exhibition program that showcases both contemporary and historical Canadian art, especially as it relates to Canadian Confederation. The **Charlottetown Festival,** which runs from the end of May to mid-October, includes the professional musical adaptation *Anne of Green Gables—The Musical (TM)* and other world-class musical theater and comedy productions. Weather permitting, the festival also offers free summer musical entertainment at noon in the amphitheater as well as near the center's main entrance. ⊠ *145 Richmond St.,* ☎ *902/566–1267 for box office; 800/565–0278.* ☉ *Daily 9–5; hrs extended May–Oct.*

❺ Confederation Landing Park. This waterfront recreation area at the bottom of Great George Street marks the site of the historic landing of the

Fathers of Confederation in 1864. Walkways and park benches offer plenty of opportunity to survey the activity of the harbor. During summer, performers in period costume stroll about the area re-creating historical events leading up to Canadian Confederation. **Founder's Hall** heritage attraction opened in 2001. Using state-of-the-art displays, this interpretation center adds insight into Charlottetown's past. Among other activities, visitors are transported back in time to the Charlottetown Conference of 1864, eventually returning to the present day with a greater appreciation for this important event in Canadian history. The adjacent **Peake's Wharf** features casual restaurants and bars, souvenir and crafts shops, and a marina where boat tours may be arranged.

NEED A BREAK?

Cows Ice Cream (⊠ Queen St., ☎ 902/892–6969; ⊠ Peake's Wharf, ☎ 902/566–4886) is the most famous ice cream on the Island. Fresh milk from PEI cows and other natural ingredients are carefully combined to create 36 flavors of premium, creamy ice cream that should be slowly savored. Cows Ice Cream can be purchased at the two Charlottetown locations, as well as at Cavendish Boardwalk, in Summerside, PEI Factory Shops in North River, Gateway Village at the approach to Confederation Bridge, and on board the PEI–Nova Scotia passenger ferry, *The Confederation.*

★ ❷ **Province House National Historic Site.** This three-story sandstone building, completed in 1847 to house the colonial government and now the seat of the Provincial Legislature, has been restored to its mid-19th-century Victorian appearance. The many restored rooms include the historic Confederation Chamber, where representatives of the 19th-century British colonies met. Special guided tours are offered for a nominal charge, historical programs may be viewed daily during the summer months, and a gift shop offers mementos. ⊠ *Richmond St.,* ☎ *902/ 566–7626.* ▣ *Donation accepted.* ☉ *Mid-Oct.–May, weekdays 9–5; June and Sept.–mid-Oct., daily 9–5; July–Aug., daily 9–6.*

❹ **St. Dunstan's Basilica.** One of Canada's largest churches, St. Dunstan's is the seat of the Roman Catholic diocese on the Island. The church is known for its fine Italian carvings and twin Gothic spires. ⊠ *Great George St.,* ☎ 902/894–3486.

❸ **St. Paul's Anglican Church.** Erected in 1896, this is actually the third church building on this site. The first was built in 1747, making this the Island's oldest parish. You can view the paintings and artwork inside the chapel. ⊠ *101 Prince St.,* ☎ *902/892–1691.*

❻ **St. Peter's Cathedral.** The murals by artist Robert Harris are found in **All Souls' Chapel,** designed in 1888 by his brother W. C. "Willy" Harris, the most celebrated of the Island's architects and the designer of many historic homes and buildings. This small chapel, which is attached to the side of the cathedral, may be open for viewing by chance; if not, you should inquire inside the cathedral. ⊠ *Rochford Sq.,* ☎ *902/566– 2102.*

❼ **Victoria Park.** At the southern tip of the city and overlooking Charlottetown Harbour are 40 beautiful acres that provide the perfect place to stroll, picnic, or watch a baseball game. Next to the park, on a hill between groves of white birches, is the white colonial **Government House,** built in 1835 as the official residence for the province's lieutenant governors (the house is not open to the public). The collection of antique cannons that still "guard" the city's waterfront provides a play area for children; runners enjoy the pathway that edges the harbor. ⊠ *Lower Kent St.* ☉ *Park daily sunrise–sunset.*

Dining

$$–$$$$ ✕ **The Selkirk.** With its wing chairs and live piano entertainment, the Selkirk is the Island's most sophisticated dining room. The imaginative menu concentrates on regional Canadian fare—locally grown potatoes, smoked Atlantic salmon, lobster, mussels, Malpeque oysters, and Canadian beef, to name a few—served with herbs straight from the garden. A four-course extravaganza aims to satisfy even the largest appetite. ⊠ *Delta Prince Edward Hotel, 18 Queen St.,* ☎ *902/894–1208. Reservations essential. AE, DC, MC, V.*

$$–$$$ ✕ **Claddagh Room Restaurant.** Some of the best seafood in Charlotte-
★ town is served here. The "Galway Bay Delight," one of the Irish owner's specialties, is a savory combination of fresh scallops and shrimp sautéed with onions and mushrooms, flambéed in Irish Mist, and doused with fresh cream. Nonseafarers can choose from other dishes featuring chicken, beef, and fresh pasta. The Olde Dublin Pub upstairs has live Irish entertainment every night in summer and on weekends in winter. This friendly pub has the largest selection of beer on tap to be found anywhere on PEI. ⊠ *131 Sydney St.,* ☎ *902/892–9661. AE, DC, MC, V.*

$$–$$$ ✕ **Culinary Institute of Canada.** Students at this internationally acclaimed school cook and present lunch and dinner under the supervision of their master chef instructor as part of their training. Here's an opportunity to enjoy excellent food and top service at reasonable prices. Located at the very end of Sydney Street, next to Charlottetown Harbour, the institute has an elegant dining room with large windows that provide lovely water vistas. Many local residents come to this tastefully decorated dining room when they want a special culinary experience. Call for a schedule. ⊠ *4 Sydney St.,* ☎ *902/894–6868. Reservations essential. AE, MC, V.*

$$–$$$ ✕ **Griffon Dining Room.** Located in the Queen Anne–style Dundee Arms Inn, this cozy restaurant is filled with antiques, copper, and brass. The French Continental cuisine includes fresh Atlantic salmon, beef tenderloin, and sea scallops. The Hearth and Cricket Pub, which serves light meals and a good selection of local and imported beers, is on the same level as the dining room. ⊠ *200 Pownal St.,* ☎ *902/892–2496 or 877/638–6333. AE, DC, MC, V.*

$–$$$ ✕ **The Merchantman Pub.** Just steps from the waterfront walking path near Confederation Landing Park, this cozy pub with antique-brick interior and original open-beam ceiling serves the best in pub food. Fresh seafood and steaks, and Thai and Cajun creations are specialties. ⊠ *Corner of Queen and Water Sts.,* ☎ *902/892–9150. AE, DC, MC, V.*

$–$$$ ✕ **Off Broadway.** Popular with Charlottetown's young professional set, this cozy spot began modestly as a crepe-and-soup joint. You can still make a meal of the lobster or chicken crepes and the soup or Caesar salad that come with them, but now the restaurant has a fairly inventive Continental menu. Fresh local ingredients are served in strongly French-influenced preparations. The private booths won't reveal your indiscretions, including your indulgence in dessert. Upstairs, with large windows overlooking the street, is the 42nd Street Lounge, where a comfortable, casual atmosphere prevails. Light fare from the restaurant kitchen is available. ⊠ *125 Sydney St.,* ☎ *902/566–4620. AE, DC, MC, V.*

$$ ✕ **Peake's Quay Restaurant and Bar.** This great summer spot on Charlottetown's restored waterfront has daily lunch and evening specials during the summer season. The large, heated patio overlooks Confederation Landing Park and the adjoining marina. Specialties include seafood chowder, fresh scallops, and Atlantic salmon. Lobster is also on the menu. There's a large selection of snack food available, and live entertainment is provided Thursday through Saturday evenings from

May until the end of September. ✉ *2 Great George St.,* ☎ *902/368–1330. DC, MC, V. Closed Nov.–early May.*

$$ ✗ **Piece a Cake Restaurant.** The young chef-owner, Wesley Gallant, cooks what he likes—and it appears that the public likes what he cooks. Up-stairs overlooking Grafton Street, near the Confederation Centre (and with a rear entrance to Confederation Mall), this eatery features Cana-dian cooking with eclectic influences. Working in an open kitchen, Gal-lant prepares fresh ingredients with spices and sauces inspired from around the world. The changing menu always includes a good selection of pas-tas. A jazz or blues group usually entertains patrons on Tuesday night. Be sure to ask for one of the six window tables. ✉ *119 Grafton St.,* ☎ *902/894–4585. AE, DC, MC, V. Closed Sun.*

$–$$ ✗ **Lone Star Cafe & Saloon.** This themed eatery (it bills itself as "the best little food house from Texas") serves hearty Tex-Mex fare—tacos, mesquite-grilled chicken, fajitas, and the like. Its casual country atmo-sphere is very popular with local residents, who come for what many consider to be the best fajitas on the Island. The café is in one of the many small strip malls that line both sides of University Avenue. ✉ *449 University Ave.,* ☎ *902/894–7827. AE, MC, V.*

Lodging

$$$–$$$$ 🛏 **Delta Prince Edward Hotel.** A member of the Delta chain of hotels
   ★ and resorts, the Prince Edward has all the comforts and luxuries of its first-rate counterparts—from whirlpool baths in some suites to a grand ballroom and conference center. Guest rooms are modern, and two-thirds of the rooms in this 10-story hotel overlook the waterfront. Lo-cated next to Peake's Wharf, the Delta Prince Edward has an ideal location from which to explore both the waterfront and historic down-town areas on foot. In addition to all the conveniences you expect in a full-service hotel, there are three dining choices. The resort also has a game room and golf simulators. ✉ *18 Queen St., Box 2170, C1A 8B9,* ☎ *902/566–2222,* 🖷 *902/566–1745,* 🆆🅴🅱 *www.deltahotels.com. 211 rooms, 33 suites. 3 restaurants, bar, indoor pool, sauna, gym, health club, coin laundry. AE, DC, MC, V.*

$$$–$$$$ 🛏 **Inns on Great George.** Closely linked with the founding of Canada
   ★ as a nation (the so-called Fathers of Confederation stayed in these build-ings during the 1864 Charlottetown Conference), this complex opened as a hotel in 1997. It includes several historic 1800s structures: the 24-room Pavilion, the five-room Wellington, and the Carriage House (a two-story house with living room and kitchen), as well as the Witter-Coombs Prime Minister's Suite and self-catering apartments. A num-ber of the restored buildings date back to 1811. Some rooms have a four-poster bed, fireplace, claw-foot or whirlpool tub, hardwood floors, and Oriental rugs. Complimentary breakfast is served in the reception area of The Pavilion each morning. ✉ *58 Great George St., C1A 4K3,* ☎ *902/892–0606 or 800/361–1118,* 🖷 *902/628–2079,* 🆆🅴🅱 *www.innsongreatgeorge.com. 29 rooms, 1 suite, 6 apartments, 1 house. AE, DC, MC, V. BP.*

$$–$$$$ 🛏 **Hillhurst Inn.** A handsome, elegant bed-and-breakfast in the heart of downtown, this grand 1897 mansion was once the home of George Longworth, a prominent Charlottetown merchant who made a fortune from building and operating ships, and has been designated a historic property. The reception area, dining room, and living room are pan-eled with burnished oak and beech, the work of the shipwrights Long-worth employed. Each of the guest rooms has period furniture, and many have exquisite handmade beds. Two rooms have whirlpool baths. Deluxe breakfast is included. ✉ *181 Fitzroy St., C1A 1S3,*

☎ *902/894–8004 or 877/994–8004,* 🆁🅰🆇 *902/892–7679,* 🆆🅴🅱 *www.hillhurst.com. 9 rooms. Air-conditioning. AE, MC, V. BP.*

$$–$$$$ 🏨 **The Shipwright Inn.** In a lovely 1860s home originally owned by the local shipbuilder James Douse are eight unique guest rooms and one housekeeping apartment. The nautical theme is continued throughout the house in both construction and decoration. All rooms have original wood floors and Victorian memorabilia. Some units have fireplaces, whirlpool baths, and balconies. Guests enjoy innkeeper Judy Hill's memorable full breakfast and afternoon tea. ✉ *51 Fitzroy St., C1A 1R4,* ☎ *902/368–1905 or 888/306–9966,* 🆁🅰🆇 *902/628–1905,* 🆆🅴🅱 *www.isn.net/shipwrightinn. 8 rooms, 1 apartment. Air-conditioning, fans. AE, MC, V. BP.*

$$$ 🏨 **Rodd Charlottetown—A Rodd Signature Hotel.** This five-story, redbrick hotel with white pillars and a circular driveway is just one block from the center of Charlottetown. The rooms have the latest amenities but retain the hotel's old-fashioned flavor (it was built in 1931) with reproductions of antique furnishings. The grandeur and charm of the Carvery Dining Room capture the elegance of an earlier era. ✉ *Kent and Pownal Sts., Box 159, C1A 7K4,* ☎ *902/894–7371 or 800/565–7633,* 🆁🅰🆇 *902/368–2178,* 🆆🅴🅱 *www.rodd-hotels.ca. 108 rooms, 7 suites. Restaurant, lounge, indoor pool, hot tub, sauna, gym. AE, DC, MC, V.*

$$–$$$ 🏨 **The Dundee Arms Inn.** Depending on your mood, you can choose to stay in either a 1960s motel or a 1904 Queen Anne–style inn. The motel is simple, modern, and neat; the inn is homey and furnished with brass and antiques. The Dundee Arms is only minutes from downtown. ✉ *200 Pownal St., C1A 3W8,* ☎ *902/892–2496 or 877/638–6333,* 🆁🅰🆇 *902/368–8532,* 🆆🅴🅱 *www.dundeearms.com. 15 rooms, 3 suites. Restaurant, pub, air-conditioning. AE, DC, MC, V.*

$$–$$$ 🏨 **Elmwood Heritage Inn.** One of the Atlantic Provinces' leading ar-
★   chitects, W. C. Harris, designed this handsome Victorian home in 1889. Originally part of a 20,000-acre estate, Elmwood was owned by Arthur Peters, grandson of Samuel Cunard, founder of the famous shipping line. Today it's in a quiet, residential area, set back from the road at the end of a 350-ft tree-lined driveway. The antiques-laden home has been restored, and the tastefully decorated rooms have either clawfoot tubs (in three rooms) or whirlpool baths. Some rooms have a working fireplace. A common living room has its own fireplace and second-floor balcony as well as a refrigerator, CD player, and a videotape collection. An elegant candlelight breakfast is included in the rate. ✉ *121 N. River Rd., C1A 3K7,* ☎ *902/368–3310 or 877/933–3310,* 🆁🅰🆇 *902/628–8457,* 🆆🅴🅱 *www.elmwoodinn.pe.ca. 6 rooms. Air-conditioning, in-room VCRs. DC, MC, V. BP.*

Nightlife and the Arts

Ceilidhs, or live traditional entertainment combining dancing, fiddling, and comedy, can be found in and around Charlottetown. For information on locations and times, contact the Visitor Information Centre (☎ 902/368–4444). The **Benevolent Irish Society Hall** (✉ 582 North River Rd., ☎ 902/892–2367) stages concerts on Friday, mid-May through October. There are a number of amateur and professional theater productions for adults and children, including dinner theaters. For schedules and cost, contact each one individually. **Eddie May Murder Mystery Dinner Theatre** (✉ Piazza Joe's, 189 Kent St., ☎ 902/569–1999) combines madcap improvisation with sleuthing and dining. **Feast Dinner Theatre** (✉ Rodd Charlottetown, corner of Kent and Pownal Sts., ☎ 902/629–2321) stages a lively show while you feast on chicken and ribs, mussels, and homemade bread. **Homefree Productions** (✉ Beaconsfield Historic House, ☎ 902/368–6603) offers a summer-long program that may include musicals and dramas, as well as children's presentations, storytelling, and concerts.

Outdoor Activities and Sports

Biking

Bicycling is a favorite sport in PEI, including in its capital. There are several companies that offer bicycle repairs and rentals as well as guided city bicycle tours, among them **Cycle Smooth** (⊠ 172 Prince St., ☎ 902/566–5530).

Golf

Although there are no courses in Charlottetown, the 18-hole **Fox Meadow Golf and Country Club** (⊠ 167 Kinlock Rd., Stratford, ☎ 902/ 569–4653) is only a 15-minute drive from downtown. A challenging par-72 championship course, it was designed by Rob Heaslip and overlooks both the community of Stratford and Charlottetown Harbour.

Water Sports

Summertime water sports are very popular throughout the Island, and several companies operate within Charlottetown. For day sailing, contact **Saga Sailing Adventures** (⊠ Charlottetown Harbour, ☎ 902/ 672–1222). You can arrange pick-up service from your hotel for north shore sea kayaking. A good way to discover the area's natural beauty is to contact **Outside Expeditions** (☎ 902/963–3366 or 800/207– 3899). **Peake's Wharf Boat Tours/Seal Watching** (⊠ 1 Great George St., Peake's Wharf, ☎ 902/566–4458) arranges seal-watching tours.

Shopping

The most interesting stores are at Peake's Wharf, in Confederation Court Mall (off Queen Street), and in Victoria Row on Richmond Street, between Queen and Great George streets. The zany **Cows** (⊠ Queen St., across from Confederation Centre, ☎ 902/892–6969) sells all things bovine—from T-shirts embellished with cartoon cows to delicious ice cream. **Great Northern Knitters** (⊠ 18 Queen St., ☎ 902/566–5302), in the Delta Prince Edward Hotel, has a terrific selection of handmade woolen sweaters. **Roots** (⊠ Confederation Court Mall, off Queen St., ☎ 902/566–1877) is an upscale leather-goods and clothing company with stores across Canada. There are a dozen factory outlet stores along the Trans-Canada Highway at North River Causeway near the western entrance to the city.

BLUE HERON DRIVE

From Charlottetown, Blue Heron Drive follows Route 15 north to the north shore, then winds along Route 6 through north-shore fishing villages, past the spectacular white-sand beaches of Prince Edward Island National Park, through *Anne of Green Gables* country, and finally along the south shore, with its red-sandstone seascapes and historic sites. The drive takes its name from the great blue heron, a stately water bird that migrates to Prince Edward Island every spring to nest in the shallow bays and marshes. The whole circuit roughly outlines Queens County and covers 190 km (118 mi). It circles some of the Island's most beautiful landscapes and best beaches, but its northern section around picturesque Cavendish and the Green Gables farmhouse is also cluttered with commercial tourist operations. For unspoiled beauty, you'll have to look beyond the fast-food outlets, tacky gift shops, and expensive carnival-type attractions and try to envision the Island's simpler days.

Prince Edward Island National Park

★ ⑩   *24 km (15 mi) north of Charlottetown.*

Prince Edward Island National Park, a narrow strip of mostly beach and dunes, stretches for more than 40 km (25 mi) along the north shore of the Island, from Cavendish to Tracadie Bay plus a separate extension, about 24 km (15 mi) further east at Greenwich. The park is blessed with nature's broadest brush strokes—sky and sea meet red-sandstone cliffs, rolling dunes, and long stretches of sand. There are six entrances to the park system off Routes 6, 13, and 15. National park information centers are at Cavendish and Brackley. The Gulfshore Highway runs through the park, giving tantalizing views of the beach and dunes. Beaches invite swimming, picnicking, and walking. Trails lead through woodlands and along streams and ponds. Among the more than 200 species of birds that pass through the area are the northern phalarope, Swainson's thrush, and the endangered piping plover. Many campgrounds span the park with varying fees and seasons. In autumn and winter, it's difficult to reach park staff—call Parks Canada (☎ 902/672–6350; 800/213–7875 for campground reservations) ahead of time for exact rates and schedules if you're planning a camping trip. ⌨ *Daily pass $3, seasonal pass $12, no charge off-season.* ☉ *Daily, full facilities open early June–mid-Sept.*

Lodging

$$$$ 🏨 **Blue Heron Hideaways Beach Houses.** Blue Heron comprises two large cottages (five- and six-bedroom) on Blooming Point (Tracadie Bay) and two beach houses plus a studio cottage on Point Deroche, 3 mi (5 km) to the east. The private 6 mi (10 km) beach is perfect for beachcombing and has sand dunes and wildlife along with rowboats and kayaks for guest use. Units are completely equipped for cooking, and have gas barbecues and CD players. Most have whirlpool baths. From mid-June to mid-September, there are weekly rentals only. ✉ *Meadowbank, R.R. 2, Cornwall, C0A 1H0*, ☎ 902/566–2427, 🖷 902/368–3798. *2 cottages with 2–4 bedrooms; honeymoon cottage; 3 villas sleep up to 10 guests. Pool, beach, boating. No credit cards. Closed Mid-Oct.–early June.*

$$$$ 🏨 **Dalvay-by-the-Sea.** Just within the eastern border of the Prince Edward Island National Park is this Victorian house, built in 1895 as a private summer home. This historic property is the only seaside country inn on Prince Edward Island. Rooms are furnished with antiques and reproductions. You can sip cocktails or tea on the porch while viewing the inn's gardens, Dalvay Lake, or the nearby beach. Canoes and rowboats are available. Breakfast and dinner are included in the room rate. In addition to the rooms in the inn, Dalvay also has eight upscale overnight cottages. As the inn is within PEI National Park, park entrance fees apply. ✉ *PEI National Park, Rte. 6, Grand Tracadie, near Dalvay Beach (Box 8), York C0A 1P0*, ☎ 902/672–2048, 🌐 *www.dalvaybythesea.com. 26 rooms, 8 cottages. Restaurant, bar, driving range, 2 tennis courts, croquet, boating, shop. AE, DC, MC, V. MAP. Closed mid-Oct.–early June.*

Outdoor Activities and Sports

GOLF

The 18 holes of the links-style, par-72 course at **Stanhope Golf and Country Club** (✉ off Rte. 6, Stanhope, ☎ 902/672–2842) are among the most challenging and scenic on the Island. It's a couple of miles west of Dalvay, along Covehead Bay.

The **Links at Crowbush Cove** (✉ off Rte. 2 on Rte. 350, Lakeside, ☎ 902/961–7300 or 800/377–8337), an 18-hole, par-72 Scottish-style course with ocean views, is about a 20- to 30-minute drive east of the national park; *Golf Digest* has rated it Canada's only five-star public golf course.

Brackley Beach

⑪ *12 km (7 mi) west of Dalvay.*

Just outside Prince Edward Island National Park, Brackley Beach offers a variety of country-style accommodations and eating establishments. The town has a national park information service building, about a mile from the toll both at the actual park entrance. Its bays and waterways attract migratory birds and are excellent for canoeing or kayaking and windsurfing. **Northshore Rentals** (⊠ Rte. 15 at Shaw's Hotel, ☎ 902/672–2022) rents canoes, river kayaks, and rowboats.

Dining and Lodging

$$–$$$ ✕ **Dunes Café.** This stunning café shares property with a pottery stu-
★ dio, art gallery, artisans outlet, and outdoor gardens. Soaring wood ceilings produce an airy atmosphere inside, and a deck overlooks the dunes and marshlands of Covehead Bay. The chef specializes in local seafood and lamb, incorporating locally grown, fresh produce, much of which comes from the café's own gardens. Reservations are recommended. ⊠ *Rte. 15 south of the national park,* ☎ *902/672–2586. AE, MC, V. Closed early Oct.–late May.*

$$$–$$$$ ✕▥ **Shaw's Hotel and Cottages.** Each room is unique in this 1860s hotel
★ with antique furnishings, floral-print wallpapers, and hardwood floors. Shaw's is one of only two remaining hotels on PEI that have continued operating for over a century. The lovely vistas of the bay and the country elegance makes this ideal for a relaxing stay or as a central base for exploring the region. Half the cottages have fireplaces. Canoes and kayaks are provided for guest use, and bicycles may be rented. If you'd like, include in your room rate a home-cooked breakfast and dinner in the Shaw's dining room, which is open to the public. The Sunday evening buffet, which features seafood, has become a popular local tradition. ⊠ *Rte. 15, Brackley Beach, C1E 1Z3,* ☎ *902/672–2022,* ₣ᴬˣ *902/672–3000,* ᵂᴱᴮ *www.peisland.com/shaws/hotel.htm. 16 rooms, 20 cottages, 3 suites. Restaurant, bar, beach, boating, playground. AE, MC, V. Closed early Oct.–May except for cottages. MAP.*

$$–$$$ ▥ **Barachois Inn.** The Victorian elegance of the 1870 Barachois Inn blends well with the surrounding historic South Rustico community. Built as the stately home for a local merchant, it has been lovingly restored with period antiques and fine art. The rooms and the spacious veranda overlook a Victorian garden and the lovely countryside leading to nearby Rustico Bay. ⊠ *Rte. 243, Box 1022, Charlottetown C1A 7M4,* ☎ *902/963–2194,* ᵂᴱᴮ *www.metamedia.pe.ca/barachois. 2 rooms, 2 suites. AE, MC, V. Closed Nov.–Apr. BP.*

Shopping

The **Cheeselady's Gouda** (⊠ Winsloe North, Rte. 223, 8 km, or 5 mi, off Rte. 2, ☎ 902/368–1506) not only demonstrates how genuine Gouda is produced (for free) but also offers samples of uniquely flavored cheeses. **The Dunes Studio Gallery** (⊠ Rte. 15 south of the national park, ☎ 902/672–2586) sells the work of dozens of leading local artists, as well as craftspeople from around the world. The pottery studio is open for viewing, and a rooftop garden offers vistas of saltwater bays, dunes, and hills.

Cavendish

⑫ *21 km (13 mi) west of Brackley.*

Cavendish is the most visited Island community outside Charlottetown because of the heavy influx of visitors to Green Gables, Prince Edward Island National Park, and the amusement park–style attractions in the area. Families with children appreciate the recreational options, which range from bumper-car rides and water slides to pristine sandy beaches. In 1908, Lucy Maud Montgomery (1874–1942) entered immortality as a beloved Canadian writer of fiction. It was in that year she created a most charming and enduring character, Anne Shirley, whom Mark Twain described as "the dearest and most lovable child in fiction since the immortal Alice [in Wonderland]." Montgomery's novel *Anne of Green Gables* is still enjoyed today, and thousands of adoring fans flock to the Cavendish area to personally experience Anne by visiting some of the homes associated with Montgomery and exploring the places described in the book.

The **Site of Lucy Maud Montgomery's Cavendish Home** is where the writer lived with her maternal grandparents following the untimely death of her mother. Though the foundation and surrounding white picket fence of the home where Montgomery wrote *Anne of Green Gables* are all that remain, the homestead fields and old apple-tree gardens provide lovely walking grounds. A bookstore and museum are also on the property, which is operated by descendants of the family. ⊠ *Rte. 6,* ☎ *902/963–2231.* 🎫 *$2.* ☉ *June and Sept.–mid-Oct., daily 10–5; July–Aug., daily 9–7.*

★ **Green Gables, Prince Edward Island National Park,** ½ km (¼ mi) west of Lucy Maud Montgomery's Cavendish home, is the green-and-white farmhouse that served as the setting for *Anne of Green Gables*. Frequently visited by Montgomery, it belonged to her grandfather's cousins. The house, farm buildings, and grounds re-create some of the settings found in the book, as do posted walking trails, the Haunted Wood, and Balsam Hollow. The site has been part of Prince Edward Island National Park since 1937. ⊠ *Rte. 6 west of Rte. 13,* ☎ *902/963–7874.* 🎫 *$5.50; lower off-season rates.* ☉ *May–late June and Sept.–Oct., daily 9–5; late June–Aug., daily 9–8; open limited schedule Nov.–Dec. and Mar.–Apr.; by appointment only in Jan. and Feb.*

There are many amusement parks throughout the Cavendish area, but **Rainbow Valley Family Fun Park** is unique. Not only is it one of the oldest attractions in the region, but as a family-operated business it provides a full day of activities for visitors of all ages. Spread over 40 acres, this clean, friendly operation includes three boating lakes, many rides, a large play port for youngsters, six waterslides, an exciting flume ride using rubber rafts, as well as live and animatronic performances. Food service is available or visitors may bring a picnic lunch. ⊠ *Rte. 6 in Cavendish,* ☎ *902/963–2221,* 🌐 *www.rainbowvalley.pe.ca.* 🎫 *$11.* ☉ *Early June–early Sept., Mon.–Sat. 9–8, Sun. 11–8.*

Dining and Lodging

Due to the relatively short distances involved on PEI (to drive the total length of the Island from North Cape to East Point is only 273 km, or 169 mi), visitors who stay in Charlottetown or anywhere in the north shore area are within minutes of all the major attractions in "Anne's Land." Accommodations in the Cavendish area are usually booked ahead—often a year in advance—during July and most of August. However, staying elsewhere in the central region puts visitors within minutes of Prince Edward Island National Park and other attractions, gives greater options in selecting a property, and often results in a lower cost.

\$\$–\$\$\$\$ ✕ **New Glasgow Lobster Supper.** Lobster suppers are held every night of the week during summer in community centers, church halls, and private restaurants. The New Glasgow Lobster Supper has been around since 1958 and is in a large, modern building edging a river. Its specialty is fresh lobster direct from a pond on the premises. Breaded scallops, hot roast beef, haddock, and ham are offered as well. All guests receive unlimited freshly baked rolls, cultivated steamed mussels, seafood chowder, garden salad, homemade desserts, and beverages. Bar service is also available, and there's a children's menu. The dining area can seat up to 500 guests at one time, and it often fills up, but because turnover is fast there isn't usually a long wait. ⊠ *Rte. 258 at New Glasgow,* ☎ *902/964–2870,* ⅎⅎ *902/964–3116. AE, DC, MC, V. Closed mid-Oct.–late May.*

\$\$\$ 🏨 **Sundance Cottages.** On a quiet little lane off Route 6 near the center of Cavendish is this friendly family operation, a collection of 20 ★ one- to four-bedroom cottages in a gently sloping field. Modern, spacious, nicely decorated, and fully equipped for self-catering, each cottage has a queen-size bed, a deck with a nice country view, a picnic table, and a barbecue. Many of the cottages have whirlpool baths, a dishwasher, and a propane fireplace. Outdoors there's a vegetable garden, where you can pick fresh vegetables for meals free of charge. A national park pass is provided for each day of stay. ⊠ *R.R. 2, C0A 1N0,* ☎ *902/963–2149 or 800/565–2149,* ⅎⅎ *902/963–2100,* ᴡᴇʙ *www.peisland.com/sundance/cottages.htm. 20 cottages. In-room VCRs, pool, hot tub, gym, mountain bikes, playground, coin laundry. AE, DC, MC, V.*

\$–\$\$\$ 🏨 **Kindred Spirits Country Inn and Cottages.** Green hills surround this lovely country estate, a short walk from Green Gables and a golf course. You can relax by its parlor fireplace and then retreat into a large room or suite, decorated in country Victorian style with local antiques. Breakfast is provided to inn guests. Surrounding extensive lawns and gardens are 14 large cottages in three different price ranges, from economy to luxury (the upper-end cottages have fireplaces and hot tubs); all are completely equipped for cooking and have cable TV. ⊠ *Memory La., Rte. 6, C0A 1N0,* ☎ ⅎⅎ *902/963–2434,* ᴡᴇʙ *www. kindredspirits.ca. 25 rooms, 14 cottages. Dining room, in-room VCRs, pool, hot tub. MC, V. Closed mid-Oct.–mid-May.*

\$ 🏨 **Bay Vista Motor Inn and Cottage.** At this clean and friendly family-oriented motel, parents can sit on the outdoor deck and take in the New London Bay panorama while children enjoy the large playground. There's a good hiking trail opposite the motel and a restaurant next door. Beaches are nearby. A three-bedroom cedar cottage is available for weekly rental. ⊠ *Rte. 6, Cavendish (reservations:* ⊠ *R.R. 2, Hunter River C0A 1N0),* ☎ *902/963–2225 or 800/846–0601,* ᴡᴇʙ *www.bayvistamotorinn.com. 28 rooms, 2 efficiencies, 1 cottage. Pool, playground, coin laundry. AE, DC, MC, V. Closed late Sept.– mid-June.*

\$ ⚠ **Marco Polo Land Campground.** There are many campgrounds in the Cavendish region, including those in the national park and provincial parks, and those in private establishments. One of the best of the latter is Marco Polo Land, which has heated swimming pools, recreational and dining facilities, a camp store, and supervised activities— including hayrides. Its serviced lots are often reserved well in advance during July and August. Situated on Route 13 in Cavendish, it's close to all the beach and amusement areas. ⊠ *Rte. 13, Cavendish (Box 9, Hunter River C0A 1N0),* ☎ *902/963–2352 or 800/665–2352; 902/ 964–2960 in winter. 500 sites. Dining room, 2 pools, miniature golf, tennis, shop, recreation room, coin laundry. MC, V. Closed mid-Oct.– late May.*

Outdoor Activities and Sports

GOLF

Green Gables Golf Course (⊠ Rte. 6, in Prince Edward Island National Park, ☎ 902/963–2488; 902/368–8045 in winter) is one of a half dozen golf courses in the north shore region. It was based on an original design by the golf-course architect Stanley Thompson and is a scenic 18-hole, par-72 course. Open May through October, the Green Gables also features a licensed lounge at the club house that serves refreshments and light meals. Tee times may be booked by phone.

SEA KAYAKING

Outside Expeditions (☎ 902/963–3366 or 800/207–3899), 8 km (5 mi) east of Cavendish in North Rustico Harbour, can gear a trip to suit either the new or experienced paddler. Tours include food, from light snacks to full-fledged lobster boils, depending on the expedition.

New London

⓭   *11 km (7 mi) southwest of Cavendish.*

This tiny village is best known as the birthplace of Lucy Maud Montgomery. It's also home to several seasonal gift and crafts shops and a tea shop. The wharf area is a great place to stop, rest, and watch fishing boats come and go. On the west side of New London Bay is **Cape Tryon Lighthouse,** one of a number of lighthouses around PEI. Constructed in 1905, this square, tapering, 39-ft tower stands picture-perfect at the end of a field with the Gulf of St. Lawrence beyond. Although this working lighthouse is not open to the public, the high cliff location (do not go beyond the fence) makes a great spot to take photographs or enjoy a leisurely picnic, and the site attracts many visitors each year. Inquire at the local tourist bureau for directions (it's at the end of a single-lane dirt road but worth the effort) to both this structure and nearby New London Rear Range light, a light station with an attached house (not open to the public).

The **Lucy Maud Montgomery Birthplace** is the modest white-and-green house overlooking New London Harbour; the author of *Anne of Green Gables* was born here in 1874. The interior of the house has been furnished with Victorian antiques to re-create the era. Among memorabilia on display are her wedding dress and personal scrapbooks filled with many of her poems and stories. ⊠ *Rtes. 6 and 20,* ☎ *902/886–2099 or 902/436–7329.* ⌐ *$2.* ☉ *Mid-May–June and Sept.–mid-Oct., daily 9–5; July–Aug., daily 9–6.*

Northwest Corner

12 km (7 mi) west of New London.

Some of the most beautiful scenery on the Island is on Blue Heron Drive along the north shore. As the drive follows the coastline south to the other side of the Island, it passes rolling farmland and the shores of Malpeque Bay. There are a couple of lovely beaches in this area. Just north of Darnley, off Route 20, is a long sand beach with a number of sandstone caves at the end. This beach—Darnley Beach—does not have developed facilities and it is often almost entirely deserted except for the seabirds. Not far from the village of Malpeque, also on Route 20, is **Cabot Beach Provincial Park,** with camping facilities (☎ 888/734–7529), a beach, and a playground. Sets used for filming the television series *Emily of New Moon* (another of L. M. Montgomery's fictional characters) may be toured. In summer the beach area is supervised during the day, and the playground is open dawn to dusk.

Woodleigh Replicas and Gardens, in Burlington, southwest of New London, is a 45-acre park with 30 scale replicas of Great Britain's best-known architecture, including the Tower of London and Dunvegan Castle. The models, some large enough to enter, are furnished with period antiques. Children especially enjoy climbing to the top of the lookout tower that crowns a small hill surrounded by flower gardens. A medieval-style maze and 10 acres of English country gardens are also on the grounds, as are food service, a picnic area, a children's playground, and a gift shop. ⊠ *Rte. 234, Burlington,* ☎ *902/836–3401.* ▦ *$8.50.* ☉ *June and Sept.–Oct., daily 9–5; July–Aug., daily 9–7.*

The **Anne of Green Gables Museum at Silver Bush** was once the home of Lucy Maud Montgomery's aunt and uncle. Montgomery herself lived here for a time and was married in the parlor in 1911. Inside the house are mementos such as photographs and a quilt the writer worked on. One of the highlights of a visit to Silver Bush is a ride in Matthew's carriage (Matthew is one of the characters in *Anne of Green Gables*). Short trips around the farm property are available as well as longer excursions. **The Shining Waters Tea Room** offers a tasty array of light dishes. The property also includes a lovely crafts shop and an antiques store. ⊠ *Rte. 20, Park Corner,* ☎ *902/886–2884.* ▦ *$2.75 (museum).* ☉ *May–June and Sept.–Oct., daily 9–5; July–Aug., daily 9–6.*

Lodging

$$–$$$ 🏠 **Malpeque Cove Cottages.** Within walking distance of Cabot Beach Provincial Park and only 21 km (13 mi) from Cavendish, these two- and three-bedroom cottages sit in an open field and have magnificent views of the rising sun over Darnley Basin. Modern and fully equipped, most have pine interiors. Each unit has a barbecue and picnic table, some have a whirlpool bath, and all have a roofed patio overlooking the harbor. From July to August, there are weekly reservations only. ⊠ *Off Rte. 20, Malpeque (Box 714, Kensington C0B 1M0),* ☎ *902/ 836–5667 or 888/283–1927,* WEB *www.malpeque.ca. 13 cottages. Coin laundry. MC, V. Closed mid-Oct.–mid-May.*

$–$$ 🏠 **Stanley Bridge Country Resort.** This collection of quality cottages, lodge units, and inn rooms overlooks picturesque New London Bay. The cottages, in a large open area, are available in price ranges from "efficiency" to "executive," and all are fully equipped for self-catering. The lodge units have kitchenettes for light meals. Two complimentary Continental breakfasts are provided per unit per day. The property's central location makes it an ideal base for exploring the whole north shore region. ⊠ *Rte. 6, Stanley Bridge (Box 8203, Kensington, C0B 1M0),* ☎ *902/886–2882 or 800/361–2882,* FAX *902/886–2940,* WEB *www.peisland.com/stanleybridge. 16 cottages, 10 lodge units, 28 inn rooms. Restaurant, lounge, pool, hot tub, gym, playground, coin laundry. MC, V. Closed late Oct.–early May. CP.*

Nightlife and the Arts

St. Mary's Church (⊠ Hwy. 104, Indian River, ☎ 902/836–4933), 5 km (3 mi) south of Park Corner, has performances by visiting artists in July and August as part of the Indian River Festival of Music. Inquire locally for schedule.

Borden-Carleton

35 km (22 mi) south of Kensington.

Once home port to the Marine-Atlantic car ferries, Borden-Carleton is now linked to the mainland via the Confederation Bridge. The 13-km (8-mi) behemoth, completed in June 1997, spans the Northumberland Strait and ends in Cape Jourimain, New Brunswick. **Gateway Village**

(☎ 902/437–8539), at the foot of the bridge near the toll booths, has an interesting display related to the unique construction techniques used in completing this amazing span. Located within the village complex are a government-run visitor information center (open year-round), a liquor store, a large number of crafts and gift shops, and several food-service outlets (including a Cows Ice Cream shop). A fascinating free interactive display, **Island Home Museum**, traces the history of the Northumberland Strait crossings. The PEI section of the Trans-Canada Highway begins here and continues through Charlottetown to the Wood Islands Ferry Terminal. Many visitors to PEI enter the province across the Confederation Bridge, explore the Island, then continue on to Nova Scotia via Northumberland Ferries Ltd. (75-minute crossing).

En Route   Prior to the late 1800s (when ferry service began), passengers and mail were taken across the strait in ice boats that were rowed and alternately pushed and pulled across floating ice by men. A monument on Route 10 in **Cape Traverse** commemorates their journeys.

Victoria

★ ⑭   *22 km (14 mi) east of Borden-Carleton.*

Victoria-by-the-Sea, as this charming community is known locally, is a picturesque fishing village filled with antiques, art galleries, and handicrafts shops. But the real beauty of Victoria is that it has retained its peace and integrity. The little shops and eateries are all owned by local people. Many of the artists and craftspeople who live here do so to escape the hectic life of larger centers. To truly appreciate Victoria, park on one of its several streets and walk. Stroll about the community, browse its shops, watch the fishing boats beside the wharf, admire the harbor lighthouses, and take time to chat with the locals. Be sure to take in a performance at the local live theater. The usually uncrowded **Victoria Provincial Park** is just outside the village. Here beach lovers enjoy the warm, calm waters of Northumberland Strait while walking on the sand flats at low tide. Changing rooms and washrooms, picnic tables, and a small play area are provided.

Dining and Lodging

$–$$$ ✕ **Landmark Café.** The funky little spot serves homemade soups, pasta, seafood dishes, and delicious desserts. Favorite dishes include scallops sautéed in garlic butter and dill as well as steamed salmon. ⊠ *Main St.,* ☎ *902/658–2286. MC, V. No lunch Wed. Closed mid-Sept.–late June.*

$ ✕ **Mrs. Profitt's Tea Shop.** This quaint, cozy tearoom on Victoria's Main Street serves a variety of fresh teas along with tasty treats. Homemade soup, sandwiches, and lobster rolls are featured. ⊠ *Orient Hotel, 34 Main St.,* ☎ *902/658–2503. AE, MC, V. Closed Mon. and late Sept.–late May.*

$–$$ ⌂ **Orient Hotel.** The small, historic hotel on Main Street has cozy guest rooms and suites, all with private baths. This is one of two hotels on PEI that have been in continuous operation for more than a century. Breakfast is served in the downstairs breakfast room. The Monkey's Freezer, an ice cream shop that's open from noon to dusk, June through September, is a fledgling business venture of the host's teenage son. ⊠ *34 Main St., Box 55, C0A 2G0,* ☎ *902/658–2503 or 800/565–6743,* ⨳ *902/658–2078,* 🌐 *www3.pei.sympatico.ca/orient. 6 rooms. AE, MC, V. Closed Oct.–late May. BP.*

$ ⌂ **Victoria Village Inn.** This Victorian house is next door to the Victoria Playhouse. A tasty Continental breakfast is served up every morning. The Actor's Retreat Café is in the inn and offers dinner and theater packages for the Victoria Playhouse. ⊠ *22 Main St., Box 1, C0A 2G0,*

☏ 902/658–2483, WEB *www.pei.sympatico.ca/victoriavillageinn. 4 rooms. MC, V. CP.*

Nightlife and the Arts

In summer, the historic **Victoria Playhouse** (✉ Howard and Main Sts., ☏ 902/658–2025; 800/925–2025 in the Maritimes) has a renowned professional theater program that celebrates maritime comedy. From late June through September, the company mounts two plays plus a Monday night Musical Showcase Series. The Playhouse, in the historic Community Hall (built 1912–14), is widely known for its intimate interior (150 seats) and excellent acoustics. Dinner packages are available.

Shopping

Island Chocolates (✉ Main St., ☏ 902/658–2320 or 800/565–2320), a chocolate factory in a 19th-century general store, sells treats made from Belgian chocolate and flavored with fruit and liqueur fillings.

Port-La-Joye–Fort Amherst National Historic Site

36 km (22 mi) east of Victoria.

In 1720 the French founded the first European settlement on the Island, Port-La-Joye; 38 years later it was usurped by the British and renamed Fort Amherst. Take time to stroll around the original earthworks of the fort; there are magnificent panoramic views. The site also includes wooded trails and a collection of antique cannons guarding the harbor, next to the picnic area. The visitor center has informative exhibits, an audiovisual presentation, a small boutique, as well as a 1720s-era café. The drive from Victoria to Rocky Point passes through the Argyle Shore to this site, which is at the mouth of Charlottetown Harbour. ✉ *Palmers La. off Rte. 19,* ☏ *902/566–7626 or 902/675–2220.* 🖾 *$2.25.* ◷ *Visitor center mid-June–Labor Day, daily 9–5; grounds May–Nov., daily dawn–dusk.*

THE KINGS BYWAY

For 375 km (233 mi), the Kings Byway follows the coastline of green and tranquil Kings County on the eastern end of the Island. The route passes wooded areas, patchwork-quilt farms, fishing villages, historic sites, and long, uncrowded beaches. In early summer, fields of blue, white, pink, and purple wild lupines slope down to red cliffs and blue sea. To get here from Charlottetown, take Route 1 east and follow the Kings Byway counterclockwise.

Orwell

★ ⑮ *27 km (17 mi) east of Charlottetown.*

For those who like the outdoors, Orwell—lined with farms that welcome guests and offer activities—is ideal. The **Orwell Corner Historic Village** is a living-history farm museum that re-creates a 19th-century rural settlement by employing methods used by Scottish and Irish settlers in the 1800s. The village contains a beautifully restored 1864 farmhouse, a school, a general store, a church, a community hall, a blacksmith shop, a refurbished shingle mill, and barns with handsome draft horses. From spring to fall the site runs many special events, including fairs and craft shows, and in summer the community hall hosts traditional music performances four evenings a week. Check locally for a schedule. ✉ *Off Trans-Canada Hwy., Rte. 1,* ☏ *902/651–8510,* FAX *902/368–6608,* WEB *www.orwellcorner.isn.net.* 🖾 *$3.50.* ◷ *Mid-June–early Sept., daily 9–5; mid-May–mid-June, weekdays 10–3; early Sept.–mid-Oct., Tues.–Sun. 9–5.*

The **Sir Andrew Macphail Homestead,** a National Historic Site, is a 140-acre farm property that contains an ecological forestry project, gardens, and three walking trails. The restored 1829 house and 19th-century outbuildings commemorate the life of Sir Andrew Macphail (1864–1938), a writer, professor, physician, and soldier. A licensed tearoom–restaurant serves traditional Scottish and contemporary fare and is open for lunch and most dinners. ✉ *Off Rte. 1,* ☎ *902/651–2789,* WEB *www.isn.net/~dhunter/macphailfoundation.html.* ☞ *Free.* ☉ *Late June–early Sept., daily 10–5; July–Aug., daily 10 AM–9 PM.*

OFF THE BEATEN PATH	**BEN'S LAKE TROUT FARM –** This pleasant attraction for the whole family is especially appreciated by aspiring young anglers. You're almost guaranteed a fish, and the staff cleans it and supplies the barbecue (for a small fee) and picnic table for a great meal. Fly fishing can also be arranged. ✉ *Rte. 24, Bellevue,* ☎ *902/838–2706.* ☞ *Catch $4 per pound.* ☉ *Apr.–Sept., daily 8–8; open weekends or by reservation in Oct.*

Lodging

$ ⊡ **Forest and Stream Cottages.** This collection of one- and two-bedroom cottages in a forest grove provides a secluded stay overlooking a large pond. You can use one of the rowboats to explore the winding stream or to take advantage of the property's nature trails. These traditional-style cottages have screened verandas, and each has a barbecue and picnic table. ✉ *Murray Harbour, C0A 1V0,* ☎ FAX *902/962–3537,* WEB *www.CanadaRentals.com. 5 cottages. Boating, playground. MC, V. Closed Nov.–Apr.*

En Route One of the Island's most historic churches, St. John's Presbyterian is in **Belfast,** off Route 1 on Route 207. This pretty white church on a hill was built by settlers from the Isle of Skye who were brought to the Island from Scotland in 1803 by Lord Selkirk. **Little Sands,** on Route 4, is home to Canada's only saltwater winery, Rossignol Estate Winery, which offers tasting for a small fee. The lighthouse at **Cape Bear** is the site of the first wireless station in Canada to receive the distress call from the *Titanic.*

Montague

20 km (12 mi) northeast of Orwell.

Montague, the business hub of eastern Prince Edward Island, is a lovely small town that straddles the Montague River and serves as a departure point for seal-watching boat tours. **Cruise Manada Seal-watching Boat Tours** ☎ 902/838–3444 or 800/986–3444, WEB www.peisland.com/cruise/manada.htm) sails past a harbor-seal colony and mussel farms. Boats leave from Montague Marina on Route 4 and Brudenell Resort Marina on Route 3 from mid-May through October. This is a great rainy-day activity. Reservations are recommended. The restored **railway station,** overlooking the marina, is used as a tourist information center as well as for a number of small crafts shops. The Confederation Trail continues past the station and is ideal for a leisurely stroll.

Dining and Lodging

$$–$$$ ✕ **Windows on the Water Café.** Overlooking the former railway station is this old house furnished with antiques and plenty of atmosphere. You can relax inside or out on the large deck in warm weather, with views of the Montague Marina. Winner of the Island Shellfish Chowder Competition, this lovely little eatery has tasty seafood, vegetarian fare, and chicken dishes. ✉ *106 Sackville St.,* ☎ *902/838–2080. AE, DC, MC, V. Closed mid-Oct.–early May.*

$ ⊞ **Roseneath Bed & Breakfast.** This fine heritage home (1868) over-
looks the Brudenell River. You can golf at the adjacent Brudenell course,
walk or bike the Confederation Trail (which crosses the property), do
a little trout fishing, or just relax and explore the 90 acres of flowers
and woodlands. The fun doesn't stop in winter—there's always snowshoeing and cross-country skiing. All the rooms have views of the river
or of the property's extensive gardens, private baths (some with claw-
foot tubs), and plenty of artwork and antiques. A family suite has two
bedrooms with a private bath. Morning brings coffee delivered to your
room and a full home-cooked breakfast downstairs. A lobster dinner
may be arranged in advance during May and June. ⊠ *R.R. 6, Cardigan, C0A 1G0,* ☎ *902/838–4590 or 800/823–8933,* FAX *902/838–4590,*
WEB *www.isn.net/~rosedew. 3 rooms, 1 family suite. Fishing, bicycles.
MC, V. Closed Oct.–late May; open off-season by reservation. BP.*

Bay Fortune

38 km (24 mi) north of Georgetown.

Bay Fortune, a little-known scenic village, has been a secret refuge for
American vacationers for two generations; they return year after year
to relax in the peace and quiet of this charming little community.

Dining and Lodging

$$–$$$$ ✕⊞ **Inn at Bay Fortune.** An enticing, unforgettable getaway, this inn
★ overlooking Fortune Harbour and Northumberland Strait is the for-
mer summer home of Broadway playwright Elmer Harris and more
recently of the late actress Colleen Dewhurst. You'll find superb din-
ing and genteel living. Local fresh-caught and fresh-harvested ingre-
dients are served in an old-time ambience. The restaurant does not serve
lunch, but a full breakfast is included in room rates. Two nearby sum-
mer houses are well-appointed, and provide housekeeping facilities that
suit families. ⊠ *Rte. 310, R.R. 4, C0A 2B0,* ☎ *902/687–3745; 860/
563–6090 off-season,* WEB *www.innatbayfortune.com. 18 rooms, 2
houses. Restaurant. Closed late Oct.–mid-May. MC, V. BP.*

$$$–$$$$ ⊞ **The Inn at Spry Point.** The sister property to the Inn at Bay Fortune,
this luxury retreat hugs the end of a 110-acre peninsula. In addition
to 4 km (2½ mi) of shoreline walking trails, the property has a 1 km
(½ mi) sandy beach. Each of the 15 guest rooms has either a private
balcony or a garden terrace. Seafood and locally grown fresh produce
are featured in the dining room, with pan-seared scallops, halibut, and
salmon taking top billing. Desserts are glorious. ⊠ *Spry Point Rd.,* ☎
902/583–2400; 860/563–6090 off-season; FAX *902/583–2176,* WEB
*www.inatsprypoint.com. 15 rooms. Restaurant. MC, V. Closed early
Oct.–late May. CP.*

Souris

14 km (9 mi) north of Bay Fortune.

The Souris area is noted for its fine traditional musicians. An outdoor
Scottish concert at **Rollo Bay** in July, with fiddling and step dancing,
attracts thousands every year. At Souris a car ferry links Prince Edward
Island with Québec's **Magdalen Islands.** Call ☎ 887/624–4437 for in-
formation about these scenic islands.

Basin Head

⑯ *13 km (8 mi) north of Rollo Bay.*

This town is noted for an exquisite silvery beach that stretches north-
east for miles, backed by high grassy dunes. The lovely sand beach has

been "discovered," but it's still worth spending some time here. Scuff your feet in the sand and hear it squeak, squawk, and purr at you. Known locally as "singing sand," it is a phenomenon found in only a few locations worldwide. The high silica content in the sand helps produce the sound. A boardwalk leads from the museum area at the top of the hill down to the beach area. There's a small take-out next to the museum where fish-and-chips and other fast food may be purchased and eaten at picnic tables overlooking the ocean. The nearby **Red Point Provincial Park** makes an excellent base for those who enjoy camping.

The **Basin Head Fisheries Museum** is on a headland overlooking the Northumberland Strait and has views of one of the most beautiful white-sand beaches on the island. The museum depicts the ever-changing nature of PEI's historic inshore fishing tradition through interesting displays of artifacts. The museum, part of the PEI Museum and Heritage Foundation, has an aquarium, a smokehouse, a cannery, and coastal ecology exhibits. ⊠ *Off Rte. 16,* ☎ *902/357-7233,* WEB *www.peimuseum.com.* ⊠ *$3.50.* ☉ *Late May–Aug., daily 9–6; Sept.–Oct., daily 9–5.*

Greenwich

54 km (33 mi) southwest of East Point.

The National Park in Greenwich is known for its superior beach and massive sand dunes. These dunes are moving, gradually burying the nearby woods; here and there the bleached skeletons of trees thrust up through the sand like wooden ghosts. To get here, follow Route 16 to St. Peter's Bay and Route 313 to Greenwich. The road ends at an interpretive center, a new extension of the Prince Edward Island National Park system. Programs at the center explain to visitors the ecology of this rare land formation. Visitors are permitted to walk along designated pathways among sand hills, through beige dunes to reach the beach. Due to the rather delicate nature of the dune system, visitors must stay on the trails and refrain from touching the flora.

Outdoor Activities and Sports

Wild Winds (⊠ Savage Harbour, ☎ 902/676-2024) is one of the best of the many deep-sea fishing boats that operate from this region of PEI; half-day trips for cod and mackerel are available.

En Route Ships from many nations have been wrecked on the reef running northeast from **East Point Lighthouse** (⊠ Off Rte. 16, East Point, ☎ 902/357-2106). Guided tours are offered, and many books about life at sea are available at the gift shop in the 1908 fog-alarm building. Due to the high erosion in this area, caution should be used when approaching the high cliffs overlooking the ocean.

LADY SLIPPER DRIVE

Many visitors to the western end of PEI tend to follow the straight, flat Route 2 most of the distance, which gives a rather boring view of the Island. To truly appreciate what the western region has to offer, divert along the coastline. Follow Route 14 to West Point and continue northward along the Northumberland Strait. Try returning along the Gulf of St. Lawrence area by using Route 12, which passes the lovely beach area of Jacques Cartier Provincial Park. Both of these highways are part of the Lady Slipper Drive. This drive—named for the delicate lady's slipper orchid, the province's official flower—winds along the coast of the narrow, indented western end of the Island, known as Prince County, through very old and very small villages that still adhere to a traditional way of life. Many of these hamlets are inhabited by Acadians, descendants of the original French settlers. The area is known for its oysters and Irish moss (the dried plants of red sea algae) but most famously for its potato farms: the province is a major exporter of seed potatoes worldwide, and half the crop is grown here.

Summerside

17 *71 km (44 mi) west of Charlottetown.*

Summerside, the second-largest city on the Island, has a beautiful waterfront area. A self-guided walking tour arranged by the Eptek Exhibition Centre is a pleasant excursion along leafy streets lined with large houses. During the third week of July, all of Summerside celebrates the eight-day **Summerside Lobster Carnival,** with livestock exhibitions, harness racing, fiddling contests, and of course, lobster suppers. Summerside has seen a renewal of the downtown area in recent years, with the addition of a number of attractions that appeal to visitors. One sign of renewal: the array of murals painted on the sides of a number of buildings in the city, most depicting historical events that helped shape the character of the community. The Confederation Trail passes through the city, and the former railway station makes an excellent starting point for walking or biking excursions. Some of the local hotels provide bicycles for their guests to explore this attractive trailway system. It takes about a half hour to drive by car from Summerside to major attractions such as Cavendish in the central region of PEI.

The **International Fox Museum and Hall of Fame** describes some unique local history. Silver foxes were first bred in captivity in western Prince Edward Island, and for several decades Summerside was the headquarters of a virtual gold rush based on fox ranching. ⊠ *286 Fitzroy St.,* ☎ *902/436–2400.* ☜ *By donation.* ☉ *June–early Sept., daily 9–5.*

Eptek Exhibition Centre on the waterfront has a spacious main gallery with changing Canadian-history and fine-arts exhibits, often with a strong emphasis on Prince Edward Island. In the same buildings are the 527-seat **Harbourfront Jubilee Theatre** and the **PEI Sports Hall of Fame.** ⊠ *130 Harbour Dr., Waterfront Properties,* ☎ *902/888–8373,* FAX *902/888–8375.* ☜ *$3.50.* ☉ *Open year-round; call for hrs.*

Spinnaker's Landing, a boardwalk along the water's edge, is lined with shops and eateries. The area has a good blend of shopping, history, and entertainment. The visitors information center is a re-created lighthouse that may be climbed for panoramic views of Bedeque Bay and the city. In summer months there's often free evening entertainment (usually at 7 PM) on the outdoor stage over the water, weather permitting. Call for a schedule of events. ⊠ *130 Harbour Dr.,* ☎ *902/ 436–6692.*

Dining and Lodging

$–$$$ ✕ **Brothers Two Restaurant.** Next to the Quality Inn Garden of the Gulf, this restaurant is popular with local residents. Service is friendly, and seating is in booths, at tables, and in summer in a roofed-patio area. As with most restaurants in PEI, fish is usually featured on the menu, and dishes such as fish-and-chips can be found along with more elaborate creations. The pride of the restaurant is the homemade bread served with each meal. ⊠ *618 Water St.,* ☎ *902/436–9654. AE, DC, MC, V.*

$$–$$$$ 🏨 **Quality Inn Garden of the Gulf.** Close to downtown, this clean, comfortable hotel is a convenient place to stay. The unusual layout features a high-ceiling courtyard with rooms on both sides. New Orleans–style decor creates a pleasant atmosphere. There's also a separate motor lodge–style building next to the main structure. A 9-hole, par-3 chip-and-putt

golf course slopes to Bedeque Bay. ⊠ *618 Water St. E, C1N 2V5,* ☏ *902/436–2295 or 800/265–5551,* FAX *902/436–6277. 92 rooms. Coffee shop, 1 indoor and 1 outdoor pool, 9-hole golf course, shop. AE, DC, MC, V.*

$$ 🏨 **Loyalist Country Inn.** Throughout this waterfront inn are detailed
★ touches that create a traditional elegance. The Loyalist combines the atmosphere of a country inn with the professionalism of a large hotel. In the heart of Summerside, the property overlooks the city waterfront, a yacht club, and a marina. The rear of the hotel faces the main downtown area, the former railway station, and the Confederation Trail— good for biking. The Prince William Dining Room has an innovative menù of seafood, steaks, and island delicacies. Thirty rooms have whirlpool baths. ⊠ *195 Harbour Dr., C1N 5R1,* ☏ *902/436–3333 or 800/361–2668,* FAX *902/436–4304. 100 rooms, 3 suites. Restaurant, lounge, indoor pool, sauna, gym. AE, DC, MC, V.*

$–$$ 🏨 **Silver Fox Inn.** A fine old Victorian house and a designated historic property, this B&B houses a tearoom, where homemade scones and Devonshire cream are served each afternoon, and a small antiques shop. Breakfasts include homemade quiche, muffins, and croissants. If you make prior arrangements, the chef will prepare dinner. Outside, a two-tier deck provides a lovely view of the garden with three koi-stocked pools. ⊠ *61 Granville St., C1N 2Z3,* ☏ *902/436–1664 or 800/565–4033,* WEB *www.silverfoxinn.net. 6 rooms. AE, DC, MC, V. CP.*

Nightlife and the Arts

The **College of Piping and Celtic Performing Arts of Canada** (⊠ 619 Water St. E, ☏ 902/436–5377 or 877/224–7473, WEB www.collegeofpiping. com) puts on a summer-long Celtic Festival incorporating bagpiping, Highland dancing, step dancing, and fiddling. The **Harbourfront Jubilee Theater** (⊠ 124 Harbour Dr., ☏ 902/888–2500 or 800/708–6505), founded in 1996, is the Island's newest professional theater. Year-round, the 527-seat main-stage theater celebrates the tradition and culture of the region with dramatic and musical productions. Call for information on current productions and schedule.

Feast Dinner Theatre (⊠ Brothers Two Restaurant, 618 Water St. E, ☏ 902/436–7674 or 888/748–1010), established in 1978, is the original dinner-theater production company in the Maritime provinces. Musical comedy is served up with heaping platefuls of Atlantic salmon, chicken, barbecue ribs, and fresh desserts.

Miscouche

10 km (6 mi) northwest of Summerside.

Many descendants of the Island's early French settlers live in this area, and a museum here commemorates their history. The **Acadian Museum/Musée Acadien,** a National Historic Site, has a permanent exhibition on Acadian life as well as an audiovisual presentation depicting the history and culture of Island Acadians. It also has a genealogical center and an Acadian gift shop. ⊠ *Rte. 2,* ☏ *902/436–2881.* 🖙 *$3.50.* ⊙ *July–Aug., daily 9:30–7; reduced hrs off-season.*

Port Hill

35 km (22 mi) north of Miscouche.

Port Hill was one of the many communities in the Tyne Valley that benefited from the shipbuilding boom of the 1800s, the era of tall-masted wooden schooners. Some beautifully restored century homes testify to the prosperity of those times.

The **Green Park Shipbuilding Museum and Yeo House** includes what was originally the home of shipbuilder James Yeo, Jr., who by the mid-1840s was the most powerful businessman on the Island. The cupola from which Yeo observed his nearby shipyard through a spyglass tops this 19th-century mansion. The modern museum building, in what has become a provincial park, details the history of the shipbuilder's craft. Those skills are brought to life at a re-created shipyard with carpentry and blacksmithing shops. The park has picnic tables and camping facilities. There's a small gift shop on site, and the museum provides an array of lectures, concerts, and activities throughout the summer. Call for schedule. ⊠ *Rte. 12,* ☎ *902/831-7947.* ⌨ *$4.* ☉ *June–Sept., daily 9–5.*

Tyne Valley

⑱ *8 km (5 mi) south of Port Hill.*

The charming community of Tyne Valley has some of the finest scenery on the Island. Watch for fisherfolk standing in flat boats wielding rakes to harvest the famous Malpeque oysters. A gentle river flows through the middle of the village, with lush green lawns and sweeping trees edging the water. The **Tyne Valley Oyster Festival** takes place here the first week of August. This three-day event includes fiddling, step dancing, oyster shucking, a talent contest, and a community dance. The festival is a good time to sample a fried-oyster and scallop dinner. Check locally for dates and times.

Dining and Lodging

$ ✕🛏 **Doctor's Inn Bed & Breakfast.** Beautifully landscaped, this 1860s village home is a joy in summer with its garden of herbs and flowers. In winter, cross-country skiers gather around the woodstove or living-room fireplace and share conversation over a warm drink. At the dining-room table, the local catch of the day is complemented by produce from the inn's own organic gardens. Dinner is prix fixe ($40 for guests, $50 for nonguests) and available by reservation only. There are free tours of the inn's gardens. ⊠ *Rte. 167, C0B 2C0,* ☎ *902/831-3057,* ⊞ *www. peisland.com/doctorsinn. 2 rooms share bath. Restaurant. MC, V. CP.*

Shopping

At **Shoreline Sweaters and Tyne Valley Studio Art Gallery** (⊠ Rte. 12, ☎ 902/831-2950), Lesley Dubey produces "Shoreline" handcrafted woolen sweaters with a lobster pattern and sells local crafts and honey May through October. The store is open 9 to 5:30 daily, noon to 5:30 Sunday. An art gallery displays works by accomplished Island artists.

Lennox Island, one of the largest Mi'Kmaq communities in the province, has a few shops that sell First Nations crafts. To get here, take Route 12 west to Route 163 and follow the road over the causeway leading to a large island projecting into Malpeque Bay. **Indian Art & Craft of North America** (⊠ Rte. 163, ☎ 902/831-2653) specializes in Mi'Kmaq ash-split baskets as well as pottery, jewelry, carvings, and beadwork. The shop, which sits on the edge of the water, has a screened-in porch where visitors may enjoy a complimentary cup of coffee along with the scenery. Earthenware figurines depicting local legends can be found at **Micmac Productions** (⊠ Rte. 163, ☎ 902/831-2277). The company is Canada's only producer of such Mi'Kmaq figurines depicting the legends and exploits of the Mi'Kmaq hero Glooscap.

O'Leary

37 km (23 mi) northeast of Tyne Valley.

The center of Prince County is composed of a loose network of small towns; some are merely a stretch of road. Many of the local residents are engaged in farming and fishing, carrying on the traditions of their forebears. Farmers driving their tractors through fields of rich, red soil, and colorful lobster boats braving the seas are common scenes in this area. This region is well known for its magnificent red cliffs, majestic lighthouses, and glistening sunsets. Woodstock, north of O'Leary, has a resort where opportunities for outdoor activities abound. The town is also a good base from which to visit one of the Island's best golf courses and a rare woolen-crafts shop.

Lodging

$$ ☑ **Rodd Mill River—A Rodd Signature Resort.** With activities ranging from night skiing to golfing, canoeing, and kayaking, this is truly an all-season resort. One of the highlights of the resort, which is inside Mill River Provincial Park, is the Mill River Golf Course. The dining room provides a perfect overview of the course. The heated pool has a 90-ft slide. ⊠ *Rte. 136, Box 399, Woodstock C0B 1V0,* ☎ *902/859–3555 or 800/565–7633,* FAX *902/859–2486,* WEB *www.rodd-hotels.ca. 80 rooms, 10 suites. Restaurant, bar, indoor pool, hot tub, sauna, 18-hole golf course, tennis court, gym, squash, windsurfing, boating, bicycles, ice-skating, cross-country skiing, tobogganing, pro shop. AE, DC, MC, V. Closed Nov.–Dec. and Apr.*

Outdoor Activities and Sports

The 18-hole, par-72 **Mill River Provincial Golf Course** (⊠ Rte. 136, ☎ 902/859–8873), in Woodstock's Mill River Provincial Park, is among the most scenic and challenging courses in eastern Canada. Ranked among the country's top 50 courses, it has been the site of several championship tournaments. Advance bookings are recommended.

Shopping

The **Old Mill Craft Company** (⊠ Rte. 2, Bloomfield, ☎ 902/859–3508) sells hand-quilted and woolen crafts July through August (reduced hours June and September). The adjacent **MacAusland's Woollen Mill** has been producing famous MacAusland blankets since 1932, the only producer of 100% pure virgin wool blankets in Atlantic Canada.

En Route   Many things in **Tignish,** a friendly Acadian community on Route 2, 12 km (7½ mi) north of O'Leary, are cooperative, including the supermarket, insurance company, seafood plant, service station, and credit union. The imposing parish church of **St. Simon and St. Jude** (⊠ 315 School St., ☎ 902/882–2049), across from Dalton Square, has a superb 1882 Tracker pipe organ, one of the finest such instruments in eastern Canada. The church is often used for recitals by world-renowned musicians.

North Cape

★ ⑲   *14 km (9 mi) north of Tignish.*

In the northwest, the Island narrows to a north-pointing arrow of land, at the tip of which is North Cape, with its imposing lighthouse. At low tide, one of the longest reefs in the world gives way to tidal pools teeming with marine life. Seals often gather offshore here. The curious structures near the reef are wind turbines at the **Atlantic Wind Test Site,** set up on this breezy promontory to evaluate the feasibility of using wind power to generate electricity.

The **Interpretive Centre and Aquarium** has information about marine life, local history, and turbines and windmills. ⊠ *End of Rte. 12,* ☎ *902/882–2991.* ☞ *$2.* ☉ *July–Aug., daily 9–8; late May–June and Sept.–mid-Oct., daily 10–6.*

Dining and Lodging

$–$$$ ✕ **Wind & Reef Restaurant.** This restaurant serves good seafood, such as Island clams, mussels, and lobster, as well as steaks, prime rib, and chicken. There's a fine view of the Gulf of St. Lawrence and Northumberland Strait. ⊠ *End of Rte. 12,* ☎ *902/882–3535. MC, V. Closed Oct.–May.*

$–$$ ☷ **Tignish Heritage Inn.** Originally built as a convent in 1868, this large inn is close to North Cape, Mile 0 of the Confederation Trail, and the facilities offered in the town of Tignish. The pastel-color rooms range in size from cozy to spacious and all feature wooden headboards and colorful comforters. Some of the bathrooms have cast-iron claw-foot tubs. ⊠ *Off Maple St. behind St. Simon and St. Jude Church, Box 398, C0B 2B0,* ☎ *902/882–2491 or 877/882–2491,* FAX *902/882–2500,* WEB *www.tignish.com/inn. 17 rooms, 1 suite. Dining room, coin laundry. AE, DC, MC, V. Closed Nov.–Mar., except for groups by reservation only. CP.*

Miminegash

20 km (12 mi) south of North Cape.

This tiny village overlooks the ocean. The **Irish Moss Interpretive Centre** tells you everything you wanted to know about Irish moss, the fan-shape red alga found in abundance on this coast and used as a thickening agent in foods. "Seaweed pie," made with Irish moss, is served at the adjacent **Seaweed Pie Café.** ⊠ *Rte. 14,* ☎ *902/882–4313.* ☞ *$1.* ☉ *Early June–Sept., daily 10–7.*

West Point

35 km (22 mi) south of Miminegash.

At the southern tip of the western shore, West Point has a tiny fishing harbor, campsites, and a supervised beach. **West Point Lighthouse,** built in 1875, is the tallest on the Island. When the lighthouse was automated, the community took over the building and converted it into an inn and museum, with a moderately priced restaurant. The lighthouse is open daily, late May through late September.

Lodging

$–$$ ☷ **West Point Lighthouse.** Few people can say they've actually spent
★ the night in a lighthouse, but here's a chance to do just that. Rooms, most with ocean views, are pleasantly furnished with local antiques and handmade quilts. This inn books up in the summer months, so make your reservations early. You can enjoy clam-digging, a favorite local pastime, or perhaps try finding the buried treasure reputed to be hidden nearby. ⊠ *Rte. 14, Box 429, O'Leary C0B 1V0,* ☎ *902/859–3605 or 800/764–6854,* FAX *902/859–1510,* WEB *www.peisland.com/west-point/light.htm. 9 rooms. Restaurant, beach, fishing. AE, DC, MC, V. Closed Oct.–May.*

En Route Lady Slipper Drive meanders from West Point back to Summerside through the **Région Évangéline,** the Island's main Acadian district. At **Cape-Egmont,** stop for a look at the Bottle Houses, two tiny houses and a chapel built by a retired carpenter entirely out of glass bottles mortared together like bricks.

Mont-Carmel

 63 km (39 mi) southeast of West Point.

This community has a magnificent brick church overlooking Northumberland Strait. **Le Village de l'Acadie** (Acadian Pioneer Village), a reproduction of an 1820s French settlement, has a church, school, and blacksmith shop. A craft shop sells locally produced goods. There are also modern accommodations and a restaurant in which you can sample authentic Acadian dishes. ⊠ *Rte. 11,* ☎ *902/854–2227 or 800/567–3228.* ☞ *$3.25.* ☉ *Early June–late Sept., daily 9–7.*

Nightlife and the Arts

La Cuisine à Mémé (⊠ Rte. 11, ☎ 902/854–2227 or 800/567–3228), a dinner theater running June 29 to September 1, features typical Acadian step dancing and fiddle music, comedy, and song. The set dinner gives a choice of chicken, salmon, or seafood casserole, with salad, dessert and coffee. The evening, which lasts from 6:30 to about 10:15 costs $29.35.

PRINCE EDWARD ISLAND A TO Z

To research prices, get advice from other travelers, and book travel arrangements, visit www.fodors.com.

AIR TRAVEL

Air Canada and its regional carriers offer daily nonstop service from Charlottetown to Halifax and Toronto, both of which have connections to the rest of Canada, the United States, and beyond. Prince Edward Air is available for private charters.

➤ AIRLINES AND CONTACTS: **Prince Edward Air** (☎ 902/566–4488).

AIRPORTS

Charlottetown Airport is 5 km (3 mi) north of town.

➤ AIRPORT INFORMATION: **Charlottetown Airport** (⊠ 250 Maple Hills Ave., ☎ 902/566–7997).

BOAT AND FERRY TRAVEL

Northumberland Ferries sails between Wood Islands and Caribou, Nova Scotia, from May to mid-December. The crossing takes about 75 minutes, and the round-trip costs approximately $49 per vehicle, $58 for a recreational vehicle; foot passengers pay $11 (you pay only when leaving the Island). There are 18 crossings per day in summer. Reservations are not accepted.

➤ BOAT AND FERRY INFORMATION: **Northumberland Ferries** (☎ 888/249–7245, WEB www.nfl-bay.com).

CAR TRAVEL

The 13-km (8-mi) Confederation Bridge connects Cape Jourimain, in New Brunswick, with Borden-Carleton, Prince Edward Island. The crossing takes about 12 minutes. The toll is $37 per car, $42.25 for a recreational vehicle; it's collected when you leave the Island.

The lack of public transportation on the Island makes having your own vehicle almost a necessity. There are more than 3,700 km (2,300 mi) of paved road in the province, including the three scenic coastal drives: Lady Slipper Drive, Blue Heron Drive, and Kings Byway. A helpful highway map of the province is available from Tourism PEI and at visitor centers on the Island.

ROAD CONDITIONS

Designated Heritage Roads are surfaced with red clay, the local soil base. The unpaved roads meander through rural and undeveloped areas, where you're likely to see lots of wildflowers and birds. A four-wheel-drive vehicle is not necessary, but in spring and inclement weather the mud can get quite deep and the narrow roads become impassable. Keep an eye open for bicycles, motorcycles, and pedestrians.

EMERGENCIES

Dial 911 for emergency police, fire, or ambulance services.
➤ HOSPITALS: **Queen Elizabeth Hospital** (✉ 60 Riverside Dr., Charlottetown, ☎ 902/894–2200 or 902/894–2095).

OUTDOORS AND SPORTS

For a publication listing golf courses in Prince Edward Island, contact **Tourism PEI** (☎ 888/734–7529). Most courses may be booked directly or by contacting **Golf Atlantic** (☎ 800/565–0001).

SHOPPING

For information on crafts outlets around Prince Edward Island, contact the **Prince Edward Island Crafts Council** (✉ 156 Richmond St., Charlottetown C1A 1H9, ☎ 902/892–5152).

TOURS

The Island has about 20 sightseeing tours, including double-decker bus tours, taxi tours, cycling tours, harbor cruises, and walking tours. Most tour companies are based in Charlottetown and offer excursions around the city and to the beaches.

DRIVING TOURS

Yellow Cab can be booked for tours by the hour or day.
➤ FEES AND SCHEDULES: **Yellow Cab** (☎ 902/892–6561).

WALKING TOURS

Island Nature Trust sells a nature-trail map of the Island. Tourism PEI has maps of the 225-km (140 mi) multiuse Confederation Trail.
➤ FEES AND SCHEDULES: **Island Nature Trust** (✉ Box 265, Charlottetown C1A 7K4, ☎ 902/566–9150). **Tourism PEI** (✉ Box 940, Charlottetown C1A 7M5, ☎ 902/368–7795 or 888/734–7529, FAX 902/566–4336, WEB www.peiplay.com).

VISITOR INFORMATION

Tourism PEI publishes an informative annual guide for visitors and maintains 10 Visitor Information Centres (VICs) on the Island. It also produces a map of the 350-km (217-mi) Confederation Trail. The main Visitor Information Centre is in Charlottetown and is open mid-May to October daily and November to mid-May weekdays.
➤ TOURIST INFORMATION: **Tourism PEI** (✉ Box 940, Charlottetown C1A 7M5, ☎ 902/368–7795 or 888/734–7529, FAX 902/566–4336, WEB www.peiplay.com). **Visitor Information Centre** (✉ 178 Water St., ☎ 902/368–4444).

5 NEWFOUNDLAND AND LABRADOR

Canada's easternmost province comprises
the island of Newfoundland, at the mouth of
the Gulf of St. Lawrence, and Labrador on
the mainland to the northwest. Humpback
whales feed near shore in the fish-rich
ocean, millions of seabirds nest in almost
300 coastal colonies, and 10,000-year-old
icebergs cruise by fishing villages. St. John's,
the capital, is a classic harbor city offering a
lively arts scene and warm hospitality.

Updated by
Ed Kirby

NEWFOUNDLAND WAS THE SITE of the first European settlement in North America. Sometime around AD 1000, a half millennium before explorers John Cabot (1497) and Gaspar Corte-Real (1500) touched down in the New World, Vikings from Iceland and Greenland built a sod hut village near Newfoundland's northern tip. They stayed only a few years and then evidence of their presence disappeared into the mists of history for centuries. Their village, part of the territory they called Vinland, was discovered only in the 1960s.

Early as they were, the Vikings were still latecomers to the area. The first people appeared in the region as the glaciers melted 9,000 years ago. The oldest known funeral monument in North America was built in southern Labrador 7,500 years ago.

When Cabot arrived, sailing under the English flag at the end of the 15th century, he reported that the fish in the ocean were so thick they could be caught with a basket. Within a decade, St. John's had become a crowded harbor. Fishing boats from France, England, Spain, and Portugal vied for a chance to catch Newfoundland's lucrative cod, which was subsequently to shape the province's history.

At one time there were 700 hardworking settlements, or "outports," dotting Newfoundland's coast, most of them devoted to catching, salting, and drying the world's most plentiful fish. Today, only about 400 of these settlements survive. Cod, Newfoundland's most famous resource, had become so scarce by 1992 that a partial fishing moratorium was declared; it's still in effect today. The cod have not yet returned, and the limited quotas may be further reduced. People have switched to catching other species, found work in other industries, or left for greener pastures. The discovery of one of the richest and largest nickel deposits in the world at Voisey's Bay in northern Labrador, near Nain, holds hope for a new industry; development is likely to begin within a few years. Several offshore oil fields are expected to go into production in the next few years, joining the Hibernia field, which began pumping oil in 1997.

For almost 400 years, before Newfoundland and Labrador joined Canada in 1949, the people had survived the vagaries of a fishing economy on their own. It was the Great Depression that forced the economy to go belly-up. After more than 50 years of confederation with Canada, the economy has improved considerably, but the people are still independent and maintain a unique language and lifestyle. E. Annie Proulx's Pulitzer prize-winning novel *The Shipping News* brought the attention of many readers to this part of the world, and a film adaptation due in 2002 promises an even wider audience. Now homegrown literary talent is finding a wider audience. Authors such as Wayne Johnston, whose novel *The Colony of Unrequited Dreams* was an artistic and commercial hit in 1999, are bringing Newfoundland and Labrador's distinctive history, ecology, and outlook to an international audience.

Visitors find themselves straddling the centuries. Old accents and customs in small towns and outports exist cheek by jowl with cable TV and the Internet. And the major cities of St. John's on Newfoundland's east coast and Corner Brook on its west coast are very much part of the 21st century.

Whether you visit an isolated outport or St. John's lively Duckworth Street, you're sure to meet some of the warmest, wittiest people in North America. Strangers have always been welcome in Newfoundland, since the days when locals brought visitors in from the cold, warmed them by the fire, and charmingly interrogated them for news of events elsewhere. Before you can shoot the breeze, though, you have to develop an ear for the strong provincial dialects. The *Dictionary of Newfoundland English* has more than 5,000 words, mostly having to do with fishery, weather, and scenery. To get started, you can practice the name of the island portion of the province—it's New-fund-*land*, with the accent on "land." However, only "livyers" ever get the pronunciation exactly right. While academics strive to preserve the old words and speech patterns, the effects of globalization combined with changes in the economy are eroding the old dialects as young people leave coastal hamlets for education and jobs in larger cities. But it is these same young people who are among the most devoted fans of Great Big Sea and other modern exponents of traditional music.

Pleasures and Pastimes

Dining
Today, despite the fishing moratorium, seafood is an excellent value in Newfoundland and Labrador. Many restaurants offer seasonal specialties with a wide variety of traditional wild and cultured species. Cod is still readily available and is traditionally prepared: panfried, baked, or poached. Aquaculture species such as steelhead trout, salmon, mussels, and sea scallops are available in better restaurants. Cold-water shrimp, snow crab, lobster, redfish, grenadier, halibut, and turbot are also good seafood choices.

Two other foods to try are partridgeberries and bakeapples. Partridgeberries, called mountain cranberries in the United States, are used for pies, jams, cakes, pancakes, and as a meat sauce. Bakeapples, also known as cloudberries, look like yellow raspberries and grow on low plants in bogs. They ripen in August, and pickers sell them by the side of the road in jars. If the ones you buy are hard, wait a few days and they'll ripen into rich-tasting fruit. The berries are popular on ice cream or spread on bread.

Only the large urban centers, especially St. John's and Corner Brook, have sophisticated restaurants. Fish is a safe dish just about everywhere, even in the most basic takeout. Excellent meals are offered in the province's network of bed-and-breakfasts, where home cooking goes hand in hand with a warm welcome.

CATEGORY	COST*
$$$$	over $32
$$$	$22–$32
$$	$13–$21
$	under $13

per person, in Canadian dollars, for a main course at dinner

Festivals and Performing Arts Events
From the Folk Festival main stage in St. John's to the front parlor, the province is filled with music of all kinds. Newfoundlanders love a party, and from the cities to the smallest towns they celebrate their history and unique culture with festivals and events throughout the summer. "Soirees" and "times"—big parties and small parties—offer a combination of traditional music, recitation, comedy, and local food, sometimes in a dinner-theater setting.

Fishing
Newfoundland has more than 200 salmon rivers and thousands of trout streams. Fishing in these unpolluted waters is an angler's dream. The Atlantic salmon is king of the game fish. Top salmon rivers in New-

foundland include the Gander, Humber, and Exploits, while Labrador's top-producing waters are the Sandhill, Michaels, Flowers, and Eagle rivers. Lake trout, brook trout, and landlocked salmon are other favorite species. In Labrador, northern pike and arctic char can be added to that list. An upturn in returning salmon in 1998 and subsequent quota increases were followed by two years of baffling low returns to many rivers. Note that nonresidents must hire a guide or outfitter for anything other than roadside angling.

Hiking

Many provincial parks and both of the national parks in the province have hiking and nature trails, and coastal and forest trails radiate out from most small communities. The East Coast Trail on the Avalon Peninsula covers 520 km (322 mi) of coastline; the trail begins in Conception Bay South and moves north to Cape St. Francis and then south all the way down to Trepassey. It passes through two dozen communities and along clifftops that provide ideal lookouts for icebergs and seabirds. You can call individual parks or the tourist information line for specifics.

Lodging

Newfoundland and Labrador offer lodgings that range from modestly priced B&Bs, which you can find through local tourist offices, to luxury accommodations. In between, you can choose from affordable, basic, and mid-price hotels, motels, and cabins. In remote areas, be prepared to find very basic lodgings for the most part (though some of the best lodging in the province can be found in rural areas). However, the lack of amenities is usually made up for by the home-cooked meals and great hospitality.

CATEGORY	COST*
$$$$	over $200
$$$	$150–$200
$$	$100–$150
$	under $100

*All prices are for a standard double room, excluding 15% harmonized sales tax (HST), in Canadian dollars.

Exploring Newfoundland and Labrador

This chapter divides the province into the island of Newfoundland, beginning with St. John's and the Avalon Peninsula and moving west, and Labrador. Labrador is considered as a whole, with suggested driving and train excursions for a number of areas.

Numbers in the text correspond to numbers in the margin and on the St. John's, Avalon Peninsula, and Newfoundland and Labrador maps.

Great Itineraries

IF YOU HAVE 3 DAYS

Pick either the west or east coast of Newfoundland. On the west coast, after arriving by ferry at **Port aux Basques** ㊻, drive through the Codroy Valley, heading north to **Gros Morne National Park** ㊲ and its fjords, and overnight in ☷ **Rocky Harbour** ㊵ or ☷ **Woody Point** ㊳. The next day, visit **L'Anse aux Meadows National Historic Site** ㊷, where the Vikings built a village a thousand years ago; there are reconstructions of the dwellings. Spend the night in ☷ **St. Anthony** ㊸ or nearby.

On the east coast, the ferry docks at Argentia. Explore the Avalon Peninsula, beginning in ☷ **St. John's** ①–⑭, where you should spend your first night. The next day visit **Cape Spear,** the most easterly point in North America, and the **Witless Bay Ecological Reserve** ⑮, where you

Newfoundland and Labrador

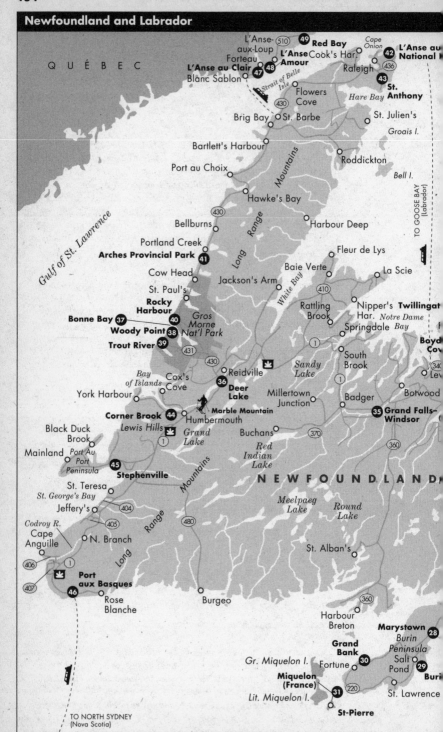

QUÉBEC

L'Anse-aux-Loup
510
49 Red Bay
Cook's Har.
Cape Onion
42 L'Anse au
National

Forteau
L'Anse Amour
Raleigh
436

L'Anse au Clair 47 48
43 St. Anthony

Blanc Sablon
Strait of Belle Isle
Hare Bay

430
Flowers Cove
St. Julien's

Brig Bay
St. Barbe
Groais I.

Bartlett's Harbour
Roddickton

Port au Choix
Bell I.

Hawke's Bay

Mountains

Bellburns
430
Harbour Deep

Portland Creek
Fleur de Lys

Arches Provincial Park 41
Baie Verte
La Scie

Cow Head
Jackson's Arm

St. Paul's
410

Rocky Harbour
Rattling Brook
Nipper's Har.
Twillingat

Bonne Bay 37
40
Gros Morne Nat'l Park
Springdale
Notre Dame Bay

Woody Point 38
South Brook
Boyd Cove

Trout River 39
431
1

430
Sandy Lake
340

Cox's Cove
Reidville
Lev.

York Harbour
36
Deer Lake
Millertown Junction
Badger
Botwood

Corner Brook 44
Marble Mountain
35 Grand Falls-Windsor

Lewis Hills
1
Humbermouth
Buchans
370

Black Duck Brook
Grand Lake
Red Indian Lake
360

Mainland
Port Au Port Peninsula
N E W F O U N D L A N D

Stephenville 45
Meelpaeg Lake
Round Lake

St. Teresa
St. George's Bay
Jeffery's
404

Codroy R.
405
480
St. Alban's

Cape Anguille
N. Branch

406
1
Long Range Mountains

407
Port aux Basques
360

46
Rose Blanche
Burgeo
Harbour Breton

Marystown 28

Burin Peninsula
Salt Pond

Gr. Miquelon I.
Grand Bank
30
29 Burin

Fortune
St. Lawrence

Miquelon (France) 31
220

Lit. Miquelon I.
St-Pierre

TO GOOSE BAY (Labrador)

Gulf of St. Lawrence

Bay of Islands

TO NORTH SYDNEY
(Nova Scotia)

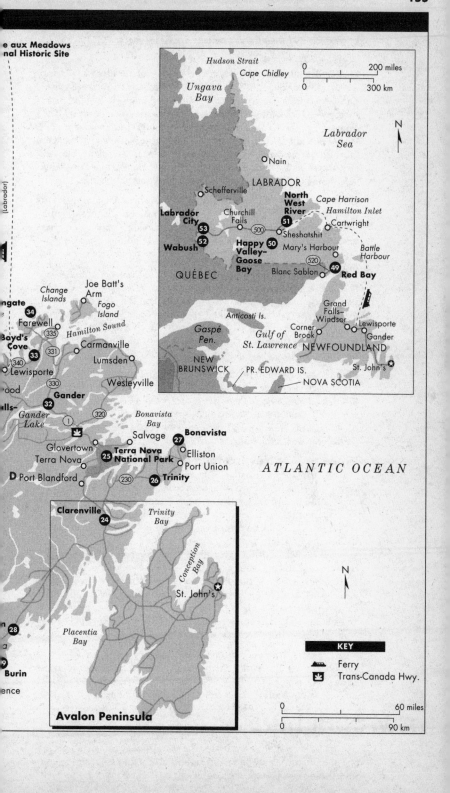

e aux Meadows
nal Historic Site

Hudson Strait

Cape Chidley

Ungava
Bay

Labrador
Sea

Nain

LABRADOR

Schefferville

North
West
River

Cape Harrison
Hamilton Inlet

Labrador
City **53**

Churchill
Falls

Cartwright

500

51

Sheshatshit

Wabush **52**

Happy
Valley-
Goose
Bay **50**

Mary's Harbour

Battle
Harbour

QUÉBEC

520

Blanc Sablon

49 **Red Bay**

Change
Islands

Joe Batt's
Arm

Fogo
Island

Anticosti Is.

Grand
Falls-
Windsor

ngate **34**

Farewell

335

Hamilton Sound

Gaspé
Pen.

Gulf of
St. Lawrence

Corner
Brook

Lewisporte

Gander

Bayd's
Cove **33**

331

Carmanville

NEWFOUNDLAND

340

Lumsden

NEW
BRUNSWICK

Lewisporte

330

Wesleyville

PR. EDWARD IS.

St. John's

ood

Gander 32

NOVA SCOTIA

lls—

320

Gander
Lake

1

Bonavista
Bay

Bonavista

Glovertown

Salvage

27

Elliston

Terra Nova

**Terra Nova
National Park 25**

Port Union

D Port Blandford

230

26 **Trinity**

Clarenville

24

Trinity
Bay

28

St. John's

Conception Bay

Placentia
Bay

9

Burin

ence

Avalon Peninsula

ATLANTIC OCEAN

N

N

KEY

Ferry

Trans-Canada Hwy.

0   200 miles
0   300 km

0   60 miles
0   90 km

can see whales, seabirds, and icebergs. Drive though **Placentia** ㉑ and spend your third day at ⌂ **Cape St. Mary's Ecological Reserve** ㉓, known for its gannets and dramatic coastal scenery.

IF YOU HAVE 6 DAYS

On Newfoundland's west coast, add southern Labrador to your trip. A ferry takes you from St. Barbe to Blanc Sablon on the Québec–Labrador border. Drive 96 km (60 mi) to **Red Bay** ㊾ to explore the remains of a 17th-century Basque whaling station; then head to **L'Anse Amour** ㊽ to see Canada's second-tallest lighthouse. Overnight at ⌂ **L'Anse au Clair** ㊼. Return through Gros Morne National Park and explore ⌂ **Corner Brook** ㊹, where you should stay overnight. The next day, travel west of **Stephenville** ㊺ to explore the Port au Port Peninsula, home of Newfoundland's French-speaking population.

On the east coast add ⌂ **Trinity** ㉖ to your must-see list, and spend the night there or in ⌂ **Clarenville** ㉔. The north shore of Conception Bay is home to many picturesque villages, including ⌂ **Cupids** ⑲ and **Harbour Grace** ⑳. Several half-day, full-day, and two-day excursions are possible from St. John's, and in each direction a different personality of the region unfolds.

IF YOU HAVE 9 DAYS

In addition to the places already mentioned on the west coast, take a drive into central Newfoundland and visit the lovely villages of Notre Dame Bay. Overnight in ⌂ **Twillingate** ㉞. Catch a ferry to ⌂ **Fogo** or the ⌂ **Change Islands.** Accommodations are available on both islands, but book ahead.

On the east coast add the Burin Peninsula and a trip to France—yes, France—to your itinerary. You can reach the French territory of ⌂ **St-Pierre and Miquelon** ㉛ by passenger ferry from Fortune. Explore romantic ⌂ **Grand Bank** ㉚, named for the famous fishing area just offshore, and climb Cook's Lookout in **Burin** ㉙, where Captain James Cook kept watch for smugglers from St-Pierre.

When to Tour Newfoundland and Labrador

Seasons can vary dramatically in Newfoundland and Labrador. In spring, icebergs float down from the north, and in late spring, fin, pilot, minke, and humpback whales arrive to hunt for food along the coast and stay until August. In summer, Newfoundland's bogs and meadows turn into a colorful riot of wildflowers and greenery, and the sea is dotted with boats and buoys marking traps and nets. Fall is a favored season: the weather is usually fine; hills and meadows are loaded with berries; and the woods are alive with moose, caribou, partridges, and rabbits. In winter, ski hills attract downhillers and snowboarders, and the forest trails hum with the sounds of snowmobiles and all-terrain vehicles taking anglers to lodges and lakes. Cross-country ski trails in provincial and national parks are oases of quiet populated by squirrels and birds.

The tourist season runs from June through September, when the province celebrates with festivals, fairs, concerts, plays, and crafts shows. The temperature hovers between 24°C (75°F) and 29°C (85°F) and gently cools off in the evening, providing a good night's sleep.

NEWFOUNDLAND

The rocky coasts and peninsulas of the island of Newfoundland present much dramatic beauty and many opportunities for exploring. Seaport and fishing towns such as St. John's and Grand Bank tell a fascinating story, and parks from Terra Nova National Park on the eastern side of the island to Gros Morne National Park on the west have impressive landscapes. The Avalon Peninsula includes the provincial capital of St. John's as well as the Cape Shore on the west side of the island. The Bonavista Peninsula and the Burin Peninsula as well as Notre Dame Bay have some intriguing sights, from Bonavista, associated with John Cabot's landing, to pretty towns such as Twillingate. The Great Northern Peninsula on the western side of Newfoundland holds a historic site with the remains of Viking sod houses. The west coast has Corner Brook, a good base for exploring the mountains, as well as farming and fishing communities.

St. John's

When Sir Humphrey Gilbert sailed into St. John's to establish British colonial rule for Queen Elizabeth in 1583, he found Spanish, French, and Portuguese fishermen actively working the harbor. As early as 1627, the merchants of Water Street—then known as the Lower Path—were doing a thriving business buying fish, selling goods, and supplying alcohol to soldiers and sailors. Today St. John's still encircles the snug punch-bowl harbor that helped establish its reputation.

This old seaport town (population 102,000), the province's capital, mixes English and Irish influences, Victorian architecture and modern convenience, and traditional music and rock and roll into a heady brew that finds expression in a lively arts scene and a relaxed pace—all in a setting that has the ocean on one side and unexpected greenery on the other.

Exploring St. John's

A walk downtown takes in many historic buildings, but a car is needed to explore farther-flung sights ranging from Cape Spear, south of St. John's, to parks and fishing villages.

A Good Walk

Begin at **Harbourside Park** ① on Water Street, where Gilbert planted the staff of England and claimed Newfoundland. When you leave, turn left on Water Street, right on Holloway Street, and then right onto **Duckworth Street** ②. The east end of this street is full of crafts shops and other stores. After walking east for five blocks, turn left onto Ordinance Street, just one of several streets that recall St. John's military past. Cross Military Road to **St. Thomas Anglican (Old Garrison) Church** ③, built in the 1830s as a place of worship for British soldiers.

Turn left as you leave St. Thomas and walk up King's Bridge Road. The first building on the left is **Commissariat House** ④, an officer's house restored to the style of the 1830s. North of Commissariat House, a shady lane on the left leads to the gardens of **Government House** ⑤. **Circular Road** ⑥, where the business elite moved after a fire destroyed much of the town in 1846, is across from the gardens in front of the house. Back on Military Road, cross Bannerman Road to the **Colonial Building** ⑦, the former seat of government and current home of the Provincial Archives. Walk west on Military Road until it becomes Harvey Road. The Roman Catholic **Basilica Cathedral of St. John the Baptist** ⑧ is on the right; you pass the Basilica Museum in the Bishop's Palace just before you get there.

Cross Harvey Road and turn left down Garrison Hill, so named because it once led to Fort Townshend, now home to fire and police stations. Cross Queen's Road and walk down Cathedral Street to Gower Street and the Gothic Revival **Anglican Cathedral of St. John the Baptist** ⑨. The entrance is on the west side on Church Hill. **Gower Street**

St. John's

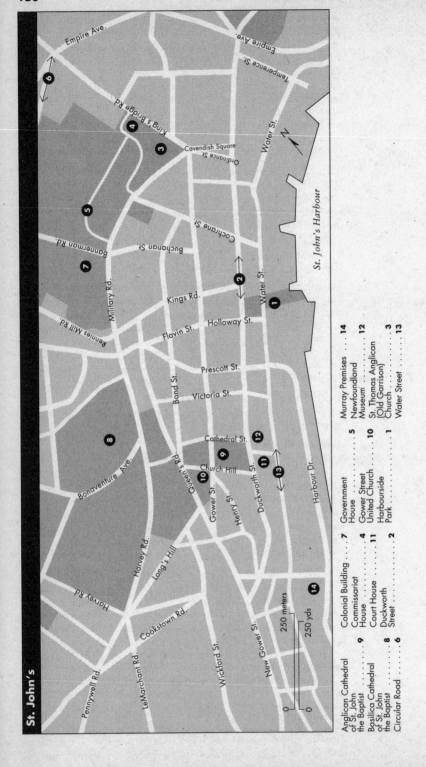

Empire Ave.

Temperance St.

Empire Ave.

King's Bridge Rd.

Cavendish Square

Ordnance St.

Water St.

St. John's Harbour

Cochrane St.

Bannerman Rd.

Buchanan St.

Military Rd.

Kings Rd.

Water St.

Rennies Mill Rd.

Flavin St.

Holloway St.

Prescott St.

Bond St.

Victoria St.

Cathedral St.

Church Hill

Queen's Rd.

Gower St.

Henry St.

Duckworth St.

Harbour Dr.

Bonaventure Ave.

Harvey Rd.

Long's Hill

Harvey Rd.

Pennywell Rd.

LeMarchant Rd.

Cookstown Rd.

Wickford St.

New Gower St.

250 meters

250 yds

Anglican Cathedral
of St. John
the Baptist **9**

Basilica Cathedral
of St. John
the Baptist **8**

Circular Road **6**

Colonial Building **7**

Commissariat
House **4**

Court House **11**

Duckworth
Street **2**

Government
House **3**

Gower Street
United Church **10**

Harbourside
Park **1**

Murray Premises ... **14**

Newfoundland
Museum **12**

St. Thomas Anglican
(Old Garrison)
Church **3**

Water Street **13**

United Church ⑩ is directly across from the cathedral on the west side of Church Hill. Continue to the bottom of Church Hill to see the Duckworth Street **Court House** ⑪, with its four turrets, each one different. Go east on Duckworth a few doors to the **Newfoundland Museum** ⑫, with exhibits on Newfoundland's natural and cultural history. Exit the museum and turn left; then go down the long set of steps to **Water Street** ⑬, one of the oldest commercial streets in North America. Turn right on Water Street to reach the last stop, the **Murray Premises** ⑭, a restored mercantile complex. It contains boutiques, a science center, offices, and—welcome after this walk—restaurants, a coffee bar, and a wine cellar.

TIMING

Downtown St. John's is compact but hilly. The walk avoids major uphill climbs. Expect to spend half a day visiting these sights, though this may vary depending on how much time you stay at each location. It's best undertaken from spring to fall.

Sights to See

❾ **Anglican Cathedral of St. John the Baptist.** A fine example of Gothic Revival architecture designed by Sir George Gilbert Scott, this church was first completed in the mid-1800s; it was rebuilt after the 1892 fire. Women of the parish operate a tearoom in the crypt from 2:30 to 4:40 daily in summer. ⊠ *22 Church Hill,* ☎ *709/726–5677,* WEB *www.infonet. st-johns.nf.ca/cathedral.* 🎫 *Free.* ⊘ *Tours June–Sept., daily 10–5.*

❽ **Basilica Cathedral of St. John the Baptist.** This 1855 Roman Catholic cathedral in the Romanesque style has a commanding position above Military Road, overlooking the older section of the city and the harbor. A museum with vestments and religious objects is next door in the Bishop's Palace. ⊠ *200 Military Rd.,* ☎ *709/754–3660,* WEB *www.delweb.rcec.com.* 🎫 *Museum $2.* ⊘ *Museum June–Sept., weekdays 9–5.*

❻ **Circular Road.** The business elite of St. John's moved here after the devastating fire of 1846. The street contains some very fine Victorian houses and shade trees.

❼ **Colonial Building.** This columned building (erected 1847–50) was the seat of the Newfoundland government from the 1850s to 1960, when the legislature moved to the Confederation Building in the north end of the city. The limestone for the building was imported from Cork, Ireland. The Colonial Building now houses the Provincial Archives, which are useful to anyone researching family or provincial history. ⊠ *Military and Bannerman Rds.,* ☎ *709/729–3065.* 🎫 *Free.* ⊘ *Mon.–Tues. and Thurs.–Fri. 9–4:15, Wed. 9–4:15 and 6:30–9:45.*

❹ **Commissariat House.** The residence and office of the British garrison's supply officer in the 1830s has been restored to reflect that era. Interpreters dress in period costume. ⊠ *King's Bridge Rd.,* ☎ *709/729–6730 or 709/729–0592.* 🎫 *$2.50.* ⊘ *Mid-June–early Oct., daily 10–5:30.*

⓫ **Court House.** The late-19th-century courthouse has an eccentric appearance: each of its four turrets is a different style. ⊠ *Duckworth St., bottom of Church Hill.*

❷ **Duckworth Street.** Once called the Upper Path, this has been St. John's "second street" for centuries. (Water Street has been the main street for just as long.) Stretching from the bottom of Signal Hill in the east to near City Hall in the west, Duckworth Street has restaurants, bars, antiques and crafts shops, and lawyers' offices. Lanes and stairways lead off the street down to Water Street and up to higher elevations.

⑤ Government House. This is the residence of the lieutenant governor, the Queen's representative in Newfoundland. According to popular myth, the moat around Government House was designed to keep out snakes, though there have never been snakes in Newfoundland. The house, so the story goes, was originally intended for the governor of a warmer colony, where serpents might be a problem. (In fact, the moat was actually designed to allow more light into the basement rooms.) The house, built in the 1830s, has a marvelous garden you can explore, but the building isn't open for tours. You can, however, enter the front porch and sign the guest book. Everyone who does so receives an invitation to the annual garden party held in early August. ⊠ *Military Rd.,* ☎ *709/720–4494,* WEB *www.mun.ca/govhouse.* ☒ *Garden free.* ☉ *Garden open daily.*

⑩ Gower Street United Church. This 1896 church has a redbrick facade, green turrets, 50 stained-glass windows, and a massive pipe organ. ⊠ *Gower St. and Queen's Rd.,* ☎ *709/753–7286,* WEB *www.infonet. st-johns.nf.ca/providers/gowerunited.* ☒ *Free.* ☉ *Daily; tours July–Aug., daily 2–5.*

① Harbourside Park. Here Sir Humphrey Gilbert claimed Newfoundland for Britain in 1583, much to the amusement of the French, Spanish, and Portuguese fishermen in port at the time. They thought him a fool, a judgment borne out a few days later when he ran his ship aground and drowned. This area, known as the Queen's Wharf, is where the harbor-pilot boat is docked. ⊠ *Water St. E.*

⑭ Murray Premises. One of the oldest buildings in St. John's, the Murray Premises dates from only 1846; the town was destroyed many times by fire. The last and worst was in 1892. This restored warehouse now houses shops, offices, and restaurants. The **Newfoundland Science Centre** (☎ *709/754–0823*), open daily, with hands-on exhibits and special demonstrations, is within the Murray Premises; admission is $4.50. ⊠ *Water St. and Harbour Dr., at Beck's Cove,* ☎ *709/754–0823,* WEB *www.sciencecentre.nf.ca.* ☉ *Weekdays 10–5, Sat. 10–6, Sun. noon–6.*

⑫ Newfoundland Museum. Three floors of displays focus on the province's cultural and natural history. There are also changing exhibits from the museum's collection. ⊠ *285 Duckworth St.,* ☎ *709/729–0917,* WEB *www.nfmuseum.com.* ☒ *$3.* ☉ *Mid-June–mid-Sept., daily 9:30–4:45; mid-Sept.–mid-June, Tues.–Fri. 9–4:45, Sat. 9:30–4:45, Sun. noon–4:45.*

③ St. Thomas Anglican (Old Garrison) Church. English soldiers used to worship at this black wooden church, the oldest in the city, during the early and mid-1800s. ⊠ *8 Military Rd.,* ☎ *709/576–6632.* ☒ *Free.* ☉ *Tours June 24–Aug. 30, daily 9:30–5:30; call ahead for off-season hrs.*

⑬ Water Street. Originally called the Lower Path, Water Street has been the site of businesses since at least the 1620s. The older architecture recalls that of seaports in southwest England and Ireland.

A Good Drive

To explore attractions outside the St. John's downtown core, begin by taking Water Street west to its intersection with Route 11, which leads you to **Cape Spear National Historic Site,** 11 km (7 mi) south of St. John's. This is the easternmost point in North America—when you stand with your back to the ocean, the entire population of North America is west of you. It's also a good place to spot whales and drifting icebergs in spring and early summer.

On the drive back to St. John's, branch off to the left through **Maddox Cove** and **Petty Harbour,** two fishing villages so picture-perfect they have served as backdrops for a couple of Hollywood movies. Continue to Route 10, turn right, and head north to Waterford Bridge Road and **Bowring Park,** a traditional English-style park. Drive east through the Waterford Valley and along Water Street, Harbour Drive, and back to Water Street; turn left up Temperance Street and right again onto Duckworth Street, and then turn right to the east end of St. John's harbor and the **Battery,** a fishing village in the city. After exploring the Battery, turn right up Signal Hill Road and drive to the top, where **Cabot Tower** has a stunning view of the coastline and the city below. The **Signal Hill National Historic Site** interpretation center is also on this road, below the tower.

Heading back down the hill, turn right at the bottom onto Quidi Vidi Road and drive to its intersection with Forest Road. Turn right, drive to Cuckold's Cove Road, and continue on to **Quidi Vidi Battery,** an old French and British fort staffed by guides in period costume in summer. Return to Quidi Vidi Road, turn right, and drive through **Quidi Vidi,** another fishing village within the city. Caution: the road is very narrow here.

The final two stops on this drive are in C. A. Pippy Park in the city's north end. Take Prince Philip Drive to Allendale Road and turn north. The first turn on the left is Nagle's Place, which brings you to **The Fluvarium,** where you can view fish underwater through a large glass window. Continue north on Allendale Road to Mt. Scio Road. Turn left and head toward the native and alpine plants at **Memorial University Botanical Garden.**

TIMING

This drive goes beyond St. John's to Cape Spear, so plan to spend between a half day and a day if you want some time at each stop. Summer, when all the attractions are open, is the best time for this tour.

Sights to See

The Battery. This tiny fishing village perches precariously at the base of steep cliffs between hill and harbor. The narrow lanes snake around the houses, making this a good place to get out and walk.

Bowring Park. An expansive Victorian park west of downtown, Bowring resembles the famous city parks of London, after which it was modeled. Dotting the grounds are ponds and rustic bridges; the statue of Peter Pan just inside the east gate was cast from the same mold as the one in Kensington Park in London. The wealthy Bowring family donated the park to the city in 1911. ✉ *Waterford Bridge Rd.,* ☎ *709/576–6134.*

Cabot Tower. This tower at the summit of Signal Hill was constructed in 1897 to commemorate the 400th anniversary of Cabot's landing in Newfoundland. The ride here along Signal Hall Road affords fine harbor and city views, as does the tower. ✉ *Signal Hill Rd.,* ☎ *709/772–5367,* WEB *www.parkscanada.pch.gc.ca/parks/newfoundland.* ✎ *Free.* ☉ *Early Sept.–mid-June, daily 9–5; mid-June–early Sept., daily 8:30–4:30; guides available on summer weekends.*

★ **Cape Spear National Historic Site.** At the easternmost point of land on the continent, songbirds begin their chirping in the dim light of dawn, and whales (in early summer) feed directly below the cliffs, providing an unforgettable start to the day. From April through July, you may well see icebergs floating by. **Cape Spear Lighthouse,** Newfoundland's oldest such beacon, has been lovingly restored to its original form and furnishings. ✉ *Rte. 11,* ☎ *709/772–5367,* WEB *www.parkscanada.pch.gc.ca/newfoundland.* ✎ *Site free; lighthouse $2.50.* ☉ *Site, daily 24 hrs; lighthouse mid-May–mid-Oct., daily 10–6:30.*

The Fluvarium. Underwater windows look onto a brook at the only public facility of its kind in North America. In season you can observe spawning brown and brook trout in their natural habitat. Feeding time for the fish, frogs, and eels is 4 PM daily. ⊠ *Nagles Pl., C. A. Pippy Park,* ☎ *709/754–3474,* ⓦⒺⒷ *www.fluvarium.nf.net.* ⌻ *$4.* ☉ *Summer, daily 9–5; call ahead for other seasons.*

Maddox Cove and Petty Harbour. These picturesque fishing villages are next to each other along the coast between Cape Spear and Route 10. The wharves and sturdy seaside sheds, especially those in Petty Harbour, harken back to a time not long ago when the fishery was paramount in the economy and lives of the residents. These villages have been the setting for several Hollywood movies.

Memorial University Botanical Garden. This 110-acre garden and natural area at Oxen Pond in C. A. Pippy Park has four pleasant walking trails and many gardens, including rock gardens and scree, a Newfoundland historic-plants bed, peat and woodland beds, an alpine house, an herb wall, and native plant collections. You can see scores of varieties of rhododendron here, as well as many kinds of butterflies and the rare hummingbird moth. Guided walks are available with advance notice. ⊠ *306 Mt. Scio Rd.,* ☎ *709/737–8590,* ⓦⒺⒷ *www.mun. ca/botgarden.* ⌻ *$2.* ☉ *May–Nov., daily 10–5.*

Quidi Vidi. No one knows the origin of this fishing village's name. It's one of the oldest parts of St. John's. The town is best explored on foot as the roads are narrow and make driving difficult. In spring, the inlet, known as the Gut, is a good place to catch sea-run brown trout.

Quidi Vidi Battery. This small redoubt has been restored to the way it appeared in 1812. Costumed interpreters tell you about the hard, unromantic life of a soldier of the empire. ⊠ *Off Cuckold's Cove Rd.,* ☎ *709/729–2977 or 709/729–0592.* ⌻ *$2.50.* ☉ *Mid-June–early Oct., daily 10–5:30.*

★ ☺ **Signal Hill National Historic Site.** In spite of its height, Signal Hill was difficult to defend: throughout the 1600s and 1700s it changed hands with every attacking French, English, and Dutch force. The French and British fought the last battle of the Seven Years' War here in 1762. A wooden palisade encircles the summit of the hill, indicating the boundaries of the old fortifications. En route to the hill is the **Park Interpretation Centre,** with exhibits describing St. John's history. In July and August, cadets in 19th-century British uniform perform a tattoo of military drills and music. In 1901 Guglielmo Marconi received the first transatlantic wire transmission near **Cabot Tower,** at the top of Signal Hill. From the top of the hill it's a 500-ft drop to the narrow harbor entrance below; views are excellent. ⊠ *Signal Hill Rd.,* ☎ *709/772–5367,* ⓦⒺⒷ *www.parkscanada.pch.gc.ca.* ⌻ *Site free; visitor center $2.50 mid-May–mid-Oct., free rest of year.* ☉ *Site daily 24 hrs. Center mid-June–Labor Day, daily 8:30–8; Labor Day–mid-June, daily 8:30–4:30.*

Dining and Lodging

$$–$$$ ✕ **Bianca's.** Modern paintings lend this bright eatery the air of an art gallery. The menu changes seasonally but emphasizes fish dishes such as salmon marinated in Scotch whisky. There's a cigar room in the back. ⊠ *171 Water St.,* ☎ *709/726–9016. AE, DC, MC, V. Closed Sun.*

$$–$$$ ✕ **The Cellar.** This restaurant in a historic building on the waterfront
★ gets rave reviews for innovative Continental cuisine that uses the best local ingredients. Menu selections include blackened fish dishes and tiramisu for dessert. ⊠ *Baird's Cove, between Harbour and Water Sts.,* ☎ *709/579–8900. Reservations essential. AE, MC, V.*

$$–$$$ ✕ **Django's.** The menu at Django's is neither hip nor adventurous, but the dishes are well made and satisfying. The lunch menu includes pastas, salads, and sandwiches; dinner fare consists mostly of chicken, seafood, and steak dishes. ⊠ *184 Duckworth St.,* ☎ *709/738–4115. AE, DC, MC, V. Closed Sun. No lunch Sat.*

$$–$$$ ✕ **Hungry Fishermen.** Salmon, scallops, halibut, mussels, cod, and shrimp top the menu here. If you're not a fish eater, try the veal, chicken, or five-onion soup. This restaurant in a historic 19th-century building overlooking a courtyard has great sauces; desserts change daily and are homemade. ⊠ *Murray Premises, 5 Beck's Cove, off Water St.,* ☎ *709/726–5790. AE, DC, MC, V.*

$$–$$$ ✕ **Margaritz Restaurant.** The fish dishes, and particularly the blackened salmon, are good choices at this pleasant restaurant. Other seafood dishes include bouillabaisse; jambalaya with shrimp, mussels, and scallops; and an appetizer of smoked-salmon pâté. You can also order steak, chicken, lamb, and pork dishes. Margaritz has separate levels for smokers and nonsmokers. ⊠ *188 Duckworth St.,* ☎ *709/726–3885. AE, DC, MC, V. Closed Sun.*

$–$$$ ✕ **Chez Briann.** Pâtés, crepes, and other French standards are served on the second floor of a downtown Victorian town house. The dark stained wood trim is well-matched by subdued decor. Heavier dishes include scallops and garlic sautéed in olive oil and served over pasta, medallions of lamb stuffed with spinach and feta, and several steak dishes. ⊠ *290 Duckworth St.,* ☎ *709/579–0096. AE, DC, MC, V. No lunch weekends.*

$ ✕ **The Big R.** A fire and changes in ownership haven't dampened the popularity of this fish-and-chips place, which draws diners from all walks of life. Be warned: lots of schoolchildren eat here at lunchtime, and it can be noisy. ⊠ *69 Harvey Rd.,* ☎ *709/722–2256. V.*

$ ✕ **Ches's.** This fish-and-chips restaurant, which has been around since the 1950s, caters to a steady stream of customers from noon until well after midnight. They come from all walks of life—politicians, students, policemen—often with a nodding acquaintance of each other, and all devoted to the cult of "fee and chee." The owner keeps the batter recipe locked in a safe. It's strictly laminated tabletops, booths, and plastic chairs, but the fish is hot and fresh. ⊠ *9 Freshwater Rd.,* ☎ *709/722–4083. MC, V.*

$ ✕ **International Flavours.** Don't be fooled by the unvarnished walls and six small tables: the place may not look like much, but the curry with chick peas—the one and only item on the menu—is delicious. The only variety comes from your ordering the dish as hot or mild as you wish. You can also buy Indian spices to use in your own curries at home. ⊠ *124 Duckworth St.,* ☎ *709/738–4636. MC, V. Closed Sun.*

$ ✕ **Pasta Plus Café.** As the name implies, pasta is a popular item on the menu; the local chain also serves curries, salads, and pizza. Try one of the curry dishes, served with banana-date chutney and rice, or the pasta stuffed with seasonally available seafood. Some of the locations have somewhat dark lighting and decor. ⊠ *233 Duckworth St.,* ☎ *709/739–6676;* ⊠ *Avalon Mall, Thorburn Rd.,* ☎ *709/722–6006;* ⊠ *Village Shopping Centre, Topsail Rd.,* ☎ *709/368–3481;* ⊠ *Churchill Sq., Elizabeth Ave.,* ☎ *709/739–5818. AE, DC, MC, V.*

$ ✕ **Velma's Place.** Velma's is the place to go downtown for traditional Newfoundland fare such as fish and *brewis* (bread and fish soaked in water and boiled) and Jigg's dinner (boiled beef served with potatoes, carrots, cabbage, and turnips). The service here is friendly, and the maritime decor tastefully transcends the usual lobster-pot kitsch. ⊠ *264 Water St.,* ☎ *709/576–2264. AE, DC, MC, V.*

$$–$$$$ ✕⌷ **Delta St. John's.** Rooms in this convention hotel in downtown St. John's overlook the harbor and the city. Rooms are standard, and have temperature control, mini-bars, and coffeemakers. Deluxe and business-zone rooms have in-room fax machines and data ports. The restaurant, Portos ($$$–$$$$), serves a delightful but pricey caribou dish in addition to Continental cuisine. ☒ *120 New Gower St., A1C 6K4,* ☎ *709/739–6404 or 800/563–3838,* FAX *709/570–1622,* WEB *www.deltahotels.com. 276 rooms, 9 suites. 2 restaurants, bar, air-conditioning, business services, convention center, meeting rooms, car rental. AE, DC, MC, V.*

$$–$$$$ ✕🖫 **Fairmont Newfoundland.** St. John's residents gather at the restaurants of this comfortable modern hotel for special occasions. The hotel
★ is noted for charming rooms that overlook the harbor, an airy atrium restaurant with live piano music, Sunday and evening buffets, and the fine cuisine of the Cabot Club. ☒ *Cavendish Sq., Box 5637, A1C 5W8,* ☎ *709/758–8164,* FAX *709/576–0544,* WEB *www.fairmont.com. 301 rooms, 14 suites. 2 restaurants, bar, minibars, no-smoking floor, room service, indoor pool, hair salon, business services, meeting rooms, free parking. AE, DC, MC, V.*

$$–$$$ 🖫 **Holiday Inn.** The surprise at this chain hotel is the location: walking trails meander around small lakes and link into the Grand Concourse. C. A. Pippy Park is directly across the street. East Side Marios serves Italian food and burgers. ☒ *180 Portugal Cove Rd., A1B 2N2,* ☎ *709/722–0506,* FAX *709/722–9756,* WEB *www.holidayinnstjohns.com. 250 rooms. Restaurant, bar, in-room data ports, no-smoking rooms, pool, gym, business services, meeting rooms, free parking. AE, DC, MC, V.*

$–$$$ 🖫 **Compton House.** A charming historic residence in the west end of
★ the city, the Victorian inn is professionally run and beautifully decorated. Twelve-foot ceilings and wide halls give the place a majestic feeling, and rooms done in pastels and chintzes add an air of coziness. Suites have fireplaces and whirlpools. ☒ *26 Waterford Bridge Rd., A1E 1C6,* ☎ *709/739–5789,* FAX *709/738–1770,* WEB *www3.nf.sympatico.ca/comptonhouse. 5 rooms, 5 suites. In-room data ports, no-smoking room, free parking. AE, DC, MC, V.*

$–$$$ 🖫 **Waterford Manor.** The Queen Anne–style inn on the river in leafy Waterford Valley has won a heritage restoration award. Waterford Manor, or The Pink House, as it was originally known because of the color of the exterior, has deep moldings, an intricately carved wooden staircase, and the original colors of the house. The King Arthur Suite has a king-size bed, a fireplace, and a whirlpool tub for two. The inn is within a few minutes' drive of Bowring Park and the downtown area. A full breakfast is included in the room rate. ☒ *185 Waterford Bridge Rd., A1E 1C7,* ☎ *709/754–4139,* FAX *709/754–4155,* WEB *www.waterfordmanor.nf.ca. 4 rooms, 3 suites. Lounge, room service, free parking. AE, MC, V. BP.*

$–$$$ 🖫 **Winterholme Heritage Inn.** The National Historic Site in the center of old St. John's is a movie star: the gorgeous dark-wood-paneled interiors were prominently featured in the 1999 film *The Divine Ryans.* Some rooms in this Queen Anne–style inn have working fireplaces. ☒ *79 Rennies Mill Rd., A1C 3R1,* ☎ *709/739–7979 or 800/599–7829,* FAX *709/753–9411,* WEB *www.winterholme.nf.ca. 11 suites. Room service, free parking. AE, DC, MC, V. CP.*

$$ 🖫 **Quality Hotel Harbour Front.** Like other properties in the chain, this harbor-front hotel has clean, comfortable rooms at reasonable prices. The restaurant, Rumpelstiltskins, has a splendid view and an unpretentious menu. ☒ *Hill O'Chips, A1C 6B1,* ☎ *709/754–7788,* FAX *709/754–5209,* WEB *www.choicehotels.ca/cn246. 162 rooms. Restaurant, no-smoking rooms, meeting rooms. AE, DC, MC, V.*

$–$$ 🖫 **The Battery Hotel and Suites.** This hotel refers to itself as "the inn with the view" with good reason: situated halfway up Signal Hill, the Battery offers an unequaled view of the harbor and downtown St. John's. Everything else about the hotel is pretty ordinary. Not all rooms have

views, so make sure you request one up front. ⊠ *100 Signal Hill Rd.,
A1A 1B3,* ☎ *709/576–0040 or 800/563–8181,* FAX *709/576–6943,* WEB
*www.batteryhotel.com. 86 rooms, 40 suites. Restaurant, bar, indoor
pool, sauna, meeting rooms, travel services. MC, V.*

$–$$ 🏨 **Prescott Inn.** Local artwork decorates the walls of this house, one
★ of the city's most popular B&Bs. The inn has been modernized, tastefully blending the new and the old. It's central to shops and downtown
attractions. Room rates include a full breakfast. ⊠ *17–21 Military Rd.,
A1C 2C3,* ☎ *709/753–7733 or 888/263–3786,* FAX *709/753–6036,* WEB
*www.prescottinn.nf.ca. 8 rooms, 14 suites. Kitchenettes (some), no-
smoking rooms, travel services, car rental. AE, DC, MC, V. BP.*

$ 🏨 **Airport Plaza Hotel.** A half mile from the airport, this hotel offers
free shuttle service to the airport and downtown. Each of the four floors
has its own color scheme, and the small rooms, some of which have
balconies, are decorated with textured wall coverings in soft pastels.
Although refurbished in 1996, the hotel still lacks an elevator. ⊠ *106
Airport Rd., A1A 5B2,* ☎ *709/753–3500 or 800/563–2489,* FAX *709/
753–3711,* WEB *www.cityhotels.ca. 98 rooms, 2 suites. Restaurant, bar,
room service, coin laundry, business services, meeting rooms, airport
shuttle, free parking. AE, DC, MC, V. BP.*

$ 🏨 **A Gower Street House.** Now a B&B, the gracious former home of
the late photographer Elsie Holloway has been designated by the Newfoundland Historic Trust as a point of interest. It's an ideal setting for
paintings by prominent local artists. The location is within walking distance of the city's main attractions. A full breakfast is included in the
rate. ⊠ *180 Gower St., A1C 1P9,* ☎ FAX *709/754–0047,* ☎ *800/563–
3959,* WEB *www.bbcanada.com/826. 4 rooms. No-smoking room, room
service. AE, MC, V. BP.*

Nightlife and the Arts

Whether it's music, theater, the visual arts, literature, or film, St. John's
has tremendous stylistic variety and vitality for such a small population. Theater settings include traditional spaces, courtyards, and the
dramatic coastline. The best-known music is Celtic-inspired traditional and traditional rock.

The Arts

The Arts and Culture Centre (⊠ Allandale Rd., ☎ 709/729–3650)
houses a 1,000-seat main theater, a library, and an art gallery that displays contemporary Canadian art. The theater hosts musical and the-
atrical events from September through June; the library and gallery are
open year-round.

The **Newfoundland and Labrador Folk Festival** (☎ 709/576–8508, WEB
www.moonmusic.nfld.com/sjfac), held in St. John's in early August, is
the province's best-known traditional music festival.

The **Resource Centre for the Arts** (⊠ LSPU Hall, 3 Victoria St., ☎ 709/
753–4531) is an innovative theater with professional main-stage and
experimental second-space productions year-round.

The **Ship Inn** (⊠ Solomon's La., between Duckworth and Water Sts.,
☎ 709/753–3870) serves as the local arts watering hole. Nighttime performances range from traditional music to flamenco dancing.

Nightlife

St. John's well-deserved reputation as a party town has been several
hundred years in the making. **Erin's Pub** (⊠ 186 Water St., ☎ 709/722–
1916) is famous for Irish music. The **Fat Cat** (⊠ 5 George St., ☎ 709/
722–6561) is the city's blues headquarters. **George Street** downtown

has dozens of pubs and restaurants; seasonal open-air concerts are held here as well.

Outdoor Activities and Sports

Golf

Neither high winds nor unforgiving temperatures can keep golfers off the links in St. John's. If you want to play, call several days in advance to book a tee time. The par-71, 18-hole Admiral's Green and the par-35, 9-hole Captain's Hill are two adjacent public courses in **C.A. Pippy Park** (⊠ 290–292 Nagle's Hill, ☎ 709/753–7110) that overlook St. John's. **Clovelley** (⊠ off Stavanger Dr., ☎ 709/722–7170) is a par-72, 18-hole course in the east end of St. John's. **The Woods** (⊠ off Rte. 2 in the city's west end, ☎ 709/229–5444) has wide, forgiving fairways on its 18-hole, par-70 layout. It caters to players of moderate skill.

Scuba Diving

The ocean around Newfoundland and Labrador rivals the Caribbean in clarity, if not temperature. There are thousands of known shipwreck sites and a wealth of sea life, plus, for the truly daring, the possibility of seeing the bottom of an iceberg. **RockWater Adventures** (⊠ 50 Pippy Pl., ☎ 709/738–6353 or 888/512–2227, WEB www.rockwater.nf.ca) organizes classes and excursions. One popular dive takes you to see wrecks of ships sunk by German U-boats during World War II off Bell Island in Conception Bay. Boats leave from the Foxtrap Marina in Conception Bay South.

Sea Kayaking

One of the best ways to explore the coastline is by sea kayaking, which lets you visit sea caves and otherwise inaccessible beaches. There's also a very good chance you'll see whales, icebergs, and seabirds. **Whitecap Adventures** (⊠ 116 Park Ave., Mount Pearl, ☎ 709/726–9283, WEB www.whitecapadventures.com) conducts half- and full-day sea-kayaking trips.

Walking

With a well-developed marked trail system that crisscrosses the city, St. John's is a walker's dream. The **Grand Concourse** (☎ 709/737–1077) covers more than 100 km (62 mi). Some trails traverse river valleys, parks, and other open areas, while others are sidewalk routes. Well-maintained trails encircle several lakes, including Long Pond and Quidi Vidi Lake, both of which are great for bird-watching. Maps are available at tourist information centers and many hotels.

Whale-Watching

The east coast of Newfoundland, including the area around St. John's, provides spectacular whale-watching opportunities with up to 22 species of dolphins and whales visible along the coast. Huge humpback whales weighing up to 30 tons come close to shore to feed in late spring and early summer. You may be able to spot icebergs and large flocks of nesting seabirds in addition to whales on many boat tours. **Adventure Tours** (☎ 709/726–5000 or 800/779–4253, WEB www.nfld.com/scademia) operates the tour boat *Scademia* from St. John's harbor. **Dee Jay Charters** (☎ 709/753–8687, WEB www.wordplay.com/deejay) takes passengers to Cape Spear on a 42-ft Cape Islander. **J & B Schooner Tours** (☎ 709/753–7245, WEB www.schoonertours.com) operates a 62-ft schooner with bar service. **Morissey's Boat Tours** (☎ 709/748–5222, WEB www.atyp.com/morisseys) conducts whale-watching excursions.

Shopping

Antiques
Murray's Antiques (✉ 414 Blackmarsh Rd., ☎ 709/579–7344) is renowned for silver, china, and fine mahogany and walnut furniture. **Polyanna Art and Antique Gallery** (✉ 214 Duckworth St., ☎ 709/726–0936) carries antiques as well as paintings and photographs.

Art Galleries
New shows by prominent and up-and-coming artists can sell out quickly. Painters such as Barbara Pratt Wangersky typify the popularity of the new generation. Native art, especially carvings from Labrador, is also a hot item. The **Art Gallery of Newfoundland and Labrador** (✉ Allandale Rd. and Prince Philip Dr., ☎ 709/737–8209), the province's largest public gallery, exhibits historical and contemporary Canadian arts and crafts with an emphasis on local artists and artisans. It's closed Monday. **Christina Parker Fine Art** (✉ 7 Plank Rd., ☎ 709/753–0580) represents local and national artists in all mediums, including painting, sculpture, drawing, and prints. **David Ariss Fine Art** (✉ 191 Water St., ☎ 709/579–4941) carries a wide variety of local painters, plus Inuit art from Labrador. **Eastern Edge Gallery** (Clift's-Baird's Cove at Harbour Dr., ☎ 709/739–1882) exhibits the works of emerging artists. **Holloway Heights Galleria** (14 Holloway St., off Duckworth St., ☎ 709/722–3777) is a small gallery that carries oils and watercolors depicting the St. John's area. **The Lane Gallery** (✉ Hotel Newfoundland, 1st floor, Cavendish Sq., ☎ 709/753–8946) features seascapes and other works by photographer Don Lane.

Books
The **Newfoundland Bookstore** (✉ 100 Water St., ☎ 709/722–5830) specializes in local publishers.

Handicrafts
Crafts stores display traditional patterns and techniques, modern interpretations of traditional favorites, and some bold experimentation. The **Cod Jigger** (✉ 245 Duckworth St., ☎ 709/726–7422) carries handmade woolen sweaters and mittens as well as Newfoundland's unique Grenfell parkas. The **Craft Council Shop** (✉ 59 Duckworth St., ☎ 709/753–2749) displays the work of local producers and showcases some innovative designs. The **Newfoundland Weavery** (✉ 177 Water St., ☎ 709/753–0496) sells rugs, prints, lamps, books, crafts, and other gift items. **NONIA** (Newfoundland Outport Nurses Industrial Association; ✉ 286 Water St., ☎ 709/753–8062) was founded in 1920 to give women in the outports a way to earn money to support nursing services in these remote communities. Homespun wool was used to create exquisite clothing. Today the shop continues to sell these fine homespun articles as well as lighter, more modern handmade items. The **Salt Box** (✉ 194 Duckworth St., ☎ 709/753–0622) carries local crafts and specializes in pottery. **Wild Things** (✉ 124 Water St., ☎ 709/722–3123) sells nature-theme crafts and jewelry.

Music
Fred's Records (✉ 198 Duckworth St., ☎ 709/753–9191) has the best selection of local recordings, as well as other music.

Avalon Peninsula

On the southern half of the peninsula, small Irish hamlets are separated by large tracts of wilderness. You can travel part of the peninsula's southern coast in one or two days, depending on how much time you have. Quaint towns line Route 10, and the natural sights are beautiful. La Manche and Chance Cove—both abandoned communi-

Avalon Peninsula

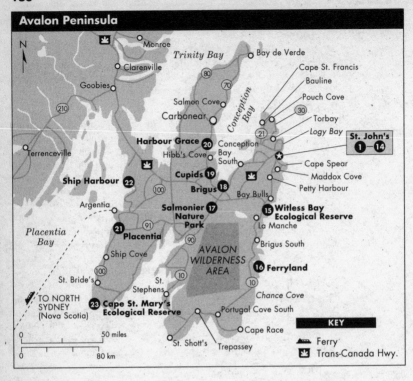

ties turned provincial parks—attest to the region's bounty of natural resources. At the intersection of Routes 90 and 91, in Salmonier, you can either head north toward Salmonier Nature Park and on to the towns on Conception Bay, or head west and then south to Route 100 to Cape St. Mary's Ecological Reserve. Each option takes about three hours. On the former route, stop in Harbour Grace; if you plan to travel on to Bay de Verde, at the northern tip of the peninsula, and down the other side of the peninsula on Route 80 along Trinity Bay, consider overnighting in the Harbour Grace–Carbonear area. Otherwise turn around and follow the same route back to Route 1.

Witless Bay Ecological Reserve

⑮ *29 km (18 mi) south of St. John's.*

Sometimes referred to as the Serengeti of the northwest Atlantic, the reserve is the summer home of millions of seabirds—puffins, murres, kittiwakes, razorbills, and guillemots—that nest on the reserve's four islands. The birds, and the humpback and minke whales that tarry here before continuing north to the summer grounds in the Arctic, feed on the billions of capelin that swarm inshore to spawn. The reserve is also an excellent place to see icebergs in late spring and early summer. The best views of birds and icebergs are from tour boats that operate here. ⊠ *Rte. 10,* ☎ *709/729–2424,* WEB *www.gov.nf.ca/parks&reserves.* ⊠ *Free.* ☉ *Daily 24 hrs.*

Outdoor Activities and Sports

Captain Murphy's Seabird and Whales Tours (☎ 709/334–2002 or 888/783–3467, WEB www.witlessbay.com) conducts interpretive wildlife tours. From mid-May to mid-October, **Gatherall's Puffin and Whale Watch** (☎ 709/334–2887 or 800/419–4253, WEB www.gatheralls.com) has six trips per day for viewing wildlife in the reserve. Shuttle service is available from St. John's hotels. **O'Brien's Bird Island Charters** (☎ 709/753–4850 or 877/639–4253, WEB www.netfx.ca/obriens) offers popular two-hour excursions featuring whale-, iceberg-, and seabird-watching.

En Route Although there are many pretty hamlets along the way from Witless Bay to Ferryland on Route 10, **La Manche,** accessible only on foot, and **Brigus South** have especially attractive settings and strong traditional flavors. La Manche is an abandoned fishing community between Tors Cove and Cape Broyle. The former residents moved to other towns after a storm destroyed part of the community in 1966. Brigus South, between Witless Bay and Cape Broyle, is a fishing village whose name is derived from an old French word for intrigue.

Ferryland

16 *43½ km (27 mi) south of Witless Bay Ecological Reserve.*

This seaside town has a long history, some of which is described in its small community museum. The major ongoing **Colony of Avalon archaeological dig** at Ferryland has uncovered the early 17th-century colony of Lord Baltimore, who abandoned the area after a decade for the warmer climes of Maryland. The site includes an archaeology laboratory and an exhibit center. Guided tours are available. ⊠ *Rte. 10, The Pool,* ☎ *709/432–3200 or 877/326–5669,* WEB *www.heritage.nf.ca/avalon.* ⊠ *$3.* ☉ *June–Oct., daily 9–7.*

Outdoor Activities and Sports

Diving excursions led by **Chance Cove Ventures** (☎ 709/363–2257, WEB www.divingtours.com) take you to explore the fascinating undersea world of shipwrecks along the southern coast of Avalon. There are more than 300 known wrecks here.

En Route In springtime, between Chance Cove and Portugal Cove South, in a stretch of land about 58 km (36 mi) long, hundreds of caribou and their calves gather on the barrens near Route 10. They migrate to this southern area from farther north in the Avalon Wilderness Area.

Salmonier Nature Park

17 *88 km (55 mi) from Ferryland, 14½ km (9 mi) north of the intersection of Rtes. 90 and 91.*

Many indigenous animal species, including moose, caribou, lynx, and otters, can be seen at this 3,000-acre wilderness reserve area. An enclosed 100-acre exhibit allows up-close viewing. ⊠ *Salmonier Line, Rte. 90,* ☎ *709/229–7189,* WEB *www.gov.nf.ca/snp.* ⊠ *Free.* ☉ *Early June–early Sept., daily noon–6; early Sept.–mid-Oct., daily 10–4.*

En Route From Salmonier Nature Park to Brigus, take Route 90, which passes through the scenic **Hawke Hills** before meeting up with the Trans-Canada Highway (Route 1). This reserve is the best representative of alpine barrens in Canada east of the Rockies. Turn off at Holyrood Junction (Route 62) and follow Route 70, which skirts Conception Bay.

Brigus

18 *19 km (12 mi) north of intersection of Rtes. 1 and 70.*

This beautiful village on Conception Bay has a wonderful public garden, winding lanes, and a teahouse. Brigus is best known as the birthplace of Captain Bob Bartlett, the famed Arctic explorer who accompanied Admiral Peary on polar expeditions during the first decade of the 20th century. **Hawthorne Cottage,** Captain Bartlett's home, is one of the few surviving examples of the picturesque cottage style, with a veranda decorated with ornamental wooden fretwork. It dates from 1830 and is a National Historic Site. ⊠ *Irishtown Rd.,* ☎ *709/753–9262; 709/528–4004 in summer.* 🖃 *$2.50.* ☉ *Mid-May–late June and early Sept.– late Oct., daily 10–6; late June–early Sept., daily 10–8; call for an appointment off-season.*

Ye Old Stone Barn Museum (the John L. Leamon Museum) displays historic town photos and artifacts, especially objects relating to its connection with the fishery. ⊠ *4 Magistrate's Hill,* ☎ *709/528–3391.* 🖃 *$1.* ☉ *Mid-June–early Sept., daily 11–6.*

Lodging

$ 🖭 **Captain Bob's Berth and Breakfast.** As the name suggests, this B&B, named for the town's most famous son, is decorated with nautical touches. Rooms have brightly colored patterned quilts, brass bedsteads, and lace-trimmed curtains. Guests can browse through books on Newfoundland in the library. A full breakfast is included in the room rate. ⊠ *6 Forge Rd., Box 2361, A1W 1C2,* ☎ *709/685–5438,* ℻ *709/834–6000. 3 rooms. AE, MC, V. Closed Oct.–May. BP.*

Cupids

⑲ *5 km (3 mi) north of Brigus.*

Cupids is the oldest English colony in Canada, founded in 1610 by John Guy, to whom the town erected a monument in 1910. Nearby flies a replica of the enormous Union Jack that flew during the tercentenary. When the wind snaps the flag, you can hear it half a mile away. In 1995 archaeologists began unearthing the long-lost site of the original colony here, and some of the recovered artifacts—including pots, pipes, and trade beads—are on display in the community museum, **Cupids Archaeological Site** (⊠ Main Rd., ☎ 709/596–1906). The site is open July through September, weekdays 8:30–4:30; admission is $2.

Lodging

$ 🖭 **Guy View Manor.** This nonsmoking ranch house is in an area near some good hiking and walking trails. A TV and telephone are available in the common room. ⊠ *First Colony Dr., A0A 2B0,* ☎ ℻ *709/528–4248,* ☎ *800/877–4248. 4 rooms. No-smoking rooms. V. CP.*

Harbour Grace

⑳ *21 km (13 mi) north of Cupids.*

Harbour Grace, once the headquarters of 17th-century pirate Peter Easton, was a major commercial town in the 18th and 19th centuries. Beginning in 1919, the town was the departure point for many attempts to fly the Atlantic. Amelia Earhart left Harbour Grace in 1932 to become the first woman to fly solo across the Atlantic. The town has two fine churches and several registered historic houses.

Lodging

$ 🖭 **Rothesay House Inn Bed & Breakfast.** This Queen Anne–style B&B was built in the early 20th century. The front of the house has a lovely porch, and the greens, yellows, and reds of the exterior are echoed in the room colors. Rooms have brass-trimmed wooden beds, wainscotting, and antiques. The hosts recommend and arrange sightseeing, whale-watching, and boat tours. A full breakfast is included in the room rate. ⊠ *34 Water St., A0A 2M0,* ☎ *709/596–2268,* ℻ *709/596–0317,* WEB *www.rothesay.com. 4 rooms. Dining room, no-smoking room, kennel. MC, V. BP.*

Route 100: The Cape Shore

This area is the site of an outstanding seabird colony at Cape St. Mary's. It's also culturally and historically rich. The French settlers had their capital here in Placentia. Irish influence is also strong here, in music and manner. You can reach the Cape Shore on the western side of the Avalon Peninsula from Route 1, at its intersection with Route 100. The ferry from Nova Scotia docks in Argentia, near Placentia.

Placentia

㉑ *48 km (30 mi) south of Route 1.*

Placentia was Newfoundland's French capital during the 1600s. The remains of an old fort built on a hill look out over Placentia and beyond to the placid waters and wooded, steep hillsides of the inlet.

Castle Hill National Historic Site, just north of town, is on what remains of the French fortifications. The visitor center has a "life at Plaisance" exhibit that shows the hardships endured by early English and French settlers. Performances of *Faces of Fort Royal,* a historical play about the French era, take place twice daily during July and August. ⊠ *Off Rte. 100,* ☎ *709/227–2401.* ⊡ *Historic site $2.50, play $2.* ☉ *Mid-June–early Sept., daily 8:30–8; early Sept.–mid-June, daily 8:30–4:30.*

Lodging

$ 🏠 **Fo'c's'le Bed and Breakfast.** Fo'c's'le is short for forecastle, the crew's sleeping quarters on a ship. And this pleasant B&B with nautical decor certainly has a touch of the old salt about it. But the real seaside action is out on the deck, where you can relax and watch seabirds. ⊠ *Rte. 91, A0B 2Y0,* ☎ ꜰᴀx *709/227–2282,* ᴡᴇʙ *www.bcity.com/focsle. 3 rooms. Dining room, no-smoking room. V. CP.*

$ 🏠 **Northeast Arm Motel.** The motel has a nice view of Northeast Arm and is situated on the main highway 10 minutes from the ferry to Nova Scotia in Argentia. Rooms are standard, without many frills. ⊠ *Main St., Dunville A0B 1S0,* ☎ *709/227–3560 or 877/227–3560,* ꜰᴀx *709/ 227–5430. 13 rooms. Bar, no-smoking rooms, coin laundry. AE, DC, MC, V.*

Ship Harbour

㉒ *34 km (21 mi) north of Placentia.*

An isolated, edge-of-the-world place, Ship Harbour has historic significance. In 1941, on a ship in these waters, Franklin Roosevelt and Winston Churchill signed the Atlantic Charter and formally announced the "Four Freedoms," which still shape the politics of the world's most successful democracies: freedom of speech, freedom of worship, freedom from want, and freedom from fear. Off Route 102, amid the splendor of Placentia Bay, an unpaved road leads to a monument to the Atlantic Charter.

Cape St. Mary's Ecological Reserve

★ **㉓** *65 km (40 mi) south of Placentia.*

Cape St. Mary's Ecological Reserve is the southernmost nesting site in the world for gannets and common and thick-billed murres. A paved road takes you within a mile of the seabird colony. You can visit the interpretation center—guides are on site in summer—and then walk to within 100 ft of the colony of nesting gannets, murres, black-billed kittiwakes, and razorbills. Most birds are March through August visitors. The reserve has some of the most dramatic coastal scenery in Newfoundland. This is also a good place to spot whales. From May through September the interpretation center hosts performances of traditional music by local artists as well as an eclectic mix of musicians from elsewhere in the province; call for information and times. ⊠ *Off Rte. 100,* ☎ *709/337–2473 or 709/729–2429,* WEB *www.gov.nf.ca/parks&reserves.* ☒ *$3 for center; site is free.* ⊘ *Center early May–late Oct., daily 9–7; site daily 24 hrs year-round.*

Lodging

$ ⌺ **Bird Island Resort.** This pleasant lodging a half hour's drive from Cape St. Mary's overlooks meadows and Placentia Bay. Rooms are standard and cottages have fully equipped kitchens. ⊠ *Off Rte. 100, St. Bride's A0B 2Z0,* ☎ *709/337–2450 or 888/337–2450,* FAX *709/334–2903. 5 rooms, 15 cottages. Gym, coin laundry. AE, MC, V.*

$ ⌺ **Capeway Motel.** The main attraction of this basic motel is its proximity to the seabird sanctuary at Cape St. Mary's. The units have cable TV and small kitchens. ⊠ *Rte. 100, General Delivery, St. Bride's A0B 2Z0,* ☎ *709/337–2163,* FAX *709/337–2028. 7 rooms. Coin laundry. MC, V.*

Clarenville and the Bonavista Peninsula

Clarenville, about two hours northwest of St. John's via the Trans-Canada Highway (Route 1), is the departure point for two different excursions: the Discovery Trail, on the Bonavista Peninsula, and Terra Nova National Park, which borders the shore of Bonavista Bay.

Clarenville

❷❹ *189 km (117 mi) northwest of St. John's.*

★ If history and quaint towns appeal to you, consider following the **Discovery Trail,** which begins in Clarenville on Route 230A. The trail includes two gems: the old town of Trinity, famed for its quaint architecture and theater festival, and Bonavista, one of John Cabot's reputed landing spots.

Lodging

$–$$$ ⌺ **St. Jude Hotel.** Rooms are spacious and comfortable, if somewhat spartan, at this modern hotel with a Mexican restaurant. Rooms fronting the highway have a good view of the bay, but those in the back are quieter. Even on a hot day, the air-conditioning can be a little too cool here. ⊠ *Rte. 1, Box 2500, A0E 1J0,* ☎ *709/466–1717 or 800/563–7800,* FAX *709/466–1714,* WEB *www.stjudehotel.nf.ca. 64 rooms. Restaurant, bar, no-smoking rooms. AE, MC, V.*

$–$$ ⌺ **Restland Motor Inn.** The bland name doesn't do justice to the lovely garden and excellent restaurant serving everything from burgers to curry dishes. The rooms in this modern property are small but comfortable. The decor is mostly bright and floral. ⊠ *Memorial Dr., A0E 1J0,* ☎ *709/466–7636 or 800/205–3993,* FAX *709/466–2743. 23 rooms. Restaurant, no-smoking rooms. AE, DC, MC, V.*

$ ⌺ **Clarenville Inn.** Formerly a Holiday Inn, the hotel in its new incarnation is still a no-surprises establishment. It's popular with families because children eat free and there's a heated swimming pool. ⊠ *Rte. 1, Box 967, A0E 1J0,* ☎ *709/466–7911,* FAX *709/466–3854. 64 rooms. Restaurant, bar, pool. AE, DC, MC, V.*

Terra Nova National Park

㉕ *24 km (15 mi) northwest of Clarenville.*

Rugged terrain, golf, sea kayaking, fishing, and camping are draws at this park on the exposed coastline of Bonavista Bay. The Terra Nova Park Lodge (87 rooms, 6 efficiencies) at Port Blandford has one of the most beautiful golf courses in Canada, and the only one where two salmon rivers cut through the 18 holes. Call ☎ 709/543–2626 for a reservation. The park also has the Marine Interpretation Center, nature walks, whale-watching and sea-kayaking tours, and a small but decent cafeteria. Eight backcountry campsites can be accessed by trails. ✉ *Trans-Canada Hwy., Glovertown A2A 1X5,* ☎ *709/533–2801, 709/533–3186 or 800/213–7275,* WEB *www.parkscanada.pch.gc.ca/parks/newfoundland.* 🎫 *Mid-May–mid-Oct., $3.25; mid-Oct.–mid-May, free.* ☉ *Site daily 24 hrs. Center June–Aug., daily 10–9; Sept.–May, weekdays 8–4:30.*

Camping

Malady Head Campground (✉ Rte. 310, ☎ 709/533–2801) has 99 sites and is open from July through September. The **Newman Sound Campground** (✉ Rte. 1, ☎ 709/533–2801), with 387 campsites, is organized in clusters around playgrounds and has a store where you can rent bicycles. Winter camping is available here.

Trinity

★ **㉖** *71 km (44 mi) northeast of Clarenville.*

Trinity is one of the jewels of Newfoundland. The village's picturesque views, winding lanes, and snug houses are the main attraction. Several homes have been turned into museums and inns. In the 1700s, Trinity competed with St. John's as a center of culture and wealth. Its more contemporary claim to fame, however, is that its intricate harbor was a favorite anchorage for the British navy. Here, too, the smallpox vaccine was introduced to North America by a local rector. On West Street an information center with costumed interpreters is open daily mid-June through October. To get here, take Route 230 to Route 239.

The **Garland Mansion** is a re-creation of a fish merchant's house that was one of the most prominent 18th-century homes in Newfoundland. Next door is a 19th-century store. ✉ *West St.,* ☎ *709/464–3706,* WEB *www3.nf.sympatico.ca/ttci.* 🎫 *$2.50.* ☉ *Mid-June–mid-Sept., daily 10–6.*

From July through Labor Day, the **Rising Tide Theatre** (☎ 709/738–3256 or 888/464–3377) conducts New-Founde-Land Trinity Pageant walking tours (Wednesday and weekends at 2) of the town that are more theater than tour. Actors in period costume lead the way.

Dining and Lodging

$–$$ ✕ **Dock Marina.** The food at this restaurant right on the wharf is standard Canadian: pasta, salads, burgers, chicken, and local seafood. Service is prompt and friendly. ✉ *Trinity Waterfront,* ☎ *709/464–2133. AE, DC, MC, V. Closed Nov.–Apr.*

$–$$$ 🏠 **Campbell House Bed & Breakfast.** Guest rooms in this mid-19th-century house are decorated with antiques; some have fireplaces. A full breakfast is included in the rate. ✉ *High St., A0C 2S0,* ☎ *877/464–7700,* ☎ FAX *709/464–3377,* WEB *www.campbellhouse.nf.ca. 6 rooms. Dining room, no-smoking room, laundry service. AE, DC, MC, V. Closed Nov.–Apr. BP.*

$–$$ ⊡ **Bishop White Manor and Eriksen Premises.** These two adjacent B&Bs with a common operator have antiques, fireplaces in some of the rooms, handcrafted furniture, and private baths. A tearoom at Eriksen Premises serves inexpensive home-style cooking. Room rates include a full breakfast. ⊠ *Bishop White Manor, Gallavan's La.; Eriksen Premises, West St. (mailing address for both: Box 58, A0C 2S0),* ☎ *709/464–3698, 709/464–3299, or 877/464–3698,* ℻ *709/464–2104,* WEB *www.trinityexperience.nf.ca. Bishop White 9 rooms, Eriksen 6 rooms. Dining room. MC, V. Closed Nov.–Apr. BP.*

$–$$ ⊡ **Fishers' Loft Inn.** The Fishers' Loft, just a few minutes from the bustle of Trinity, overlooks a harbor where whales sometimes swim among small fishing boats and icebergs drift by farther out in the bay. Rooms here are bright and airy, with down duvets, handcrafted furniture, and original artwork. Four rooms have cathedral ceilings. The owners pack you a lunch and give you a map and guidance for hiking in the area. ⊠ *Mill Rd., Port Rexton A0C 2H0,* ☎ *877/464–3240,* ☎ ℻ *709/464–3240,* WEB *www.fishersloft.com. 8 rooms, 4 suites. Dining room, in-room data ports, no-smoking rooms. AE, DC, MC, V. Closed Nov.–Apr.*

$ ⊡ **The Hangashore B & B.** This restored 19th-century house is the summer home of renowned Newfoundland fiddler Kelly Russell and his folklorist spouse, Tonya Kearly, who calls a mean dance at the couple's regular Wednesday traditional dance sessions. Browse the collection of rare Newfoundland books. The walls feature a changing collection of contemporary local art. Breakfast is included in the room rate. ⊠ *1 Ash's Lane (mailing address: 51 Monkstown Rd., St. John's A1C 3T4),* ☎ *709/464–3807 or 888/754–7377. 3 rooms. AE, MC, V.*

$ ⊡ **Peace Cove Inn.** This restored inn, once a schooner captain's residence, is one of the few remaining modified Second Empire houses with the front and back mansard roofs and bonneted windows in Newfoundland. Rooms are large and have antiques and private baths. ⊠ *Trinity E. Rd. (Box 123, Port Rexton A0C 2H0),* ☎ *709/464–3738,* ℻ *709/464–2167,* WEB *www.atlanticadventures.com. 6 rooms. Dining room, no-smoking rooms. MC, V. Closed Nov.–Apr.*

$ ⊡ **Sherwood Suites.** This accommodation has both housekeeping units and motel suites. The housekeeping units have a fully equipped kitchen, a private patio, two bedrooms, a living room, and cable TV. The motel suites have private entrances and cable TV. ⊠ *Rocky Hill Rd., Port Rexton A0C 2H0,* ☎ ℻ *709/464–2130,* WEB *www.sherwoodsuites.nfld. net. 10 housekeeping units, 4 motel suites. No-smoking rooms, playground, coin laundry. V. Closed Oct.–May.*

Nightlife and the Arts

The **Rising Tide Theatre** stages the Summer in the Bight festival. Outdoor Shakespeare productions, dinner theater, and dramas and comedies fill the bill. The troupe's theater, styled like an old mercantile warehouse, is on the waterfront. Fees vary, so call for details.

Outdoor Activities and Sports

Atlantic Sailing Charters and Tours (☎ 709/464–2133 or 709/781–2255) operates a 46-ft motorized sailboat for whale-watching or just cruising Trinity Bight.

Shopping

Trinity Crafts (⊠ Church Rd., ☎ 709/464–3823) specializes in locally made quilts, woolens, and knitted goods.

Trinity Folk Art (⊠ Water St., ☎ 709/464–3760) sells a wide array of crafts from all over the province, including Innu tea dolls from Labrador.

Bonavista

㉗ *28 km (17 mi) north of Trinity.*

No one knows exactly where explorer John Cabot landed when he came to Atlantic Canada in 1497, but many believe it to have been at Bonavista. The **Ryan Premises National Historic Site** on the waterfront depicts the almost 500-year history of the commercial cod fishery in a restored fish merchant's property. ⊠ *Off Rte. 230,* ☎ *709/468–1600 or 800/213–7275,* WEB *www.parkscanada.pch.gc.ca/parks/newfoundland.* 🖭 *$2.50.* ☼ *June 1–Oct. 1, daily 10–6.*

The **Cape Bonavista Lighthouse,** on the point about 1 km (½ mi) outside town, has been restored to its condition in 1870. ☎ *709/468–7444,* WEB *www.nfmuseum.com.* 🖭 *$2.50 (includes Mockbeggar Plantation).* ☼ *Mid-June–early Oct., daily 10–5:30.*

The **Mockbeggar Plantation** teaches about the life of an outport merchant in the years immediately before Confederation. ⊠ *Off Rte. 230,* ☎ *709/729–0592 or 709/468–7300.* 🖭 *$2.50 (includes Cape Bonavista Lighthouse).* ☼ *Mid-June–early Oct., daily 10–5:30.*

Burin Peninsula, Gander, and Notre Dame Bay

The Burin Peninsula's history is tied to the rich fishing grounds of the Grand Bank, which established this area as a center for European fishery as early as the 1500s. By the early 1900s, one of the world's largest fishing fleets was based on the Burin Peninsula. Today its inhabitants hope for a recovery of the fish stocks that have sustained their economy for centuries. Marystown is the peninsula's commercial center.

Gander, in east-central Newfoundland, is known for its airport and its aviation history. North of it is Notre Dame Bay, an area of rugged coastline and equally rugged islands that were once the domain of the now extinct Beothuk tribe. Only the larger islands are inhabited. Before English settlers moved into the area in the late 18th and early 19th centuries, it was seasonally occupied by French fisherfolk. Local dialects preserve centuries-old words that have vanished elsewhere. The bay is swept by the cool Labrador Current that carries icebergs south through Iceberg Alley; the coast is also a good whale-watching area.

The journey down to the Burin Peninsula is a three- to four-hour drive from the intersection of Routes 230 and 1 through the craggy coastal landscapes along Route 210.

Marystown

㉘ *283 km (175 mi) south of Bonavista.*

Marystown is built around beautiful Mortier Bay, so big it was considered large enough for the entire British fleet during the early days of World War II. Shipbuilding is the main industry. Of note is the 20-ft statue of the Virgin Mary that looks out over the bay.

Lodging

$ 🏨 **Hotel Marystown.** Substantial renovations have upgraded this property, the largest hotel on the Burin Peninsula. Rooms are standard but comfortable with pastel shades, double beds, and cable TV. ⊠ *Ville Marie Dr., A0E 2M0,* ☎ *709/279–1600 or 800/563–2489,* FAX *709/279–4088,* WEB *www.cityhotels.ca. 131 rooms. Restaurant, bar, kitchenettes (some), room service, business services, meeting rooms. AE, DC, MC, V.*

Burin

29 *17 km (11 mi) south of Marystown.*

Burin, a community built amid intricate cliffs and coves, was an ideal setting for pirates and privateers, who used to lure ships into the rocky, dead-end areas in order to plunder them. When Captain James Cook was stationed here to chart the coast in the 1760s, one of his duties was to watch for smugglers bringing in rum from the island of St-Pierre. Smuggling continues to this day. Cook's Lookout, a hill overlooking Burin, is where Cook kept watch. Trail directions for the hill are available at **Island Treasure Woodcrafts** (☎ 709/891–2516) on Main Street.

Heritage Museum, considered one of the best community museums in Newfoundland, gives you a sense of what life was like in the past in this fishing community. It has a display on the 1929 tidal wave that struck Burin and the surrounding coastal communities, and a gallery for traveling exhibits. ⊠ *Seaview Dr. off Rte. 221,* ☎ *709/891–2217,* WEB *www.schooner.nf.ca.* ☉ *Mid-May–July and early Sept.–early Oct., daily 10–6; early July–early Sept., daily 10–8.*

Lodging

$ 🛏 **Sound of the Sea Bed and Breakfast.** The sound of waves crashing on the shore drifts into this B&B to create an utterly relaxing experience. Each room in this former merchant's home matches color schemes to wooden furniture: the lighter colors go with the birch furniture, the medium colors with pine, and the darker colors with the antique walnut furniture. The owners can help arrange boat tours. ⊠ *11A Seaview Dr., A0E 1E0,* ☎ *709/891–2115,* FAX *709/891–2377. 3 rooms. No-smoking room, coin laundry. MC, V. BP.*

Grand Bank

30 *62 km (38 mi) from Burin.*

One of the loveliest communities in Newfoundland, Grand Bank has a fascinating history as an important fishing center. Because of trading patterns, the architecture here was influenced more by Halifax; Boston; and Bar Harbor, Maine, than by the rest of Newfoundland. A sail-shape building holds the **Southern Newfoundland Seamen's Museum,** which provides insight into the town's past. ⊠ *54 Marine Dr.,* ☎ *709/832–1484.* 🖼 *$2.50.* ☉ *May–mid-June and early Sept.–Oct., daily 9–4:45; mid-June–early Sept., daily 9:30–4:45.*

Lodging

$ 🛏 **Granny's Motor Inn.** The rooms here may be small, but they are comfortable, and the location is convenient, with easy access to the ferry to St-Pierre. It's also close to the town's soccer field—a five-minute walk after dinner lets you catch the most popular sport on the Burin Peninsula. ⊠ *Grandview Blvd., A0E 1W0,* ☎ *709/832–2355 or 888/275–1098,* FAX *709/832–0009. 10 rooms. Restaurant, bar, room service, coin laundry. AE, DC, MC, V.*

$ 🛏 **Thorndyke Bed and Breakfast.** This 1917 Queen Anne–style mansion, a former sea captain's house, is a designated historic structure. The blown-glass objects, colored panels, and sun porch have been part of the house since it was first built. The ferry to St-Pierre is a five-minute drive away. A full breakfast is included in the price. ⊠ *33 Water St., A0E 1W0,* ☎ *709/832–0820. 4 rooms. No-smoking rooms. V. Closed Oct.–Apr. BP.*

St-Pierre and Miquelon

31 *70-min ferry ride from Fortune.*

The islands of St-Pierre and Miquelon, France's only territory in North America, are a ferry ride away. If you crave French cuisine or a bottle of perfume, this is the place. Shopping and eating are both popular pastimes here. The bakeries open early, so there's always piping hot fresh bread for breakfast. Bargain hunters can find reasonably priced wines from all over France, so a good pocket guide is most helpful. An interesting side trip via boat takes you to see seals, seabirds, and other wildlife, plus the huge sandbar (formed on the bones of shipwrecks) that now connects formerly separate Great and Little Miquelon. Visitors to the islands should carry proof of citizenship; people from outside the United States and Canada have to show valid visas and passports. Because of the ferry schedule, a trip to St-Pierre means an overnight stay in a modern hotel such as **Hotel Robert** (☎ 508/412419) or a pension, the French equivalent of a B&B. Call the **St-Pierre tourist board** (☎ 800/565–5118) for information about accommodations.

A passenger ferry operated by **Lloyd G. Lake Ltd./St-Pierre Tours** (☎ 709/832–2006, 709/722–4103, or 800/563–2006) leaves Fortune (south of Grand Bank) daily at 2:15 PM from mid-June to late September; the crossing takes 70 minutes. The ferry leaves St-Pierre at 1 PM daily; round-trip is $55.

Gander

32 *367 km (228 mi) north of Grand Bank.*

Gander, a busy town of 12,000 people, is notable for its aviation history. It also has many lodgings and makes a good base for travel in this part of the province. During World War II, **Gander International Airport** (✉ James Blvd.) was chosen by the Canadian and U.S. air forces as a major strategic air base because of its favorable weather and secure location. After the war, the airport became an international hub for civilian travel; today it's a major air-traffic control center. The **Aviation Exhibition** in the airport's domestic passengers' lounge (☎ 709/256–3905) traces Newfoundland's role in the history of air travel. It's open daily 8 AM–midnight.

The **North Atlantic Aviation Museum** gives an expansive view of Gander's and Newfoundland's roles in aviation. In addition to viewing the expected models and photographs, you can climb into the cockpit of a real DC-3 parked outside next to a World War II Hudson bomber and a Canadian jet fighter. ✉ *On Rte. 1, between hospital and visitor information center,* ☎ *709/256–2923.* ⊡ *$3.* ☉ *June–Sept., daily 9–9; Oct.–May, weekdays 9–5.*

Gander River Tours (☎ 709/679–2271) organizes salmon-fishing trips, canoeing excursions, and guided tours of the river and wilderness areas around Gander from April to November.

Lodging

$–$$ 🏨 **Hotel Gander.** The largest hotel in Gander has comfortable rooms and a decent dining room that serves standard Canadian fare. Children under 12 can stay and eat for free here. The staff can arrange a round of golf or a tour of the area. ✉ *100 Trans-Canada Hwy., A1V 1P5,* ☎ *709/256–3931 or 800/563–2988,* FAX *709/651–2641,* WEB *www.hotelgander.com.* 154 rooms. *Bar, dining room, no-smoking rooms, room service, indoor pool, coin laundry. AE, DC, MC, V.*

$–$$ 🏨 **Sinbad's Hotel and Suites.** Near nightclubs and restaurants, Sinbad's is popular with young couples. The hotel also has a lively bar of its own. Rooms are spacious and have standard amenities such as hair dryers, irons, and cable TV. ✉ *Bennett Dr., A1V 1W6,* ☎ *709/651–2678 or 800/563–8330,* FAX *709/651–3123,* WEB *www.sinbadshotel.nf.ca. 103 rooms, 9 suites. Bar, dining room, kitchenettes (some), no-smoking rooms. AE, DC, MC, V.*

Boyd's Cove

③③ *66 km (41 mi) north of Gander.*

Between 1650 and 1720, the Beothuks' main summer camp on the northeast coast was at the site of what is now Boyd's Cove. The coastline in and near Boyd's Cove is somewhat sheltered by Twillingate Island and New World Island. Short causeways link the shore to the islands.

The **Boyd's Cove Beothuk Interpretation Centre** offers a fresh look at the lives of the Beothuks, an extinct First Nations people who succumbed in the early 19th century to a combination of disease and battle with European settlers. The center uses traditional Beothuk building forms and adjoins an archaeological site that was inhabited from about 1650 to 1720, when pressure from settlers drove the Beothuk from this part of the coast. ✉ *Rte. 340,* ☎ *709/656–3114 or 709/729–0592,* WEB *www.nfmuseum.com.* ⊠ *$2.50.* ⊙ *Mid-June–early Oct., daily 10–5:30.*

Twillingate

③④ *31 km (19 mi) north of Boyd's Cove.*

The inhabitants of this scenic old fishing village make their living from the sea and have been doing so for nearly two centuries. Colorful houses, rocky waterfront cliffs, a local museum, and a nearby lighthouse add to the town's appeal. Every year on the last weekend in July, the town hosts the **Fish, Fun and Folk Festival** (☎ 709/884–2678, WEB www.fishfunfolkfestival.com), where fish are cooked every possible way.

One of the best places on the island to see icebergs, Twillingate is known to the locals as Iceberg Alley. These majestic and dangerous mountains of ice are awe-inspiring to see while they're grounded in early summer. **Twillingate Island Boat Tours** (☎ 709/884–2242 or 800/611–2374) specializes in iceberg photography in the local waters. An iceberg interpretation center is right on the dock.

Lodging

$　🏠 **Evening Sun Inn Bed and Breakfast.** You can relax on the deck and watch the sun set over the bay at this B&B. The inn has one standard room and a suite with a private entrance, a living room, and a kitchenette. Arctic terns nest nearby, and a short walk along a trail brings you to an excellent spot for watching whales and icebergs. ✉ *319 Bayview St., A0G 4M0,* ☎ *709/884–2103,* FAX *709/884–2176. 2 rooms. No-smoking room, laundry service. V. BP.*

$　🏠 **Toulinguest Inn Bed and Breakfast.** In this traditional home on the waterfront, rooms are old-fashioned but comfortable. You can wind down in the living room. ✉ *56 Main St., A0G 4M0,* ☎ *709/884–2080 or 709/256–8406,* FAX *709/256–8410. 3 rooms. Closed Oct.–Apr. No-smoking rooms, coin laundry. V. BP.*

Grand Falls–Windsor

③⑤ *95 km (59 mi) west of Gander.*

This central Newfoundland town is an amalgamation of the paper-making town of Grand Falls, the quintessential company town founded by British newspaper barons earlier this century, and Windsor, once an important stop on the railway. The paper mill still ships newsprint all over the world, but the railway is no more.

The **Loggers' Exhibit** (✉ Rte. 1, ☎ 709/292–4522), a re-creation of a logging camp 2 km (1 mi) west of town, tells of the hard lives of those who supplied wood for the paper mill.

Lodging

$–$$ 🏨 **Mount Peyton Hotel.** This lodging establishment has hotel and motel rooms, housekeeping units with kitchenettes, and a good steak house. The rooms are comfortable, if unremarkable, and have coffeemakers, hair dryers, and irons and ironing boards. ✉ *214 Lincoln Rd., A2A 1P8,* ☎ *709/489–2251 or 800/563–4894,* FAX *709/489–6365,* WEB *www.mountpeyton.com. 130 rooms, 32 housekeeping units, 4 suites. 2 restaurants, bar, kitchenettes (some), no-smoking rooms, meeting rooms. AE, DC, MC, V. Motel rooms closed Sept.–Mar.*

OFF THE
BEATEN PATH

CHANGE ISLANDS AND FOGO ISLAND – These islands give the impression of a place frozen in time. Modernity came late to these outposts of the past, where old expressions and accents still survive. You can take a ferry (☎ 709/486–0733) from Farewell to either the Change Islands or Fogo Island. To get to Farewell, take Route 340 to Route 335, which takes you through scenic coastal communities.

If you choose to stay overnight, **Hart's Bed and Breakfast** (☎ 709/621–3133) is on the Change Islands and **Alma's Bed and Breakfast** (☎ 709/627–3302) is in Stag Harbour on Fogo Island.

The Great Northern Peninsula

The Great Northern Peninsula is the northernmost visible extension of the Appalachian Mountains. Its eastern side is rugged and sparsely populated. The Viking Trail—Route 430 and its side roads—snakes along its western coast through a national park, fjords, sand dunes, and communities that have relied on lobster fishing for generations. At the tip of the peninsula, the Vikings established the first European settlement in North America a thousand years ago. For thousands of years before their arrival, the area was home to native peoples who hunted, fished, and gathered berries and herbs.

Deer Lake

③⑥ *208 km (129 mi) west of Grand Falls–Windsor.*

Deer Lake was once just another small town on the Trans-Canada Highway, but the opening of Gros Morne National Park in the early '70s and the construction of a first-class paved highway passing right through to St. Anthony changed all that. Today, with an airport and car rentals available, Deer Lake is a good starting point for a fly–drive vacation.

☺ The **Newfoundland Insectarium** holds an intriguing collection of live and preserved insects, spiders, scorpions, and the like. It's in a suburb of Deer Lake, off Route 430. ✉ *Rte. 430, Reidville,* ☎ *709/635–4545,* WEB *www.newfoundlandinsectarium.nf.ca.* ✉ *$6.* ☉ *Mid-June–mid-Sept., daily 9–9; mid-Sept.–mid-June, Tues.–Fri. 9–5, weekends 10–5.*

Lodging

$ 🏨 **Deer Lake Motel.** The guest rooms here are clean and comfortable, and the food in the café is basic, home-cooked fare. Seafood dishes are exceptionally well prepared. ✉ *Rte. 1, Box 820, A0K 2E0,* ☎ *709/635–2108 or 800/563–2144,* FAX *709/635–3842,* WEB *www.deerlake-*

motel.com. 54 rooms, 2 suites. Restaurant, bar, café, no-smoking rooms, meeting rooms. AE, MC, V.

Gros Morne National Park

★ ③⑦ *46 km (29 mi) north of Deer Lake on Rte. 430.*

Because of its geological uniqueness and immense splendor, this park has been named a UNESCO World Heritage Site. Among the more breathtaking visions are the expanses of wild orchids in springtime. Camping and hiking are popular recreations, and boat tours are available. To see Gros Morne properly you should allow yourself at least two days. An excellent **interpretation center** (☎ 709/458–2417) in Rocky Harbour has displays and videos about the park. Scenic **Bonne Bay,** a deep, mountainous fjord, divides the park in two. You can drive around the perimeter of the fjord on Route 430 going north.

③⑧ **Woody Point,** a charming community of old houses and imported Lombardy poplars, is in the south of the park, on Route 431. The **Tablelands,** rising behind Norris Point, are a unique rock massif that was raised from the earth's mantle through tectonic upheaval. Its rocks are toxic to most plant life, and Ice Age conditions linger in the form of persistent snow and moving rock glaciers. A **Discovery Centre** (⊠ Rte. 431, on the outskirts of Woody Point heading west toward Trout River, ☎ 709/458–2417) offers educational programs on the park's geology and natural history.

③⑨ The small community of **Trout River** is at the western end of Route 431 on the Gulf of St. Lawrence. You pass the scenic **Trout River Pond** along the way. The **Green Gardens Trail,** a spectacular short or long hike, is also nearby, but be prepared to do a bit of climbing on your return journey. The trail passes through the Tablelands barrens and descends sharply to a coastline of eroded cliffs and green meadows.

Head to the northern side of the park, along coastal Route 430, to visit ④⓪ **Rocky Harbour** with its range of restaurants, lodgings, and a luxurious indoor public pool and large hot tub—the perfect place to soothe tired limbs after a strenuous day.

The most popular attraction in the northern portion of Gros Morne is the boat tour of **Western Brook Pond.** You park at a lot on Route 430 and take a 45-minute walk to the boat dock through an interesting mix of bog and woods. Cliffs rise 2,000 ft on both sides of the gorge, and high waterfalls tumble over ancient rocks. Hikers in good shape can tackle the 16-km (10-mi) hike up **Gros Morne Mountain,** at 2,644 ft the second-highest peak in Newfoundland. Weather permitting, the reward for your effort is a unique arctic landscape and spectacular views. The park's **northern coast** has an unusual mix of sand beaches, rock pools, and trails through tangled dwarf forests known locally as tuckamore. Sunsets seen from **Lobster Cove Head Lighthouse** are spectacular. Keep an eye out for whales, and visit the lighthouse museum, devoted to the history of the area. ⊠ *Gros Morne National Park, via the Viking Trail (Rte. 430),* ☎ *709/458–2417,* ℻ *709/458–2162,* 🕸 *www.parkscanada.pch.gc.ca/grosmorne.* 🎫 *Mid-May–mid-Oct., $5; free rest of yr.* ☉ *Mid-May–mid-June, daily 9 AM–5 PM; mid-June–Labor Day, daily 9–9, Labor Day–Canadian Thanksgiving Day, daily 9–5.*

Dining and Lodging

$–$$ ✕ **Fisherman's Landing.** The food here is good, but the service can be a bit slow at lunchtime. Staples of Canadian fare such as hot turkey sandwiches, deep-fried chicken, and burgers are on the menu. The fish is usually a good choice, but make sure that it's fresh and not frozen. ⊠ *Main St., Rocky Harbour,* ☎ *709/458–2060. AE, MC, V.*

$–$$ ✕ **Seaside Restaurant.** Fresh seafood is prepared in traditional Newfoundland style at the Seaside Restaurant. You can enjoy the familiar fish-and-chips, cod, and lobster, or you can try something more adventurous in the form of batter-dipped panfried cod tongue. The tongue, denser than a fillet, has a unique combination of textures: the top has the consistency of a clam, and the underside is jellylike. Huge windows give diners a view of Bonne Bay. ⊠ *Main St., Trout River,* ☎ *709/451–3641. AE, MC, V. Closed Nov.–May.*

$–$$$ ⌂ **Gros Morne Resort.** Guest rooms in the front of this hotel overlook the ocean; those in the rear face the mountains. All of the rooms are well-appointed, spacious, and have balconies. The resort is in St. Pauls, a small community encircled by Gros Morne Park. ⊠ *Rte. 430, Box 100, St. Pauls, A0K 4Y0,* ☎ *709/243–2606 or 888/243–2644,* FAX *709/243–2615. 8 rooms, 12 suites. 2 restaurants, 2 bars, minibars, hair salon. AE, MC, V.*

$–$$$ ⌂ **Sugar Hill Inn.** This small hostelry in Gros Morne National Park has quickly developed a reputation for fine wining and dining (for guests only) because of host Vince McCarthy's culinary talents and educated palate. Guided cross-country skiing and snowmobiling treks are available. ⊠ *115–129 Sexton Rd., Box 100, Norris Point A0K 3V0,* ☎ *709/458–2147 or 888/299–2147,* FAX *709/458–2166,* WEB *www. sugarhillinn.nf.ca. 3 rooms, 3 suites. Dining room, no-smoking rooms, hot tub, sauna, coin laundry. AE, MC, V. Closed Nov.– mid-Jan.*

$–$$ ⌂ **Gros Morne Cabins.** These modern log chalets, which overlook the Gulf of St. Lawrence, are near restaurants and stores in Rocky Harbour. Cabins can accommodate up to four people and have kitchens and TVs. ⊠ *Main St., Rocky Harbour A0K 4N0,* ☎ *709/458–2020 or 888/603–2020,* FAX *709/458–2882. 22 cabins. Grocery, playground, coin laundry. AE, DC, MC, V.*

$–$$ ⌂ **Victorian Manor Bed and Breakfast.** This modified Queen Anne house situated in Woody Point, one of the prettiest towns in the vicinity of Gros Morne, has been in the same family since it was built in the 1920s. Much of the furniture and decor of the original home, such as the valanced curtains and chandeliers, have been retained. The Victorian Manor has B&B rooms, efficiency units, and a separate guest house. The suite has a whirlpool tub. ⊠ *Water St., Woody Point A0K 1P0,* ☎ FAX *709/453–2485,* WEB *www.grosmorne.com/victorianmanor. 3 rooms, 1 suite, 3 efficiencies, 1 house. Dining room, no-smoking rooms. MC, V.*

$ ⌂ **Crocker Cabins.** These standard cabins are in Trout River in the quieter, less-developed southern part of the park. The cabins can accommodate four people. ⊠ *57 Duke St., Trout River A0K 5P0,* ☎ FAX *709/ 451–3236. 4 cabins. Fishing, playground, coin laundry. AE, MC, V.*

$ ⌂ **Frontier Cottages.** These well-appointed log cabins can hold up to six people and are ideal if you wish to do your own cooking while visiting Gros Morne. The kitchen has lots of cooking gear, and the wooden table seats six. There's a great view of the hills from the deck. It's a good idea to bring a pre-paid long-distance calling card because there are no telephones in the cabins, just a pay phone in the grocery. ⊠ *Rte. 430, Box 172, Wiltondale A0K 4N0,* ☎ *709/453–7266 or 800/668– 2520,* FAX *709/453–7272. 6 cabins. Restaurant, grocery, miniature golf, snowmobiling, playground, coin laundry. AE, DC, MC, V.*

$ ⌂ **Ocean View Motel.** The wonderful views of Rocky Harbour more than make up for the lackluster motel rooms. This is also the home base for Bontour, which conducts sightseeing boat trips. ⊠ *Main St., Rocky Harbour A0K 4N0,* ☎ *709/458–2730 or 800/563–9887,* FAX *709/*

458–2841, WEB *www.oceanviewmotel.com. 44 rooms. Restaurant, no-smoking rooms, meeting rooms. AE, DC, MC, V.*

$ ⊡ **Shallow Bay Motel and Cabins.** Shallow Bay, which has standard rooms and small cottages, is near the northern boundary of the park. Comedic dinner-theater productions from the Gros Morne Theatre Festival are held here. ⊠ *Main St., Cow Head A0K 2A0,* ☎ *709/243–2471 or 800/563–1946,* FAX *709/243–2816,* WEB *www3.nf.sympatico. ca/sb.motel. 35 rooms, 17 cottages. Restaurant, pool, sauna, miniature golf, coin laundry, meeting rooms. AE, DC, MC, V.*

CAMPING

To make reservations at any of the following **campgrounds** at Gros Morne, call ☎ 709/458–2417. **Berry Hill,** in the forest on Route 430, 4 km (2½ mi) north of Gros Morne, has 152 sites, kitchen shelters, playgrounds, and showers. **Lomond,** a partly exposed area on Route 431, has 29 sites, kitchen shelters, a playground, and showers. Also on Route 431 is **Trout River,** with 35 sites, kitchen shelters, showers, and a playground. **Green Point,** 10 km (6 mi) north of Rocky Harbour on Route 430, is close to the ocean and partly sheltered. It has 18 sites and kitchen shelters, but no showers. In the northern part of the park near Cow Head, **Shallow Bay** is sheltered from the ocean by sand dunes and trees. It has kitchen shelters, showers, and a huge sandy beach.

Nightlife and the Arts

The **Gros Morne Theatre Festival** (☎ 709/243–2899) provides summer entertainment in Cow Head and other venues throughout the park. Most productions are comedies, though there are some dramas based on local stories, plus an outdoor children's show.

Outdoor Activities and Sports

Gros Morne Adventures (☎ 709/458–2722 or 800/685–4624, WEB www.grosmorneadventures.com) has sea kayaking up the fjords and land-locked ponds of Gros Morne National Park, as well as a variety of hikes and adventures in the area.

Bon Tours (☎ 709/458–2730 or 800/563–9887, WEB www.oceanview-motel.com) runs sightseeing boat tours of Western Brook Pond in Gros Morne National Park and on Bonne Bay. **Tableland Boat Tours** (☎ 709/451–2101) leads tours on Trout River Pond near the southern boundary of Gros Morne National Park.

Arches Provincial Park

❹ *20 km (12 mi) north of Gros Morne National Park.*

Arches Provincial Park is a geological curiosity: the action of undersea currents millions of years ago cut a succession of caves through a bed of dolomite that was later raised above sea level by tectonic upheaval. This free park, open mid-June–mid-September, is not staffed. ⊠ *Rte. 430,* ☎ *709/729–2429,* WEB *www.gov.nf.ca/parks&reserves.*

En Route Continuing north on Route 430, parallel to the Gulf of St. Lawrence, you'll find yourself refreshingly close to the ocean and the wave-tossed beaches. The **Long Range Mountains** to your right reminded Jacques Cartier, who saw them in 1534 as he was exploring the area on behalf of France, of the long, rectangular-shape farm buildings of his home village in France. Small villages are interspersed with rivers where salmon and trout grow to be "liar-size." The remains of Maritime Archaic and Dorset people have been found in abundance along this coast, and **Port au Choix National Historic Site** has an interesting interpretation center about them. An archaeological dig also has discovered an ancient village. Ask at the interpretation center for directions. ⊠ *Off*

Rte. 430, ☎ 709/458–2417; 709/861–3522 in summer, WEB
www.parkscanada.pch.gc.ca. 🖅 $2.75. ☉ Mid-May–mid-June daily
9–5; mid-June–Labor Day, daily 9–9; Labor Day–Canadian Thanksgiving Day, daily 9–5.

L'Anse aux Meadows National Historic Site

★ ⑫ 210 km (130 mi) northeast of Arches Provincial Park.

Around the year AD 1000, Vikings from Greenland and Iceland founded
the first European settlement in North America near the northern tip
of Newfoundland. They arrived in the New World 500 years before
Columbus, but stayed only a few years and were forgotten for centuries.
It was only in 1960 that the Norwegian team of Helge and Anne Stine
Ingstad discovered the remains of the Viking settlement's long sod huts.
Today L'Anse aux Meadows is a UNESCO World Heritage Site. The
Canadian Parks Service has a fine visitor center and has reconstructed
some of the huts to give you a sense of centuries past. An interpretation program introduces you to the food, games, and way of life of
that long-ago time. ⊠ Rte. 436, ☎ 709/623–2608; 709/458–2417 in
winter; FAX 709/623–2028 summer only. 🖅 $5. ☉ Mid-May–mid-June,
daily 9–5; mid-June–Labor Day, daily 9–8; Labor Day–Canadian
Thanksgiving Day, daily 9–5.

☯ Two kilometers (one mile) east is a second Viking attraction, **Norstead.**
This reconstruction of an 11th-century Viking port, with its chieftain's
hall, church, and ax-throwing arena, is a good follow-up to a stop at
L'Anse aux Meadows; it's aimed more at children, but the Viking
boat-building course is designed for all ages. ⊠ Rte 436, ☎ 709/454–
8888. 🖅 $7. ☉ Early June–late Sept., daily 10–6.

Dining and Lodging

$ ✕ **Smith's Restaurant.** Don't let the modest facade and roadside loca-
tion of Smith's Restaurant fool you—inside, huge windows frame a
magnificent view of a shallow harbor, protected by an island dotted
with grazing sheep, and seabirds circling overhead. The food's not bad,
either. Try the Mediterranean chowder, halibut, or cod and walk it off
with a stroll on the deck. The attached store sells crafts and books. ⊠
Rte. 436, St. Lunaire–Griquet, ☎ 709/623–2431, AE, DC, MC, V.

$ ✕🏠 **Tickle Inn at Cape Onion.** This refurbished, century-old fisherman's
house on the beach is probably the northernmost residence on the island of Newfoundland. The Franklin stove in the parlor is good to relax
by after exploring the coast or L'Anse aux Meadows (about 45 km,
or 28 mi, away). The inn serves seafood, baked goods, and homemade
jams. ⊠ R.R. 1, Box 62, Cape Onion A0K 4J0, ☎ 709/452–4321 June–
Sept.; 709/739–5503 Oct.–May, WEB www3.nf.sympatico.ca/adams.
tickle. 4 rooms share bath. Dining room, no-smoking room. MC, V.
CP, MAP.

$ 🏠 **Southwest Pond Cabins.** These basic cabins are a 10-minute drive
from L'Anse aux Meadows. ⊠ Rte. 430, Box 58, St. Lunaire–Griquet
A0K 2X0, ☎ 709/623–2140 or 800/515–2261, FAX 709/623–2145. 8
cabins. Grocery, playground, coin laundry. AE, DC, MC, V. Closed
Nov.–mid-May.

$ 🏠 **Valhalla Lodge Bed & Breakfast.** Comfortable and inviting, the Val-
halla is 8 km (5 mi) from L'Anse aux Meadows. Some fossils are part
of the rock fireplace. Hot breakfasts are included in the room rate, and
other meals can be arranged. E. Annie Proulx, author of The Shipping
News, stayed here while writing the novel. ⊠ Gunner's Cove, St.
Lunaire–Griquet A0K 2X0, ☎ 709/623–2018 or 877/623–2018; 709/
896–5476 in winter; FAX 709/623–2144, WEB www.valhalla-lodge.com.
5 rooms. No-smoking room. MC, V. CP.

$ 🖬 **Viking Nest/Viking Village Bed & Breakfast.** Each room at the Viking Nest is named after a famous person or boat from Viking legends or history. The Snorri, with a queen-size bed and private bath, is named for the first European born in the New World, at L'Anse aux Meadows. The Saga-Siglar, also with a queen-size bed, takes the name of a Viking longboat. All the guest rooms look out on the water. A full breakfast is included in the price. The Viking Village is a new five-room inn on the same property. The Viking settlement at L'Anse aux Meadows is only 1 km (½ mi) away. ⊠ *Box 127, Hay Cove A0K 2X0,* ☎ *877/858–2238,* ☎ FAX *709/623–2238,* WEB *www.bbcanada.com/2671. html. 9 rooms. No-smoking rooms. MC, V. BP.*

St. Anthony

43 *16 km (10 mi) south of L'Anse aux Meadows.*

The northern part of the Great Northern Peninsula served as the setting for *The Shipping News,* E. Annie Proulx's Pulitzer Prize–winning novel. St. Anthony is built around a natural harbor on the eastern side of the Great Northern Peninsula, near its tip. If you take a trip out to the lighthouse, you may see an iceberg or two floating by.

The **Grenfell Mission** was founded by Sir Wilfred Grenfell, a British medical missionary who established nursing stations and cooperatives and provided medical services to the scattered villages of northern Newfoundland and the south coast of Labrador in the early 1900s. It remains the town's main employer. The main foyer of the **Charles S. Curtis Memorial Hospital** (⊠ 178–200 West St., ☎ 709/454–4010) has a decorative tile mural depicting scenes from the life of Grenfell.

The **Grenfell Historic Properties,** comprising a museum, house, and interpretation center, focus on Dr. Grenfell's life and work. ⊠ *West St.,* ☎ *709/454–4010,* WEB *www3.nf.sympatico.ca/grenfell.* 🎟 *$5.* ☉ *May–Sept., daily 9–8.*

Dining and Lodging

$ ✕ **Light Keeper's Cafe.** Good seafood and solid Canadian fare are served in this former lighthouse keeper's home overlooking the ocean. The ocean here is cold, which means the seafood—if fresh—will be succulent. Halibut, shrimp, and cod are usually good bets. If the fish isn't fresh, stick with a nonseafood dish such as pork chops. ⊠ *Fishing Point Rd.,* ☎ *709/454–4900. MC, V. Closed Oct.–Apr.*

$–$$ 🖬 **Tuckamore Country Inn.** The Scandinavian-style lodges of the Tuckamore Country Inn provide a comfortable base point from which to explore the wilderness of the area. Adventure packages, which are not covered in the basic lodging fee, include sea kayaking, wilderness viewing, and snowmobiling. This is about an hour away from St. Anthony. ⊠ *1 Southwest Pond, Box 100, Main Brook A0K 3N0,* ☎ *709/865–6361 or 888/865–6361,* FAX *709/865–2112,* WEB *www.tuckamore-lodge.nf.net. 5 rooms, 3 suites. No-smoking rooms, sauna, laundry service, airport shuttle. DC, V.*

$–$$ 🖬 **Vinland Motel.** Some rooms at this standard motel in the center of town have whirlpool baths. The restaurant isn't great, so look for other places nearby. ⊠ *West St., A0K 4S0,* ☎ *709/454–8843 or 800/563–7578,* FAX *709/454–8468. 43 rooms. Restaurant, bar, lounge, sauna, gym, coin laundry, meeting rooms. AE, DC, MC, V.*

Outdoor Activities and Sports

Northland Discovery Tours (⊠ behind the Grenfell Interpretation Centre, off West St., ☎ 709/454–3092 or 877/632–3747, WEB www3.nf. sympatico.ca/paul.alcock) offers boat tours to see whales, icebergs, and seabirds; land tours for viewing caribou, moose, and rare plants; salmon fishing; and snowmobile excursions.

Shopping

Be sure to visit the **Grenfell Handicrafts** store (⊠ 227A West St., ☎ 709/454–4010) in the Grenfell Historic Properties complex. Training villagers to become self-sufficient in a harsh environment was one of Grenfell's aims. A windproof cloth that villagers turned into well-made parkas came to be known as Grenfell cloth. Mittens, caps, and coats are embroidered with motifs such as polar bears.

The West Coast

Western Newfoundland is known for the unlikely combination of world-class Atlantic salmon fishing and papermaking at two newsprint mills. This area includes Corner Brook, a major center. To the south, the Port au Port Peninsula west of Stephenville shows the French influence in Newfoundland; the farming valleys of the southwest were settled by Scots. A ferry from Nova Scotia docks at Port aux Basques in the far southwest corner.

Corner Brook

44 *50 km (31 mi) southwest of Deer Lake.*

Newfoundland's second-largest city, Corner Brook is the hub of the island's west coast. Mountains fringe three sides of the city, which has beautiful views of the harbor and the Bay of Islands. The town is also home to one of the largest paper mills in the world; you may smell it while you're here. Captain James Cook, the British explorer, charted the coast in the 1760s, and a memorial to him overlooks the bay.

Corner Brook is a convenient hub and point of departure for exploring the west coast. It's only a three-hour drive (allowing for traffic) from the Port aux Basques ferry from Nova Scotia. The town enjoys more clearly defined seasons than most of the rest of the island, and in summer it has many pretty gardens. The nearby Humber River is the best-known salmon river in the province.

The north and south shores of the Bay of Islands have fine paved roads—Route 440 on the north shore and Route 450 on the south—and both are a scenic half-day drive from Corner Brook. On both roads, farming and fishing communities exist side by side.

Dining and Lodging

$$–$$$ ✕ **13 West.** Start your meal off with oysters for an appetizer and chase them with one of the wonderful salmon specials: strawberry salmon, mango salmon, blackened salmon, or salmon with rosemary and peppercorns. For those not interested in seafood, the rack of lamb and pork tenderloin are good choices. ⊠ *13 West St.,* ☎ *709/634–1300. AE, MC, V.*

$–$$$ ✕🏨 **Glynmill Inn.** This Tudor-style inn was once the staff house for the
★ visiting top brass of the paper mill. Rooms are cozy, and the dining room serves basic and well-prepared Newfoundland seafood, soups, and specialty desserts. There's also a popular steak house in the basement. ⊠ *1 Cobb La., Box 550, A2H 6E6,* ☎ *709/634–5181; 800/563–4400 in Canada; FAX 709/634–5106,* WEB *www.glynmillinn.ca. 58 rooms, 23 suites. 2 restaurants, bar, no-smoking rooms, meeting rooms. AE, DC, MC, V.*

$–$$ ✕🏨 **Best Western Mamateek Inn.** The restaurant, which serves good Newfoundland home-cooked food, is known for its exquisite view of the city. Sunsets seen from here are remarkable. Rooms are more modern than those at the Glynmill Inn. ✉ *Maple Valley Rd., Box 787, A2H 6G7,* ☎ *709/639–8901 or 800/563–8600,* FAX *709/639–7567,* WEB *www. bestwestern.com. 55 rooms. Restaurant, bar, in-room data ports, no-smoking rooms, coin laundry, business services, meeting rooms. AE, DC, MC, V.*

$–$$　🏨 **Holiday Inn.** There's nothing special here, aside from the convenient location in town. The outdoor pool is heated, and some rooms have minibars. The restaurant is average, aside from good seasonal fish dishes. ✉ *48 West St., A2H 2Z2,* ☎ *709/634–5381,* FAX *709/634–1723,* WEB *www.holidayinncornerbrook.com. 99 rooms, 2 suites. Restaurant, lobby lounge, no-smoking rooms, room service, pool, gym. AE, D, DC, MC, V.*

$　🏨 **Comfort Inn Corner Brook.** This is a comfortable, modern motel with pastel decor and beautiful views of the city or the Bay of Islands. ✉ *41 Maple Valley Rd., Box 1142, A2H 6T2,* ☎ *709/639–1980,* FAX *709/ 639–1549. 80 rooms. Restaurant, no-smoking rooms, meeting rooms. AE, DC, MC, V.*

Outdoor Activities and Sports

Strawberry Hill Resort (☎ 709/634–0066 or 877/434–0066, WEB www. strawberryhill.net) in Little Rapids, 12 km (7 mi) east of Corner Brook on Route 1, was once an exclusive retreat for the owner of the Corner Brook mill. Here you can enjoy Newfoundland's finest sport salmon fishing.

The growing **Marble Mountain Resort** (✉ Rte. 1, ☎ 709/637–7600 or 888/462–7253, WEB www.skimarble.com), 5 km (3 mi) east of the city in Steady Brook, has 27 downhill runs and five lifts capable of moving 6,500 skiers an hour, as well as a large day lodge, ski shop, day-care center, and restaurant. The vertical drop is 1,600 ft.

Stephenville

45　*77 km (48 mi) south of Corner Brook.*

The former Harmon Air Force Base is in Stephenville, a town best known for its summer festival. It also has a large modern paper mill. To the west of town is the Port au Port Peninsula, which was largely settled by the French, who brought their way of life and language to this small corner of Newfoundland.

The **Stephenville Festival** (☎ 709/643–4982 WEB www.stf.ca), held mid-July to mid-August, is the province's major annual summer the-atrical event, with a mix of light musicals and serious drama.

En Route　As you travel down the Trans-Canada Highway toward Port aux Basques, Routes 404, 405, 406, and 407 bring you into the small Scottish communities of the **Codroy Valley.** Some of the most productive farms in the province are nestled in the valley against the backdrop of the Long Range Mountains and the Lewis Hills, from which gales strong enough to stop traffic hurl down to the coast.

Port aux Basques

46　*166 km (103 miles) south of Stephenville.*

Port aux Basques was one of seven Basque ports along Newfoundland's west coast and in southern Labrador during the 1500s and early 1600s and was given its name by the town's French successors. It's now the main ferry port connecting the island to Nova Scotia. In J. T. Cheeseman Provincial Park, 15 km (9 mi) north of town on the Trans-Canada Highway, and at Grand Bay West you may see the endangered piping plover, which nests in the sand dunes along this coast.

Lodging

$–$$ 🏨 **Hotel Port aux Basques.** There's nothing special about the rooms here, but this is a good choice for families—children stay free and pets are permitted. This hotel is closer to the ferry than any other in town. ✉ *1 Grand Bay Rd., A0M 1C0,* ☎ *709/695–2171 or 877/695–2171,* FAX *709/695–2250,* WEB *www.gatewaytonewfoundland.com. 50 rooms. Restaurant, bar, no-smoking rooms, meeting rooms. AE, DC, MC, V.*

$–$$ 🏨 **St. Christopher's Hotel.** This clean, comfortable hotel has quiet, air-conditioned rooms and good food. Rooms have satellite TV. ✉ *Caribou Rd., Box 2049, A0M 1C0,* ☎ *709/695–7034 or 800/563–4779,* FAX *709/695–9841,* WEB *www.stchrishotel.nf.net. 52 rooms, 3 suites. Restaurant, bar, no-smoking rooms, playground, meeting rooms. AE, DC, MC, V.*

$ 🏨 **Caribou Bed and Breakfast.** All the rooms here are decorated in slate blue and neutral, soothing colors. The Caribou tends to be a quiet B&B because people have an early breakfast before catching the nearby ferry. A full breakfast is included in the room rate. ✉ *42 Grand Bay Rd., A0N 1K0,* ☎ *709/695–3408,* WEB *www.bbcanada.com/2225.html. 5 rooms. No-smoking rooms. MC, V. Closed Nov.–Apr. BP.*

LABRADOR

Isolated from the rest of the continent, Labrador has remained one of the world's truly wild places, although its two main centers of Labrador City–Wabush and Happy Valley–Goose Bay have all the amenities of larger urban areas. Labrador, steeped in history, is a place where the past invades the present and life evolves as it did many years ago: a composite of natural phenomena, wilderness adventure, history, and culture. This vast landscape—293,347 square km (113,261 square mi) of land and 8,000 km (5,000 mi) of coastline—is home to 30,000 people. The small but richly diverse population has a history that in some cases stretches back thousands of years; in other cases—the mining towns of Labrador West, for example—the history goes back less than four decades.

The Straits

The Straits in southeastern Labrador were a rich hunting-and-gathering ground for the area's earliest peoples, the Maritime Archaic tribes. The oldest industrial site in the New World is here—the 16th-century Basque whaling station at Red Bay.

L'Anse au Clair

47 *5 km (3 mi) from Blanc Sablon, Québec (ferry from St. Barbe, Newfoundland, docks in Blanc Sablon).*

In L'Anse au Clair—French for "clear water cove" —anglers can try their luck for trout and salmon on the scenic Forteau and Pinware rivers. The French place name dates from the early 1700s when this area was settled by French speakers from Québec. Ask at the local museum for directions to The Doctor's Path where, in the 19th century, the local doctor searched out herbs and medicinal plants.

Lodging

$–$$ 🏨 **Northern Light Inn.** Loads of bus-tour passengers make this a stop in summer because the Northern Light is the only accommodation of any size along Route 510. The hotel is pretty ordinary, but the food is decent and the rooms are air-conditioned. Rooms have cable TV and telephones, and there's a gift shop. ✉ *58 Main St./ Rte. 510, A0K 3K0,*

☎ 709/931–2332 or 800/563–3188, FAX 709/931–2708. 49 rooms, 5 suites. Restaurant, bar, coin laundry, meeting rooms. AE, DC, MC, V.

L'Anse Amour

48 19 km (12 mi) east of L'Anse au Clair.

The elaborate **Maritime Archaic Indian burial site** (⊠ Rte. 510) discovered near L'Anse Amour is 7,500 years old. A plaque marks a site that is the oldest known aboriginal funeral monument in North America. The **L'Anse Amour Lighthouse** (☎ 709/927–5825; ☜ $2.50, ⊙ mid-June–early Oct., daily 10–5:30), constructed in 1857, is 109 ft tall, the second-tallest in Canada; you can climb it.

En Route The **Labrador Straits Museum** provides a glimpse into the history and lifestyle of the area. ⊠ *Rte. 510 between Forteau and L'Anse au Loup,* ☎ 709/931–2067. ☜ $2. ⊙ *Mid-July–mid-Sept., daily 9–5:30.*

Red Bay

49 35 km (22 mi) from L'Anse Amour.

The area's main attraction lies at the very end of Route 510: Red Bay, the site of a 16th-century Basque whaling station and a National Historic Site. Basque whalers began harpooning migrating whales from flimsy boats in frigid waters a few years after Cabot's discovery of the coast in 1497. Between 1550 and 1600 Red Bay was the world's whaling capital.

★ The **Red Bay National Historic Site** has a visitor center that interprets the Basque heritage with film and artifacts. A boat takes you on a five-minute journey over to the excavation site on Saddle Island. ⊠ *Rte. 510,* ☎ 709/920–2142, WEB *parkscanada.pch.gc.ca.* ☜ *Visitor center $5; boat to island $2. ⊙ Mid-May–mid-June, daily 9–5; mid-June–Labor Day, daily 9–8; Labor Day–Canadian Thanksgiving Day, daily 9–5.*

Coastal Labrador

Along the southern coast, most villages are inhabited by descendants of Europeans, whereas farther north they are mostly Inuit and Innu. Over the years the European settlers have adopted native skills and survival strategies, and the native peoples have adopted many European technologies. In summer the ice retreats and a coastal steamer delivers goods, but in winter small airplanes and snowmobiles are the only ways in and out.

You can tour central coastal Labrador aboard a car ferry from Lewisporte, Newfoundland. A second vessel, a coastal freighter known as the *Cruising Labrador,* travels from St. Anthony, Newfoundland, to Nain, Labrador's northernmost settlement. This trip takes two weeks to complete. Both vessels carry all sorts of food and goods for people living along the coast. The coastal freighter stops at a number of summer fishing stations and coastal communities. Reservations are required.

Battle Harbour National Historic Site

12 km (7 mi) by boat from Mary's Harbour.

This island site has the only remaining intact outport fishing merchant's premises in the province. Settled in the 18th century, Battle Harbour was the main fishing port in Labrador until the first half of the 20th century. After fires destroyed some of the community, the people moved to nearby Mary's Harbour. The site also contains the oldest Anglican church in Labrador. Accommodations are available. ⊠ *Southern Labrador coast, accessible by boat from Mary's Harbour,* ☎ FAX *709/ 921–6216,* WEB *www.seascape.com/labrador/battleharbour.* ⊠ *$3.50; boat from Mary's Harbour $10 one-way.* ☉ *June–Sept., daily 10–6.*

Jones Charters and Tours (☎ 709/921–6249) offers an air and small-boat package from either St. John's or Happy Valley–Goose Bay.

Lodging

$–$$ ⊺ **Battle Harbour Inn.** This is the only game in town as far as lodging is concerned. The restored two-story house is clean and comfortable, but a bit rustic. ⊠ *Box 135, Mary's Harbour A0K 3P0,* ☎ FAX *709/ 921–6216. 5 rooms share 2 baths. Dining room. MC, V. Closed Oct.– May.*

Happy Valley–Goose Bay

50 *525 km (326 mi) from Labrador City.*

Happy Valley–Goose Bay is the chief service center for coastal Labrador. Anyone coming to Labrador to fish will probably pass through here. The town was founded in the 1940s as a top-secret air base used to ferry fleets of aircraft to Europe. It's still used as a low-level flying training base by the British, Dutch, and German air forces.

Lodging

$–$$ ⊺ **Aurora Hotel.** Rooms at this basic hotel, the best in town, are bright and decorated with pastels. The Aurora is a five-minute drive from the airport. ⊠ *382 Hamilton River Rd., A0P 1C0,* ☎ *709/896–3398 or 800/563–3066,* FAX *709/896–9608,* WEB *www.aurorahotel.com. 37 rooms, 3 suites. Bar, dining room, room service, meeting rooms. AE, MC, V.*

Outdoor Activities and Sports

Ski Mount Shana (⊠ Rte. 520, ☎ 709/896–8162), with 10 downhill runs, is between Happy Valley–Goose Bay and North West River. The vertical drop is 525 ft.

North West River

51 *32 km (20 mi) northeast of Happy Valley–Goose Bay.*

North West River was founded as a Hudson's Bay trading post in the 1830s. The town was also the starting point for the Wallace–Hubbard expedition of 1903. Leonidas Hubbard and Dillon Wallace were American adventurers who attempted a journey from Lake Melville to Ungava Bay along a previously untraveled route. They took a wrong turn, got lost, and Hubbard died in the wilderness from starvation. His wife, Mina, never forgave Wallace and completed her husband's journey in 1905. Her book, *A Woman's Way Through Unknown Labrador,* is still considered a classic. These and other stories are examined at the **Labrador Heritage Museum** (☎ 709/497–8898). Call ahead for an appointment.

Labrador West

Labrador West's subarctic landscape is challenging and unforgettable. The two towns here were founded in the 1950s to exploit the huge iron-ore deposits. The best way to see this area is to ride the **Québec North Shore and Labrador Railway** (☎ 418/968–7808 or 709/944–8205), which leaves Sept-Isles, Québec, three times a week in summer and twice a week in winter. The seven- to eight-hour trip to the area takes you through nearly 600 km (372 mi) of virgin forest, past spectacular waterfalls and majestic mountains.

Wabush

⑤② *525 km (326 mi) west of Happy Valley–Goose Bay.*

The modern town of Wabush has all the amenities of larger centers, including accommodations, sports and recreational facilities, good shopping, and some of the warmest hospitality found anywhere.

Outdoor Activities and Sports
The **Smokey Mountain Alpine Skiing Center** (✉ Rte. 500, ☎ 709/944–2129), west of Wabush, is open mid-November to late April and has slopes for beginners and advanced skiers. The vertical drop is 1,000 ft.

Labrador City

⑤③ *525 km (326 mi) west of Happy Valley–Goose Bay.*

Labrador City has all the facilities of nearby Wabush. Each March, Labrador City and Wabush play host to a 192-km (120-mi) dogsled race.

Outdoor Activities and Sports
The **White Wolf Snowmobile Club** (☎ 709/944–7401 or 709/944–6833) organizes a mid-March snowmobile rally that includes tours to see the world's largest caribou herd (about 600,000 animals). White Wolf also maintains an extensive groomed trail system all winter; snowmobile rentals are available.

NEWFOUNDLAND AND LABRADOR A TO Z

To research prices, get advice from other travelers, and book travel arrangements, visit www.fodors.com.

AIR TRAVEL
Air Canada flies into Newfoundland. Canada 3000 has international service to Deer Lake, Gander, St. John's, and Stephenville. Regional connectors include Air Labrador, Provincial Airlines, and airNova.
➤ AIRLINES AND CONTACTS: **Air Canada** (☎ 800/776–3000). **Air Labrador** (☎ 888/247–2262). **airNova** (☎ 888/247–2262). **Canada 3000 Airlines** (☎ 877/973–3000). **Provincial Airlines** (☎ 709/576–1666; 800/563–2800 in Atlantic Canada).

AIRPORTS
The province's main airport is St. John's International Airport (YYT). Other airports in Newfoundland are at Stephenville (YJT), Deer Lake (YDF), St. Anthony (YAY), and Gander (YQX); airports in Labrador are in Happy Valley–Goose Bay (YYR), Wabush (YWK), and Churchill Falls (ZUM).
➤ AIRPORT INFORMATION: **St. John's International Airport** (✉ Airport Rd. off Portugal Cove Rd., St. John's, ☎ 709/772–0011).

BOAT AND FERRY TRAVEL
Marine Atlantic operates a car ferry from North Sydney, Nova Scotia, to Port aux Basques, Newfoundland (crossing time is six hours), and, from June through September, from North Sydney to Argentia, three times a week (crossing time 12–14 hours). In all cases, reservations are required.

Another car ferry, operated by the provincial government, travels from Lewisporte in Newfoundland to Cartwright, on the coast of Labrador, and then through the Hamilton inlet to Happy Valley–Goose Bay. Reservations are required. The trip takes 33 hours one-way, and two regularly scheduled return trips are made weekly.

To explore the south coast of Labrador, catch the ferry at St. Barbe on Route 430 in Newfoundland to Blanc Sablon, Québec. From here you can drive to Mary's Harbour along Route 510. Tourism Newfoundland and Labrador has information about ferry schedules.
➤ BOAT AND FERRY INFORMATION: **Marine Atlantic** (✉ Box 250, North Sydney, NS B2A 3M3, ☎ 800/341–7981; 902/794–8109 TTY). **Tourism Newfoundland and Labrador** (☎ 800/563–6353).

BUS TRAVEL
DRL Coachlines runs a trans-island bus service in Newfoundland. Buses leave at 8 AM from St. John's and Port aux Basques. Small buses known as outport taxis connect the major centers with surrounding communities.
➤ BUS INFORMATION: **DRL Coachlines** (☎ 709/738–8088).

CAR TRAVEL
In winter, some highways may close during and after severe snowstorms. For winter road conditions on the west coast, call the Department of Works, Services, and Transportation. A 24-hour hot line provides winter road conditions throughout the province; calls cost 75¢. You can also log on to the Government of Newfoundland and Labrador Web site (www.gov.nf.ca/roads) for information on road conditions.

Route 500 links Labrador City with Happy Valley–Goose Bay via Churchill Falls. Conditions on this 526-km (326-mi) unpaved wilderness road are best from June through October. If you plan on doing any extensive driving in any part of Labrador, you should contact the Department of Tourism, Culture, and Recreation for advice on the best routes and road conditions.

Newfoundland has an excellent highway system, and all but a handful of secondary roads are paved. The province's roads are generally uncrowded, adding to the pleasure of driving. Travel time along the Trans-Canada Highway (Route 1) from Port aux Basques to St. John's is about 13 hours, with time out for a meal. The trip from Corner Brook to St. Anthony at the northernmost tip of the island is about five hours. The drive from St. John's to Grand Bank on the Burin Peninsula takes about four hours. If you're heading for the southern coast of the Avalon Peninsula, pick up Route 10 just south of St. John's and follow it toward Trepassey.

EMERGENCY SERVICES
➤ CONTACTS: **Department of Tourism, Culture, and Recreation** (☎ 709/729–2830 or 800/563–6353). **Department of Works, Services, and Transportation** (☎ 709/635–4144 in Deer Lake; 709/292–4444 in Grand Falls–Windsor and Central Newfoundland; 709/466–4160 in Clarenville; 709/729–7669 in St. John's; 709/896–7888 in Happy Valley–Goose Bay depot in Labrador; 900/451–3300 for 24-hour hot line, with cost of 75¢).

EMERGENCIES
➤ CONTACTS: **Medical emergencies, police** (☎ 911 or 0).
➤ HOSPITALS: **Captain William Jackman Hospital** (✉ 410 Booth Ave., Labrador City, ☎ 709/944–2632). **Charles S. Curtis Memorial Hospital** (✉ West St., St. Anthony, ☎ 709/454–3333). **General Hospital** (✉ 300 Prince Philip Dr., St. John's, ☎ 709/737–6300). **George B. Cross Hospital** (✉ Manitoba Dr., Clarenville, ☎ 709/466–3411). **James**

Paton (✉ 125 Trans-Canada Hwy., Gander, ☎ 709/651–2500). **St. Clare's Mercy Hospital** (✉ 154 Le Marchant Rd., St. John's, ☎ 709/778–3111). **Western Memorial** (✉ Brookfield Ave., Corner Brook, ☎ 709/637–5000).

OUTDOORS AND SPORTS

FISHING

Seasonal and regulatory fishing information can be obtained from the Department of Tourism, Culture, and Recreation.

➤ CONTACTS: **Department of Tourism, Culture, and Recreation** (✉ Box 8730, St. John's A1B 4K2, ☎ 709/729–2830).

TOURS

ADVENTURE

Local operators offer sea kayaking, ocean diving, canoeing, wildlife viewing, mountain biking, white-water rafting, heli-hiking, and interpretive walks in summer. In winter, snowmobiling and caribou- and seal-watching expeditions are popular. In spring and early summer, a favored activity is iceberg-watching. Before choosing an operator, contact the Department of Tourism, Culture, and Recreation to make sure you're calling an established outfit.

Eastern Edge Kayak Adventures leads east-coast sea-kayaking tours and gives white-water kayaking instruction. Maxxim Vacations in St. John's organizes packaged adventure and cultural tours. Tuckamore Wilderness Lodge, in Main Brook, uses its luxurious lodge on the Great Northern Peninsula as a base for viewing caribou, seabird colonies, whales, and icebergs, and for winter snowmobile excursions. Wildland Tours in St. John's has three weeklong guided tours that view wildlife and visit historically and culturally significant sites across Newfoundland.

➤ FEES AND SCHEDULES: **Department of Tourism, Culture, and Recreation** (✉ Box 8730, St. John's A1B 4K2, ☎ 709/729–2830). **Eastern Edge Kayak Adventures** (☎ 709/782–5925, WEB www.kayakeeo.hypersource.com). **Maxxim Vacations** (☎ 709/754–6666 or 800/567–6666, WEB www.maxximvacations.com). **Tuckamore Wilderness Lodge** (☎ 709/865–6361 or 888/865–6361, WEB www.tuckamore-lodge.nf.net). **Wildland Tours** (☎ 709/722–3123, WEB www.wildlands.com).

BY BUS

Fleetline Motorcoach Tours in Holyrood runs island-wide tours. Local tours are available for Port aux Basques, the Codroy Valley, Corner Brook, the Bay of Islands, Gros Morne National Park, the Great Northern Peninsula, and St. John's. McCarthy's Party in St. John's has guided bus tours across Newfoundland, learning vacations, and charter services.

➤ FEES AND SCHEDULES: **Fleetline Motorcoach Tours** (☎ 709/229–7600). **McCarthy's Party** (☎ 709/781–2244 or 888/660–6060, WEB www.newfoundland-tours.com).

WALKING

On the St. John's Haunted Hike, Reverend Thomas Wickam Jarvis (actor Dale Jarvis) leads popular walking tours of the supernatural on summer evenings; tours begin at the west entrance of the Anglican Cathedral on Church Hill.

➤ FEES AND SCHEDULES: **St. John's Haunted Hike** (☎ 709/576–2087).

TRAIN TRAVEL

Iron Ore Company of Canada's Québec North Shore and Labrador Railway has service between Sept-Isles, Québec, and Labrador City in Labrador.

➤ TRAIN INFORMATION: **Iron Ore Company of Canada's Québec North Shore and Labrador Railway** (☎ 418/968–7808 or 709/944–8205).

VISITOR INFORMATION

The Department of Tourism, Culture, and Recreation distributes brochures from its offices in the Confederation Building, West Block, St. John's. The province maintains a 24-hour, tourist-information line year-round that can help with accommodations and reservations.

From June until Labor Day, a network of Visitor Information Centres, open daily 9–9, dots the province. These centers carry information on events, accommodations, shopping, and crafts stores in their area. The airports in Gander and St. John's operate in-season visitor-information booths. The city of St. John's operates an information center in a restored railway carriage next to the harbor.

➤ TOURIST INFORMATION: **Department of Tourism, Culture, and Recreation** (✉ Box 8730, St. John's A1B 4K2, ☎ 709/729–2830; 800/563–6353 for tourist-information line).

FRENCH VOCABULARY

One of the trickiest French sounds to pronounce is the nasal final *n* sound (whether or not the *n* is actually the last letter of the word). You should try to pronounce it as a sort of nasal grunt—as in "huh." The vowel that precedes the *n* will govern the vowel sound of the word, and in this list we precede the final *n* with an *h* to remind you to be nasal.

Another problem sound is the ubiquitous but untransliterable *eu*, as in *bleu* (blue) or *deux* (two), and the very similar sound in *je* (I), *ce* (this), and *de* (of). The closest equivalent might be the vowel sound in "put," but rounded.

Words and Phrases

English	French	Pronunciation

Basics

English	French	Pronunciation
Yes/no	Oui/non	wee/nohn
Please	S'il vous plaît	seel voo **play**
Thank you	Merci	mair-**see**
You're welcome	De rien	deh ree-**ehn**
That's all right	Il n'y a pas de quoi	eel nee ah pah de **kwah**
Excuse me, sorry	Pardon	pahr-**dohn**
Sorry!	Désolé(e)	day-zoh-**lay**
Good morning/ afternoon	Bonjour	bohn-**zhoor**
Good evening	Bonsoir	bohn-**swahr**
Goodbye	Au revoir	o ruh-**vwahr**
Mr. (Sir)	Monsieur	muh-**syuh**
Mrs. (Ma'am)	Madame	ma-**dam**
Miss	Mademoiselle	mad-mwa-**zel**
Pleased to meet you	Enchanté(e)	ohn-shahn-**tay**
How are you?	Comment ça va?	kuh-mahn-sa-**va**
Very well, thanks	Très bien, merci	tray bee-ehn, mair-**see**
And you?	Et vous?	ay **voo**?

Numbers

English	French	Pronunciation
one	un	uhn
two	deux	deuh
three	trois	twah
four	quatre	**kaht**-ruh
five	cinq	sank
six	six	seess
seven	sept	set
eight	huit	wheat
nine	neuf	nuff
ten	dix	deess
eleven	onze	ohnz
twelve	douze	dooz

thirteen	treize	trehz
fourteen	quatorze	kah-**torz**
fifteen	quinze	kanz
sixteen	seize	sez
seventeen	dix-sept	deez-**set**
eighteen	dix-huit	deez-**wheat**
nineteen	dix-neuf	deez-**nuff**
twenty	vingt	vehn
twenty-one	vingt-et-un	vehnt-ay-**uhn**
thirty	trente	trahnt
forty	quarante	ka-**rahnt**
fifty	cinquante	sang-**kahnt**
sixty	soixante	swa-**sahnt**
seventy	soixante-dix	swa-sahnt-**deess**
eighty	quatre-vingts	kaht-ruh-**vehn**
ninety	quatre-vingt-dix	kaht-ruh-vehn-**deess**
one-hundred	cent	sahn
one-thousand	mille	meel

Colors

black	noir	nwahr
blue	bleu	bleuh
brown	brun/marron	bruhn/mar-**rohn**
green	vert	vair
orange	orange	o-**rahnj**
pink	rose	rose
red	rouge	rooje
violet	violette	vee-o-**let**
white	blanc	blahnk
yellow	jaune	zhone

Days of the Week

Sunday	dimanche	**dee**-mahnsh
Monday	lundi	**luhn**-dee
Tuesday	mardi	**mahr**-dee
Wednesday	mercredi	**mair**-kruh-dee
Thursday	jeudi	**zhuh**-dee
Friday	vendredi	**vawn**-druh-dee
Saturday	samedi	**sahm**-dee

Months

January	janvier	**zhahn**-vee-ay
February	février	**feh**-vree-ay
March	mars	marce
April	avril	a-**vreel**
May	mai	meh
June	juin	zhwehn
July	juillet	**zhwee**-ay
August	août	oot
September	septembre	sep-**tahm**-bruh
October	octobre	awk-**to**-bruh
November	novembre	no-**vahm**-bruh
December	décembre	day-**sahm**-bruh

Useful Phrases

Do you speak . . . English?	Parlez-vous . . . anglais?	par-lay **voo** **ahn**-glay
I don't speak . . . French	Je ne parle pas . . . français	zhuh nuh parl **pah** frahn-**say**
I don't understand	Je ne comprends pas	zhuh nuh kohm-prahn **pah**
I understand	Je comprends	zhuh kohm-**prahn**
I don't know	Je ne sais pas	zhuh nuh say **pah**
I'm American/ British	Je suis américain/ anglais	zhuh sweez a-may-ree-**kehn**/ahn-**glay**
What's your name?	Comment vous appelez-vous?	ko-mahn voo za-pell-ay-**voo**
My name is . . .	Je m'appelle . . .	zhuh ma-**pell** . . .
What time is it?	Quelle heure est-il?	kel air eh-**teel**
How?	Comment?	ko-**mahn**
When?	Quand?	kahn
Yesterday	Hier	yair
Today	Aujourd'hui	o-zhoor-**dwee**
Tomorrow	Demain	duh-**mehn**
This morning/ afternoon	Ce matin/cet après-midi	suh ma-**tehn**/set ah-pray-mee-**dee**
Tonight	Ce soir	suh **swahr**
What?	Quoi?	kwah
What is it?	Qu'est-ce que c'est?	kess-kuh-**say**
Why?	Pourquoi?	**poor**-kwa
Who?	Qui?	kee
Where is . . .	Où se trouve . . .	oo suh **troov**
the train station?	la gare?	la gar
the subway?	la station de?	la sta-**syon** duh
station?	métro?	may-**tro**
the bus stop?	l'arrêt de bus?	la-**ray** duh **booss**
the airport?	l'aérogare?	lay-ro-**gar**
the post office?	la poste?	la post
the bank?	la banque?	la bahnk
the hotel?	l'hôtel?	lo-**tel**
the store?	le magasin?	luh ma-ga-**zehn**
the cashier?	la caisse?	la **kess**
the museum?	le musée?	luh mew-**zay**
the hospital?	l'hôpital?	lo-pee-**tahl**
the elevator?	l'ascenseur?	la-sahn-**seuhr**
the telephone?	le téléphone?	luh tay-lay-**phone**
Where are the rest rooms?	Où sont les toilettes?	oo sohn lay twah-**let**
Here/there	Ici/là	ee-**see**/la
Left/right	A gauche/à droite	a goash/a drwaht
Straight ahead	Tout droit	too drwah

Is it near/far?	C'est près/loin?	say pray/lwehn
I'd like . . .	Je voudrais . . .	zhuh voo-**dray**
a room	une chambre	ewn **shahm**-bruh
the key	la clé	la clay
a newspaper	un journal	uhn zhoor-**nahl**
a stamp	un timbre	uhn **tam**-bruh
I'd like to buy . . .	Je voudrais acheter . . .	zhuh voo-**dray** **ahsh**-tay
a cigar	un cigare	uhn see-**gar**
cigarettes	des cigarettes	day see-ga-**ret**
matches	des allumettes	days a-loo-**met**
dictionary	un dictionnaire	uhn deek-see-oh-**nare**
soap	du savon	dew sah-**vohn**
city map	un plan de ville	uhn plahn de **veel**
road map	une carte routière	ewn cart roo-tee-**air**
magazine	une revue	ewn reh-**vu**
envelopes	des enveloppes	dayz ahn-veh-**lope**
writing paper	du papier à lettres	dew pa-pee-**ay** a **let**-ruh
airmail writing paper	du papier avion	dew pa-pee-**ay** a-vee-**ohn**
postcard	une carte postale	ewn cart pos-**tal**
How much is it?	C'est combien?	say comb-bee-**ehn**
It's expensive/ cheap	C'est cher/pas cher	say share/pa share
A little/a lot	Un peu/beaucoup	uhn peuh/bo-**koo**
More/less	Plus/moins	plu/mwehn
Enough/too (much)	Assez/trop	a-say/tro
I am ill/sick	Je suis malade	zhuh swee ma-**lahd**
Call a . . . doctor	Appelez un . . . médecin	a-play uhn mayd-**sehn**
Help!	Au secours!	o suh-**koor**
Stop!	Arrêtez!	a-reh-**tay**
Fire!	Au feu!	o fuh
Caution!/Look out!	Attention!	a-tahn-see-**ohn**

Dining Out

A bottle of . . .	une bouteille de . . .	ewn boo-**tay** duh
A cup of . . .	une tasse de . . .	ewn **tass** duh
A glass of . . .	un verre de . . .	uhn **vair** duh
Ashtray	un cendrier	uhn sahn-dree-**ay**
Bill/check	l'addition	la-dee-see-**ohn**
Bread	du pain	dew pan
Breakfast	le petit-déjeuner	luh puh-**tee** day-zhuh-**nay**
Butter	du beurre	dew burr
Cheers!	A votre santé!	ah vo-truh sahn-**tay**
Cocktail/aperitif	un apéritif	uhn ah-pay-ree-**teef**

Dinner	le dîner	luh dee-**nay**
Special of the day	le plat du jour	luh plah dew **zhoor**
Enjoy!	Bon appétit!	bohn a-pay-**tee**
Fixed-price menu	le menu	luh may-**new**
Fork	une fourchette	ewn four-**shet**
I am diabetic	Je suis diabétique	zhuh swee dee-ah-bay-**teek**
I am on a diet	Je suis au régime	zhuh sweez oray-**jeem**
I am vegetarian	Je suis végé-tarien(ne)	zhuh swee vay-zhay-ta-ree-**en**
I cannot eat . . .	Je ne peux pas manger de . . .	zhuh nuh **puh** pah mahn-**jay** deh
I'd like to order	Je voudrais commander	zhuh voo-**dray** ko-mahn-**day**
I'm hungry/thirsty	J'ai faim/soif	zhay fahm/swahf
Is service/the tip included?	Le service est-il compris?	luh sair-**veess** ay-teel com-**pree**
It's good/bad	C'est bon/mauvais	say bohn/mo-**vay**
It's hot/cold	C'est chaud/froid	say sho/frwah
Knife	un couteau	uhn koo-**toe**
Lunch	le déjeuner	luh day-zhuh-**nay**
Menu	la carte	la cart
Napkin	une serviette	ewn sair-vee-**et**
Pepper	du poivre	dew **pwah**-vruh
Plate	une assiette	ewn a-see-**et**
Please give me . . .	Merci de me donner . . .	Mair-**see** deh meh doe-**nay**
Salt	du sel	dew sell
Spoon	une cuillère	ewn kwee-**air**
Sugar	du sucre	dew **sook**-ruh
Waiter!/Waitress!	Monsieur!/Mademoiselle!	muh-**syuh**/mad-mwa-**zel**
Wine list	la carte des vins	la **cart** day van

MENU GUIDE

French	English

General Dining

French	English
Entrée	Appetizer/Starter
Garniture au choix	Choice of vegetable side
Selon arrivage	When available
Supplément/En sus	Extra charge
Sur commande	Made to order

Breakfast

French	English
Confiture	Jam
Miel	Honey
Oeuf à la coque	Boiled egg
Oeufs au bacon	Bacon and eggs
Oeufs sur le plat	Fried eggs
Oeufs brouillés	Scrambled eggs
Tartine	Bread with butter or jam

Appetizers/Starters

French	English
Anchois	Anchovies
Andouille(tte)	Chitterling sausage
Assiette de charcuterie	Assorted pork products
Crudités	Mixed raw vegetable salad
Escargots	Snails
Jambon	Ham
Jambonneau	Cured pig's knuckle
Pâté	Liver puree blended with meat
Quenelles	Light dumplings
Saucisson	Dried sausage
Terrine	Pâté in an earthenware pot

Soups

French	English
Bisque	Shellfish soup
Bouillabaisse	Fish and seafood stew
Julienne	Vegetable soup
Potage/Soupe	Soup
Potage parmentier	Thick potato soup
Pot-au-feu	Stew of meat and vegetables
Soupe du jour	Soup of the day
Soupe à l'oignon gratinée	French onion soup
Soupe au pistou	Provençal vegetable soup
Velouté de . . .	Cream of . . .
Vichyssoise	Cold leek and potato cream soup

Fish and Seafood

French	English
Bar	Bass
Bourride	Fish stew from Marseilles
Brandade de morue	Creamed salt cod
Brochet	Pike
Cabillaud/Morue	Fresh cod
Calmar	Squid
Coquilles St-Jacques	Scallops
Crabe	Crab
Crevettes	Shrimp
Daurade	Sea bream

Écrevisses	Prawns/crayfish
Harengs	Herring
Homard	Lobster
Huîtres	Oysters
Langouste	Spiny lobster
Langoustine	Prawn/lobster
Lotte	Monkfish
Lotte de mer	Angler
Loup	Catfish
Maquereau	Mackerel
Matelote	Fish stew in wine
Moules	Mussels
Palourdes	Clams
Perche	Perch
Poulpe	Octopus
Raie	Skate
Rascasse	Scorpion-fish
Rouget	Red mullet
Saumon	Salmon
Thon	Tuna
Truite	Trout

Meat

Agneau	Lamb
Ballotine	Boned, stuffed, and rolled
Blanquette de veau	Veal stew with a white-sauce base
Boeuf	Beef
Boeuf à la Bourguignonne	Beef stew
Boudin blanc	Sausage made with white meat
Boudin noir	Sausage made with pig's blood
Boulettes de viande	Meatballs
Brochette	Kabob
Cassoulet	Casserole of white beans, meat
Cervelle	Brains
Châteaubriand	Double fillet steak
Côtelettes	Chops
Choucroute garnie	Sausages and cured pork served with sauerkraut
Côte de boeuf	T-bone steak
Côte	Rib
Cuisses de grenouilles	Frogs' legs
Entrecôte	Rib or rib-eye steak
Épaule	Shoulder
Escalope	Cutlet
Foie	Liver
Gigot	Leg
Langue	Tongue
Médaillon	Tenderloin steak
Pavé	Thick slice of boned beef
Pieds de cochon	Pig's feet
Porc	Pork
Ragoût	Stew
Ris de veau	Veal sweetbreads
Rognons	Kidneys
Saucisses	Sausages
Selle	Saddle

Tournedos	Tenderloin of T-bone steak
Veau	Veal
Viande	Meat

Methods of Preparation

À point	Medium
À l'étouffée	Stewed
Au four	Baked
Bien cuit	Well-done
Bleu	Very rare
Bouilli	Boiled
Braisé	Braised
Frit	Fried
Grillé	Grilled
Rôti	Roast
Saignant	Rare
Sauté/poêlée	Sautéed

Game and Poultry

Blanc de volaille	Chicken breast
Caille	Quail
Canard/Caneton	Duck/duckling
Cerf/Chevreuil	Venison
Coq au vin	Chicken stewed in red wine
Dinde/Dindonneau	Turkey/Young turkey
Faisan	Pheasant
Lapin	Rabbit
Lièvre	Wild hare
Oie	Goose
Pigeon/Pigeonneau	Pigeon/Squab
Pintade/Pintadeau	Guinea fowl/Young guinea fowl
Poularde	Fattened pullet
Poulet/Poussin	Chicken/Spring chicken
Sanglier/Marcassin	Wild boar/Young wild boar
Volaille	Fowl

Vegetables

Artichaut	Artichoke
Asperge	Asparagus
Aubergine	Eggplant
Carottes	Carrots
Champignons	Mushrooms
Chou-fleur	Cauliflower
Chou (rouge)	Cabbage (red)
Choux de Bruxelles	Brussels sprouts
Courgette	Zucchini
Cresson	Watercress
Épinard	Spinach
Haricots blancs/verts	White kidney/green beans
Laitue	Lettuce
Lentilles	Lentils
Maïs	Corn
Oignons	Onions
Petits pois	Peas
Poireaux	Leeks
Poivrons	Peppers

Pomme de terre	Potato
Pommes frites	French fries
Tomates	Tomatoes

Sauces and Preparations

Béarnaise	Vinegar, egg yolks, white wine, shallots, tarragon
Béchamel	White sauce
Bordelaise	Mushrooms, red wine, shallots, beef marrow
Bourguignon	Red wine, herbs
Chasseur	Wine, mushrooms, shallots
Diable	Hot pepper
Forestière	Mushrooms
Hollandaise	Egg yolks, butter, vinegar
Indienne	Curry
Madère	With Madeira wine
Marinière	White wine, mussel broth, egg yolks
Meunière	Brown butter, parsley, lemon juice
Périgueux	With goose or duck liver puree and truffles
Poivrade	Pepper sauce
Provençale	Onions, tomatoes, garlic

Fruits and Nuts

Abricot	Apricot
Amandes	Almonds
Ananas	Pineapple
Cacahouètes	Peanuts
Cassis	Black currants
Cerises	Cherries
Citron/Citron vert	Lemon/Lime
Figues	Figs
Fraises	Strawberries
Framboises	Raspberries
Fruits secs	Dried fruit
Groseilles	Red currants
Marrons	Chestnuts
Melon	Melon
Mûres	Blackberries
Noisettes	Hazelnuts
Noix de coco	Coconut
Noix	Walnuts
Pamplemousse	Grapefruit
Pêche	Peach
Poire	Pear
Pomme	Apple
Pruneaux	Prunes
Prunes	Plums
Raisins blancs/noirs	Grapes green/purple
Raisins secs	Raisins

Desserts

Coupe (glacée)	Sundae
Crêpe	Thin pancake
Crème brûlée	Custard with caramelized topping

Crème caramel	Caramel-coated custard
Crème Chantilly	Whipped cream
Gâteau au chocolat	Chocolate cake
Glace	Ice cream
Mousse au chocolat	Chocolate mousse
Sabayon	Egg-and-wine-based custard
Tarte aux pommes	Apple pie
Tarte tatin	Caramelized apple tart
Tourte	Layer cake

Alcoholic Drinks

À l'eau	With water
Avec des glaçons	On the rocks
Kir	Chilled white wine mixed with black-currant syrup
Bière	Beer
blonde/brune	*light/dark*
Calvados	Apple brandy from Normandy
Eau-de-vie	Brandy
Liqueur	Cordial
Poire William	Pear brandy
Porto	Port
Vin	Wine
sec	*dry/neat*
brut	*very dry*
léger	*light*
doux	*sweet*
rouge	*red*
rosé	*rosé*
mousseux	*sparkling*
blanc	*white*

Nonalcoholic Drinks

Café	Coffee
noir	*black*
crème	*with steamed milk/cream*
au lait	*with steamed milk*
décaféiné	*caffeine-free*
Express	Espresso
Chocolat chaud	Hot chocolate
Eau minérale	Mineral water
gazeuse/non gazeuse	*carbonated/still*
Jus de . . .	. . . juice
Lait	Milk
Limonade	Lemonade
Thé	Tea
au lait/au citron	*with milk/lemon*
glacé	*Iced tea*
Tisane	Herb tea

INDEX

NOTES